THE Administrative Professional

Patsy J. Fulton-Calkins, Ph.D., CPS
Formerly University of North Texas, Denton

Dianne S. Rankin
Educational Media Development
Monticello, Kentucky

Kellie A. Shumack, Ph.D.
Foundations and Secondary Education
Auburn University

SOUTH-WESTERN
CENGAGE Learning

Australia • Brazil • Japan • Korea • Mexico • Singapore • Spain • United Kingdom • United States

SOUTH-WESTERN
CENGAGE Learning

The Administrative Professional:
Technology and Procedures
Fourteenth Edition
Patsy J. Fulton-Calkins
Dianne S. Rankin
Kellie A. Shumack

Vice President of Editorial, Business:
Jack W. Calhoun
Vice President/Editor-in-Chief:
Karen Schmohe
Senior Acquisitions Editor: Jane Phelan
Developmental Editor: Karen Hein
Senior Content Project Manager:
Cliff Kallemeyn
Senior Media Editor: Mike Jackson
Senior Frontlist Buyer: Kevin Kluck
Senior Rights Specialist, Text:
Mardell Glinski-Schultz
Senior Rights Specialist, Photo:
Deanna Ettinger
Production Service: Integra Software
Services
Senior Art Director: Tippy McIntosh
Internal Designer: Ke Design; Mason, OH
Cover Designer: Ke Design; Mason, OH
Cover Image: Getty Images; iStock

Photos, pp. 16, 33, 50, 68, 83, 98, 121, 139,
160, 183, 213, 233, 252, 272, 295, 314:
iStock Photo/© Feng Yu

Art figures, pp. 2, 54, 110, 129, 132, 134,
158, 168, 180, 218, 219, 220, 221, 229, 276:
© Cengage Learning

For product information and technology assistance, contact us at
Cengage Learning Customer & Sales Support, 1-800-354-9706

For permission to use material from this text or product,
submit all requests online at **www.cengage.com/permissions**
Further permissions questions can be emailed to
permissionrequest@cengage.com

Microsoft, Windows, Windows Live, Access, Excel, Outlook, PowerPoint,
SharePoint, Word, and Internet Explorer are either registered trademarks or trademarks of Microsoft Corporation in the United States and/
or other countries.

Mac is a registered trademark of Apple Inc.

Firefox is a registered trademark of the Mozilla Foundation.

QuickBooks is a trademark of Intuit Inc., registered in the United States
and other countries.

Lotus Notes is a trademark of International Business Machines
Corporation in the United States, other countries, or both.

GroupWise is a registered trademark of Novell, Inc., in the United States
and other countries.

ISBN-13: 978-0-538-73104-1
ISBN-10: 0-538-73104-4

South-Western Cengage Learning
5191 Natorp Boulevard
Mason, OH 45040
USA

Cengage Learning is a leading provider of customized learning solutions
with office locations around the globe, including Singapore, the United
Kingdom, Australia, Mexico, Brazil, and Japan. Locate your local office at:
international.cengage.com/region

Cengage Learning products are represented in Canada by
Nelson Education, Ltd.

For your course and learning solutions, visit **www.cengage.com/school**

Visit our company website at **www.cengage.com**

Purchase any of our products at your local college store or at our
preferred online store **www.cengagebrain.com**

Printed in the United States of America
2 3 4 5 6 7 14 13 12 11

Pick Up the Call

.... *Introducing The Administrative Professional, Technology & Procedures 14e*

with a brand new look! This edition is sharp and focused, and it targets the skills and best practices in the administrative assistant's work world. The basic elements that have made The Administrative Professional the market leader are retained, but many significant improvements have been made.

New to This Edition:

- Brand new approach and content for six chapters — 1 Entering the Workforce — 2 Becoming a Professional — 3 Managing and Organizing Yourself — 4 Working Ethically — 5 Understanding the Workplace Team — 14 Understanding Financial Responsibility — 16 Leading with Confidence

- Significant enhancements made throughout other chapters

- Dynamic features that give a real-world perspective to each chapter

- Action-oriented, career focused end-of-chapter activities

- Value-added website with videos and interactive eBook

> "The readability is good, with excellent examples to help understand the topics."
>
> ~Tricia Troyer
> Waubonsee Community College

... *to Get Organized for Success*

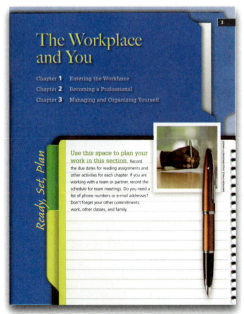

Parts openers provide space to plan and organize your schedule.

A real job posting will hook your interest right from the start.

New Career-Focused Features

Pick up the call —meet the Savvy Admin a "Dear Abby" approach to handling difficult workplace issues.

Dear Savvy Admin

Dear Savvy Admin:
My boss is hopelessly disorganized. He loses documents I give him. He doesn't seem to be able to look up a phone number without my help. He doesn't get back to me with information the company president requests. I like him and want to keep working here, but our work styles are very different. What can I do?

Babysitting the Boss

Workplace Wisdom offers practical advice on communication, ethics, decision-making, and other topics.

workplace wisdom

We all know how aggravating it can be to deal with a person who "doesn't have it together." It puts pressure on you when you cannot rely on someone who has trouble meeting deadlines and remembering commitments. It is even more aggravating to be that disorganized person. Here are some great reasons to get organized:

- To save time
- To meet deadlines
- To improve overall job performance
- To reduce the strain on those who depend upon you
- To get control of your environment and your life

Show Respect for Others

Using the proper degree of formality for different communication situations will make listeners more open to receiving your message. The degree of formality that is considered appropriate when speaking with coworkers, managers, and clients will vary from company to company. In some companies, coworkers (and managers in particular) are addressed by their titles and last names: "Good morning, Mr. Luongo." In other companies, coworkers and clients are addressed more informally by their first names.

Observe the custom followed at your company. However, do not be overly friendly or informal with coworkers or clients you do not know well even if you address them by their first names. Be especially sensitive to the degree of formality you use when talking with coworkers or clients from other cultures. In many parts of the United States, direct and concise communications are considered appropriate.

For example, you might say to a coworker, "Great. Call me when you have the final results." To a client or coworker from another culture, this message may seem abrupt or rude. A more appropriate message might be, "That's great news, Mr. Haddad. Will you please call me when you have the final results?"

> "This text is very relevant"
> ~Teresa Moore
> Volunteer State CC

Special emphasis is given to topics that address professional habits and attitudes.

Deliver a *Dynamic* and *Real World* Perspective

Communicating @ Work Tips on listening, speaking, taking messages and more

People @ Work Focuses on the people you interact with on the job, from the mailroom to the CEO

Technology @ Work Addresses new technologies and issues such as security updates

Writing @ Work Stresses the importance of effective written communication

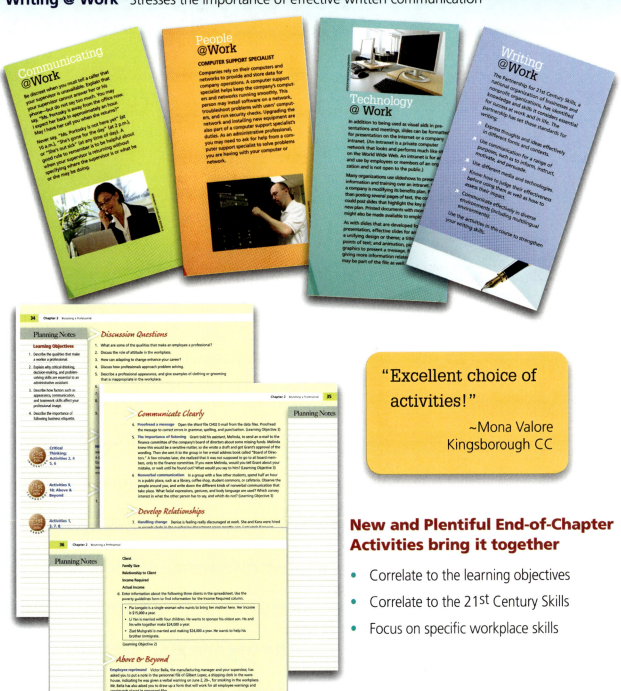

> "Excellent choice of activities!"
>
> ~Mona Valore
> Kingsborough CC

New and Plentiful End-of-Chapter Activities bring it together

- Correlate to the learning objectives
- Correlate to the 21st Century Skills
- Focus on specific workplace skills

New Value-Added Website

©Mark Wagg, iStock

www.cengage.com/officetech/fultoncalkins

Administrative Professional 14e offers a feature-packed CourseMate website with tools and activities to enhance learning. CourseMate includes:

- An interactive eBook with bookmarking, text highlighting, notetaking, zoom, search, and more.

- Interactive learning tools listed below.

- Engagement Tracker that will enable instructors to map student participation in the web resources.

Student Resources

- Learning Objectives
- Flashcards
- Chapter quizzes
- Web links
- Data files
- Videos with interactive quizzes
- Cool Tools with activities for podcasts, blogs, wikis, etc.

Instructor Resources

- Instructor's Manual
- **Exam**View® test bank
- PowerPoint® presentations

Good luck in your administrative professional studies . . . we wish you the best in work and life.

About the Authors

Patsy Fulton-Calkins, Ph.D., CPS. Patsy has taught at the high school, community college, and university levels, including CPS review courses. Patsy has administrative experience at the college level, including division chairperson, vice-president of instruction, president, and chancellor.

Dianne S. Rankin, is a consulting editor, writer, and developer of instructional materials for websites, ancillaries, and textbooks for business education publishers. Dianne has taught at the high school and community college levels and continues to teach computer classes for businesses and organizations. In addition, Dianne has had first-hand experience as an administrative assistant.

Kellie A. Shumack, Ph.D. is an assistant professor at Auburn University, Montgomery teaching Foundations and Secondary Education. Kellie has worked as an administrative assistant and has taught at both the secondary and postsecondary levels in courses such as Computer-Based Instructional Strategies and Curriculum Integration of Technology. Kellie was awarded the 2010 Delta Pi Epsilon Outstanding Doctoral Research Award for her work in researching professional development needs in Business Education.

Contributing Authors

Lauri Harwood
Business Consultant and Trainer
Cincinnati, Ohio

Barbara Norstrom
Professor Office Systems
Technology
Kaskaskia Community College
Centralia, Illinois

Karin M. Stulz, M.A.E.
Assistant Professor
Northern Michigan University
Marquette, Michigan

Reviewers

Jack Adams
San Diego City College

Nancy Backlund
Modesto Junior College

Sharon Buss
Hawkeye Community College

Janel C. Doyle
Bowling Green Technical
College

Veronica Dufresne
Finger Lakes Community
College

Margaret A. Fisher
Florida State College,
Jacksonville

Susan M. Kanda
Baker College

Alysia Martinez
Gateway Technical College

Amy McAnally
Central Texas College

Teresa Moore
Volunteer State Community
College

Diane Penn-Mickey
Northern Virginia Community
College

Marcel M. Robels
Eastern Kentucky University

Jan Sorahan
Central Community College

Cindy Thompson
University of Arkansas Community
College, Morrilton

Tricia Troyer
Waubonsee Community
College

Mona Valore
Kingsborough Community College

Brief Contents

Contents

Communication—The Key to Success 103

Records Management, Travel, and Finances 189

Career Success 277

Part I

Professional Profile

Randall Fullington

Student Services Assistant
English Department
University of Colorado
Boulder, Colorado

Randall Fullington is the student services assistant in the English Department at the University of Colorado at Boulder. "I work to ensure that the faculty and students receive the information, supplies, and support they need throughout the school year. If I'm doing my job, faculty and students can focus on their teaching and studies while not having to worry about the minor (and sometimes major) day-to-day administrative issues."

Randall advises new administrative professionals to listen, ask questions, be friendly, and be patient. "On your first day, you won't know how to do everything you are required to do, and your coworkers and boss will understand this. Listen carefully and ask questions to learn the ins and outs of your job. Don't be too hard on yourself if you make mistakes. All of your colleagues are constantly learning how to do their jobs better, so be patient with yourself as you learn how to do your assignments."

"If I'm doing my job, faculty and students can focus on their teaching and studies while not having to worry about . . . administrative issues."

Appropriate self-presentation in the workplace is extremely important from the get-go. "My philosophy is to dress and act in a way that doesn't elicit any response from the people I work with, unless it's a compliment," says Randall. "A clean desk also demonstrates efficiency and professionalism. People will trust you more if your work space indicates to them that you get the job done.

"The number-one thing I do to get and stay organized is to find a procedural system that works and stick to that system. I have to sort through a lot of paperwork and procedures. In order to ensure that I don't misplace documents or forget steps, I always try to follow the same processing and filing procedures."

Randall loves his job because he works with a diverse group of people he respects: "Every day, I get to interact with students and faculty who share a similar passion for discussing literature, current events, and history."

The Workplace and You

Ready, Set, Plan

Use this space to plan your work in this section.
Record the due dates for reading assignments and other activities for each chapter. If you are working with a team or partner, record the schedule for team meetings. Do you need a list of phone numbers or e-mail addresses? Don't forget your other commitments: work, other classes, and family.

Do I qualify?

Administrative Assistant

Fortune 1000 company is looking for an experienced professional to support a division president by performing advanced, diversified, and confidential administrative duties, including:

- Complete word processing tasks such as correspondence, reports, memos, proposals, charts, and agreements
- Provide administrative support to new employees
- Learn and use the company work order management system
- Work with the finance team to track budgets, provide reporting, and complete capital funding request forms
- Participate in and support firm-wide projects
- Identify challenges and solicit assistance for resolution

©MARK WRAGG, ISTOCK

CHAPTER

1

Entering the Workforce

The World of Office Administration

In offices all around the world, the demand for administrative assistants is strong and growing. These essential office workers are respected and valued in business, industry, government, education, law, medicine, science, and the arts. Employees throughout the organization rely on administrative assistants to keep offices organized and operating efficiently.

An administrative assistant is usually "Information Central" for the department, perhaps reporting to the department head, but assisting others as well. Assistants schedule meetings and appointments, handle calls, correspondence, faxes, and e-mails, keep records and files, and manage many other administrative details.

Learning Objectives

1. Assess the demand for administrative assistants and describe their work and work settings.

2. Describe and begin developing the skills, knowledge, attitudes, and traits employers expect of an administrative assistant.

3. Describe the responsibilities of the employer and employees in a work relationship.

4. Describe the culture and structure of business organizations.

Today both women and men are choosing office administration as a career and as a means of advancing within a company or field. The work can be very rewarding in itself. It can also serve as an introduction to a business or industry, from which the administrative assistant can move to other positions or occupations. Either way, administrative assistants need a wide range of skills, traits, and attitudes to succeed.

What Do Administrative Professionals Do?

Administrative assistants support organizations in many ways. Figure 1-1 lists some of their most common responsibilities.

Figure 1-1 Typical Responsibilities of Administrative Professionals

- Relieve management of administrative detail
- Coordinate work flow
- Compose correspondence and reports
- Maintain the supervisor's calendar
- Arrange travel
- Recruit, hire, train, and supervise secretarial or clerical staff as required
- Do Internet research
- Meet and greet clients and visitors
- Coordinate and maintain records
- Set up and facilitate meetings and conferences
- Maintain and distribute staff weekly schedules
- Manage projects
- Answer the telephone
- Perform general clerical duties such as faxing, mailing, and filing

Source: Some data are from the International Association of Administrative Professionals (IAAP), "Administrative Support Job Descriptions," http://www.iaap-hq.org/resources/keytrends/JobDescriptions.html (accessed March 11, 2010).

Most administrative assistants are required to be at the office during business hours, generally working 37.5 to 40 hours a week. Some may work part-time, but rarely are administrative assistants allowed to work from home because, by its nature, the work is very office-centered. The administrative professional is almost always expected to be in the office to respond to requests and keep things running. There are exceptions, of course, such as working at an off-site conference, but most administrative assistants are responsible for covering "home base."

The Growing Job Market

According to data from the U.S. Department of Labor (DOL), administrative assistant is one of the largest occupations in the United States, and it is among those expected to add the largest numbers of new jobs in the coming years. In 2008, administrative assistants held more than 4.3 million jobs. By 2018, some 471,600 new jobs are expected to open. Figure 1-2 on page 6 gives details about this projected growth.

Growth is predicted because administrative professionals work in areas of the economy that are expanding, such as health care, social services, and legal services. Some of this growth is occurring because the roles of administrative assistants are expanding as they take on more kinds of work that used to be done by other professionals.

Where the Jobs Are DOL reports that about 90 percent of administrative assistants work in the service sector. The service sector includes activities that provide a service rather than a product, such as medical and legal services, hospitality and tourism, government, insurance and finance, education, the arts, and social services. The remaining 10 percent work in businesses in the manufacturing and construction industries. Figure 1-3 on page 6 shows employment of administrative assistants during 2008 by specialty.

Temporary Administrative Assistants The demand for temps is growing rapidly because businesses often have seasonal or temporary increases in workloads. Temporary staffing also saves the

Figure 1-2 **Predicted Job Growth through 2018**

Predicted Job Growth 2008–2018			
Occupational Title	**Total Jobs, 2008**	**New Jobs**	**Percentage Increase**
Secretaries and administrative assistants	4,348,100	471,600	11%
Executive secretaries and administrative assistants	1,594,400	204,400	13%
Legal secretaries	262,600	48,400	18%
Medical secretaries	471,100	125,500	27%
Secretaries, except legal, medical, and executive	2,020,000	93,300	5%

Source: U.S. Department of Labor, *Occupational Outlook Handbook, 2010–11 Edition*, "Secretaries and Administrative Assistants," http://www.bls.gov/oco/ocos151.htm (accessed February 15, 2010).

employer certain costs of permanent employees, such as health insurance benefits and retirement plans. According to DOL, in 2008 more than a million administrative assistants worked for employment services, mostly temporary staffing agencies.[1]

Working for a temporary agency has advantages. Some temporary positions lead to long-term jobs, a situation known as temp-to-hire. Some staffing agencies offer free training to make their workers more marketable to client companies, and some provide health insurance benefits.

Temporary agencies give people more control over when and where they work because a temporary worker is free to turn down an assignment. Working short-term job assignments allows workers to try different employment settings to see which they prefer.

Still, there are drawbacks to temporary employment. Temporary workers often earn less than full-time employees, and they are typically the first to

Figure 1-3 **Employment by Specialty, 2008**

Secretaries, except legal, medical, and executive	46%
Executive secretaries and administrative assistants	37%
Medical secretaries	11%
Legal secretaries	6%

Source: U.S. Department of Labor, *Occupational Outlook Handbook, 2010–11 Edition*, "Secretaries and Administrative Assistants," http://www.bls.gov/oco/ocos151.htm (accessed February 15, 2010).

be laid off when an organization needs to reduce its staff.

Virtual Administrative Assistants   The Internet and e-mail have created a niche for freelance administrative assistants, also called **virtual assistants**. These self-employed administrative assistants work from a home office to provide off-site administrative and/or personal assistance to clients. This arrangement is popular with individuals and small start-up companies that may not require the services of a full-time administrative assistant.

Virtual assistants have their own offices, often in their homes, equipped with a computer and appropriate software, an Internet connection, and an e-mail account as well as fax and telephone equipment for teleconferencing. Most people who start their own virtual assistant service have at least five years of experience in an office as an assistant, sometimes with special expertise such as legal secretarial experience.

Education and Training

A generation ago, a high school diploma was considered enough prior training for beginning administrative assistants, and that is still the case in some offices. However, the roles of administrative assistants have grown to include a great deal more responsibility and increasing technical skills. Associate's degrees are available through programs in office technology or office administration at community and technical colleges. Many temporary placement agencies also provide formal training in computer and office skills. Some employers require a college degree in business or a related field.

Most administrative assistants polish and refine their skills on the job. Many take courses offered by professional organizations such as

1 U.S. Department of Labor, *Career Guide to Industries, 2010–11 Edition*, "Employment Services," http://www.bls. gov/oco/cg/cgs039.htm (accessed February 15, 2010).

the International Association of Administrative Professionals (IAAP) or by local colleges. Administrative assistants can also earn a variety of professional credentials, some of which are described in Chapter 2. Many seek online training, especially in new office technologies. Retraining and continuing education are essential to the on-going success of the administrative professional. The more you know, the more valuable you will be to your employer.

Legal and medical secretaries need highly specialized expertise, including knowledge of legal or medical terminology and an understanding of procedures in their field. Legal secretaries prepare legal documents such as complaints, motions, and subpoenas. They often teach new lawyers how to prepare documents to submit to the courts, and they may assist with legal research. Medical secretaries record medical histories, handle insurance claims, and arrange laboratory tests. Some help to prepare medical articles, speeches, and conference proceedings.

Employer Expectations

Employers expect all their employees to have the knowledge and skills they need to do their jobs. They also expect employees to have the interpersonal skills needed to work well with coworkers and customers.

Organizations seek employees who are responsible and accountable for completing the work assigned to them. They want people who manage their time well, have strong thinking and problem-solving skills, and are committed to advancing the goals of the organization.

Employers look for workers with a combination of skills, knowledge, attitudes, and personal traits, including:

- Technical skills
- Interpersonal skills
- Communication skills
- Teamwork and collaboration skills
- Customer focus

Virtual assistants work from a home office.

- Problem-solving and critical-thinking skills
- Professionalism (a professional attitude)
- Productivity
- A strong work ethic

Technical Skills

Technical skills are the ability to *apply* specialized knowledge and procedures, such as the use of specific software to get the job done. In many occupations, the ability to learn new software is essential. Technical skills change, so the employee must be able to adapt and learn new skills.

Administrative professionals are expected to know how to use word processing, database management, spreadsheet, and presentation software. In some offices, they must be able to use desktop publishing and project management software. Many organizations have proprietary software applications that are not taught in schools and colleges and that are learned on the job. Some proprietary applications are built on familiar tools, such as *Microsoft Excel®* and *Microsoft Access®*.

As an administrative professional, you will be expected to learn new skills based on what you already know. For example, word processing is a basic office skill. You may be familiar with *Microsoft Office® 2007* but take a job in a group that uses *Microsoft Office® 2010*. Your employer will expect you to be able to use *Office 2010*. Or you may never have used a particular phone system, but your employer will expect you to learn how to use it quickly with no formal training.

A few other technical skills are required. In addition to having good keyboarding skills, you should be good at spelling, punctuation, and grammar. You will also need to learn to use general office equipment efficiently. You may be expected to troubleshoot problems with peripheral equipment such as scanners, printers, copiers, and fax machines, and you probably will be expected to train and guide others in their use as well.

What's in a Name?

Administrative assistants go by many job titles. Although your coworkers may not be familiar with the term *administrative professional,* it is important that you realize the professional nature of this work.

Although some *admins* (another popular term) see their jobs as a stepping-stone to other positions, many administrative professionals choose this work as their *profession.* Generally, they expand their role and are given more responsibilities, but they remain in the profession they have chosen.

You will hear other terms for administrative professional, among them:

- ⬈ Administrative associate
- ⬈ Secretary
- ⬈ Executive secretary
- ⬈ Office manager
- ⬈ Executive assistant

Interpersonal Skills

Every employee needs good interpersonal skills. One of the most common reasons that people fail to advance in their careers or are let go from their jobs is the inability to get along with others. Furthermore, good interpersonal skills make the work environment more pleasant, less stressful, and more satisfying.

As an administrative professional, you will interact with many people each day, in person, by e-mail, and on the telephone. You should treat supervisors, coworkers, and customers with courtesy, respect, and consideration.

Communication Skills

You will learn about effective speaking, listening, writing, and presentation skills in coming chapters. It is very important to develop and improve these skills throughout your career. In survey after survey, year after year, employers rank strong communication skills among the skills they look for most when hiring.

The workplace runs on efficient conversations and e-mails in which ideas are exchanged, questions answered, and decisions made. You need to be able to express your thoughts and ideas effectively when speaking and writing and to be skilled in asking questions. You also need to listen well to ensure you understand what others are saying as well as their attitudes and intentions.

Teamwork and Collaboration Skills

Many tasks in today's workplace are accomplished by groups or teams. An understanding of how teams work and how to be an effective team member will help you in your career.

By definition an administrative professional is a team member who helps and supports others. People who choose this occupation generally work closely with one or more people. In addition to this daily supporting role, from time to time you may be asked to manage special projects with others. You may serve on teams to solve problems or to complete assignments.

Working collaboratively in a group or team requires a particular set of skills. You will learn more about teamwork in Chapter 5.

Customer Focus

Employers look for employees who are genuinely committed to serving customers. Exceptional customer service turns occasional customers into loyal customers and attracts new business through word of mouth.

Many administrative assistants are the face of the office—the first person most visitors meet. How you conduct yourself reflects on the organization. In every case, you want to appear professional, pleasant, cooperative, and helpful. You will learn more about interacting with customers in Chapter 6.

Problem-Solving and Critical-Thinking Skills

Every workplace has problems and challenges. Your employer will expect you to use your critical-thinking skills to anticipate problems so they can be prevented. If they cannot be prevented, you will need to be able to work out ways of solving them.

Versatility and adaptability are also tremendous assets. Employers want employees who accept and cooperate with change as the company grows. The ability to analyze situations critically will help you see the bigger picture—the events that are causing the change—so you can respond positively and productively.

You will read more about these skills and qualities in Chapter 2. Remember the excellent advice to be part of the solution, not part of the problem.

Professionalism

Have you ever had this experience? You walk into a huge discount store and one employee stands out. That person gives you his or her full attention, walks with you to the section of the store you are looking for, and smiles at you if you happen to meet again. That employee is a professional.

Professionalism comprises a number of qualities and skills, including good judgment, initiative, discretion, organizational ability, the ability to work independently, and a professional appearance (your work space and yourself). Professionals are proud of doing their work well and proud to represent their organization.

You will read more about professionalism in Chapter 2 and throughout this text.

Productivity

Employers look for employees who are productive. Productivity is not the same as being busy, nor even as completing all the day's assignments. Productivity is not just a matter of the quantity of work you do but also of the quality—not just how much you do but how well you do it.

As an administrative professional, your role is to support your supervisor and others and to ensure that the office runs smoothly. You will need to become skilled at setting priorities, completing the most important tasks first, always meeting deadlines, and refocusing on a task after an interruption. All these skills take planning and effort.

Technology @Work

Set a goal to become an expert in the most common multipurpose software your group uses (word processing, spreadsheet, presentation, e-mail/calendar, etc.) so you can support people by answering their questions, solving problems, and making their documents look professional.

When the group upgrades software or gets a new program, become an expert user. Be proactive in learning to use new software—and the phone system, copier, and printer. Because of your central role, people will ask you for help and expect you to be able to provide it.

Communicating @Work

A discussion about a work topic is not over when the participants walk away from each other, hang up, or close the e-mail. They must verify that they understood the exchange the same way (decisions, follow-up items, timing, who will do what, and so on).

Verbally recapping the outcomes of a conversation is always a good idea. After every business discussion, you should record the key points.

Send an e-mail to participants summarizing any decisions that were made and any actions to be taken. Note tasks and deadlines in your calendar or personal information management software.

You will also need to develop strategies for avoiding procrastination. Putting off tasks you dislike can lead to a crisis or missed deadline that can cause problems for the people you support.

You will need to learn to track multiple projects to make sure you are on schedule and to follow up to ensure tasks are completed correctly. You will learn more about organizing yourself and managing your time in Chapter 3.

Strong Work Ethic

Most supervisors prefer to hire someone who has a strong work ethic—someone who takes pride in working effectively and efficiently. This professional quality is discussed more fully in Chapter 2.

Discipline yourself to get to work a few minutes early every morning so that you are settled when the workday begins. You should be at your desk and on task first thing in the morning, and you should stay on task throughout the day, working as efficiently as you can.

Throughout the day, there will be distractions and temptations. At most companies, it is all right to take an occasional brief break to talk with a coworker about things other than business. You want to be on friendly terms with everyone. Just keep it short.

Employer/Employee Responsibilities

The employer/employee relationship should be a cooperative effort in which you share values and goals and are equally dedicated to meeting the needs of the organization and its customers or clients. Employees should be committed to helping their employer produce high-quality products or services.

As an employee, you owe your employer hard work, loyalty, and goodwill. You are expected to be honest, conscientious, and committed. You should come to work punctually every day with a positive attitude, well rested, and prepared to put in a full day's work.

In the most successful organizations, employers and employees support each other. Your employer is making a considerable investment in you. The employer pays you, of course, and many employers offer training and benefits such as health, disability, and life insurance and paid vacation, holidays, and sick days. (You will learn about employee benefits in Chapter 14.) Employers have significant overhead expenses, including rent, utilities, taxes, liability insurance, equipment, and supplies. Your work contributes to the profits that pay these expenses. When you work productively, the money spent on your salary and benefits is a good investment.

In many organizations, you will have a formal job description that outlines your duties and your role in the organization. Nearly every job description for an administrative professional ends (or should end) with the words "other duties as assigned." When your supervisor asks you to do something, you should never take the attitude, "That's not my job," unless the request is illegal, unethical, or completely unreasonable.

Your employer should provide a safe and healthy work environment so that you are comfortable and able to focus on your job. Your employer should give you the tools, equipment, and supplies you need to get your work done. Training should be available, usually on the job, to help you master the skills you need to perform well.

©iStock

A good employer will offer frequent, constructive comments on your performance to help you learn the job the way the employer wants it done. In many jobs, you will have a formal performance appraisal, typically once a year, to help you understand what you are doing well and how you can improve to become an outstanding employee through training and development. Chapter 15 provides more information about performance evaluations.

The Work World of the Administrative Professional

Learning about the culture, structure, and management of the organization you work for will help you perform your job better. It will help you understand

- Your position in the organization.
- Your position relative to others.
- Acceptable behaviors and actions.
- How the organization is run.
- Why things are done the way they are.
- What to expect.

Dear Savvy Admin

Dear Savvy Admin:

My boss is hopelessly disorganized. He loses documents I give him. He doesn't seem to be able to look up a phone number without my help. He doesn't get back to me with information the company president requests. I like him and want to keep working here, but our work styles are very different. What can I do?

Babysitting the Boss

Dear Babysitting the Boss:

Isn't it nice to be needed? Think of it as job security. In the meantime, keep a copy of documents you give him with a sticky note attached indicating when you gave it to him. When he asks you for it, you can say, "Oh, you already have it, Pete. I gave it to you Tuesday. But I have a copy if you can't find yours."

Have you set up his frequently used phone numbers in *Microsoft Outlook®*? You can show him how easy it is to find the numbers.

Try e-mail alerts and gentle reminders such as "Subject: Reminder from Sarah: Albert needs sales data by Friday." It might take more than one reminder. But remember that your job is to make him look good.

Savvy Admin

Office Culture and Language

Every organization has its own culture, which reflects the key values, beliefs, and attitudes that drive the organization and define its style of doing business. The culture may be formal and strict or casual and laid-back. Most cultures are somewhere in between. You will absorb this atmosphere as you work, but by paying careful attention, you can learn about it more quickly and more quickly fit in.

Culture is expressed in symbols such as the dress code and unwritten rules that may not be discussed but that show up in employees' attitudes. Southwest Airlines, for example, is known for having a relaxed, informal culture. Employees have an upbeat attitude and are dedicated to helping each other and to providing excellent customer service.

You will also find that every office has its own terminology. If you are working in a law or medical office, you will need to learn legal or medical terms. The same is true of working for an architect, an engineer, or a performing artist. Make it your goal to acquire and maintain a good working knowledge of the field.

Types of Organizations

The businesses you work for as an administrative professional may be organized in different ways. The three basic forms are a sole proprietorship, a partnership, and a corporation.

- **Sole proprietorship** A **sole proprietorship** is owned and controlled by an individual. The owner receives all the profits and is responsible for all the debts.

- **Partnership** A **partnership** is an association of two or more people as co-owners of a business. Business decisions, profits, and losses are shared among the partners according to the terms of the partnership agreement. Partnerships are largely being replaced by limited liability companies.

- **Corporation** **Corporations** are legal entities formed by following a formal process of incorporation established by state statutes. Corporations may be publicly or privately owned. They are owned by investors called **shareholders** (or stockholders) who have purchased stock representing a portion or share of the company. An **S-corporation** is a type of corporation that has 75 or fewer stockholders.

The investment of stockholders may be affected by actions, decisions, policies, or practices of the business. For example, if the business is mismanaged or has financial problems, the stock price may decrease, and the stockholder may lose money on the investment.

States recognize variations on these three basic forms, such as these common types of businesses:

- **Limited liability company** A **limited liability company** (also called a limited liability corporation, or LLC) combines the tax advantages of a partnership with the limited liability of a corporation. An LLC must include two or more members. The LLC can own property, borrow and lend money, enter into contracts, and elect or appoint managers or agents. An advantage of an LLC is that the individuals owning it are protected from personal liability for what the corporation does or fails to do. Professionals such as medical doctors, accountants, and lawyers often operate as an LLC.

- **Nonprofit corporation** **Nonprofit corporations** are formed to engage in civic, charitable, educational, or artistic endeavors. These corporations are generally exempt from federal, state, and local income taxes and qualify as charitable organizations for donors. Examples are hospitals, schools, charities, and arts organizations.

- **Government entity** **Government entities** (offices, departments, and agencies) carry out the functions of state, local, and national government. Examples are regulatory agencies, safety services, public schools and universities, government-run social

workplace wisdom

The tone of the workplace and the formality of working relationships are determined by top management. One way that tone and formality are expressed is in how people address each other. Because information like this is unwritten, you will need to observe those around you to determine what people in your organization generally do.

A good rule of thumb is to address your supervisor and other higher-level personnel with a courtesy title such as *Mr.* or *Ms.* followed by a surname. Do not use first names unless invited to do so. Address people the way they want to be addressed. If your coworker prefers to be called William, call him William, not Bill. Words like *honey* and *dear* have no place at work.

services such as the U.S. Department of Veterans Affairs, legislative bodies such as city councils, and numerous other departments, commissions, bureaus, and boards.

Formal Organizational Structures

Large companies are usually under the control of a board of directors that is charged with looking after the interests of shareholders. Boards of directors are responsible for establishing policies and setting goals that guide the management of the organization. The directors typically meet monthly or every two or three months. In addition to making policy decisions, boards hire, evaluate, and dismiss (if necessary) the chief executive officer (CEO) of the corporation.

Boards generally provide oversight through committees that deal with specific aspects of the business, such as a personnel committee or a finance committee. Directors may not put themselves in a position in which their private interests and duties conflict with the duties they owe the company. When these interests and duties differ, this is called a conflict of interest.

The board of directors assists the CEO and other officers in determining the direction the organization will take. It holds the CEO responsible for the organization's overall performance in a nonprofit setting and/or for its profitability in a for-profit enterprise. The board also holds the CEO responsible for following official policies and procedures and operating the organization within ethical guidelines.

In addition to the CEO, a company may have a CFO (chief financial officer), COO (chief operating officer), and CIO (chief information officer). These top executives may have presidents and vice presidents reporting to them. In large organizations, managers at lower levels, such as the human resources director and the director of engineering, are responsible for day-to-day operations as well as carrying out upper management's strategies and decisions and achieving the goals they set for the organization.

Management Responsibilities

Every organization has leaders and managers. The top executives described above are the company's

People @Work

Every chapter of *The Administrative Professional* has a People @ Work feature that describes an occupation with which an administrative assistant can expect to interact. This first chapter introduces the subject-matter experts, sometimes called SMEs (rhymes with *sneeze*). These are the people who do the work you support, such as lawyers, architects, chiropractors, police officers, and museum curators.

SMEs can be a useful resource in helping you acquire a thorough knowledge of the field you are working in. Look through trade journals, explore websites—and ask the SMEs about their work. The more you know, the better support you can provide.

key leaders, who set the direction for the organization. You will read more about leadership in Chapter 16.

Management is considered a subset of leadership, and the responsibilities associated with these two roles overlap. Although the textbook covers the characteristics of effective leaders and the responsibilities of effective managers separately, understand that the most effective managers are also effective leaders.

Some key functions of management are planning, organizing, managing information, recruiting and hiring, and evaluating.

Planning   Planning sets the direction of an organization. A major part of planning is establishing goals and objectives. Although most organizations have goals and objectives, they may be very loosely defined or not defined at all. Defining goals in writing and establishing measurable results are key to successful planning.

Strategic planning, also called **long-range planning**, is the process of defining the organization's long-term mission, assessing the current business environment, anticipating changes in the environment, and developing strategies for achieving the mission. Organizational plans are generally written for a one-year period and a three- to five-year period.

The overall goals of an organization may be set by boards of directors and top-level executives (presidents and executive vice presidents). Once these goals have been determined, they are distributed to the managers in the organization. The managers, along with their work groups, then set objectives for their work units. Managers are held responsible by upper administration for achieving the objectives that have been established.

Assume you supervise two administrative staff members. What is your involvement in the planning process? First, you review the strategic plan with the personnel who report to you and go over the long-range objectives. You talk with them about the directions the unit needs to take to support the plan, and you set unit objectives that support the overall objectives of the organization. The unit then develops a plan that specifies how the objectives will be accomplished—what actions will occur, who is accountable, when the tasks will be completed, what financial resources are necessary, and how the tasks will be evaluated.

Organizing   After the plans are developed, the work is organized. Organization brings together people and systems to accomplish the plans and objectives in an effective manner.

Organization of people often involves teamwork. Once a team receives an assignment, the team leader and members determine the responsibilities of each team member and accomplish the tasks.

A **system** is a group of independent but interrelated elements that make a unified whole, such as the departments or units in a business. Information flows between the different elements that make up the system. The leader of a unit (a department, group, or team) helps the unit members understand how their work affects the activities of other units in the system. The effectiveness of an organization requires that the systems be well defined.

Managing Information   Organizations generate a staggering amount of information: about products, personnel, finances, and so on. If information is to be of value, it must be accurate, complete, relevant, and timely. Systems must be developed that allow information to be stored properly, used effectively, and distributed to the necessary groups both inside and outside the organization.

Recruiting and Hiring   Organizations usually establish procedures through their human resources departments that outline how they will recruit employees. Managers and supervisors within departments then have the responsibility for recruiting and employing.

Writing @Work

The Partnership for 21st Century Skills, a national organization of businesses and nonprofit organizations, has identified knowledge and skills it considers essential for success at work and in life. The partnership has set these standards for writing:

- ↗ Express thoughts and ideas effectively in different forms and contexts.

- ↗ Use communication for a range of purposes, such as to inform, instruct, motivate, and persuade.

- ↗ Use different media and technologies.

- ↗ Know how to judge their effectiveness before using them as well as how to assess their impact.

- ↗ Communicate effectively in diverse environments (including multilingual environments).

Use the activities in this course to strengthen your writing skills.

©iStock

Evaluating   Once plans have been set into motion, they must be periodically evaluated. Without evaluation, plans may not be carried out, with no one asking why. Organizations suffer, and even go out of business, because of an inability to adhere to plans and deliver a product or service that customers need.

Management Challenges

The American workforce is changing rapidly. You may be working with people of all ages and all ethnic, national, and racial backgrounds. White Americans, especially white men, dominated American culture and workplaces for generations, but government projections show that whites will no longer be the major racial group by 2042.[2] As new laws have been passed to encourage equal opportunities for women and minorities, this diversity has grown and is now embraced as a positive force in economics as well as in society.

The diversity of the workforce is only one way that employment is changing. You will experience many other changes throughout your career. Organizations and people change for many reasons. They may decide to change to improve what they do or how they do it. They may be forced to change to stay competitive in changing economic times. Whatever the reason, you will be happier and more successful if you accept change and cooperate when those above you implement it. Having a professional attitude toward change is discussed in more detail in the next chapter.

2 U.S. Census Bureau, "An Older and More Diverse Nation by Midcentury," August 14, 2008, http://www.census.gov/Press-Release/www/releases/archives/population/012496.html (accessed February 18, 2010).

Understanding Your Organization

The most valuable administrative professionals know a great deal about the company or organization they work for and the department or group they support, knowledge they begin to accumulate even before they are hired. Chapter 15 describes information you should gather about a company or organization before applying for a job there. Once hired, you should also learn about the group or department you support and your role in the group.

- What do they produce, or what services do they provide?
- Which departments do they interact with?
- How do they contribute to the organization's goals?
- What does the group need most from you?
- Do your coworkers have advice for you based on how the person who held your position before you did the work?

Learn about the structure and culture of your organization and some basic information about the industry in general. A variety of sources are available for acquiring this knowledge. They include company publications such as brochures and annual reports, the company website, and newspaper and magazine articles. Look for articles from the business section of local newspapers and from financial publications such as *Fortune* and *Forbes* magazines and *The Wall Street Journal*. Observe your supervisor and coworkers; they are valuable resources for learning about your organization.

Key Terms

corporation

government entity

limited liability company

long-range planning

nonprofit corporation

partnership

S-corporation

shareholder

sole proprietorship

strategic planning

system

virtual assistant

Summary

- Nearly 472,000 new jobs for administrative assistants are expected to open by 2018.

- Administrative professionals perform a wide and expanding range of tasks to keep offices running efficiently and smoothly.

- Employers look for technical, interpersonal, communication, collaboration, and teamwork skills, as well as skills in customer relations, problem solving, and critical thinking.

- The employee's responsibilities include honesty, conscientiousness, and professional behavior. The employer's responsibilities include providing a safe and healthy work environment and the tools and equipment needed to perform the job.

- Every organization has its own culture, which reflects the key values, beliefs, and attitudes that drive the organization.

- The businesses you work for may be organized in one of three basic forms: a sole proprietorship, a partnership, or a corporation. Your employer could also be a nonprofit organization or government entity.

- Boards of directors are responsible for establishing policies and setting goals that guide the management of the organization.

- Top executives and managers are responsible for planning, organizing information, recruiting and hiring, and overseeing operations of a business.

- Learning about the organization where you work will help you perform your job better and will increase your value to the company.

Bookmark It. *For convenient access to activities, links, and valuable career resources for administrative professionals, visit the companion website for this text:*

www.cengage.com/officetech/fultoncalkins

Discussion Questions

1. Why is the job market for administrative professionals growing? What effect do you think the economic downturn of 2008–2009 had on this field?

2. Where do administrative professionals work? Name at least two factors that would be the same and two factors that would be different in the various settings.

3. What technical skills do administrative assistants need?

4. Why are interpersonal and communication skills especially important for someone in an administrative assistant role?

5. List several types of nonprofit organizations. Brainstorm some typical tasks an administrative assistant might do in each setting.

6. In a work relationship, what are the employer's responsibilities to employees?

7. How would you describe the culture of the institution in which you are taking this class? How does your class reflect this culture?

Critical Thinking

How can you help? You are Pastor Helmut Rieg's administrative assistant at Grace Lutheran Church. An elderly neighbor, Lester Beddinghaus, has called to complain that trees on church property are shedding leaves onto his lawn. He wants the church to rake the leaves so he won't have to pay his lawn service to do it. Pastor Rieg has told you that the church is under no legal obligation to remove the leaves, but he would like to find a way to resolve the problem. With a partner, discuss how you might help.

Meanwhile, Mr. Beddinghaus has called you three times to complain about the leaves. You have assured him that you are working on a solution, but he seems to be lonely and in need of someone to listen. How can you listen to his concerns without letting him take too much of your time? How can you gracefully end a telephone conversation in which he goes on and on? How can you discourage him from calling so often?

Build Workplace Skills

1. **Self-improvement plan** Create a *Word* file named CH01 Skills. Create a three-column table with seven rows. Title the table **ADMINISTRATIVE ASSISTANTS**. Label the columns as shown:

Skills, Attitudes, and Traits	Importance	Ways to Improve

Using the information in this chapter, in the first column, list what you consider to be the six most important skills, qualities, attitudes, and traits administrative professionals need. In the second column, explain why each skill, quality, attitude, or trait is important. In the third column, describe how you plan to improve your abilities in each of the six areas during this course. (Learning Objective 2)

Planning Notes

Learning Objectives

1. Assess the demand for administrative assistants and describe their work and work settings.

2. Describe and begin developing the skills, knowledge, attitudes, and traits employers expect of an administrative assistant.

3. Describe the responsibilities of the employer and employees in a work relationship.

4. Describe the culture and structure of business organizations.

Critical Thinking; Activities 1, 5, 8

Activities 2, 12

21st Century Skills CAREER **Activities 2, 3, 4, 6, 7, 9, 10, 11**

2. **Interpersonal skills**   Ask five employed people you know about the topic of interpersonal skills at work. What is their best advice for getting along well with others at the workplace? Can they describe a situation from their own work experience in which interpersonal skills were especially important?

   Select one situation from your interviews to share with your classmates. Include a title for the situation, the name of the person you interviewed (if you have permission to share his or her name), and a brief account of the situation. If the situation reflects poorly on an employee, do not use real names. Save the document as a single-file web page that can be posted and viewed by your classmates. (Learning Objective 2)

3. **21st Century Skills**   Go to the website of the Partnership for 21st Century Skills. The companion website for the textbook has a link to this site. Explore the Route 21 section of the site. Read about each of the three skills areas. Pick one area and write a scenario in which an administrative professional applies (or does not apply) some of the skills. For example, you might pick the Learning and Innovation skills area and write about someone using Communication and Collaboration skills. Include details to make your scenario realistic. (Learning Objective 1)

4. **Employee responsibilities**   Keiko works as an administrative assistant for Mr. Alvarez. Keiko often arrives at work late and is very tired from watching movies late into the previous night. She tries to appear as if she is working very hard whenever Mr. Alvarez can see her. When he is away from his office, Keiko often reads a magazine or shops on the Internet. She knows she has deadlines for finishing her work, but she is not committed to meeting them. Keiko reasons, "I will get paid the same amount whether the work is finished on time or not, so why hurry?"

   Does Keiko behave in the manner her employer has a right to expect? Why or why not? What behaviors or attitudes would you suggest Keiko change? (Learning Objective 3)

5. **Business organization and culture**   Select a business to research. The business can be one with which you are somewhat familiar, such as a local company, or a large, nationally known company. Talk to employees, read newspaper or magazine articles, or search the Internet to find information about the company. Create a short report that gives the following information:

   - Company name
   - Structure (partnership, corporation, etc.)
   - Main company location(s)
   - Primary products or services offered
   - Corporate culture (values, mission statement, causes supported, or other information from the About Us, History, or similar pages of the company website) (Learning Objective 4)

❯ *Communicate Clearly*

6. **Introduce yourself**   Write a note or e-mail to your instructor. Introduce yourself (your educational background, other classes you are enrolled in, your part-time or full-time job, hobbies, family, and so on). Explain why you are taking this course, your goals for the course, and your career goals.

7. **Are you qualified?**   Look at the sample job posting for an administrative assistant on page 4 of this chapter. Select two of the qualifications and list your experience in

each area. Use your lists to write two sentences that you could use in a cover letter to convince the employer that you have the necessary qualifications for the job. (Learning Objective 2)

8. **Project memo**   Your supervisor has asked you to create a final copy of a memo announcing a special project. Open the *Word* file CH01 Memo from the data files. Edit the memo to correct errors in keyboarding, punctuation, spelling, and word usage.

Develop Relationships

9. **Mentoring**   With a partner, research mentoring on the Internet. Discuss how the two of you can mentor each other during this class. Come up with concrete ideas, not generalities, and document your plan in a *Word* file.

10. **Good cubicle neighbors**   You are the office manager at Buferd Real Estate Company. Maggie, a new administrative assistant, has complained to you that she is having trouble concentrating because her neighbor in the next cubicle, Morgan, has the radio on all day playing sixties oldies.

    In a small group, discuss how you might approach resolving this problem. Would it be best done in a casual conversation with Morgan? An e-mail? Would it be better to have an informal meeting in your office with just Maggie and Morgan? Would you wait and bring it up in the next meeting of all the administrative assistants? Write a summary of the group's recommendations for addressing this issue.

Use Technology

11. **Job opportunities**   Start a collection of local help-wanted ads for administrative professionals. Copy at least three online ads into a *Word* file. Label each ad with the website at which you found it, the date, and the type of organization. Make it a point to look for new ads throughout this class, and add to your *Word* file every week. (Learning Objectives 1 and 2)

12. **Online planners**   Administrative professionals are busy, and a planner is essential for being organized, keeping up with your workload, and planning ahead. As an assignment for this course, use an online planner or organizer software during this session of school to keep track of all your classes and other responsibilities. If you use *Microsoft Outlook* for e-mail, but have not used the calendar function, learn how to use it. You might also look on the Internet at the many companies that offer free electronic organizers and services. If an online organizer is not for you, find a calendar or planner template (or create one), print it, and use it during this semester or quarter. (Learning Objective 2)

Above & Beyond

A day in the life   Arrange to interview an administrative professional at a company or organization that interests you. The interview can be on the phone or in person. Try to arrange to job-shadow the person for some or all of a workday. Prepare a short list of questions before your interview in order to learn what a "day in the life" of this job is like. Note the tasks done by the administrative professional and describe the work setting. Write a short report to summarize your experience. (Learning Objective 1 and 2)

Executive Administrative Assistant Wanted

Company president seeks highly motivated, detail-oriented individual to manage the office. Duties include:

- Schedule meetings, update calendar items, and screen phone calls
- Prepare and manage confidential correspondence and records
- Arrange travel plans
- Organize and schedule events and meetings

The successful candidate must be dependable and have excellent organizational, time management, and communication skills.

©MARK WRAGG, ISTOCK

Do I qualify?

2

Becoming a Professional

What Is a Professional?

Administrative assistants perform balancing acts in their jobs. As an administrative assistant, you are committed to helping others function well in their own positions. To do this, you need to be able to take direction and conform to established practices and policies. Your position also calls for the initiative, thinking skills, and good judgment to recognize potential problems, assess situations, and act creatively. A professional administrative assistant can do both of these things—help others do their jobs well and know when to take the initiative and act decisively.

Throughout *The Administrative Professional*, you will learn how to fulfill your role professionally and project a professional image. Your professionalism (or lack of it) shows in everything you do at work, and becoming a true professional is a key to your success as an administrative assistant.

Learning Objectives

1. Describe the qualities that make a worker a professional.

2. Explain why critical-thinking, decision-making, and problem-solving skills are essential to an administrative assistant.

3. Describe how factors such as appearance, communication, and teamwork skills affect your professional image.

4. Describe the importance of following business etiquette.

A **professional** looks, speaks, writes, and behaves in a manner that reflects well on the employer as well as the employee. A professional sets an example for others through a strong work ethic, positive attitude, and dedication to continuing improvement.

Work Ethic

One of the most valued traits in an administrative assistant is a strong **work ethic**. A person with a strong work ethic does not have to be told to work hard. This determination comes naturally from an inner drive to accomplish as much as possible. Such an employee is self-motivated, taking pride in the job and the company as well as in the work produced. A good administrative assistant demonstrates a strong work ethic by being punctual, conscientious, and persistent—sticking with a project until it is completed.

If the people around you at work do not seem to be motivated by this inner drive, do not let their attitudes affect your behavior. What should matter to you is how effective you are, rather than how ineffective others may be. The inefficiency of those around you may make your job harder, but it is a waste of energy to worry about their shortfalls. Focus on your own strengths and honor your own values. Your attitude at work should be a question of "How much can I accomplish?" rather than "How little can I get away with doing?"

Arriving at work on time and meeting deadlines are two of the basic values behind a strong work ethic. An administrative assistant arrives at work organized and ready to tackle the day's to-do list. Your employer should be able to rely on you to complete projects with little supervision. Employers value administrative professionals who stick with a project until it is done and done well.

You will have days when you are tired or not feeling well, when you are preoccupied with personal concerns, or when you simply feel blue or discouraged. Working hard can be a good "cure" for personal problems. Make up your mind not to let personal concerns affect your behavior at work.

Always give your employer your best effort, no matter what may be going on in your personal life.

A strong work ethic will help you be successful as an administrative professional.

Throwing yourself wholeheartedly into your work can help to take your mind off a problem, a bad mood, or even a headache.

A strong work ethic does not mean that you avoid social interaction in the workplace, but that you keep it under control. Your relationships with coworkers are essential to your success, so you want to be friendly and sociable without letting such interactions keep you from your work.

A Positive Attitude

Human resources experts know that a worker's attitude is as important as skills for success on the job. If you come to work in the wrong frame of mind, your negative attitude can affect your performance all day. It can also influence those around you. Others want to be around you when you have a positive attitude. They are more likely to cooperate with a positive coworker than with one who brings a negative attitude to work. Think about jobs you have had or group class projects you have worked on. You probably preferred working with others who were enthusiastic and positive about the work.

Make a promise to yourself to bring a positive attitude to work every day. Everyone has occasional complaints about work or coworkers, but it is important not to let any resentments you have affect your work. This kind of behavior only perpetuates problems. It can also make matters worse. No one wants to listen to the worker who seems always to be complaining about problems instead of trying to fix them. There will be problems you cannot solve, but this should not affect your overall attitude and performance.

Figure 2-1 Special Attributes of the Administrative Assistant

> **The Administrative Assistant**
>
> - Has a professional manner and a high energy level.
> - Exhibits a positive attitude.
> - Is a competent administrator.
> - Possesses leadership qualities.
> - Has excellent organizational and communication skills.
> - Demonstrates good judgment (common sense).
> - Manages stress well.
> - Continually upgrades her/his professional development.
> - Accepts new ideas and challenges.
> - Is a highly motivated, creative thinker who changes with the times and technology.

Source: Association of Administrative Assistants, "Is This for You?" http://www.aaa.ca/what_is.php (accessed February 18, 2010).

Find ways to accept situations you cannot change. Your workplace may not be perfect, but you can overcome many problems by taking pride in yourself, your work, and your organization, doing everything in your power to make it better.

The highly respected Association of Administrative Assistants, which was founded in 1951 in Canada, has a list of what it calls the special attributes employers expect in a valued administrative assistant (see Figure 2-1).

Self-Confidence

Having **self-confidence** means believing in yourself and your abilities. Most of us have to develop self-confidence over time through learning, growing, and refining new skills. When you are constantly striving to improve, you will have small successes that will build your self-confidence. Give yourself credit when you do something well. Forgive yourself when you make mistakes. Both are part of the learning process.

A self-confident person can accept and admit mistakes, learning from them and thinking about how to prevent similar failures. If you observe self-confident people around you, you will find that they are not afraid to take responsibility for mistakes or to admit their own weaknesses. Everyone makes mistakes and everyone has weaknesses. Self-confidence is not a matter of being arrogant or "full of yourself." It is believing in your own ability to be self-motivated and self-directed.

When you do not understand something, it is important to ask questions rather than to hide your confusion. When you are open to learning new information, new procedures, and new skills, you will not need to impress others with how much you already know. You can share your knowledge with others without feeling that you have to impress them by knowing everything. No matter how long you have been on the job, the people and situations around you have things to teach you that will make you a better worker.

Handling Change

The world around us is always changing. So is the workplace. Organizations change projects, products, schedules, and services. They change leadership and goals. People come and go. Technology evolves to provide new tools and processes for getting work done. Just as you are getting comfortable with your supervisor, you may find yourself reporting to someone else who has different priorities and expectations. Just as you feel highly skilled at using a software package, your company may upgrade to a new version or select a different application altogether. You may become very comfortable working with a coworker who gets promoted or laid off, leaving you to adjust to a new coworker who may be very different. Worse yet, the coworker may not be replaced, and you may be expected to pick up that person's workload in addition to your own.

Complaining and resisting will only make the situation more difficult for everyone. The more graciously you adjust to and cooperate with changes, the more valuable you will be to your employer.

The more self-confidence you gain, the more comfortable you will become in taking risks and managing change in the workplace. The right attitude will help you accept changes, adapt to them, and learn from them.

Handling Feedback and Criticism

A good employer will provide honest and constructive information, often called **feedback**, to make you aware of how well you are doing and how you might improve your performance. Ideally, you will receive feedback not only at formal performance appraisals but also informally between appraisals, as you do your job.

In giving you feedback, your employer may point out mistakes you have made and suggest how you might have done things differently. A valuable professional quality is the ability to handle such feedback and criticism, even unfair criticism, with

Positive Self-Talk

From high school basketball players to Olympic gymnasts, many athletes are taught to use positive self-talk to help them succeed. *I can make this free throw. I can see myself doing every step of my routine perfectly.*

Self-talk is the running commentary that people keep up all the time inside their heads. It's the characteristic things they say to themselves about their performance.

Negative self-talk (*I did a terrible job on that project. There's no way I can meet that deadline.*) sets people up for failure. It "creates a self-fulfilling prophecy," says Margaret Moore, co-director of the McLean/Harvard Medical School Institute of Coaching. "We stop looking for solutions and assume defeat. Instead of looking at our options, we tell ourselves that we can't handle the things that face us."[1]

Positive self-talk can do more than help people win at sports. It can build self-confidence and self-esteem. It can help to control fear and reduce stress. Positive self-talk can help you manage yourself at work, and it can help you improve yourself and become what you want to be.

Strive to make positive self-talk a habit. Use it, as Olympic athletes do, not only to keep a healthy, confident frame of mind but to improve your performance. When you face a challenge—a presentation to your department, for example, or a performance appraisal on which a promotion hinges—visualize it, step by step, before you take it on. Talk yourself through it. See yourself succeeding.

1 Margaret Moore, "How Do You Spot Negative Self-Talk?" *Psychology Today*, August 23, 2009, http://www.psychologytoday.com/blog/life-changes/200908/ how-do-you-spot-negative-self-talk (accessed March 14, 2009).

poise and to learn from it. Chapter 15 suggests tips for conducting yourself when receiving feedback from your employer.

If your organization does not offer formal feedback, regularly ask your supervisor and coworkers how you can improve your performance. This is vital information for growing in your job.

Staying Organized

Organizational skills enable you to use your time well, keep track of documents and projects, prioritize tasks, and finish projects on time. Using your time well is essential to success at any job. Because you support others in the office, your organizational skills can make any workplace more efficient and effective. If you are disorganized, the entire office may suffer from the confusion and delays disorder creates. You will learn more about organizational skills in Chapter 3.

Thinking Skills

In any office, problems arise every day and decisions must be made. Most are small, but some are large and can have a substantial effect. A person who thinks issues through and can help solve problems is a valuable employee. The abilities to think critically, make decisions, and solve problems are valuable skills that can be practiced and improved.

Critical Thinking

Critical thinking is breaking problems or questions down into small parts and examining them to find solutions or reach conclusions. A critical thinker

- **Describes the real issue.** Before you can solve a problem, you must be able to recognize the real problem and describe it. Break a large problem into smaller parts to help determine the main problem.

- **Distinguishes between facts and opinion.** Ask yourself if what a person asserts as fact really *is* fact.

- **Recognizes bias.** A person who is biased can't judge something impartially because of a personal preference. Try to put aside your own preferences and look at an issue objectively. You must also look for signs of bias when you consider others' opinions.

- **Asks questions and keeps an open mind.** Stay open to new ideas and points of view.

- **Weighs new information.** Evaluate information— and its sources—before accepting it as true.

- **Considers implications and possibilities.** Consider whether the new evidence means that you should adjust your conclusions.

- **Supports opinion with evidence.** Do not expect your opinions to be accepted without support. Explain the logical reasons for your conclusions.

Critical thinking is required to make decisions and solve problems at work.

Making Decisions

The ability to make decisions enhances your productivity at work. To make a good decision:

1. Decide what your goal is. What do you want to be different as a result of the decision?

2. Identify barriers to meeting the goal.

3. Determine strategies to overcome the barriers.

4. Evaluate the costs, benefits, and consequences of each strategy. What is the worst that could happen? What is the best that could happen? Are the risks worth the result?

5. Choose the best strategy.

After you implement the decision, evaluate the outcome. Use that information to help you make the next decision.

JACK HOLLINGSWORTH/BRAND X PICTURES/GETTY IMAGES

The administrative assistant must think critically about situations and problems.

Decision Making and Problem Solving in Action

Suppose you have been told to reduce your budget by 15 percent (goal) even though department expenditures are already stretched (barrier). You consider several strategies to overcome the barrier:

- Eliminate one job in the department.
- Cut costs in supplies and office technology.
- Give smaller raises to department personnel for the next two years.

You then evaluate the costs, benefits, and consequences of each strategy and choose the best one:

- Layoffs will have a negative long-term financial effect.
- Technology is critical to the success of the department.
- You decide to give department personnel smaller raises for the next two years.

Suppose sales are declining and morale is low, and you are part of a task force investigating the situation. Your group determines that the problem is poor leadership.

To collect information, group members observe how managers perform their jobs, interview employees for their perspectives, and read about leadership to get ideas for improving the situation. The group brainstorms these options:

- Institute a leadership training program that addresses the specific problems your task force has identified.
- Set up a mentoring program for less effective leaders.
- Replace less effective leaders.

When evaluating the possible solutions, you realize that instituting a leadership training program can both address the current problem and provide a basis for shaping leadership in the future. You recommend that option.

Solving Problems

Because business situations are always changing, problems do not always get solved or stay solved. Employees spend time looking for the best way to address a situation or solve a problem.

Effective problem-solvers follows these steps:

1. **Identify the problem.** Recognize that the problem exists. Until you identify the problem, you cannot make any changes to solve it.

2. **Collect information.** Observe the problem in action. Ask the people involved for their perspectives, and research the situation.

3. **Determine the options.** Use *brainstorming* to generate options. Make sure everyone who is involved understands the problem or issue. (You can also brainstorm on your own.) Record ideas without discussion or comment. When you run out of ideas, discuss the suggestions, combine ideas, and so on.

4. **Weigh the pros and cons of each option.** Set up criteria for the solution and test each option against it.

5. **Choose the best option.** Many times there is not a right or wrong answer. Choose the best option given the circumstances and the results of your evaluation.

6. **Evaluate the solution.** After an appropriate amount of time, revisit the problem to see if the option you selected has been successful for solving the problem.

Knowing When to Act

The administrative assistant's role requires being supportive *and* being independent. An extremely valuable thinking skill is the ability to evaluate a situation and determine if you should get involved. You need to know when and how to handle situations on your own, when to offer suggestions (and when to stand back), and what to do when you don't agree with a decision.

Handling Situations on Your Own   As you get to know your supervisor, you should understand clearly when you are expected to solve a problem or make a decision yourself. You should also understand when the supervisor wants to handle a situation personally.

Most supervisors are grateful to administrative assistants who can be relied on to take care of small daily problems without troubling them. Others may want to make all the decisions. The best supervisors delegate easily and are proud of their assistant's ability to solve problems and make decisions.

When your supervisor wants you to solve a problem on your own, it doesn't necessarily mean that you should not trouble her, him, or other coworkers with questions. Thinking through a problem with others makes it more likely that you will find the best solution. Organizations need every employee's best contribution.

Offering Suggestions   In many offices, employees are encouraged to suggest changes that might improve procedures or make operations more efficient. Some supervisors, however, resent such employee input. When you have been in a position for a while, you should have a good understanding of when to make suggestions and when not to.

People @Work

HUMAN RESOURCES ASSOCIATE

A human resources associate works in the human resources (HR) department of an organization. Human resources associates are responsible for recruiting, screening, hiring, orienting, and training employees. They may provide new employees with the employee manual, if one exists, and any other written or unwritten policies such as dress codes.

An HR associate may also manage employee benefit programs. Duties may include making employees aware of medical and other benefits and rules and policies for vacation, sick leave, and personal leave.

As an administrative assistant, you may interact with a human resources associate when providing information for personnel files or are receiving training.

workplace wisdom

There is a difference between thinking critically and being critical. The dictionary lists two very different meanings for the word *critical*:

- Characterized by careful, exact evaluation and judgment
- Inclined to judge severely and find fault

Critical thinkers know to set aside their own biases and look at situations and problems objectively.

People who are *critical*, on the other hand, have a reputation for judging situations from their own limited point of view—usually to their own advantage.

Being critical often involves no thinking skills at all!

You should present your ideas as simply and clearly as possible, giving concrete examples of how your plan would work. If the supervisor decides against your plan, accept this decision gracefully.

Your Professional Image

©ISTOCK

Presenting a professional appearance to your coworkers and outsiders is essential to your success. Your appearance dress, speech, writing, and conduct all have an impact on how professional you appear.

Appearance

You should come to work every day looking clean, tidy, and well-groomed. For details of what is meant by *well-groomed*, consider the State of Utah's grooming guidelines for job applicants:[2]

- Keep hair clean, trimmed, and combed. Men should be clean shaven and/or keep mustache or beard neatly trimmed.

- Women should use makeup sparingly.

- Keep fingernails neat, clean, and trimmed.

- Keep teeth brushed and breath fresh.

- Beware of food odors. Use a breath mint if needed.

- Be freshly bathed and use deodorant.

- Use perfumes/colognes sparingly or none at all.

2 State of Utah, "Find a Job at Virtual Career Fair Utah," *Virtual Career Fair Utah*, http://virtualcareerfairutah .com/employmentguide.php (accessed February 22, 2010).

Dear Savvy Admin

Dear Savvy Admin:

My boss is very effective in her job. She treats me well and has taught me a great deal about our business. What bothers me about her is her appearance. She wears conservative suits and high-heeled pumps in an office where the standard is business casual. Because of some comments she has made, I wonder if she thinks I ought to dress the way she does. If I did, I would look out of place. How do I discuss this with her without offending her?

Underdressed

Dear Underdressed:

Unless your boss brings up the subject, just continue to follow the company dress code. If she wants to overdress, it really is her business. You risk offending her if you offer unwanted advice about her appearance.

She may have started working when a business suit and high heels were standard dress. Obviously this habit has done her no harm, since you say she is very effective at her job. Appreciate her good qualities and let her taste in clothing go.

Savvy Admin

It may not seem fair, but people often judge others by how they look. People form first impressions during the first few seconds of meeting someone. Because not much can be said in this short time, this early judgment is based mostly on appearance. Whether or not they realize it, people may think that the quality of a person's work will match the quality of the person's appearance. Your appearance may be seen as reflecting your attention to detail, your level of motivation, and your sense of commitment and professionalism.

Your own attitude and confidence level may also be affected by the clothes you wear. If you dress more casually, you may tend to behave more casually as well.

You and your clothing should always be neat, tidy, and inconspicuous. Stick to comfortable, practical, simple, and professional shoes and attire. Jewelry and other accessories should not be too large or too flashy. Avoid wearing strong perfumes and colognes— some people are allergic to fragrances, and others find them objectionable.

Your shoes should be shined, your hair should be neatly styled, and your hands should be modestly manicured. Overly long or elaborate fingernails can reduce your efficiency, especially in keyboarding.

If you have tattoos or other body art, wear clothing that conceals it if possible. If you have lip, brow, or nasal piercings for facial jewelry, leave the jewelry at home. You have a right to express your own individuality, but you do not want to express it in this way on the job.

You should never wear tight or revealing clothes to work, no matter how casual the dress code may be. If there is no written code, observe how others dress in the workplace, and if you are still in doubt, ask.

Typically, inappropriate attire includes:

- T-shirts
- Tank tops
- Halter tops
- Midriff tops
- Shirts or blouses with words on them
- Tops with bare shoulders or revealing necklines
- Sweatshirts and sweatpants

Communication Skills

Communicating clearly with your supervisor, your coworkers, clients, and the public is an essential element in your professional presentation. How you express yourself influences the confidence others have in you.

Written Communication   Writing, formatting, editing, and proofreading skills are essential to an administrative professional. If you are writing to a supervisor or coworker, your writing contributes to that person's impression of you. If you are writing to an outsider, your communication contributes to the receiver's impression of the organization.

Professional business writing has several qualities. For instance, it should be clear. The reader should be able to understand it easily. The information it contains should be accurate, and it should provide all the information the reader needs. Professional business writing is also always courteous. Letters, reports, and other documents should be formatted attractively, with a professional look and an arrangement that helps make the document easy to read. You will learn more about business writing skills in Chapter 7.

Listening and Verbal Communication   Being a good listener is a professional quality. Effective listeners pay careful attention to what the speaker is saying, even if it is repetitive or not very interesting. They don't interrupt, they don't let their attention wander, and they don't miss important points. You will learn more about good listening skills in Chapter 7.

When talking to coworkers, your supervisor, and customers, adopt a pleasant, professional manner. Speaking clearly, directly, and simply makes it more likely that you will be understood. Strive to keep strong emotions such as anger from showing in your voice. Speak at a normal volume and speed—not too loud or soft and not too slow or fast. You will learn more about effective verbal communication in Chapter 7.

Nonverbal Communication   *Nonverbal communication* includes facial expressions, gestures, and body language, all of which

Communicating @Work

In many offices, it is the administrative assistant who welcomes, orients, and trains new employees. She or he may do this independently in small offices or in cooperation with the human resources department in larger organizations. Administrative assistants are often responsible for preparing the new employee's work space and computer equipment and ensuring the employee has the tools and supplies needed to do the job.

As part of orientation, the administrative assistant is often the one who explains office policies and procedures, sets up the employee's personnel file, and makes sure government-required documents are in place. The admin often prepares or arranges for identification badges and access cards or keys.

In many small offices, it is the administrative assistant who goes over the employee handbook (if one exists), health care forms, and other benefit forms. In small organizations, administrative assistants often keep track of time cards and use of benefits such as vacation and sick time taken.

affect how people interpret what you say. For instance, looking people in the eye when you talk with them shows that you are focused on communicating with them. It also gives an impression of sincerity. These nonverbal messages are reinforced by a posture that's erect but relaxed and a facial expression that's politely attentive and changes in response to what they say. You will learn more about nonverbal communication in Chapter 7.

Teamwork Skills

It is rare for a worker in any job to do everything alone. You will find that many tasks are completed and many goals are reached through cooperation with and support from others.

When you are assigned to a team, make sure you understand exactly what your role is and how your effort contributes to the whole. Never let yourself fade into the background, expecting other team members to carry the weight without you. You are accountable for your share of the responsibility, your share of the work, and your share of the credit for whatever you accomplish.

In Chapter 5, you will read more about the skills that make an effective team member. Do your best to develop and model these skills. Think carefully about your strengths and talents, and actively look for ways to contribute.

Working in teams is a great way to learn from others. Make up your mind to learn something from everyone on the team. At the same time, your team members will be learning from you. Working on a team is also a good opportunity to build relationships with others and promote your professional image.

Professional Organizations

Membership in a professional organization has many advantages. Joining one or more of these organizations can enhance your career by giving you opportunities to interact with and learn from colleagues in your field. Local chapter meetings, national conferences, online forums, and other venues offer opportunities for *networking*, making contacts with people who may help you

Technology @Work

Many young people start their MySpace™, Facebook, and Twitter™ profiles when they are teenagers and have not yet entered the workforce.

Keep in mind that the information you reveal, the words you use, and the images you post online are there for everyone to see.

Make sure your online images, profiles, and words are ones you would want a potential employer and your coworkers to see. Making jokes that might be offensive, expressing yourself in an unprofessional way, or showing yourself in silly or compromising situations may seem like harmless fun when you are in high school. However, that sort of image can reflect badly on you in the workplace.

in an activity, such as professional growth. You can form relationships with other administrative professionals to exchange information, advice, and news. Networking can lead to interviews and jobs.

Professional organizations enable you to improve your knowledge and skills through certification and classes, workshops, seminars, and other types of training, both in-person and online. They represent and promote the profession to the public. They also help you keep current in your field by providing the very latest news. Professional publications, career advice, online job centers, and discounts on products and services are some other advantages of membership.

One of the largest and best-known organizations is the International Association of Administrative Professionals (IAAP), which may have a local chapter in your area. Other valuable national and international organizations are the American Society of Administrative Professionals (ASAP), the Association of Executive and Administrative

Professionals (AEAP), and the Association of Administrative Assistants (AAA).

Similar associations serve specific specialties. They include:

- NALS (originally called the National Association of Legal Secretaries; now referred to by its acronym)
- Legal Secretaries International Inc. (LSI)
- The International Virtual Assistants Association (IVAA)
- A free peer networking club on the website of VACOC, the Virtual Assistance Chamber of Commerce
- The Association of Health Care Administrative Assistants (AHCAA)

The companion website for this text has links to all the professional organizations listed here.

Business Etiquette

Etiquette refers to the rules and customs that guide polite behavior in a particular setting. **Business etiquette** refers to accepted professional behavior in the workplace and at business functions.

Business etiquette includes unwritten rules that make social interactions in the workplace run smoothly and cordially. For example, no one will tell you that you are expected to treat everyone— customers, people who come to the office to deliver or repair things, supervisors, and coworkers—with courtesy and respect. Good manners are based on mindfulness of other people and their feelings. Say *please*, *thank you*, and *I'm sorry*. If you follow the golden rule and treat others the way you would like to be treated, you will find that they will be more willing to work with you and help you.

Credentials for Administrative Assistants

A professional credential can improve your chances in the job market, command higher salaries, and count for college credit. Several professional organizations have credentials programs for administrative professionals:

- IAAP offers two widely recognized credentials. The Certified Professional Secretary (CPS) designation covers office technology, office systems, administration, and management. The more advanced CAP certification (Certified Administrative Professional) covers those areas as well as advanced organizational management.

- NALS also offers two certifications. Accredited Legal Secretary (ALS) is the basic certification, and Professional Legal Secretary (PLS) is the advanced certification.

- LSI offers the Certified Legal Secretary Specialist (CLSS) designation in real estate, intellectual property, criminal law, civil litigation, probate, and business.

SCOTT T. BAXTER/PHOTODISC/GETTY IMAGES

- IVAA offers the Certified Virtual Assistant (CVA), Certified Real Estate Support Specialist (CRESS), and EthicsCheck designations.

All these credentials require passing an exam. To sit for most exams, candidates must have a certain number of years of professional experience. A post-secondary degree, an approved course, or another recognized certification may substitute for some or all of the professional experience requirement.

When you ask someone for a favor or assistance, saying "Would you please . . ." is more polite than giving a directive. For example, instead of saying, "Shut down the computer before you leave," say, "Please remember to shut down the computer."

Thank people when they help you or compliment you. Even if it is a small favor such as opening a door for you or helping you carry a heavy box, express your gratitude with a smile. Thanking others for their efforts goes a long way toward creating a positive working environment.

When you have made a mistake or have offended someone, do not hesitate to apologize. Learn to say you are sorry for even the smallest mistake and take responsibility for your behavior and actions. Do what you can to make up for the mistake.

Handling Introductions

First impressions are always important. When you are being introduced to others:

1. Stand up.
2. Smile and establish eye contact.
3. Shake hands firmly, not with a crushing grip and not with a limp grip.
4. Say hello, repeating the other person's name so you will remember it.
5. Exchange a few words with the person.

When the meeting or conversation ends, let new acquaintances know you enjoyed meeting them.

When you are making introductions, introduce the person of lower rank to the person of higher rank. For example, you might say to your supervisor, "Anna, have you met Frank Fallows? He comes in twice a month to take care of the plants and the fish tank. Frank, this is Mrs. Warner, the office manager."

Follow these additional steps when you are introducing yourself:

1. Smile and establish eye contact.
2. Greet the person and state your name and position.
3. Shake hands.
4. Repeat the person's name.

It is always good etiquette to remember the names of people to whom you are introduced, even if you see them only occasionally. If you forget someone's name, admit it rather than guess or have an awkward conversation in which you avoid using the person's name.

Greeting People

Greeting people appropriately is an important courtesy in the office. When you pass people

Writing @Work

Taking the time to thank other people can contribute to building relationships. It is easy to send a quick e-mail to thank someone for her or his assistance. E-mailing thanks has its advantages. For instance, you can do it right away, when the other person's effort is fresh in your mind—and theirs.

A formal keyed letter of thanks is more appropriate in some business contexts, especially if you have just met the person or have a more impersonal relationship. For instance, the follow-up letter you send after a job interview should include a thank you for the opportunity to interview.

A brief handwritten note is a more personal means of expressing your appreciation. Because e-mail and letters are sent so often, a handwritten note stands out.

When you want to thank someone in writing, think about the recipient. Decide which type of message that person would prefer.

©ISTOCK

in the hall, it is appropriate to greet them. Acknowledging someone's presence with a polite *hello* shows your good manners. Learning and using people's names shows that they matter to you. Asking how someone is doing can show that you care about them and about their well-being.

When you receive a visitor in your office, remember that how you treat a visitor creates the first impression not only of you but also of your company. Greet the person graciously with a simple *good morning* or *good afternoon*. Make sure you have the person's name right, and address the person by name.

Determine the purpose of an unscheduled visit. Avoid blunt questions such as "What do you want?" A more appropriate question is "How can I help you?"

Be pleasant even to a difficult visitor. Be wary of visitors who try to avoid your inquiries with evasive answers such as "It's a personal matter." An appropriate response to such a statement is "My employer sees visitors only by appointment. I will be happy to set one up for you."

Business Meals

A good deal of business takes place at business meals. Whether you are having lunch with a business associate or dinner with a prospective client, good table etiquette reflects well upon you. Follow these rules for the table:

- Silence your cell phone before the meal. If you forgot to do this and it rings, silence it and do not look at or take the call. Focus your attention on the people at the meal.

- If you are the host, suggest that the guests order first.

- Order dishes that are easy to eat. Avoid ordering the most expensive meal on the menu or making several changes to a menu item.

- Use the bread plate on your left and the beverage glasses on your right.

- Do not use the communal bread plate, knife, or butter dish for your own use. Take a roll or piece of bread from the main bread dish and put it on your own bread plate. Do the same with the butter. Use your own bread knife or regular knife to butter your bread.

- Break a roll or piece of bread in half or into smaller pieces before you butter it or start eating it.

- Place your napkin in your lap.

- Sit up straight and keep your elbows off the table.

- Avoid chewing with your mouth open and speaking with food in your mouth.

- Do not dominate the conversation.

- Use the utensils in the order they are placed, starting with the outside. For example, use the left-most fork for your salad.

- If you use the wrong utensil, don't call attention to your mistake. Ask the server for a replacement if necessary.

- Once you pick up a utensil, do not place it on the table. When you have finished using it, place it on your plate.

- When you finish your meal, lay your knife and fork diagonally across the plate. Do not push the plate away from you.

- When your host signals the end of the meal, place your napkin on the table and thank the host.

- If you are unsure about anything, watch the host and other guests for guidance.

Etiquette experts advise that it is customary to wait until the major portion of the meal is over to raise business matters. This will not be true at every meal, of course, so follow the lead of your supervisor or coworkers. Be prepared to make small talk until business is discussed.

Key Terms

business etiquette

critical thinking

feedback

professional

self-confidence

work ethic

Summary

- Becoming a true professional is a key to your success as an administrative assistant.

- Professional attitudes, values, and skills include a strong work ethic, a positive attitude, self-confidence, the ability to handle change and accept criticism, and organizational skills.

- Employers expect administrative assistants to be good problem solvers who can make decisions.

- Critical thinking is a valuable skill that can be practiced and improved. Good critical thinkers can assess a situation and determine when and how to handle it.

- To be seen as professional, you must be dressed and groomed professionally every day.

- Good written, verbal, and nonverbal communication skills are very important in any office setting.

- Working effectively in teams is important for administrative assistants.

- Belonging to a professional organization is a good way to gain skills and experience that will contribute to your professional image.

- Business etiquette makes social interactions in the workplace run smoothly and cordially. Knowing and following business etiquette marks you as a professional.

Bookmark It. *For convenient access to activities, links, and valuable career resources for administrative professionals, visit the companion website for this text:*

www.cengage.com/officetech/fultoncalkins

Planning Notes

Learning Objectives

1. Describe the qualities that make a worker a professional.

2. Explain why critical-thinking, decision-making, and problem-solving skills are essential to an administrative assistant.

3. Describe how factors such as appearance, communication, and teamwork skills affect your professional image.

4. Describe the importance of following business etiquette.

 Critical Thinking; Activities 2, 4, 5, 6

 Activities 9, 10; Above & Beyond

 Activities 1, 3, 7, 8

Discussion Questions

1. What are some of the qualities that make an employee a professional?

2. Discuss the role of attitude in the workplace.

3. How can adapting to change enhance your career?

4. Discuss how professionals approach problem solving.

5. Describe a professional appearance, and give examples of clothing or grooming that is inappropriate in the workplace.

6. Why is business etiquette important? How can you learn business etiquette?

7. Discuss the importance of eye contact and handshakes in introductions.

8. What should you do if your employer does not provide feedback on your work through a formal evaluation?

9. Why is working effectively in teams important for success as an administrative assistant?

Critical Thinking

What will you say? Your company hired a new records clerk last fall, and you were assigned responsibility for her orientation and for mentoring her. Moira is a quick learner, and she is efficient and organized. She is neat and well-groomed, but she has an outrageous punk hairstyle and an eyebrow ring. The receptionist is leaving, and Moira has asked your advice about applying for the position. As Moira's mentor, what will you say to her? (Learning Objectives 2, 3)

Build Workplace Skills

1. **Introductions** In a group with several classmates, write scripts for making introductions. Include examples of how to introduce yourself when you are new on the job, how to introduce a new employee to coworkers, and how to introduce a new client to your boss. Role play making introductions before a group of your classmates. (Learning Objective 4)

2. **Thinking critically** You have just started working in a law firm, and a newly hired lawyer asks you to arrange for her to attend a daylong continuing legal education (CLE) seminar that costs $150. Whom will you talk to about the lawyer's request? List all the questions you need to ask so you can meet the law firm's rules and the lawyer's preferences. (Learning Objective 2)

3. **What should you wear?** Describe what you would wear the first day if you were working on a temporary assignment as an administrative assistant to a federal judge. Describe what you would wear if you were assigned to a hip, youthful advertising agency. (Learning Objective 3)

Communicate Clearly

4. **Proofread a message**   Open the *Word* file CH02 E-mail from the data files. Proofread the message to correct errors in grammar, spelling, and punctuation. (Learning Objective 3)

5. **The importance of listening**   Grant told his assistant, Melinda, to send an e-mail to the finance committee of the company's board of directors about some missing funds. Melinda knew this would be a sensitive matter, so she wrote a draft and got Grant's approval of the wording. Then she sent it to the group in her e-mail address book called "Board of Directors." A few minutes later, she realized that it was not supposed to go to all board members, only to the finance committee. If you were Melinda, would you tell Grant about your mistake, or wait until he found out? What would you say to him? (Learning Objective 3)

6. **Nonverbal communication**   In a group with a few other students, spend half an hour in a public place, such as a library, coffee shop, student commons, or cafeteria. Observe the people around you, and write down the different kinds of nonverbal communication that take place. What facial expressions, gestures, and body language are used? Which convey interest in what the other person has to say, and which do not? (Learning Objective 3)

Develop Relationships

7. **Handling change**   Denise is feeling really discouraged at work. She and Kara were hired as records clerks in the purchasing department seven months ago. Last week Kara was promoted to a supervisory position, and Denise will now report to her. Kara has noticed that Denise seems resentful and is barely speaking to her. When Kara gave Denise an assignment yesterday, she failed to complete it. If you were Kara, what would you say to Denise? Write a draft that addresses the problem in a way that will make Denise feel more comfortable with the situation. (Learning Objectives 1, 2, 3)

8. **Soliciting feedback**   Adam is a new front office assistant in a dental practice. The office manager, Ms. Spivey, is always very busy. Adam would like to start getting feedback on how well he is doing his work. In a group, brainstorm some ways that Adam could solicit feedback from Ms. Spivey even though she is busy. Discuss your ideas and list the ones you think would be most effective. (Learning Objective1)

Use Technology

9. **Professionalism**   With a partner, select one of the attitudes or values described in this chapter. Using *Microsoft PowerPoint®* presentation software and clip art, create a good and bad workplace example of the attitude or value. Use the software's narration function to add voiceovers to the scenarios. (Learning Objective 1)

10. **Immigration spreadsheet**   The immigration lawyer you work for has asked you to create a spreadsheet for clients trying to qualify to sponsor a family member who wants to come to the United States.

    a. Go to the U.S. Citizenship and Immigration Services website. A link is provided on the website for this book.

    b. Find the most recent poverty guidelines for sponsorship (Form I-864P).

    c. Create a spreadsheet with five column headings:

Client

Family Size

Relationship to Client

Income Required

Actual Income

d. Enter information about the following three clients in the spreadsheet. Use the poverty guidelines form to find information for the Income Required column.

- Pia Longalo is a single woman who wants to bring her mother here. Her income is $15,000 a year.
- Li Yan is married with four children. He wants to sponsor his oldest son. He and his wife together make $24,000 a year.
- Ziad Muhgrabi is married and making $24,000 a year. He wants to help his brother immigrate.

(Learning Objective 2)

> Above & Beyond

Employee reprimand Victor Bella, the manufacturing manager and your supervisor, has asked you to put a note in the personnel file of Gilbert Lopez, a shipping clerk in the warehouse, indicating he was given a verbal warning on June 2, 20--, for smoking in the workplace. Mr. Bella has also asked you to draw up a form that will work for all employee warnings and reprimands placed in personnel files.

Create a form to include pertinent information, such as the date, the name and title of the employee, the name and title of the supervisor, the subject of the reprimand, and whether it was verbal or written. Include space for any other details you think would be important. (Learning Objective 2)

Administrative Assistant Wanted

Engineering firm seeks administrative assistant to join our award-winning team. Must be able to meet deadlines and handle large work volume and multiple tasks in a fast-paced work environment. Job duties include:

- Tracks department schedules and projects
- Schedules, tracks, and manages contract due dates
- Reviews projects after completion to assess efficiency of processes
- Monitors orders, inventories, and budgets
- Schedules and facilitates meetings
- Prepares correspondence, presentations, reports, special projects, technical papers, and related material as requested

Do I qualify?

©MARK WRAGG, ISTOCK

CHAPTER

3

Managing and Organizing Yourself

Goals and Accountability

Meeting goals and accounting for your productivity in the workplace require self-discipline. **Self-discipline** is your own control over what you do, as well as how and when you do it. As you grow in experience throughout your career, you will likely gain a greater understanding of how to organize and manage yourself. Applying this understanding can make all the difference in your personal as well as your professional life. In this chapter, you will learn how to make self-discipline part of your own lifestyle.

Set Goals for Yourself

Why set goals? You may have heard the old saying that if you don't know where you're going, you're unlikely to get there. You need to clarify the results you are seeking and focus on exactly what you want to accomplish before you can figure out how to get to the desired results.

Learning Objectives

1. Explain steps for setting and meeting goals and priorities.

2. Describe strategies and tools for organizing your work area.

3. Describe strategies and tools for managing your workload.

4. Identify life management skills that improve job performance.

Setting clear, attainable goals is a key to success in your private life as well as your work life, and each helps to support the other. The word *goal* dates back to the sixteenth century and probably referred originally to the finish line in a race. The meaning of the term has expanded to include any result you are trying to reach, whether physical, intellectual, professional, or financial.

Long-Term and Short-Term Goals

Your more ambitious goals may take some time to reach, which is why they are called long-term goals. An example would be earning a college degree. Your short-term goals would be the various steps you need to reach the bigger goal: getting admitted to college, taking required classes, working hard at your studies, and earning good grades.

Make sure there are long-term plans among your goals to give yourself more meaningful challenges. Step back from the day-to-day challenges you face and think about where you would like to be in five years.

Clear Goals

Your goals need to be clear and concrete. State them simply and specifically. Do not generalize or be vague. Compare the examples in the following chart.

Vague Goal	Clearer Goal
I will work more efficiently.	I will use the mail merge feature of my word processing program to prepare 100 personalized letters.
I will do a better job this year.	I will achieve an "exceeds expectations" rating in at least two areas of my performance appraisal this year.

Realistic, Positive Goals

Your goals need to be realistic and reachable, and you should describe them in positive terms. As a short-term goal, for example, instead of saying, "I will not waste time this afternoon," set the goal "I will finish this spreadsheet by 3 p.m."

Make your goals challenging, but within your reach. You want to choose ambitious goals, but

Discussing your goals with someone whose judgment you trust can be helpful.

not beyond the realm of what it is in your power to achieve. Be willing to work hard to reach your goals, without discouraging yourself by overreaching.

Set goals that really matter to you—goals you really want to meet. There will be delays, obstacles, and setbacks, so stay flexible and be willing to adapt your plan. When you find yourself off the mark, reexamine and revise your strategies. Look upon missteps as temporary setbacks. Keep trying and do not give up.

Align Your Goals

In addition to being clear, realistic, and reachable, your goals should be aligned with those of your supervisor, your coworkers, and the organization that employs you. Make sure your goals contribute meaningfully to the goals of your department and the mission of your company. If goals are not in synch, they can work at cross-purposes, reducing the chances of success for others as well as you.

Remember that as an administrative professional, your role is to support others. You are part of a team working toward common goals that will be reached more easily if your own goals directly and indirectly support those of others. Knowing that you have made a significant contribution to other people's success can be very rewarding.

Adjust Your Priorities

It is important to stick to the goals you have set. However, it would be a mistake to be too strict about this general rule. You need to be firm but flexible. Your priorities may change from day to day and from hour to hour depending on the needs of your company and your department. Your top priority may have been completing the sales report; however, if your supervisor asks you to do something he or she considers more urgent, realign your goals to match those of your supervisor. Move that sales report down a notch. Finish your supervisor's priority as efficiently as you can and then refocus on the sales report.

Stay Motivated

Motivation is fed by progress as well as by incentives. **Progress** means forward movement toward a goal. Stopping to measure your progress can encourage you to stay on track. Take time to focus on what you have accomplished rather than fretting about how far you have to go. Going back to the origins of the word *goal* as probably a finish line, a runner will be more inspired by thinking, "I've completed a whole mile!" than by thinking, "I still have four miles to go!"

Measure Your Progress   Taking the time to pause and measure your progress is important to keeping you focused on what you want to achieve, even if it is still a long way off. If you take the time to feel the satisfaction of reaching smaller goals, more ambitious goals will seem more reachable. For example, if your goal is to earn an associate's degree, completing your first class with a good grade should encourage you to continue.

Pausing to assess how far you have come serves several purposes. Accomplishing small steps along the way can motivate you to keep going forward. If you find that a certain step or strategy did not get you closer to your goal, it is time to reassess, rethink, and reenergize your efforts.

Be flexible. If one strategy doesn't move you toward your goal, think of others that might.

The Role of Incentives   An **incentive** is a reward or encouragement. It need not be a material reward such as a bonus or a raise. Many strong incentives have no material value. Their value lies in the sense of accomplishment you feel.

Of course, being paid for your work is an incentive, as is staying employed. Impressing a client or your supervisor with excellent service reinforces your commitment to doing it again. The satisfaction of gaining ground can be one of the most powerful incentives to keep striving. There is no harm in promising and giving yourself small, tangible rewards. For example, you might say to yourself, "If I walk a mile after work, I'll have a frozen yogurt." The walk may also clear your mind to help you generate ideas for solving problems.

Resist Interference   Most offices are not quiet, peaceful places where you can easily focus on a single task or project without interruptions and obstacles. It is the nature of office work that phones ring, visitors arrive, e-mail inboxes fill, coworkers ask questions, and your supervisor

People @Work

OFFICE MANAGER

As an administrative professional, you may work under the supervision of an office manager. Office managers plan, coordinate, and supervise the work of administrative assistants and other support staff. They develop schedules, make assignments, set deadlines, and oversee work to be sure it is done properly and on schedule.

Office managers frequently monitor and adjust workloads and job responsibilities to ensure that work is done efficiently. They may redesign job duties, shift them from one person to another, and create or eliminate job positions with the approval of company managers. Many companies fill office manager positions by promotion from their administrative or office support staff.

pages you. **Interference** is anything that stands in the way of progress, whether it is demands from other people or your own temptation to waste time on things that will not help you reach your goal.

Take Advantage of Opportunities

An **opportunity** is a good chance, prospect, or timing. For example, if your long-term goal is to be promoted to office manager, and the person doing that job offers to mentor you, take full advantage of the opportunity and learn all you can. Perhaps one of your goals is to get an office in your workplace instead of a cubicle so that you will have more space and privacy. When a nearby office becomes free, ask whether you might have it.

Perhaps you have not yet met the CEO and really want to impress her. When you run into her in the break room, engage her in conversation about something positive your department is working on. Impress her with your professionalism

and sincere interest in the project. These are all opportunities.

Accountability Leads to Results

In the word *accountability*, you can see the root word *account*, which originally meant a financial record of debits and credits. When you are accountable in the workplace, you are a credit to your employer and yourself.

Accountability means more than taking responsibility for your work—more even than taking responsibility for your mistakes. **Accountability** is an obligation to answer to others regarding your behavior, the completion of a task or responsibility, or adherence to a standard. You are also accountable to yourself, your own standards, your own commitments, your own goals. On its website, OfficeTeam, the temporary staffing service for administrative assistants, offers advice on how to increase your accountability in the office, shown in the feature below.

Becoming More Accountable

Build your accountability quotient— and your manager's trust in you—by doing the following:

- **Make deadlines a priority.** Work with your manager to set realistic timeframes on projects. Then make sure you always meet your deadlines.

- **Complete the circle.** Make sure projects stay on track from start to finish. If you encounter setbacks during the process, take the lead in seeing they're resolved.

- **Keep in mind the chain of accountability.** You're accountable to your manager, who, in turn, is accountable to his or her boss. Always be aware that your mistakes reflect poorly on your supervisor, and on the flip side, your successes make him or her look good. The more you can make your manager shine in front of others, the more valuable you'll be.

- **Let the buck stop with you.** If coworkers or clients are having trouble finding help, try to point them in the right direction or find a solution for them, even if the matter doesn't directly involve you. By lending a helping hand you'll develop a reputation as the person who gets things done.

- **Polish your projects.** Try to make your work as accurate as possible before it reaches others. Sometimes it helps to put written communications such as memorandums and reports aside for a few hours before proofreading them again and sending them on. You'll be able to catch errors that you might otherwise miss.

Keep your work area neat and organized, with a minimum of personal items.

Workstation Organization

In Chapters 1 and 2, you learned about the importance of maintaining a strong professional appearance in your dress, your behavior, your communications, and your work area.

A neat and orderly desk is especially important to administrative professionals because their workspace tends to be in a high-traffic area where more people are likely to see it. The impression your work area makes on your coworkers, clients, customers, and the general public reflects on the professionalism of your organization.

Overall Appearance

For a professional look, keep personal items at your workstation to a minimum. A family picture, a plant, or a paperweight might be fine, but don't overdo, and follow any rules set by your organization.

Your organization will probably have staff or a service that cleans employees' workstations. Regardless, make sure your work area is always neat. Your desk should be clean and your work area free of dust. Placing dust covers over your computer equipment at the end of each day reduces the amount of cleaning that needs to be done and helps keep it in good repair.

If you have drinks at your desk or occasionally eat a snack or lunch there, keep these items well away from your equipment and any documents you are working on. Use a coaster to protect the desk surface, and keep some napkins or paper towels at your workstation in case of spills.

Organizational Aids and Supplies

A trip to any office supply store will reveal a wide variety of organizing systems and tools from planners, discussed later in this chapter, to fasteners, notebooks, filing systems, and sticky notes. Every worker can benefit from a planner. You will learn over time from your own experience which other devices and supplies help you to stay organized.

Many administrative assistants find it helpful to have an inbox and an outbox on their desks. With an inbox, your supervisor and coworkers will know where to put a document for your attention if you happen to be away from the desk or on the telephone. An outbox may be all you need for finished documents and projects that will be forwarded to others.

If your work is too complicated to rely on an outbox, a vertical file may help you to keep track of things. In this handy file, you can keep sturdy, wide folders of outgoing work by category. For example, you may have one file labeled "To Be Signed," another labeled "To Be Notarized," and others labeled for specific attention, such as "To Be Discussed with Supervisor," "To Be Entered in Database," or "To Be Faxed."

This sort of system will keep items from getting lost in the outbox pile and will remind you of the next step in the process. If you want to clear your desk completely at the end of the day, save a deep desk drawer where you can store this vertical file.

For some people, different-colored files or color-coded labels help to distinguish between important projects and urgent ones or to distinguish certain types of projects from others. It may also help you to use color-coded stickers on documents indicating that you have completed handling them and they are ready for the shredder or recycle bin.

A clear, orderly filing system is essential to any office. You will learn how to manage, organize, and maintain files in Chapter 11, Managing Records, and Chapter 12, Handling Mail and Retaining Records.

Ready-to-Go Principle

Arrange your work area for efficiency and comfort. Adjust your chair to a comfortable height. Position your computer keyboard and mouse within easy reach. Place your desk lamp and computer monitor so you can read and see the screen without strain.

Clear your desk of everything you do not need. Clutter has a way of piling up and making it harder to find things. Your work space should be set up to let you get right to work with as little preparation as possible. Place tools and supplies you use frequently, such as your stapler and flash drive, within easy reach. Put everything you use *where* you use it, so you will not waste time searching for what

you need. Arrange documents and files you refer to often in a desk drawer, clearly labeled.

At the end of each day, clear your desk and prepare a to-do list for the next day, putting the most urgent matters first. Keep this list in a particular place, so that it is always there when you arrive in the morning. The most important guides and reminders can be posted on the wall above your desk, as long as they look neat and orderly.

At the end of each week, clear your entire work space, leaving out only what you will need for the following week. Throw away items that are unneeded or outdated. Shred sensitive documents, such as forms with people's personal information on them, if you no longer need them.

Manage Your Workload

If you try to work without planning and organizing, you are doing yourself a great disservice. You may think that you have a good memory and plenty of self-discipline. You may think that you can complete tasks or projects "on autopilot." However, planning and organizing can help even the most organized person to be still more efficient.

workplace wisdom

We all know how aggravating it can be to deal with a person who "doesn't have it together." It puts pressure on you when you cannot rely on someone who has trouble meeting deadlines and remembering commitments. It is even more aggravating to be that disorganized person. Here are some great reasons to get organized:

- To save time
- To meet deadlines
- To improve overall job performance
- To reduce the strain on those who depend upon you
- To get control of your environment and your life

Use a Planner

Few people have such good memories that they do not need to make notes about tasks and appointments. That's why nearly everyone needs a planner.

You have probably used a planner in school or at previous jobs. Whether print or electronic, a planner is essential for organizing your work and for tracking appointments and other commitments for your supervisor or other workers, if these tasks are your responsibility.

Your office may require you to use a certain type of planner or planning software. If not, take some time to explore the various options that are available. Some people like to use paper planners. Others prefer an electronic planner on their workstation computer. Still others favor a PDA, and some people use a combination of planners.

If you use an electronic planner such as *Microsoft Outlook*, invest some time in learning about its features. Use the software help feature, take an online tutorial, or check out a book from the library.

Use your planner to record appointments, meetings, assignment due dates, and reminders. Enter important dates and tasks as soon as you become aware of them so that you will not forget to enter them later.

Make a backup copy of your planner data. For a printed planner, you can photocopy essential pages. In deciding how often to make a backup, consider what the impact would be if you lost the data and how much time and effort it would take to replace it.

Many people use a PDA for a planner.

Avoid Procrastination

When you put things off in order to avoid doing something you find difficult or boring, that is called **procrastination**. The first step to getting something done is starting. So even if you know you cannot finish a project that you have been postponing, promise yourself that you will apply yourself to it for half an hour a day, or some other length of time that suits your schedule and your attention span, until it is finished.

If you break tasks into smaller steps, you can get the reward of making progress, and the tasks will seem more manageable. There are difficult and boring parts to any job. Try to think of more efficient ways to manage them. Discipline yourself to work on them a little at a time.

Prioritize Your Work

Making lists of things you need to do can be a very effective way of organizing your work. A daily to-do list, for example, is a simple and invaluable tool. With a daily to-do list, you can tell at a glance what you need to accomplish that day and in what order, and you can tell which tasks can wait until another day if necessary. A simple paper list works well for many people. Others like to keep a list in their word processing or planning software so they can use features such as cut and paste to easily reorder items.

Besides keeping a daily to-do list, setting aside time every day or so to look at the larger picture of your workload is time well spent. This is your opportunity to set priorities and to organize how you are going to address projects and tasks and in what order. It will keep you from wasting time on things that can wait or things that do not matter as much as your more urgent priorities. A **priority** is something that merits your attention ahead of other tasks.

In prioritizing your work, it can help to organize tasks into four categories that reflect their importance and urgency. An *urgent* task is one that requires immediate attention. An *important* task is one that you or your company places value on, a task that leads to growth or opportunities. Figure 3-1 shows

Figure 3-1 Time Management Categories

Urgent and Important
- Getting rid of a computer virus
- Booking plane reservations for your supervisor's last-minute trip
- Preparing for your annual performance evaluation next week

Important, but not Urgent
- Developing a relationship with the new paralegal
- Researching new virus protection software
- Planning the presentation you will give next month

Urgent, but not Important
- Filing correspondence
- Helping a coworker move her office
- Rescheduling patient appointments that are set for the second week of January (which is three months away) because your supervisor has just told you that he will be on vacation that week

Neither Urgent nor Important
- Going through four-year-old correspondence files
- Surfing the Internet for sales on office supplies
- Shopping for a new pair of jeans at lunch

examples for these four categories. This system was developed by Stephen Covey.

As an administrative professional, you will probably spend most of your time on tasks that are both urgent and important because other people will set many tasks and priorities for you. You will need to spend time on tasks that are urgent, but not important, for the same reason. At the same time, though, it is important to think about and work in time for tasks that are important, but not urgent.

Referring to Figure 3-1, you can see that researching new antivirus software for the office is a task that doesn't have to be done today or tomorrow, but it is important in the long run. The sooner you purchase new software, the less time you will have to spend—unpredictable and uncontrollable amounts of time—getting rid of a virus and undoing the damage it has caused. So spending time on tasks that are important, but not urgent, can reduce the amount of time you have to spend on tasks that are urgent, but not important.

Spending time on important, but not urgent, tasks has other benefits besides the significant benefit of saving you time and work. Developing a good working relationship with the new paralegal isn't something that you should, or could, accomplish in a day. But it's something that could have tremendous value for both of you in the long run. It will help ensure that your interactions will be pleasant and profitable. It will benefit the company and contribute to your reputation as an employee who gets along well with others. You might gain new responsibilities, and your relationship could turn out to be a valuable professional association that will benefit you in your career.

Tasks that are important, but not urgent, may be set for you, but it is also important to set them for yourself. You may determine that reorganizing the filing system would save you and others a considerable amount of time and effort. Or you may decide to volunteer to give a presentation at the next IAAP chapter meeting. Seek and plan for activities that will improve the way you do your job and will contribute to your personal and professional growth.

Make Neatness a Habit

Neatness should become a habit rather than just a goal, because neatness will help you feel relaxed and in control. The key to keeping things in order is to put them away right after you use them. There is not much use in having a place for everything if everything is not in its place. Discipline yourself to return the stapler to the place where you always keep it. When you make this a habit, you will not spend time searching for the stapler. . . or anything else.

©ISTOCK

Control Paper and E-mail

Piles of letters, memos, and other documents and e-mail messages can accumulate quickly. You open a piece of mail and put it in a pile, thinking, "Oh, this can wait." The document quickly grows into an overwhelming mountain of items you thought could wait.

You have probably heard the common advice to handle a piece of paper only once. It is good advice, but it is not always possible, practical, or even desirable. What you should do at once when you receive a document is make a decision as to how you will handle it.

- Act on it at once if it needs immediate action or if you have the time.

- Keep it on hand if you will deal with it later that day.

- If it doesn't need to be dealt with that day, and if you have more pressing priorities, determine a time when you will handle it and note it in

Dear Savvy Admin

Dear Savvy Admin:

As hard as I try, it seems that I never get everything on my to-do list done each day. I'm getting tired of staying late and giving up so many breaks and lunch hours for work. Any advice?

Overworked

Dear Overworked:

Take a good, hard look at your to-do list. Is the amount of work you give yourself each day reasonable? Does it all need to be done that day, or can some wait?

Are you doing your work as efficiently as possible? Could your work or work area be organized in a better way?

If the answer to these questions is yes, then your workload is too heavy, and it's time to get help. Keep a log for a week of your assignments, what you get done, and the time it takes. Then speak to your supervisor. Some responsibilities may need to be reallocated or another person hired. Part-time help for a few hours a day or week might make the difference.

Savvy Admin

your to-do list or planner. You may find it helpful to have an action file for items that won't be dealt with immediately but will be disposed of in the next few days.

- If it isn't your responsibility, forward it to someone who can handle it.

- If it needs to be filed, file it at once, if possible. Non-urgent filing can wait, but set a specific time for it so it doesn't accumulate. Think before you create a file for a document or before you add it to an existing file. Will you really need to refer to it again?

- If you don't need the document, throw it away. Set up a few minutes at the end of each week to clean out saved e-mail messages that no longer have any purpose.

Organize Files

E-mail programs allow you to set up folders that can help you organize messages you really do need to save. Depending on the kind of work you do, it may help you to have folders named "From John Jones" or "From Su-kyong Kim" so that you do not have to wade through as many messages to find what you need. You can also set up folders for e-mails related to a specific issue or task, such as an "Employee Benefits Committee" folder where you put all the messages from any sender that relate to that project.

E-mails can be organized by date, sender, or subject. You can personalize the way your e-mail program makes you aware of new messages (often in bold until you open them and then in normal text after they have been opened). You can also flag important messages with various symbols to help you find them.

You will learn about organizing and managing paper as well as electronic files in Chapter 11, and you will learn about retaining and disposing of records in Chapter 12.

Streamline Repetitive Tasks

In most jobs, there are certain tasks that you do over and over again, sometimes daily, sometimes several times a day. Over time, you are likely to get faster at doing them and to find ways of performing them more efficiently. Think actively about ways to streamline this sort of work. Observe what your coworkers do, or ask their advice.

Luckily, both hardware and software can help you to work more efficiently by automating all or part of the process. As you get to know various software systems, you will also learn how to automate certain steps to speed up keyboarding and/or entering data. There are dozens of shortcuts and automations for commands in word processing software, which you have probably mastered in keyboarding classes.

You are also probably familiar with creating templates in word processing software to speed up the keying of documents. These tools will be covered thoroughly in Chapter 12.

In spreadsheet software such as *Microsoft Excel*, you can use macros to record, save, and run an automatic series or sets of commands or steps. This will enable to you to format rows, columns, cells, functions, and calculations with fewer steps. You can find excellent online training on how to use macros in all of your worksheets so that the cells, formats, and formulas are inherent in the document without your having to enter each command in a series.

In your e-mail program, set up your address book to include groups of people who commonly receive the same messages. It will be much easier to communicate quickly with them all by selecting the group instead of individual e-mail addresses.

Technology @Work

Your telephone system probably allows you to assign a code or number for a phone number you frequently call. If you take the time to program the system with shortcuts, which may be single digits, you can dial the telephone numbers you have entered without entering the entire number. Most fax machines can also be programmed in this way, shortening the time it takes to send a fax to someone.

Machines can also be programmed to send a message with a single command to each person in a group, such as your company's board members, specific team members working on a project, or heads of departments. It takes some time to set up group numbers for telephones and fax machines, but in the long run, having them programmed into the device will save you time and effort.

Manage Projects

When you have a long-term project to manage, the first step is to think through and write out your objectives. Plan carefully, considering the information, materials, and supplies you may need. Think about research and resources that would help you complete the project. If the budget is tight, you may have to make do with what you have, but it does not hurt to ask your supervisor if you could have something that would make your work easier, including help.

Try to anticipate what could go wrong and what you can do to prevent problems along the way. Break the project into smaller steps and give yourself deadlines for completing them well in advance of the project due date. Ask trusted coworkers how they would approach the project. They may have some good ideas that had not occurred to you.

Handle Time Wasters

Some of the biggest time wasters at work are disorganization and the failure to do tasks efficiently. By organizing your work and finding efficient ways to do it, you can reduce this waste and save yourself a good deal of time.

Interruptions While some time wasters can be controlled or prevented, others cannot. Interruptions, another big time waster, are the rule rather than the exception for administrative professionals. To minimize their effects, learn to take them in stride and to refocus quickly on your work after you address them. Something as simple as putting a check mark where you were in a document can help you get back on track after answering someone's question that has interrupted your work.

Other People Another distraction, of course, is other people. Sometimes people really do need to interrupt your work to ask a question or bring something to your attention. And a little friendly conversation with fellow employees each day is part of workplace life. Still, there seem to be chatty people in every workplace who will prolong a talk when other employees need to get back to work. Look for graceful ways of ending such conversations. For example, you might say, "I'm sorry, Don. This report is due in an hour. May I stop by your desk to talk about this after I finish it?"

Trouble Focusing If you are like most people, you will have trouble focusing on work at times. Doing something else, even briefly, often helps. Get away from your desk for a few minutes. Take a break, perhaps for a walk outside. Have a short talk with someone, or switch to another task.

Make Downtime Productive

Most administrative assistants have some **downtime**; that is, time when they are not accomplishing a specific task, such as when they are waiting for new software to install, a fax to print, or a long document to make its way through the copier. Challenge yourself to use your downtime productively. While you are on hold on the telephone, put your desk drawer in order. Take a notepad to the copier with you and use the time to jot down ideas

Writing @Work

E-mail and instant messaging (IM) make work more efficient—but they can also *create* work, unless you use them in a thoughtful way.

Sometimes people send more messages about a topic than they need to because it's so quick and easy to do (or because it's a welcome distraction from work). These exchanges can also readily move onto nonwork topics. Besides the time put into responding to such messages, each one is an interruption that takes you away from what you were doing. Opt out of too-lengthy messaging cycles in the same graceful way that you would an in-person conversation.

While e-mail is often the quickest and easiest option for contacting someone, that isn't always the case. Sometimes making a phone call takes less time than composing a message. Similarly, a face-to-face conversation might save several e-mails going back and forth.

©ISTOCK

for that report you need to write. Tidy up the area around the copier so the next user will not find a mess. Even if the clutter is not your own, it helps the organization if you use this time to accomplish something for everyone's good.

If the business where you work has seasonal or weekly ups and downs, you may find yourself with more free time at some times than others. Use these slow periods to learn new skills. Explore new software or software you already know to discover functions and commands you have not tried before. For example, experiment with using macros in *Microsoft Excel*. You will probably find that they come in handy in streamlining and automating some spreadsheets. Or go online to learn more about your industry or field that will help you advance in your career.

You may find that, at times, your coworkers are very busy and you are not. This is the time to volunteer to help. "Do you have anything I can help you with?" is a question most people welcome with gratitude. Offering assistance builds relationships in the workplace. If you choose to sit at your desk daydreaming or surfing the Internet while others are struggling to meet a deadline, you give the impression that you are only out for yourself and are not concerned about your coworkers or the overall good of the company. Remember that your success, and your continued employment, depends upon the success of the company.

Life Management

Your employer understands that you have a personal life and that it can be difficult to juggle your private duties with your professional ones. If you let things get out of hand in one setting, the other suffers as well. The more order you put into your private life, the more energy you will have to focus on your employer's business. The more order you put into your professional life, the less it will interfere with life at home.

The need not to let personal problems affect your work was discussed in Chapter 2. It is also important not to permit the demands of personal life, routine or otherwise, to intrude too much on your work time. While making an appointment to get your car repaired or to see your dentist is usually okay, spending extended work time on personal obligations is not. Nor is over-frequent requests for personal time off—coming in late, leaving early, being gone

for part of the day, or taking the entire day. Most employers understand that children get sick, wallets get lost, dangerous natural gas leaks happen that need to be fixed during business hours, and so forth. Be certain that this kind of request for personal time off is rare. You do not want to make a habit of it.

Take Care of Yourself

To be effective on the job, you need to feel well. Make sure that you are eating a healthful diet, controlling your weight, exercising, and getting enough sleep.

A healthful diet has a number of benefits. It can help you feel well and reach or maintain your ideal weight. In addition, a healthful diet may reduce your risk of cardiovascular disease, type 2 diabetes, osteoporosis, stroke, certain kinds of cancer, and other medical problems. It is also essential in the management of many diseases.

Communicating @Work

Do not encourage family and friends to call you at work, and avoid making personal calls from work. There are, of course, exceptions. Your child's school may call to advise you that your child has a fever. Your employer will understand that you need to take this call. In most cases, however, the needs of family and friends can be handled before and after business hours. If a long-lost friend happens to contact you at work, cordially arrange to talk with the person after work. Keep such conversations as brief as possible.

Many businesses ask you for your work number, but avoid giving them this information, or at least discourage them from using it. Your barber may think he is doing you a favor by reminding you of tonight's scheduled haircut, but the receptionist where you work has better things to do than to forward your personal calls or take your personal messages. Use your planner to record personal appointments so that you do not need a reminder call.

Make time for exercise, even it's only walking. It's no secret that exercise helps you manage your weight. It also improves your mood, boosts your energy level, and helps you sleep better. Like eating well, getting regular exercise can help you guard against and manage a host of diseases.[1]

Taking care of yourself also means making time for activities that you enjoy. The demands of work, family, and other obligations can consume large amounts of time. Setting aside time for yourself is not selfish. It will help you maintain a good work–life balance and perform better on the job.

Regular exercise has many benefits.

Manage Relationships

Successfully managing your relationships with different kinds of people is a skill that can be developed with time, experience, and thoughtful effort. Taking the time to think about yourself—to truly know what you want and what you don't, what you'll do and what you won't—is a good way to start. Knowing these things and being faithful to them will shape your interactions with others.

You should also spend some time thinking about your negative emotions and what triggers them. When you understand what sorts of things make you impatient or angry, you can better control those emotions when they begin. Controlling your emotions is very important in both personal and work relationships. When you control your emotions, you can step back and consider the best way to respond, instead of mindlessly reacting.

Get to know the people with whom you have relationships. Be interested, be observant, and pay attention to what they say and do. Try hard to understand their requests, problems, and so on, from their point of view. At work, strive to put your relationships on a professional level, adopting the professional attitude described in Chapter 2.

Cope with Stress

Stress is the worry and anxiety you feel when you react to pressure from others or yourself. Stress is, of course, a common occurrence in people's professional and personal lives. Most administrative assistants are under pressure to be efficient and effective in their jobs because their work supports what others do.

Stress can have many different causes. It can be short-term (provoked, for instance, by knowing you are going to be late for an important appointment) or long-term (caused by a death in one's family or an illness, for example). Long-term stress can increase your risk for some health problems, such as depression.

A few other facts about stress are important to know. What is stressful for one person may not stressful for another, and people's reactions to stress vary. Ways to manage stress include the following:

- Set aside at least 15 minutes a day to do something for yourself.

- Talk about the stressful situation with a friend or family member who is a good listener.

- Make time for physical activity such as walking, yoga, or tennis.

- Get enough sleep.

- Use positive self-talk (see Chapter 2).

- Set realistic limits on what you try to accomplish each day and on the demands of others.

- Develop your own strategies for coping with stress.

1 Mayo Clinic Staff, "7 Benefits of Regular Physical Activity," MayoClinic.com, http://www.mayoclinic.com/health/exercise/hq01676 (accessed March 18, 2010).

Key Terms

accountability

downtime

incentive

interference

opportunity

priority

procrastination

progress

self-discipline

stress

Summary

- Self-discipline is essential to ensure productivity and accountability in the workplace.

- Achieving your aims in life requires setting clear, attainable goals, staying motivated, measuring progress, reinforcing success through incentives, resisting interference, and taking advantage of opportunities.

- To succeed as an administrative professional, you need to be accountable to your employer, your coworkers, customers and clients, and yourself.

- A neat and orderly work space gives a professional impression and promotes productivity.

- Organizational aids such as planners and to-do lists are essential to managing your workload.

- To manage your workload effectively, avoid procrastination, prioritize, control paper and e-mail clutter, organize your files, and streamline repetitive tasks.

- Time wasters on the job include disorganization, the failure to do tasks efficiently, interruptions, other people, and trouble focusing on work.

- You should make effective use of downtime, including multitasking and assisting coworkers.

- A healthy diet, weight control, exercise, and adequate sleep will help you to be an efficient, productive worker.

- Life management skills include balancing personal and professional commitments, managing relationships, and coping with stress.

Bookmark It. *For convenient access to activities, links, and valuable career resources for administrative professionals, visit the companion website for this text:*

www.cengage.com/officetech/fultoncalkins

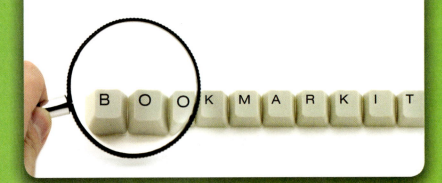

Discussion Questions

1. Why is setting goals and priorities important?

2. What does accountability mean? To whom are you accountable, and in what ways?

3. What is the ready-to-go principle?

4. List and explain three techniques for managing your workload.

5. Explain the "four categories" method of organizing your work. Give an example of your own (not from the text) for each category.

6. Identify three time wasters.

7. Give two examples of what would probably be a reasonable use of personal time at work. Give two examples of what would not be a reasonable use of personal time there.

8. Name three benefits of a healthful diet and three benefits of exercise.

9. What is stress, and what causes it? Identify three ways of managing stress.

Critical Thinking

In Jeremy's absence   Your department has two administrative assistants, you and Jeremy Wyler. Jeremy has just learned that he has leukemia. He will need to miss large amounts of work time for doctors' appointments and therapy sessions. In a small group, brainstorm ways to help reassign his work so it doesn't all fall on you. How would you plan this project? Who should be involved? What are some issues to keep in mind? For example, people could donate sick days and personal days, but how much responsibility should employees shoulder, and when should your employer take over? (Learning Objective 3)

Build Workplace Skills

1. **Setting goals**   List two long-term and two short-term goals that are related to your education or career and that are important to you. They can be goals that you are currently working towards or goals that you would like to achieve in the future. State each goal simply, specifically, and in positive terms. Make a timeline for reaching each goal with steps along the way. (Learning Objective 1)

2. **Ergonomics on the job**   *Ergonomics* is the design and arrangement of equipment and work areas for the user's protection and comfort. As an administrative professional, you are likely to spend a lot of time working at a computer. If you follow ergonomic guidelines in arranging your workstation and using your computer equipment, you will work more comfortably and will be less likely to develop medical problems such as back pain and carpal tunnel syndrome from working.

    Visit the U.S. Occupational Health and Safety Administration website to learn about ergonomics for computer workstations. A link is provided on the website for this book. As far as possible, follow the guidelines at the site to arrange your workstation at school, work, or home to follow ergonomic guidelines. Send an e-mail to your instructor describing the results. (Learning Objective 2)

Planning Notes

Learning Objectives

1. Explain steps for setting and meeting goals and priorities.

2. Describe strategies and tools for organizing your work area.

3. Describe strategies and tools for managing your workload.

4. Identify life management skills that improve job performance.

Activities 2, 7, 11, 12

Critical Thinking; Activities 6,10

21st Century Skills CAREER
Activities 1, 3, 4, 5, 8, 9; Above & Beyond

Planning Notes

3. **Organizing at work** In a small group, discuss methods and tips for organizing your work and your work area that you have found useful. Develop a list of the best methods and tips. The list should include at least a dozen items. (Learning Objectives 2, 3)

4. **Prioritize your work** Make a list of tasks for the next week. Use the "four categories" method described on page 44 to organize them according to their urgency and importance. Be sure to include tasks that are important, but not urgent.

   Return to this assignment at the end of the week. Which tasks did you start or accomplish? Was the four-categories method useful? Do you have another method that you prefer to use? If so, describe the advantages of this method. (Learning Objective 3)

Communicate Clearly

5. **Time management** Keep a log of how you spend your time for the next three days. At the end of that time, review the log. Did the results surprise you? Did you accomplish everything you wanted to accomplish? What time wasters did you encounter? Which were within your control, and which were not?

   Write a short essay in which you analyze how you used your time, answer the questions in this activity, and explain any changes you might make as a result of your analysis. Submit the essay to your instructor. (Learning Objective 3)

6. **Edit a letter** Open the *Word* file CH03 Seminar Letter from the data files. Edit the letter to correct errors in spelling, capitalization, grammar, word usage, and number usage.

7. **Stress** Do research to learn about causes of stress and ways of managing stress. The companion website for this book has a link to the American Psychological Association's Psychology Health Center, which has numerous articles about stress. You will also find other useful articles online. Choose an article that interests you. Create a *PowerPoint* presentation to use in communicating the main points of the article to your class. (Learning Objective 4)

Develop Relationships

8. **A new coworker** Mike Scialdone, the administrative assistant you've worked with for the past five years, is leaving the company; and Nancy Ramirez, an administrative assistant from another department, is being transferred to take his place. You do not know Nancy, but you have heard some comments about her from other employees in the office. For instance, you have heard that Nancy doesn't let anyone know when she is leaving for a break or lunch. She goes whenever she wants to, and she takes breaks at unusual times. In your department, you and Nancy will be required to cover for each other during breaks and lunches. You have also heard that Nancy is a hard worker, but she does only her own work and doesn't offer to help others. While you and Mike are each responsible for your own assignments, over time you have made it a practice to share your work, always helping each other.

   Think about how you will start your relationship with Nancy. How will you handle the requirement to cover breaks and lunch? What will you do about the arrangement for helping each other with work? (Learning Objective 4)

9. **Dealing with interruptions** Your company recently hired a new administrative assistant, Maryam Arjmand. On her first day, you stopped by her desk to meet her. During your conversation, you told her that if you could do anything to help her in settling in, just to let you know. Since then, Maryam has called you whenever she has a question. Sometimes the questions are about items are urgent; but on other occasions, they are not. Assisting her usually takes just a few minutes, but sometimes it takes longer.

   Maryam probably calls you about eight times a day. Helping her so much is affecting your ability to get your work done. There are two administrative assistants in Maryam's department who you know would be happy to help her. Maryam, however, doesn't know them very well and is more comfortable asking you. How can you continue to assist Maryam and to encourage her to ask questions about things she doesn't understand while controlling the inroads her interruptions make on your time? (Learning Objective 4)

10. **Helping Jeremy** Review the Critical Thinking activity. In a small group, brainstorm what helping Jeremy might mean in different business cultures. For example, suppose you are part of a small, friendly office. People know each other's families, and they go to social events together. Or suppose your organization is very business-oriented, and people don't show interest, or get involved, in personal issues outside work. (Learning Objective 3)

Use Technology

11. **Online tutorial** Take an online tutorial for software that you use in school or at work. Identify at least three things you learn from the tutorial that will help you do your work more efficiently. Make a list of these items. (Learning Objective 3)

12. **Assess your diet and fitness** Visit the MyPyramid Tracker website at the link provided on the website for this book (or a similar website). Register on the site and use it to track your physical activity and diet for today. Continue to enter data about your physical activity and diet for the next three days. What recommendations, if any, does the assessment tool make regarding your physical activity and diet? Since this information is personal, you are not asked to submit it to your instructor. (Learning Objective 4)

Above & Beyond

Plan for your absence Document the key things you do on your job so that someone else could do them if you were absent for more than two days. If you aren't currently working, do this for a previous job or for the tasks and activities you do each day related to school and family. Plan this document and use headings to categorize the tasks and information.

Planning Notes

Part 2

Shereatha Bradley

Librarian Service Assistant
Public Library of Cincinnati and Hamilton County
Cincinnati, Ohio

Shereatha Bradley is a librarian service assistant for the Public Library of Cincinnati and Hamilton County in Cincinnati, Ohio. She helps patrons with reference queries, maintains patron records, helps organize departments to make them more user-friendly, and guides visitors within the library.

"I work at the main branch of the library, and our facility takes up two large city blocks downtown. Even with hundreds of patrons coming in every day, our staff tries to take the time to acknowledge every visitor and make sure that each person—old or young, rich or poor—is treated equally, feels welcome, and receives good service."

"Even with hundreds of patrons coming in every day, our staff tries to . . . acknowledge every visitor and make sure that each person . . . receives good service."

When helping patrons over the phone, Shereatha makes sure that they feel valued. "I try to help callers with whatever they need and project a friendly tone and demeanor. I have a deep voice, which means that I have to make sure my inflections are clear for patrons to hear me and know that I'm listening and responding to their requests. That's the most important thing."

Shereatha emphasizes that it takes a team effort to help every patron in such a large facility. "Here's a common example: Say a woman comes into the library and heads straight to the information desk, where I work. I give her the information she's looking for, but she also needs a library card. I then lead her to the circulation desk where that can be taken care of. We also lead her to the book she's looking for and finally back to the circulation desk again to check out. Now, it took several staff members' help to make sure that this patron received excellent customer service, was satisfied, and moved efficiently through the library."

The Workplace Environment

Ready, Set, Plan

Use this space to plan your work in this section. Record the due dates for reading assignments and other activities for each chapter. If you are working with a team or partner, record the schedule for team meetings. Do you need a list of phone numbers or e-mail addresses? Don't forget your other commitments: work, other classes, and family.

Administrative Assistant

National nonprofit organization seeks assistant to support the work of its legal affairs department. The ideal job candidate must have:

- Excellent written and oral communication skills
- Understanding of and commitment to the mission and philosophy of the company
- Excellent interpersonal skills
- Flexibility and adaptability
- Ability to maintain confidentiality of sensitive information
- Experience with federal, state, and local lobbying and gift/gratuities rules

© MARK WRAGG, ISTOCK

Do I qualify?

CHAPTER

4

Learning Objectives

1. Understand basic ethical terms and concepts.

2. List characteristics of ethical businesses and organizations.

3. Describe resources and methods for making ethical decisions at work.

4. Identify unethical workplace behaviors and steps for working ethically.

Working Ethically

Ethics: The Basics

Ethics are guidelines or accepted beliefs about what is right or wrong, good or bad. Business ethics apply these principles to day-to-day decisions and activities in the workplace.

People's decisions and actions each day affect how others perceive them. Can others depend on you to act fairly? Do they consider your decisions to be based on a thoughtful process? Do they count on you to do the right thing? In a similar way, the reputation of a business is impacted by the decisions and actions of its employees, managers, and owners.

Understanding business ethics is especially important for administrative professionals because of the nature of this trusted position. For example, often administrative assistants are knowledgeable about confidential information and sensitive issues. This chapter will help you better understand the significance of ethics in the workplace and the responsibility you have as an employee.

Values, Morals, and Character

Values, or personal beliefs about what is right and wrong, are derived from a number of sources, beginning with parents and other family members. Other influences include religious groups, education, and the media. For example, students are often penalized if they turn in assignments late, so they learn the value of punctuality. Figure 4-1 lists some common sources of values.

Culture affects values. For example, if you belong to a culture that considers the development of personal relationships important, you may tend to try to establish such relationships with customers and with fellow employees. If, on the other hand, you belong to a culture in which people tend to keep others at a distance, you may be more reserved and less likely to attempt to form close associations on the job.

When people enter the workforce, they bring with them their value system and integrate it into the company value system as well as the rules and policies of their employer. As situations arise that require judgment, employees rely on their sense of right and wrong to choose how to react. These decisions continue to shape their values.

Morals are similar in meaning to values and are generally considered to be principles or rules for behaving in the right manner. **Character** refers to a combination of personal standards of behavior or traits, such as integrity and moral strength. Character implies consistency of behavior traits. Strong character is what people want in their leaders.

Core values are long-term attributes; they don't change from day to day or situation to situation. Because each person has different educational and

Figure 4-1 Sources of Values

- Parents
- Grandparents, aunts, and uncles
- Brothers and sisters
- School, teachers, and classmates
- Church, religious leaders, and fellow parishioners
- The media
- Culture and society

©STOCKPHOTO.COM/CLAUDIA DEWALD

life experiences, core values are not the same for everyone.

Businesses and organizations (and professions) also have core values, which form the cornerstone of the institution's ethics program. These values are reflected in communications and in the way employees, customers, and other stakeholders are treated. Figure 4-2 on page 58 lists the core values of IAAP.

Whole Foods Market, which consistently ranks among the top 100 companies to work for as reported by *Fortune* magazine, is an example of a business with core values. Those values include satisfying and delighting customers, creating wealth through profits and growth, supporting team member happiness and excellence, and caring about communities and the environment.[1]

Many organizations (and professions) also have a **code of ethics**, a written pledge to make responsible, moral decisions. Employees are expected to respect their company's code of ethics, and its values and ethical policies, when conducting business for the company.

1 Whole Foods Market, "Our Core Values," http://www.wholefoodsmarket.com/company/corevalues.php (accessed April 6, 2010).

Figure 4-2 IAAP Core Values

Integrity	■ Demonstrate honesty, accountability, and high ethical standards.
Respect	■ Listen, understand, and acknowledge member feedback.
Adaptability	■ Embrace positive change. ■ Nurture diversity, creativity, and visionary thinking.
Communication	■ Be approachable at all levels. ■ Communicate openly. ■ Build strong relationships.
Commitment	■ Be steadfast in goals.

Source: IAAP, "About IAAP," http://www.iaap-hq.org/aboutus (accessed March 22, 2010).

Laws and Ethical Standards

Many laws have their origins in the common ethical beliefs of a society. For instance, most people believe that it is wrong to steal or to cause physical harm to others. When many people in a community, state, or nation agree on an ethical principle, it is often made into law.

But while laws and ethical standards may be similar, they are not the same. For example, it is illegal to jaywalk, or cross the street in a reckless and irresponsible way, but there is nothing unethical about this behavior. Similarly, it is not illegal, but it is unethical, to take credit for work that someone else has done.

Sometimes laws are not ethical, and sometimes ethical behavior is against the law. In the United States, it was legal at one time to own slaves and illegal for women to vote. During the 1960s, civil rights activists like Rosa Parks and Martin Luther King, Jr., intentionally violated laws that enforced or promoted segregation.

Many laws are made with the intent to force people to act ethically. An example is the Civil Rights Act of 1964, which forbids discrimination on the basis of sex as well as race.

Characteristics of Ethical Organizations

Employees are more likely to enjoy going to work each day when they know they'll be treated fairly, that they will not be harassed, and that other workers will play by the rules. A strong ethical climate helps ensure that employees and other **stakeholders**, or those persons who have a vested interest in the company, are respected. Stakeholders include employees, owners, customers, suppliers, distributors, and the community. Employees, for example, expect to be paid well and to be treated fairly. Companies that do not pay their employees a fair wage or treat them fairly can expect to have a high turnover rate, which adversely affects the business. Owners, including shareholders, have an interest in the company's showing a profit. Investors expect the company to be open and honest about its financial condition. Customers who buy the company's products and services provide the financial resources for it to make a profit. Pleasing its customers with an excellent product or service and standing behind that product or service are top priorities for successful businesses. You can see that maintaining an ethical climate is frequently in the best interests of a business or organization.

Several characteristics distinguish ethical organizations. They include being environmentally responsible, promoting diversity within the organization, providing a safe environment for workers, offering fair and equitable pay, being socially responsible, and respecting the law.

Environmentally Responsible

Ethical organizations work to preserve the environment for future generations by reducing the impact of their operations on the environment. For example, many companies recycle paper, plastics, electronics, and other items. Some companies have adopted alternative energy sources, such as solar, wind, or methane. Some use hybrid or electric vehicles in their fleets.

NetApp, a manufacturer of data storage systems, is an example of a company with a comprehensive environmental policy. Through an energy management program, NetApp has reduced energy use and has increased energy efficiency throughout its facilities. Its "reduce, reuse, recycle" program reduces the volume of many types of disposable materials at its offices, from beverage cans to electronics. A trip reduction program for employees includes features such as a guaranteed ride home for workers who use public transit, telecommuting, and reserved carpool parking.[2]

Diverse Workforce

A diverse workforce benefits companies in several ways. It helps them meet the needs of their global customers and an increasingly diverse U.S. population. Studies have shown that groups and teams with diverse members are more creative and make better decisions. Diversity also helps a company attract and retain talented employees.

All organizations must comply with laws that promote equal treatment and prohibit discrimination (described in the "Workers' Rights" section on pages 60–61. Ethical organizations, however, go further than the law requires. They make hiring decisions based on merit and are committed to providing equal employment opportunities. They create environments that are attractive to all employees. They are intolerant of discrimination, maintain a policy against sexual harassment, provide diversity training for their employees, and hold managers accountable for consistently supporting and ensuring diversity.

Diversity at work encompasses a number of differences. They include race and ethnicity, physical ability, age, sexual orientation, and gender.

Race and Ethnicity
The Census Bureau projects that by 2042, minority groups, which today make up a third of the population, will become the majority.[3]

This growing racial and ethnic diversity is reflected in the labor force, both in locations that traditionally have been centers of immigration and diversity and in places that have not.

Physical Ability
As of 2007, more than one in six U.S. citizens over age 5 had a disability. Among working-age people with disabilities, the employment rate was 36.2 percent, less than half that of individuals without disabilities.[4] The federal government, state and local governments, and many companies and organizations have programs, policies, and initiatives for employing people with disabilities. Aircraft manufacturer Boeing is an example. When a disability imposes a barrier that keeps an employee from performing a job in the traditional way, Boeing reviews the situation and tailors the work arrangements as needed.[5]

Age
There was a time when many companies in the United States had a mandatory retirement age. The Age Discrimination in Employment Act protects individuals age 40 or older from age-based employment discrimination. Today, many older workers are choosing to stay in or return to the workforce rather than retiring. From 1997 to 2007, the employment of workers age 65 and older increased 101 percent, and the Census Bureau

2 NetApp, "Environmental Responsibility," http://www.netapp.com/us/careers/life/environmental-responsibility.html (accessed April 8, 2010).

3 U.S. Census Bureau, "An Older and More Diverse Nation by Midcentury," August 14, 2008, http://www.census.gov/Press-Release/www/releases/archives/population/012496.html (accessed February 18, 2010).

4 Rehabilitation Research and Training Center on Disability Statistics and Demographics, "Population Statistics" and "Employment," *Annual Disability Statistics Compendium: 2009,* http://disabilitycompendium.org (accessed March 25, 2010).

5 Boeing, "Employment—Culture — Diversity," http://www.boeing.com/employment/culture/diversity.html (accessed April 8, 2010).

Ethical organizations safeguard the environment.

projects that it will continue to rise as baby boomers move into this age category.[6] Ethical organizations value the experience, knowledge, and loyalty of their older workers and see age as no bar in hiring.

Sexual Orientation

Federal law does not protect gay, lesbian, bisexual, and transgender (GLBT) persons from discrimination in employment, though many state laws and municipal ordinances do. Businesses and organizations, however, are gradually adapting their workplace policies to consider sexual orientation in the same category as they do other types of diversity.[7]

Many organizations promote a workplace that accepts GLBT employees and treat them equally with other employees. For example, some companies provide employees in same-sex partnerships and marriages with the same benefits as employees in traditional marriages, such as health insurance.

Gender

Women make up nearly half the U.S. workforce. While women have made great strides in equal employment in the past few decades, inequities still exist, particularly in pay, representation in leadership positions in organizations, and advancement opportunities. Ethical employers work to eliminate pay gaps and to promote qualified female employees to higher-level positions. They also offer family-friendly policies and benefits, such as day care, flexible jobs and hours, and telecommuting.

Workers' Rights

Workers are entitled to a safe and healthful working environment. The U.S. Occupational Safety and Health Administration (OSHA) sets and enforces standards for safe and healthful working conditions. An ethical organization takes these requirements very seriously. For example, it may provide extensive training and state-of-the-art safety equipment. It may also use ergonomics in designing work areas and purchasing equipment

so that employees can work not only safely, but comfortably, and in a pleasant environment.

State and federal laws set standards for minimum wages and require equal pay for equal work. If employees are unionized, an organization is legally required to bargain in good faith for wages, benefits, and working conditions.

People @Work

SEXUAL HARASSMENT COMPLIANCE OFFICER

If you work for an organization that provides training for employees on what constitutes sexual harassment, you may receive your training from a sexual harassment compliance officer. Sexual harassment compliance officers provide policy information and guidance when an organization responds to incidents of sexual harassment. An officer takes complaints of sexual harassment and sex discrimination and investigates each complaint thoroughly. She or he provides remedies and works with external representatives regarding complaints. The sexual harassment compliance officer also works with management to provide a working environment free of sexual harassment and sexual discrimination.

© 2010 TETRA IMAGES/JUPITERIMAGES CORPORATION

6 Bureau of Labor Statistics, "Older Workers," http://www.bls.gov/spotlight/2008/older_workers, July 2008 (accessed March 25, 2010).

7 Todd Henneman, "Diversity Training Addresses Sexual Orientation," *Workforce Management* Online, December 2004, http://www.workforce.com/section/11/feature/23/90/44/239046.html, July 2008 (accessed March 27, 2010).

An ethical organization offers its employees fair and equitable pay. This attitude coincides with the best interests of the company. Most employers compete for the best workforce. To retain highly qualified individuals, they must pay the market or above the market price. An ethical organization wants its employees to be pleased with their pay and benefits as well as their working conditions. A good compensation plan attracts capable employees, motivates employees to perform effectively, and helps retain capable employees.

Federal law protects workers from being discriminated against because of their age, a disability, gender, race or ethnicity, religion, or pregnancy. These rights are guaranteed for hiring, promotion, firing, and pay. In addition to complying with these laws, ethical organizations, as noted above, do not tolerate any type of discrimination. They uphold clearly stated policies and procedures committed to equal employment. They publish grievance policies that are also clearly stated and are distributed to all employees.

Socially Responsible

Social responsibility refers to the obligation of a business to contribute to the greater good of the community. Communities rely on the support of local companies for financial stability and growth. Businesses have a legal and ethical obligation not to harm the citizens of the community. This includes properly disposing of harmful wastes and using pollution controls for factories. An ethical company is a good neighbor.

Businesses make choices about pollution, employee health and safety, the sponsorship of charitable endeavors and employee volunteer programs, and other issues and needs. They may, for example, choose to give employees time off for volunteering or a convenient way to financially support worthy causes. After the September 11 attacks, the flooding in New Orleans following Hurricane Katrina in 2005, and the 2010 earthquake in Haiti, corporations were among the first to send millions of dollars in aid for people in need.

Whistleblowing

A *whistleblower* is a person, usually an employee, who discloses to the public or to authorities wrongdoing in a company or government department. In 1988, the National Whistleblowers Center was formed to help those who report fraud and abuse. Persons who step forward and report abuse and/or fraud have sometimes lost their jobs in the process.

The Sarbanes-Oxley Act of 2002 made it a crime to retaliate against corporate whistleblowers in publicly traded companies. The National Whistleblowers Center is an advocate for those persons who have stepped forward even in the face of retaliation by their employers. The center

identifies whistleblowers as the most important corporate resource for detecting and preventing fraud. The organization also supports and lobbies for legislation that protects whistleblowers. Some companies have incorporated hotlines where employees can anonymously report unethical behavior.

© ISTOCKPHOTO.COM\WILLIE B. THOMAS

Respect for the Law

An ethical company has respect for the law. It abides by all federal, state, and local laws. If it is an international company, it also abides by the laws of the country or countries in which it does business. Numerous laws affect businesses, including hiring, firing, interstate trade, taxes, fair competition, and EPA requirements. In addition to abiding by the law itself, an ethical company makes sure its employees know, understand, and follow the laws that affect its business.

Making Ethical Choices

At work, you will face many ethical choices. Some of these choices will be easy to make. The right or wrong answer will be clear. For others, the answer will not be so easy. To make good ethical decisions at work, you can rely on your own personal values, guidance from your employer, and a four-step process for working through an ethical problem and finding a solution.

Personal Values

People rely on their personal values when making ethical decisions. While each person has his or her own core values, some values are widely shared. Five of these common values are honesty, fairness, respect, responsibility, and compassion.

- **Honesty**—Be honest. Don't deceive, cheat, or steal. Consider how you feel when someone lies to you. Being honest not only means telling the truth, but also giving the relevant information. Hiding information from others is also being dishonest.

- **Fairness**—Being fair means acting without prejudice or favoritism. Be fair in your dealings with coworkers, customers, and supervisors. Listen to others. Don't blame others, and do not take advantage of others.

- **Respect**—Respect others. Respect cultural differences and diversity in the workplace. Try to understand differences in opinions and find common ground and consensus in decision making.

  Respect also means listening with an open mind to the opinions of others. Learning to be tactful is very important in showing respect. The more

respectful you are toward others, the more respect they will show toward you. It is possible to have disagreements without disrespecting each other. There will be people at work that you like more than others, but you must be respectful to everyone.

- **Responsibility**—Take responsibility and be accountable for your duties and actions. Always try to do your best. When you make a mistake, own up to it and correct it.

- **Compassion**—Be kind and considerate toward others. Use your manners. Show understanding and caring for your coworkers. Send thank-you notes, sympathy notes, and congratulations notes when appropriate. Try to put yourself in another person's situation to understand how that person might act and feel. Avoid hurting others' feelings.

Writing @Work

How can you apply ethics in your workplace writing? Here are several suggestions:

- ⤢ Make sure your content is accurate. Check and recheck your facts.

- ⤢ Honesty is important. Avoid questionable language.

- ⤢ Under no condition should your writing contain obscenities or off-color language.

- ⤢ Use the editing process as a means of ensuring your messages are courteous and professional. Setting aside a document and reviewing it later will help keep you from sending messages that you will later regret.

- ⤢ Take pains not to offend any group in your writing, and avoid language that could be perceived as sexist.

- ⤢ Don't use humor, unless you know your correspondent well. Keep in mind that many jokes can be offensive to different people or groups.

©ISTOCK

Ethics Training

Some companies give their employees formal ethics training. An ethics training class or program will help you understand the core values, code of ethics, and ethical policies of your organization. You can also expect instruction on what is legal and what is not. Ethics training helps employees recognize ethical dilemmas and ethical ways to handle problems. It often includes scenarios about common ethical dilemmas in the workplace. Employees may explore these problems through role-plays, group conversations, watching videos, or other means.

Ethical training requires employees to examine how they are making ethical decisions and helps them to improve those skills. It may present a set of steps for ethical decision making and may introduce resources, such as an ethics officer, or company procedures to follow when an ethical problem arises.

Whether your employer provides ethical training or not, you should make yourself aware of your company's ethical standards. They may be formally stated in a code of ethics, core values, an ethics policy, or a code of conduct. They may also be less formally reflected in the workplace culture and in the business's actions. In addition, you should be aware of procedures your company expects you to follow when you are confronted with an ethical issue.

©ISTOCK

Dear Savvy Admin

Dear Savvy Admin:

My supervisor is always asking me to lie. He tells me to tell callers he is out for the day when he is in his office. He also has me say to vendors that their checks are in the mail when I know they are not. I am very uncomfortable about being asked to lie like this. I work in a small office, and there is no one I can talk to here. Can you give me some advice on handling this situation?

Caught in the Middle

Dear Caught in the Middle:

You can truthfully say to callers that your supervisor is unavailable and offer to take a message. When it comes to telling vendors that their checks are in the mail when they are not, you should talk to your supervisor about how uncomfortable you feel relaying this message. If he continues to insist, this may be a sign of cash flow problems and a more serious issue of the company's staying in business. It may be time to update your resume and look for alternate employment.

Savvy Admin

A Four-Step Process

For some ethical problems, the right choice isn't immediately clear. Suppose, for instance, that your supervisor, whom you like and respect, has a problem with alcohol that is affecting her work. You may have to choose between telling the company and protecting your supervisor. When you are in situations like this, you can follow a set of steps, like the steps for problem solving and decision making that you learned about in Chapter 2, to help you reach a good decision:

1. Evaluate the problem and understand the options.

2. Know the stakeholders—the consequences will affect them.

3. Strive to do the right thing. Don't be driven by the desire for immediate gratification.

4. Be in harmony with your employer's values.

Ethical training teaches that limiting oneself to *either–or* choices is a mistake. There may be other choices available that will allow a more ethical way to proceed. In this example, you might investigate the company's policies regarding substance abuse. It may turn out that your company works with the employee to address the problem rather than dismissing that person. You might choose to disclose the information to someone in authority at the company whose judgment you trust. You may think about your relationship with your supervisor and decide that you can talk with her about the problem and suggest that she seek help.

An Ethical Character

Making ethical decisions in your personal life will help you make ethical decisions in your professional life. Ethical and unethical behaviors tend to be consistent. In addition, ethics can and do become better and stronger with repeated ethical decisions and actions. Being around people who have good values and seeing ethical actions take place make people stronger and more willing to take ethical actions.

People's decisions influence their actions. Their decisions and actions become habits, and their habits contribute to their reputation. All of these combined make up their character. The more people make ethical decisions, the easier they are to make. The reverse is unfortunately also true. The more people make unethical decisions, the easier it is to make them again. They also become habits and build a poor character.

In Stephen Covey's book *The 7 Habits of Highly Effective People*, the second habit is "Begin with the End in Mind." Think about how your daily decisions and actions will build your reputation.

At the end—your retirement—what will people say about your career? You might want them to say that you were competent at your job; were fair, honest, and compassionate in your relationships with customers and colleagues; were of great value to the organization; and will be missed.

Find someone in your company who appears to be honest, compassionate, fair, and trustworthy. Follow that person's lead. Think of yourself as a role model for someone else. Would you be a good role model to someone recently hired in your company? If the answer is no, what can you do to improve yourself so you would be a good role model for a new employee?

Working Ethically

Most people want to work ethically. They want to do the jobs they've been hired to do and to live up to the expectations of their supervisors, coworkers, and customers. When things are going well, working ethically can be easy. It's when circumstances aren't ideal that the temptation

Ethical Guidelines

Texas Instruments has received many awards for its policies regarding the environment, employee well-being, and other ethical issues. When hired, employees receive the following Ethics Quick Test on a business-card-sized pamphlet to carry with them:

Ethics Quick Test

Is the action legal?

Does it comply with our values?

If you do it, will you feel bad?

How will it look in the newspaper?

© 2010 DAJ/JUPITERIMAGES CORPORATION

If you know it's wrong, don't do it!

If you're not sure, ask.

Keep asking until you get an answer.

Source: Texas Instruments, "Corporate Social Responsibility," http://www.ti.com/corp/docs/company/citizen/ethics/quicktest.shtml (accessed 12/20/2009).

to lie, cut corners, or cover up can arise. As an administrative professional, you will sometimes be overworked. You will be under pressure to meet deadlines and produce results. You will experience stress from your job or your personal life. These situations occur for everyone, and they will also occur for you. You need to prepare yourself so you can handle them without losing your sense of perspective or taking actions that you will regret.

Honesty

Dishonesty at work is a common ethical problem. Dishonesty means not only lying but also withholding information or misrepresenting the truth. These actions are always unethical; they are also sometimes illegal. Be honest with your supervisor, coworkers, and clients. When you make a mistake that your supervisor needs to know about, tell your supervisor, even if you think it makes you look bad. If patients are waiting for their appointments and you know there will be an hour's delay, say so.

Confidentiality

As an administrative professional, you will work with private and sensitive information. Working ethically means protecting the confidentiality of that information. Protecting confidentiality is also sometimes a legal requirement. If you work in a health care facility, for example, you will be required to comply with laws such as the Health Insurance Portability and Accountability Act of 1996 (HIPAA), which prohibits communication of a patient's medical and billing information, except for certain purposes, without the patient's written consent. Similar protections exist for client information in legal offices and for company information and personal and financial data of employees and clients in many other types of businesses.

While breaches of confidentiality are sometimes intentional, they can also occur through ignorance and carelessness. Take the time to make yourself thoroughly aware of the ways in which confidentiality needs to be protected in your office. Learn the requirements of the law, and always follow standard company procedures for storing, maintaining, and releasing confidential data.

Working ethically also means maintaining confidentiality of information that isn't formally protected but that people assume is private. Forwarding someone's e-mail to another reader without first getting permission from the writer is an example of unethical behavior.

workplace wisdom

Many people aren't aware of some of the ways in which confidentiality of information may be violated. Here are some examples:

- Discussing private information on a cell phone
- Using a client's name as the subject line in an e-mail
- Posting a birthday list that includes birth dates
- Leaving a note on your desk that contains confidential information
- Releasing more information than was requested
- Leaving an employee's file displayed on a computer
- Discussing a patient's medical condition with a family member

Taking Credit for Others' Work

Working ethically also means not taking credit for work that isn't one's own. When this is done with respect to another person's words or ideas, that is known as plagiarism. Like breaches of confidentiality, plagiarism is sometimes intentional, but it can also occur through carelessness or lack of understanding. It is easy, when you have a lot of work to do or are under a deadline, to hastily write down material from a source and to forget to note that it is a quotation. And people are often not aware, for instance, that copying and pasting material from the Internet is plagiarism and is often also a violation of copyright laws. Always provide the source for the following kinds of information, regardless of the medium in which it is provided:

- Direct quotations
- Paraphrasing, or restating material in your own words
- Factual information that isn't widely available or generally known

Respecting the Employer's Resources

Most people would never consider stealing something from a friend. Yet taking from an employer—taking home office supplies, running personal errands on company time, or taking a sick day to go to an amusement park—is a common ethical problem.

Petty Theft Employee theft costs companies billions of dollars each year. For retailers, losses from employee theft exceed those from shoplifting. Taking home notebooks, copy paper, staplers, and other office supplies is stealing. So is using an office copier for personal copying. Duplicating company software to use at home is illegal and unethical. Using the company mail system to mail personal packages is stealing from the company and is highly unethical.

Misuse of Time The importance of attending to company business while at work was discussed in earlier chapters. Surfing the Internet, reading or writing personal e-mail, browsing through catalogs, and reading the newspaper should be done in time away from work. It is appropriate to have a little communication on matters that are not related to

work with other employees. Occasional personal phone calls are usually permissible. Abuse of that privilege is unethical.

Calling in sick when one is not is a common unethical practice. Attendance is extremely important. When employees aren't at work, their work doesn't get done. Other people may need to do it for them. Employee absences affect coworkers and supervisors. Coming in late and leaving early can become a habit—a very bad habit, as can taking long breaks or lunch hours.

Technology @Work

It is unethical to use company time for personal business. Are you spending time on these sites instead of performing work?

- ↗ News sites
- ↗ Banking sites
- ↗ Entertainment sites
- ↗ Shopping sites
- ↗ Sports sites
- ↗ Auction sites
- ↗ Stock trading sites
- ↗ Employment sites
- ↗ Social networking sites

Communicating @Work

Gossip divides people and forces employees to take sides. Do not be a part of the gossip circle.

↗ Do not pass on half-truths.

↗ Verify information before repeating it.

↗ Do not divulge company business under any conditions.

↗ Make your gossip good news gossip.

↗ Consider the image that others have of you. What do you think of coworkers who spread malicious gossip or talk about confidential information?

Substance Abuse

Drug and alcohol abuse in the workplace is not tolerated. Employees who abuse drugs and/or alcohol use more sick days, are late more often than other employees, are more likely to be injured on the job or injure someone else, and cause low employee morale. Some companies have mandatory drug testing prior to employment. If there is an accident on the job, a drug test may be required.

Personal Behavior Outside Work

Unethical behavior outside work can wreak havoc on one's professional life. The Technology @ Work feature in Chapter 2 warned against posting inappropriate personal information on social networking sites. Some job recruiters search for applicants' names on these sites and on the Internet at large. In some cases, applicants aren't hired and employees are fired for what they have posted. A mayor was fired for posting a provocative picture of herself. A young woman who posted comments about how boring her job found herself out of a job.

Employees can also be fired for doing something illegal in their personal lives. Examples are getting caught with illegal drugs or receiving a citation from the police for driving while intoxicated.

For the most part, companies do not try to dictate what their employees do in their personal lives. A few companies, citing rising health care costs, forbid their employees from smoking, drinking, and using drugs not only in the workplace but outside it. These companies sometimes do blood tests to detect any violations of their policies regarding drugs. Such companies usually have a policy about drinking, smoking, or drug use that prospective hires know before they accept a position with the company.

Key Terms

character

code of ethics

core values

ethics

morals

stakeholders

values

Summary

- Ethics are guidelines or accepted beliefs about what is right or wrong, good or bad. Business ethics apply these principles to day-to-day decisions and activities in the workplace.

- Personal values come from many sources including parents, teachers, religious leaders, and society. People apply their core values in making ethical decisions.

- A strong ethical climate helps ensure that companies will treat employees and other stakeholders fairly.

- Ethical organizations are environmentally responsible, have a diverse workforce, provide a safe environment for workers, offer fair and equitable pay, are socially responsible, and respect the law.

- Incorporating the core values of honesty, fairness, respect, responsibility, and compassion into your decisions and actions will help you make ethical choices. For difficult decisions, a four-step process can help.

- Working ethically requires you to make responsible choices in terms of honesty, confidentiality, giving credit to others' work, and respecting your employer's resources.

- Unethical behavior in one's personal life can have detrimental effects on one's professional life.

Bookmark It. *For convenient access to activities, links, and valuable career resources for administrative professionals, visit the companion website for this text:*

www.cengage.com/officetech/fultoncalkins

Discussion Questions

1. What role do values play in making ethical decisions?

2. What is the difference between laws and ethical standards?

3. What are the characteristics of an ethical organization?

4. What might you learn in an ethics training class or program?

5. Name the four steps in the process for making ethical decisions.

6. Explain how carelessness and ignorance can result in breaches of confidentiality.

7. What does respecting your employer's resources mean?

Critical Thinking

Recommending a friend   There is a job opening in your office, and you have been asked to serve on the hiring committee. An old friend of yours has applied. You know your friend really needs a job. You also know she was let go by her last employer. You suspect that it was because she spent too much time on the phone and e-mailing friends. You know she will expect you to put in a good word for her if you are on the committee. Do you serve on the hiring committee? Do you recommend her? Do you share your suspicions with the committee? How will you respond if she asks you to be a reference? Work in a small group. Use the four-step process described in the "Making Ethical Choices" section of the chapter to answer these questions. (Learning Objective 3)

Build Workplace Skills

1. **Values**   Write a short essay describing your values. What are the sources of your values? How has culture affected them? Describe at least one ethical decision that you have made at work, at school, or in your personal life by applying your values. (Learning Objective 1)

2. **Ethical companies**   Use the Internet to find and report on three companies that have codes of ethics on their websites. What is the code of ethics of each company? Does the company provide a list of values? Does it outline an ethics policy with respect to hiring, the environment, social responsibility, or other ethics topics? Write a summary of each company's code of ethics and any values and ethics policies. (Learning Objectives 1, 3)

3. **Ethics training**   You are the administrative assistant to the director of human resources. The company is going to institute an ethics training program, and she has asked you to research programs and identify three good prospects. The programs should cover common ethical problems encountered in an office environment, particularly related to confidentiality. Work in a small group to research and choose the programs. Assemble materials from the programs you have selected for the director's review, and write an evaluation that compares them. (Learning Objective 3).

Planning Notes

Learning Objectives

1. Understand basic ethical terms and concepts.

2. List characteristics of ethical businesses and organizations.

3. Describe resources and methods for making ethical decisions at work.

4. Identify unethical workplace behaviors and steps for working ethically.

 Critical Thinking; Activities 3, 4, 5, 6

 Activities 2, 9, 10

 Activities 1, 7, 8; Above and Beyond

Communicate Clearly

4. **News release**   Open the *Word* file CH04 News Release from the data files. Edit the news release to correct errors in keyboarding, punctuation, spelling, capitalization, and word usage. (Learning Objective 2)

5. **Two conversations**   Locate the sound file CH04 Exchange from the data files. Play the file to hear a short conversation between Mark and his supervisor, Ms. Ramirez, and a second conversation between Mark and his coworker, Courtney. What unethical workplace behaviors are taking place? Did Mark make the right decision? (Learning Objective 4)

6. **Volunteer project**   At your company, employees can propose volunteer projects that the company will sponsor through funding and inviting employees to participate. Choose a volunteer project that you think is important. Write an e-mail to your instructor in which you propose the project to the company. Use your persuasive skills to convince the company that the project is worthwhile. Be sure to do any research that is needed to give your employer an accurate idea of the work to be done and the cost.

Develop Relationships

7. **Doing personal work**   You are the administrative assistant to a physician with a private practice. You are very good at spelling, grammar, and proofreading. The physician has left a handwritten paper on your desk with a note to key the paper and correct spelling and grammar errors. You are to do this on company time. When you look at the paper, you can see that it is a term paper for her 15-year-old son. What do you do? Use one of the methods described in the "Making Ethical Choices" section of the chapter to decide. (Learning Objectives 3, 4)

8. **Misuse of time**   You are an administrative assistant in a large complex. Your offices open at 8:00 a.m. and close at 5:00 p.m. each day. All office personnel are required to punch in and out on a time clock. Many of the office workers in your area stop working at 5:00, go to the restroom or chat, and then punch out at 5:08. In this way, they get paid for an extra quarter hour. You do not feel this is right. What do you do? Use one of the methods described in the "Making Ethical Choices" section of the chapter to decide. (Learning Objectives 3, 4)

Use Technology

9. **How much does it cost?**   You may think that taking a few Post-It® Notes for personal use or arriving to work a few minutes late doesn't matter. Create a spreadsheet in *Microsoft Excel*. Complete the following calculations to see how much employee theft costs a fictitious company of 30 employees over the course of one week. Over the course of a year? Does this change your opinion?* (Learning Objective 4)

   • Three workers each take home two packs of Post-It® Notes, at a cost of $.67 per pack.

   • Three workers arrive at work 15 minutes late, at a cost of $11/hour.

   • Four workers take an extra half-hour for lunch, at a cost of $14/hour.

   • Three employees play computer games for a total of 4 hours each, at a cost of $10/hour.

- One employee sends three personal packages at the company's expense, at a cost of $7, $4.50, and $12.
- One worker makes 300 personal copies on the company photocopier, at a cost of $.05/copy.
- Three workers call in sick for one 8-hour day when they are healthy, at a cost of $10/hour.
- Ten workers send three personal e-mails each, which take a total of 7 hours, at a cost of $10/hour.

*Adapted from Doris Humphrey, *Quick Skills*: *What Your Employer Expects* (Cincinnati: South-Western, 2001), 37.

10. **Best companies to work for**   Use library resources or the Internet to find *Fortune* magazine's most recent annual listing of the ten best companies to work for. Pick three of the companies and write a paragraph on each one explaining why it was picked as one of the best companies to work for. (Learning Objective 2)

> *Above & Beyond*

Ethical role model   Pick an employed person whom you admire for his or her ethics. Interview that person face-to-face, by e-mail, or on the phone. Ask the person to describe her or his values. What are some ethical decisions that he or she has had to make at work? What method(s) were used to resolve them? Write a summary of your interview. Be ready to report on it to the class. (Learning Objective 3)

Planning Notes

Do I qualify?

Administrative Assistant

Program and construction management firm seeks administrative assistant. Duties include:

- Work on an administrative team to support eight managers
- Research, track, and report new business leads
- Arrange and facilitate meetings and events
- Represent the firm at industry events as needed

This position requires strong communication skills and the ability to work with many different personalities and management styles.

©MARK WRAGG, ISTOCK

CHAPTER

5

Understanding the Workplace Team

Teams at Work

Understanding how teams function in the workplace and their significance to the everyday operations of an organization is important for the administrative professional. It is important because workplace teams, in whatever form, are a reality. You will be asked to work on formal and informal teams throughout your lifetime. Teams may take the form of groups or departments or projects, but in the long run, they all have one thing in common—there is some common goal, and everyone is working toward that goal.

If you do an Internet search of the term *teamwork*, you will get "hits" about teamwork in sports or teamwork in averting or responding to tragedy. Although those situations are not from a business perspective, they share the same concepts of collaboration and cooperation.

Learning Objectives

1. Describe benefits of teams and identify common types of workplace teams.

2. Describe the general process by which teams operate.

3. Describe qualities and skills for being an effective team member, supporter, or leader.

4. List qualities of effective teams and identify team challenges.

Individuals are working together for a common goal, resources are shared, some responsibilities are shared and others are not, and everyone ultimately gets credit for successes and failures.

Teams are groups of employees who work together towards a common goal—simply put, people who work together to get a job done. The ideas you will read about in this chapter are generally transferable to any team situation you will encounter at work, at school, in sports teams, or at home. Teamwork is a very practical concept and an area in which you already have much experience.

Benefits of Teams for Organizations

Teams are vital to the health and efficiency of many organizations. They bring together skills and experiences that exceed those of an individual. Approaching a problem or process through the use of teams can result in greater creativity, more options, and better decisions and solutions, leading to improved productivity and quality.

Employees who serve on effective teams enjoy having greater responsibility and being able to contribute to the organization in a "bigger" or different way than they would normally in their jobs. As a consequence, they may have more job satisfaction, perform better, and be more likely to stay with the company.

Being part of a successful workplace team can have valuable benefits.

Benefits of Teams for Employees

Employees sometimes have mixed feelings about serving on teams. They are concerned, for instance, about their time being wasted, having teammates who won't do their share of the work, or being held responsible along with the rest of the team if it fails. Belonging to an effective team, however, can have several valuable benefits:

- You will gain insight, ideas, help, information, and more from those you come in contact with, and those around you will also gain insight, ideas, help, information, and more from their connection with you.

- Teams allow for cross-training on different tasks. This experience gives team members opportunities to learn new skills that can make their jobs more interesting and help them perform their jobs better. New skills can also be useful later in their careers.

- As a team collaborates on a project, all the members have the advantage of seeing the whole process, which makes the team better at problem solving and gives team members a new perspective on the tasks that other people perform.

- Teams often get to see the "big picture." Learning about the organization as a whole helps you in your job.

- They are fun. People on successful teams enjoy being a part of something bigger than themselves and get deep enjoyment and satisfaction from being on a team.

Being able to work on, support, and eventually lead a team is a fundamental workplace skill. Regardless of how you participate, you will have unique challenges and opportunities as you seek to assist the team in accomplishing its goal.

Types of Teams

Most administrative professionals work in a team environment—in a small office, in a department or division, or directly with an executive, for example. In addition to this general supporting role, you may sometimes be asked to serve on or lead a formal team.

Workplaces have many different types of teams. Some are ongoing and permanent, such as a finance committee. Others are temporary, set up for a specific task or purpose and disbanded once it has been achieved. An example is a task force set up to address the problem of increased employee absenteeism.

Committees and task forces are discussed in Chapter 10. Three other common types of workplace teams are described below. As you read about them, consider the common threads that emerge—communication, collaboration, a commitment to clearly defined goals, and shared responsibility for the outcome.

Project Teams   Teams that are developed for a clearly defined project with a beginning and an end are called **project teams**. This type of team might report to a task force, which has multiple ongoing projects to achieve a larger goal. A project team usually has a set budget and a schedule for how and when the work will be completed. Because companies constantly have to develop new products, services, or methods in order to stay productive, project teams are important to organizations and continue to gain in importance.[1] Examples of project teams are teams that find a new market niche, develop a new client service, or improve a process.

Cross-Functional Teams   **Cross-functional teams** are composed of individuals from a number of different functional groups within an organization (such as the engineering, marketing, and quality control departments). They are usually brought together to solve a problem or work on a project that requires their expertise. A cross-functional team is a type of project team and has a matrix structure; that is, resources are temporarily borrowed from all over the company to accomplish a goal. As an administrative professional, you might be part of a cross-functional team formed, for example, to make a plan for implementing the use of new software across the company.

Virtual Teams   **Virtual teams** primarily meet electronically, crossing time, distance, and organizational boundaries in order to operate as a team. Virtual teams are valuable to organizations because they can save time and money, and they open up collaborative opportunities that wouldn't be possible or practical by any other means. An uncertain economy and a competitive marketplace make virtual teams an attractive option for many companies.

1 Anthony T. Cobb, *Leading Project Teams: An Introduction to the Basics of Project Management* (Thousand Oaks, Calif.: Sage, 2006), 2.

workplace wisdom

What is a project? That may seem like an easy question, but consider how projects differ from ongoing work. Ongoing work, such as producing a product, is part of the normal operation of a company or unit. It usually has predictable costs and schedules, since it is work that is usually repetitive and has a history. Projects are less predictable and more stressful to manage because they are new and there is less evidence available to predict costs, schedules, and resource requirements.* Two examples of projects are a community cleanup endeavor and the creation of a company child-care program to reduce absenteeism and increase company morale.

*Source: James P. Lewis, *Team-Based Project Management* (New York: Amacom, 1998), 10–11.

While virtual teams may be spread across the country or around the world, they may also operate in closer proximity to one another, in the same region or city or even the same building. Such teams meet virtually some or all of the time for convenience and to accommodate different schedules and locations. Employees who telecommute may be part of virtual teams.

Virtual teams use many different types of technologies to communicate and collaborate. They include e-mail, blogs, wikis, web conferencing, phone calls, and instant messaging. These technologies are discussed in Chapters 9 and 10.

The Team Process

Knowing what to expect when you are asked to serve on or lead a workplace team will help you to be an effective member or leader from the start. While the team process is not the same within all organizations or teams, you will find there are many similarities, key elements, and transferable skills.

Early Meetings

In businesses, organizational leadership (such as a manager, supervisor, or CEO) forms teams and puts a leader into place to guide them. The leadership style of that leader will determine much of the process of them. Leadership will be discussed in more detail in Chapter 16. The type of team also determines how the team operates—whether the mission of the team is ongoing or short-term.

After the leader finds a meeting time that is most convenient for as many team members as possible, a time is set for the first meeting. If all the team members are not from the same department or work area in an organization, the team starts out with introductions and then moves on to defining the team's goal and the roles of team members.

The leader sets the stage for the work of the team by clearly defining what the team is supposed to accomplish. These broad goals may then be discussed at length and broken down into more specific and practical objectives. Procedures for team communication; where, when, and how often

©ISTOCK

Writing @Work

Providing regular progress reports is part of the team process. As an administrative professional, you may be asked to prepare **status reports** to be sent to administrators or supervisors. A status report is often prepared as e-mail or a memo. It generally includes a brief summary of the team's progress since the last report was made and the team's objectives for the period until the next report is due. Status reports may also include

- ↗ The overall deadline for completing the work.

- ↗ Any upcoming interim deadlines.

- ↗ A general statement about whether the project is on schedule.

- ↗ Questions for which the team does not need an immediate answer.

- ↗ Problems that are not urgent or confidential that the administrator or supervisor should be made aware of.

- ↗ Other brief information that may be useful to the recipient.

the team will meet; and the roles of individual members will probably also be discussed in the first, or the first few, team meetings. Initial work assignments might also be made.

Team Roles

The team leader may assign formal roles or may ask for volunteers to fill them. Some examples of formal roles are vice chairperson and record keeper. As the team proceeds in its work, members will also gradually assume **informal roles**. Informal roles are not articulated or assigned. They are roles that team members recognize as needing to be filled and accordingly take on, often because they are skilled in that area. For example, you may be particularly good at settling conflicts. When disagreements arise between teammates, you may step in and use your skills to help resolve them. Figure 5-1 gives other examples of informal roles.

As an administrative professional, you should take on informal roles when you see something that needs to be done on your team, especially if it is something you do well. Besides showing that you are a committed and engaged member of the team, this is a chance for others to see your potential as a leader and for you to assume some responsibility that will prepare you for future leadership opportunities.

Team Norms

Over time, a team will begin to establish **team norms**, which are habits or unwritten rules of operation for the team. These rules either may not be stated at all or may be discussed and established within the team but just not formally written down. It is important for the dynamics of the team that team norms be followed. Here are some examples of team norms:

- A team doesn't talk about the details of the project outside team meetings. This might be a norm when the project topic is somewhat controversial.

Figure 5-1 Informal Team Roles

Role	Description
Clarifier	Interprets ideas, discussions, and issues by asking questions, giving examples, and restating ("So what you are saying is…")
Facilitator	Quite often, but not always, also serves as the team's leader. The facilitator keeps meetings on topic and helps the team reach agreements and understand issues.
Initiator	Offers ideas and suggestions to get the team started and to move it along
Summarizer	Pulls together related ideas and draws conclusions for the team
Supporter	Praises the efforts of other team members and helps build and sustain morale

- If a team member isn't going to be at a meeting, that person e-mails his or her contribution to the leader before the meeting.

- A team may elect to defer certain questions to a particular team member because of that person's expertise (such as budgeting questions referred to the team member from the business office).

- Team members agree to let everyone speak, without interruption or criticism, on each new issue presented or discussed.

- The team may spend the first ten minutes or so of a meeting socializing. Members can arrive during this time without being considered late.

Stages of Team Development

In 1965 Bruce Tuckman, a respected educational psychologist, identified a model for team development that is still widely accepted today. Initially it consisted of four stages; later he added a fifth stage. Tuckman believed that teams go through the following stages as they operate and develop.[2] You may recognize these stages from teams you are on now or have belonged to in the past.

1. **Forming** At this stage, all the members are seeking to get to know the team and are avoiding conflict.

---

2 Teaching Effectiveness Program, "Basic Group Theory: Tuckman's Five Stages of Group Development." University of Oregon, http://www.uoregon.edu/-tep/resources/crmodel/strategies/basic_group_theory.html (accessed April 10, 2010).

2. **Storming** As important issues are discussed, people begin to have conflicts and let their opinions be known.

3. **Norming** The conflicts are over. Everyone knows each other better and can listen and appreciate what each member has to offer the team. Now real progress can be made in solving the problem at hand.

4. **Performing** Everyone trusts one another enough to work independently. Roles are flexible, and the team changes easily according to need. This is the most productive stage in the team's development. Not every team reaches this stage.

5. **Adjourning** The work is done. The team disbands with a feeling of loss because of the positive group relationships they have had but also with a sense of satisfaction.

Developing Ideas

Brainstorming encourages teams to come up with innovative ideas. In a brainstorming session, team members build on what others say, and any and all ideas are encouraged. The main rule is that no idea is ever criticized or evaluated during the brainstorming session. Instead, the team evaluates ideas after the session is over. This environment helps promote the involvement of all team members and gets people to think outside established patterns.

Starbursting is a form of brainstorming that consists of asking questions instead of generating answers. The words *who, what, when, where,* and *why* are written each on the tip of a star. Then participants pose questions (no answers, just questions) about the topic (the product, problem, or whatever the team's purpose is) starting with those words. This technique helps participants understand all the different aspects of a problem and see potential solutions.[3]

[3] Mind Tools, "Starbursting," http://www.mindtools.com/pages/article/newCT_91.htm (accessed April 10, 2010).

Contributing to the Team

Being an effective team member requires certain qualities and skills that can be developed and improved over time with practice. Supporting a team in your role as an administrative professional requires many of the same skills and qualities as being a good team member. You will be expected to act with discretion and keep the confidences of team members. The support a team receives is essential to its **cohesion** (the ability to "stick together" and operate as one), efficiency, discipline, and ability to achieve its goals.

Reliability and Commitment

For a team to be successful, its members must be reliable in carrying out their responsibilities, and they need to be committed to the team and its goals. Commitment is demonstrated in both a team member's attitude and in that person's actions. You can show your fellow team members that you are reliable and committed in ways like these:

- Getting to meetings on time
- Being prepared
- Doing the work the team assigns you
- Taking part wholeheartedly in the team's activities
- Meeting deadlines

Actions like these earn the trust of other team members, which is another important element of a team's success. Mistrust results when members have the real or mistaken perception that someone isn't interested or isn't doing his or her fair share of the work. You may believe you are doing your work well, but if you are always late, make a lot of personal phone calls at work, and have missed several team meetings, your teammates may doubt your commitment to the team and may begin to write you off as unreliable. Team leaders may also overlook you when assigning important tasks.

Doing your part to earn the trust of your fellow team members also involves investing in relationships with them. People who know each other well work better as a team.

Technology @ Work

When brainstorming as a team, try using *mind maps*. Mind maps let you visually represent a problem, help clarify points, and allow you to see the problem differently. You can create a mind map in a word processing program using shapes and lines, or you can access free online mapping tools (examples of sites are provided on the website for this text). Before starting your mind map, develop a list of words to help your team get started brainstorming.

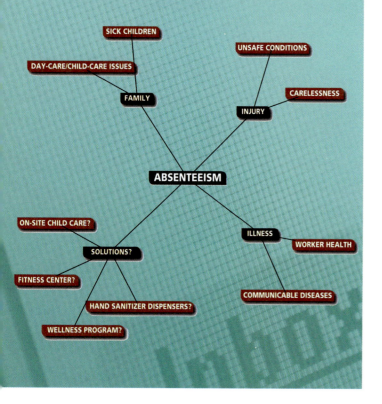

Listening and Speaking Skills

Because teams work and act so closely together, you need good communication skills to be an effective team member. They include the ability to listen attentively to what other team members have to say and to express your ideas and opinions clearly and assertively.

Listen carefully when other people on your team are speaking. Focus your attention on the speaker. You may think that you know what the speaker's point is going to be, but you may not be right. Continue listening so that you do not miss something important. Take notes if you need to. Wait until the speaker has finished before deciding what you are going to say. Ask questions if there is something you don't understand. Chapter 7 discusses skills for effective listening.

As a member of a team, you will be expected to share your opinions and ideas. It's a good idea to think and plan a little before contributing so that you can express yourself directly and clearly. Writing a few brief notes to organize your thoughts may be helpful.

Look at the person to whom you're speaking. If you're addressing the team, glance from one person to another. Be positive and straightforward. Say what you think, but in a way that shows respect for your teammates' thoughts and points of view. Be proactive: try to be ready to suggest a solution when you have a question or concern.

If you are reluctant to speak during team meetings, remember that you were chosen for the team because someone believed that your contributions would be valuable. Stay focused on the goal of the team and how you can contribute to that goal. Examine what makes you reluctant. Are you adequately prepared for meetings? Make it a habit to review the minutes from the last meeting and the agenda for the upcoming one. Do you find it difficult to speak in front of others? Mentally rehearse what you are going to say and use your notes to help you stay focused. The more you contribute, the easier it will become.

Other Skills

Being an effective team member requires several other skills and qualities discussed in other chapters of *The Administrative Professional*. They include the following:

- Written communication skills
- Interpersonal relations

Communicating @Work

Do's and don'ts of being in a team meeting:

- ↗ **Do** listen well to everyone.
- ↗ **Do** try to understand everyone's point of view.
- ↗ **Don't** interrupt anyone.
- ↗ **Don't** dominate the discussion.
- ↗ **Don't** talk off-topic.
- ↗ **Don't** demonstrate a negative attitude.
- ↗ **Don't** text, check e-mail, or surf the Internet on your cell phone or computer.

- ■ The ability to handle criticism with poise
- ■ Problem-solving and decision-making skills
- ■ Conflict resolution skills
- ■ Leadership skills

Being the Leader

Besides serving as a member of a team and supporting a team in your capacity as an administrative professional, you may sometimes have the opportunity to lead a team. For example, you may be asked to lead a grievance committee within your organization or to lead the silent auction team for the company fundraiser for college scholarships. It is important for you to accept these opportunities for leadership. They will enable you to develop and improve your skills at leading and managing people and organizing and managing time and projects. Leadership in some form is a natural progression in any career.

If you are able to select the members of your team, choose members with the knowledge, skills, and backgrounds needed to help the team meet its goal. If you know the people from whom you're

selecting your team, consider their strengths and weaknesses and what they might contribute. Chapter 8 provides additional suggestions on selecting members of a team. If you can choose the size of your team, five to seven members is a good range for effective problem solving and decision making.

Start out by setting ground rules and establishing expectations. By creating a good foundation, you help to eliminate problems in the future, begin to establish a rapport with your team members, and create a precedent for communication and collaboration.

Make sure the purpose and goals of the team are clearly defined and clearly communicated to all members. This sets the focus for the team and helps prevent confusion about what the team is doing. Some leaders start each meeting with the team goal, have it placed at the top of all meeting agendas, or even have it posted on the conference room wall. These actions help members stay focused on the goal.

Expected Team Behaviors

To help establish an open, collaborative climate on your team, try setting ground rules such as these:

- ↗ Only one person talks at a time.
- ↗ Be on time for meetings.
- ↗ *Listen* to the person talking.
- ↗ No side discussions.
- ↗ Deal with issues, not personalities.
- ↗ Keep your commitments.

Source: James P. Lewis, *Team-Based Project Management* (New York: Amacom, 1998), 82.

As the team leader, you will have certain administrative tasks. They will include making work assignments, tracking and reporting on the team's progress, and keeping the team on schedule. You will also be responsible for team meetings. The leader's role in planning, organizing, and conducting meetings is discussed in Chapter 10.

Model openness so that you can encourage an open, cooperative, and collaborative climate. Encourage team members to ask questions. Show that you are receptive to others' ideas and will not become defensive when your ideas are criticized.

Another important task of leaders is to motivate their team members. Establishing a rapport and building on that relationship can help accomplish this. A positive rapport and good relationships translate into trust, and trust is an important element when inspiring everyone on your team to participate.

In her book *Management Basics*, Sandra Gurvis argues that "genuine praise is a powerful motivator."[4] The key to this motivational concept is the word *genuine*. In contrast, flattery, as defined by clergyman and reformer Henry Ward Beecher, "is praise insincerely given for an interested purpose."[5] Genuine praise is something you might say about someone even when

4 Sandra Gurvis, *Management Basics: A Practical Guide for Managers*, 2nd ed. (Avon, Mass.: Adams Business, 2008), 110.

5 Henry Ward Beecher, *Eyes and Ears* (Boston: Ticknor and Fields, 1862), 409.

©ISTOCK

Dear Savvy Admin

Dear Savvy Admin:

I'm in charge of my department's United Way campaign, and one of my coworkers won't contribute. We are at 99 percent, and I'm afraid I'll be blamed for not getting 100 percent. What do I do?

Anxious Chairman

Dear Anxious Chairman:

Of course, you cannot force someone to contribute to a charity. You can, however, politely try to find out the person's objections and seek to satisfy them. For example, does this person prefer to support an agency that isn't listed? If so, see if United Way does provide funding for the agency or suggest another agency with similar functions. If all efforts fail, you can report attempting to satisfy all non-contributors and know you've done your best. In most cases, people have legitimate reasons for not contributing, and their opinion should be respected. Be sure not to discuss anyone's charitable contribution or lack thereof with others.

Savvy Admin

that person isn't around to hear it. Be quick to notice your team members' positive contributions and offer genuine praise.

Leaders need to see each member of the team as an individual and to get to know each member's skills and strengths. One way to do this is to ask the right questions and listen effectively. If you ask good questions, you will find out what team members are enthusiastic about and what they believe they excel in or can do well.

Effective Teams and Team Challenges

Good leadership has a lot to do with the success of a team. Organizational support—from the supervisor or manager to whom the team reports, for example—is also important. As a team leader or team member, knowing the characteristics of successful teams and being aware of common challenges that teams encounter will help you shape your team into an effective one.

Characteristics of Effective Teams

Certain characteristics distinguish well-functioning teams from unsuccessful ones. The following list is used by managers to assess the competence of teams.

An effective team has:

- Clear and realistic goals.
- A proper mix of skills.

- A proper level of education and skills among team members.
- Adequate tools to do the job.
- Discipline (such as a communication plan and regular meetings).
- Cohesion and the capacity to reach consensus readily.
- Effective leadership.
- A structure appropriate to the work that needs to be done.
- The ability to integrate diversity.
- The ability to achieve the desired results.
- The ability to work with customers effectively.[6]

Effective teams have several other characteristics as well. Individuals focus on team goals rather than personal goals. Each member takes responsibility for the team's success or failure in reaching its goals. Members respect and trust one another, and they show it. Finally, people on effective teams take ownership of the team's performance and efficiency.

Team Challenges

Teams often encounter challenges as they proceed in their work. The team leader is usually the person most responsible for meeting these challenges. If you are a team member, however, you can also play a part in helping to resolve problems and getting the team back on track.

Conflict It is not at all unusual for conflict to occur on a team. Teams are often intentionally designed to include a diversity of members and viewpoints. While in some instances, conflict isn't productive, at other times it can help identify problems or issues the team has not considered and can help the team grow to new levels.

6 J. Davidson Frame, *Project Management Competence* (San Francisco: Jossey-Bass, 1999), 158.

People @ Work

PROJECT MANAGER

Project managers oversee and manage all the details associated with completing a project. They carry out the project plans by identifying the resources that are needed (including people) as well as managing the day-to-day operations of the project. Project managers have financial duties that include projecting and tracking team hours and expenses, and they perform other duties related to management of the project budget. It is the project manager's responsibility to manage the team in such a way that the project is finished on time, all project goals are met, and project documents are complete. The project manager also reviews any deliverables prepared by the team. The project manager has the technical understanding of the project necessary to be a good leader and manager.

Project managers have several additional tasks. They facilitate team meetings and discussions, communicate with clients, continually seek opportunities to increase customer satisfaction, and serve as mentors and leaders to the project team. Like team leaders, project managers may moderate team conflict, challenge others on the team to take leadership roles, and inspire and motivate teammates to work together and to their fullest potential.

As an administrative assistant, you may work with a project manager to help the project team complete its goals. This will require having a broad understanding of the team's overall goal and working to support the team in achieving it through tasks such as obtaining needed resources, communicating with team members, arranging meetings and reserving facilities, and preparing agendas, reports, and budgets.

When conflict occurs on your team, take some time to explore the perspectives of team members and to discover the underlying causes. Taking a step back and looking at the conflict objectively from your perspective and the perspectives of others will help in resolving the conflict and will build better team relationships and dynamics. Skills and guidelines for resolving conflict are presented in Chapter 10.

If you find that you are in the wrong, make a sincere apology and move on. Not holding a grudge is important for staying focused on the task at hand and not being distracted by petty disagreements.

Conflict can have positive results for a team.

Groupthink   While working well together and agreeing with one another can make for a comfortable team relationship, problems can occur when conformity becomes more important than exploring differing viewpoints and contrary ideas. You may have been part of teams in which you felt pressured to agree with what other members were saying. You may have had doubts or different ideas that you were reluctant to express or that were set aside by the team as not important. A situation like this is known as **groupthink**. First described by psychologist Irving Janis, groupthink has been identified as a factor in some disastrously poor decisions.

Groupthink can be addressed in several ways. For instance, the leader can bring new members onto the team to shake up the structure, or the team can be broken temporarily into smaller groups.

Other Challenges   Two other common challenges for teams are the reluctance of some members to contribute to team discussions and the tendency of some members to dominate them. Chapter 10 provides specific suggestions on how leaders can encourage contributions and manage discussions so that everyone is heard.

Key Terms

cohesion

cross-functional team

groupthink

informal roles

project team

status report

team

team norms

virtual team

Summary

■ As an administrative professional, you will be asked to work on formal and informal teams throughout your career. Teams have benefits for companies and organizations and for you as a team member or leader.

■ Three common types of teams that you may encounter at work are project teams, cross-functional teams, and virtual teams.

■ Understanding the general process by which teams operate will prepare you to be an effective team member and leader.

■ As a team member, you should be reliable and committed, listen attentively to what your teammates have to say, and be positive and straightforward in expressing your opinions and ideas.

■ Team leaders have many responsibilities. Conscientiously fulfilling them will have a lot to do with the success of your team.

■ Many teams face challenges as they proceed in their work. Some common challenges include conflict, groupthink, the reluctance of some members to contribute to team discussions, and the tendency of some members to dominate them.

Bookmark It. *For convenient access to activities, links, and valuable career resources for administrative professionals, visit the companion website for this text:*

www.cengage.com/officetech/fultoncalkins

Planning Notes

Learning Objectives

1. Describe benefits of teams and identify common types of workplace teams.

2. Describe the general process by which teams operate.

3. Describe qualities and skills for being an effective team member, supporter, or leader.

4. List qualities of effective teams and identify team challenges.

Critical Thinking; Activities 1, 2, 4, 5, 6, 7, 9; Above & Beyond

Activities 10, 11, 12

Activities 3, 8

Discussion Questions

1. Name and describe the types of teams discussed in this chapter.

2. What are team norms? Give three examples of norms from teams you have belonged to or have observed.

3. Briefly describe a time when you were on a team. What made it a positive or negative experience?

4. What are some qualities of an effective team member?

5. Why is visually representing a problem helpful for a team?

6. What are some qualities of an effective team?

7. What are three common challenges that teams often face? Briefly describe each challenge.

Critical Thinking

Meeting virtually   You are an administrative assistant for an insurance company. Your supervisor, Mr. Hinder, wants you to learn the new office budgeting system and the new procedures for basic insurance claim underwriting. You know that several other administrative assistants from offices in four cities and two states must also learn the new procedures. It makes sense to you to do this as a team. You also wonder if these meetings could take place virtually. You know Mr. Hinder doesn't like to spend money unnecessarily, and you don't relish the prospect of several months of weekend or overnight travel. Mr. Hinder is accustomed to traditional face-to-face meetings, and he doesn't know much about computers.

Form a team with three or four classmates. Make a written plan to convince Mr. Hinder of the benefits of doing your training as a team and of making that team a virtual team. (Learning Objective 1)

Build Workplace Skills

1. **Team project**   Form a team with three or four classmates to redesign your school's website. As a team, you will need to analyze the site and determine what needs to be changed and how the site could be more user-friendly. You will need to consider the needs of different users—prospective and current students, parents, faculty, and staff.

   Have an initial team meeting. Using *Microsoft Word*, prepare a document in which you identify the purpose of the team, the specific goals to be accomplished, team members' responsibilities, and a time frame. (Learning Objective 2)

2. **Team roles**   Review the description of informal roles in this chapter. For the team you joined in activity 1, which informal role(s) do you think you are most qualified to assume? Why? If you were put on a team today, what informal role would you naturally assume? Why? What is another informal role that could be added to the list? (Learning Objectives 2, 3)

3. **Team leader**   Your supervisor has asked you to lead a team to plan the annual company outing to an amusement park three months from now. The outing will include a company-sponsored cookout and picnic for employees, with games and prizes for the winners. Make a plan for how you will accomplish this goal. From which departments of the company will you draw your team members? What skills and experience should they have, and how many members should there be? Include a list of tasks that your team will need to complete. (Learning Objective 3)

Communicate Clearly

4. **Keeping the team informed**   In your team from activity 1, you are the member assigned to consider the needs of prospective students in the website redesign. Since you will be out of town for the next meeting, write an e-mail to the rest of the team explaining what you believe are the most important website changes that need to be made for your assigned group of website visitors. (Learning Objective 3)

5. **Website qualities**   Make a list of qualities you think are necessary for a good website. The list can be drawn from your own experience, research, or both. Meet with your teammates and present your list. Together, develop a common list of the most important qualities for your school's website. (Learning Objective 2)

6. **Status report**   Open the *Word* file CH05 Status Report from the data files. Edit the status report to correct errors in keyboarding, grammar, punctuation, spelling, number usage, and word usage. (Learning Objective 3)

Develop Relationships

7. **Team assessment**   Considering the qualities of effective teams presented in this chapter, make a checklist to determine if your team (from activity 1) is operating well. Evaluate your team based on this checklist. (Learning Objective 4)

8. **Unprepared team member**   Someone on your team (from activity 1) isn't doing her work. This person doesn't contribute much in discussions, and it appears that she isn't doing anything outside of team meetings to contribute to the work of the team. What should you do if you are the team leader? What should you do if you are a team member? (Learning Objectives 3, 4)

9. **Icebreaker**   Icebreakers are activities intended to create a comfortable atmosphere in a group and to help people get to know each other. Research icebreakers on the Internet. Some links are provided on the website for this text. Choose an icebreaker for the first public team meeting about redesigning the school website from activity 1. Participants will be from all around your campus and will include professors, staff, and other students.

Use Technology

10. **Concept mapping**   In your team from activity 1, create a map of the website your team is designing using a free online mapping tool. Links to some of these tools are provided on the website for this text. (Learning Objective 2)

11. **Survey says**... Design a short survey of student opinions about the school website from activity 1. Ask, for example, if students are satisfied with the ease of navigating the site or if there are features they think should be added. Survey 10–20 students. Set up an *Excel* spreadsheet and design several charts to show the results of your survey. (Learning Objective 2)

12. **Website creation** Use *Word*, web design software, or a free website design site to create one or more pages for the website you mapped in activity 10. Post your pages or completed site for the class to review. (Learning Objective 2)

Above & Beyond

Self-directed work teams You are one of three administrative professionals employed by the county court of appeals, each of you working for two of the judges. The volume of cases that the court hears has been steadily increasing over the past year, and producing decisions and correspondence in a timely way has become a problem.

The court administrator is thinking that having the three of you work together as a team and determine your own workload, instead of working for individual judges, might be the solution to this problem. He has asked you to do some research on self-directed work teams. Write a brief report for your supervisor in which you explain what a self-directed work team is, apply the concept to the situation at the court, and make a recommendation for or against this approach. Be sure to include reasons for your recommendation. (Learning Objective 1)

Administrative Assistant

Insurance agency seeks an administrative assistant to provide customer service support for established and prospective clients. Candidate must:

- Provide excellent customer service to all internal and external clients
- Possess strong organizational skills and excellent communication skills
- Be capable of working effectively with people in difficult situations
- Maintain a database, process forms, and prepare correspondence
- Handle incoming phone calls and e-mails
- Be proficient using *Microsoft Office*

Do I qualify?

©MARK WRAGG, ISTOCK

CHAPTER 6

Developing Customer Focus

Customer Focus

A **customer** is someone who buys or uses the products or services of a company or organization. Customers may also be called *clients* or *buyers*. **Customer service** can be demonstrated in a number of ways, and it is often defined as the ability of an organization to consistently give customers what they want and need. Many successful businesses and organizations are committed to providing high-quality customer service to all their customers. This attitude and commitment is called **customer focus**. Organizations with a customer focus know the importance of providing excellent customer service to attract and maintain customers. Customer service is not simply a job or a department; it is a way of thinking within an organization.

In your career as an administrative professional, you may work for a variety of organizations including businesses, nonprofit organizations,

Learning Objectives

1. Define customer focus and explain the differences between external and internal customers.

2. Describe strategies for developing customer focus.

3. Develop skills for providing effective customer service.

4. Describe how to handle difficult customer service situations.

IMAGE COPYRIGHT YURI ARCURS 2010. USED UNDER LICENSE FROM SHUTTERSTOCK.COM

Having a customer focus should be a goal for all employees.

and government entities. Although different types of organizations may have different goals, most organizations cannot achieve their goals without a focus on effective service to their external and internal customers.

External and Internal Customers

Everyone within an organization has a role to play in developing an environment that is focused on the customer. Although many people are aware of the importance of providing service to external customers, individuals sometimes forget the importance of internal customer service.

External Customers
The most recognized customers of a business or other organization are its external customers. **External customers** are the people or other organizations that buy or use the products and services provided by the organization. For example, a consumer who buys a new washing machine is an external customer of an appliance store. A student who visits a nonprofit public library is an external customer of the library.

Internal Customers
In addition to considering the needs of external customers, an organization must also recognize the importance of internal customers. **Internal customers** are departments or employees within an organization who use the products or services provided by others within the organization.

Employees in the printing services department of a company, for example, serve the needs of other employees. These employees are the internal customers of the workers in the printing services department. Without the services this department provides, others in the company would not be able to do their work. Even employees who have no direct contact with external customers, like those in printing services, must have a customer service focus for the entire organization to be effective.

Importance of Customer Focus

A major goal of business is to make a profit. An effective customer focus is vital to achieving this goal. External customers who are not satisfied with the service they receive are likely to take their business elsewhere in the future. When many customers take this action, lower sales may result in lower profits. However, customers who are pleased with the service they have received are more likely to buy from the company again. Increased sales and profits can be a major benefit of providing effective customer service. Excellent external customer service can lead to customer satisfaction, customer loyalty, and customer retention.

Effective internal customer service is essential for a business to provide good external customer service. The relationships among managers, employees, associates, and peers are all important when developing an internal customer focus. Developing strong relationships with those who depend on you to provide answers or services is essential to creating an environment that puts customers first. By developing positive relationships with internal customers, you are showing that you value their importance to the organization. Excellent internal customer service can lead to employee satisfaction, employee loyalty, and employee retention as well as a higher level of external customer service.

Customer Focus Strategies

To be successful as an administrative professional, you must understand the importance of customer focus in all your relationships. You should practice the same high standards of service with both internal and external customers. **Strategies** (plans of action for achieving goals) for developing a customer focus are discussed in this section.

Show Respect for Customers

You may have heard the statement "The customer is always right." Although the intent of the statement is to show the importance of customers, the statement should not be taken literally. Customers are people, and people are not always right. If a customer comes to you with a concern, you should give it serious attention.

Consider this simple but realistic situation: Assume you have recently taken a test. When you get your test back, you have received no credit for a question you think you answered correctly. You talk with your instructor. She explains that your answer is not correct and refers you to a source for the correct answer. In this situation, you are the customer—you receive the services of your school and instructor. If the instructor had agreed that you were right when you were not, you would have gone away with incorrect information.

Even when the customer is not right, the customer deserves to be shown respect and to have his or her complaint or question heard. Show the customer that you are sincere and serious about providing assistance. In the example above, the instructor listened to your question. She then referred you to a source where you could get the correct answer, which helps you learn. Perhaps the best principle to follow is that the customer should always be treated fairly and with respect. Customers should be given an explanation if there is a question about a product or service.

Seek Customer Input

An effective customer focus strategy is seeking input from customers. Take the time to ask questions. Give customers the opportunity to

Nonprofit Organizations and Customer Service

Nonprofit organizations and government entities seek to provide products or services to groups of people. Even though these organizations may not be trying to make a profit, effective customer service is important for achieving their goals.

Consider public schools as an example. The goal of an elementary school may be to provide quality instruction in a safe, friendly environment that is conducive to learning. School staff members must consider the students' needs and wants (provide effective customer service) if they are to accomplish their goal.

© 2010 MONASHEE FRANTZ/JUPITERIMAGES CORPORATION

express their opinions (both positive and negative) about the quality of products and services the business provides. After asking questions, take the time to listen to the information you receive.

Problems can provide learning opportunities for you or your organization. Use problem situations to obtain information from customers. A customer concern or complaint is really just a request for action. If you listen to the customer, he or she will often have ideas about how to solve the problem.

Customers may also give you ideas about how a problem can be avoided in the future. Asking for a customer's feedback gives her or him an opportunity to participate in the process of improving a situation. Sometimes a customer will recognize issues that you may not see. Allowing the customer to participate in solving a problem is a positive step toward reestablishing goodwill.

Go the Extra Mile

Have you ever been disappointed in a product or service that you purchased? When you brought your concerns to the attention of a customer service representative, did he or she listen intently to your concern? Were you offered a solution to your problem and given something extra for your trouble? Perhaps you purchased a sweater from an online store, and the company sent the sweater in the wrong color. When you called the customer service line, the representative explained how to return the incorrect merchandise and gave you a voucher for 20 percent off your next order.

If something similar has happened to you, how did you feel about the situation? Perhaps you recognized

that errors sometimes occur and were happy to give the company a second chance. Doing something special or extra that is not required of you as part of your job or obligations to the customer can help the company maintain a valued external customer or help you build a good relationship with an internal customer. Although keeping customers happy is important, never do anything that violates company ethics or standards to keep a customer happy. A good question to ask yourself is, Would I be comfortable explaining what I did to my supervisor the next day? Know the actions you can take to maintain customers, such as giving discounts on orders or reduced fees, by talking with your supervisor ahead of time.

Maintain Effective Relationships

Maintaining effective relationships strengthens your ability to provide excellent customer service. Have you ever been working with a colleague who has exhausted his knowledge of a problem but then says, "I know someone here who has some experience with this. Let me see if she can help us." It is likely that these individuals have worked together in the past, providing each other with support and assistance.

When you are helpful and provide assistance to your internal customers, they are likely to return the favor by providing you with excellent service as well. These two-way relationships continue to

workplace wisdom

When someone you have just met immediately calls you by name, how do you feel? Do you feel as if the person is interested in you and your concerns? Most people would answer "yes." When someone takes the time to learn your name and then use it, you tend to think that the individual and the company care about you.

Quickly learn the names of coworkers when you start a new job. Welcome new workers who join your organization by remembering their names. Greet coworkers in a friendly manner.

Jot down the names of customers you talk with by phone. Use the customer's name frequently in the conversation.

grow and eventually develop into solid working relationships built on customer focus practices.

Take Responsibility

Everyone occasionally makes an error or mistake. However, the mature individual willingly takes responsibility for his or her mistakes and learns from them. When you make a mistake, do you admit it or try to hide the fact that you have made a mistake? If you answered honestly, you probably had to say that there have been times when you did not admit you made a mistake.

Admitting you made a mistake is difficult for anyone. However, refusing to admit to being wrong can damage your reputation and label you as dishonest. When you or your company makes a mistake, the key is to apologize quickly for the error and then solve the problem. When a mistake is made, take the time to determine what went wrong and how you can prevent the same mistake in the future. If you skip this step, it's possible you will repeat the mistake in the future.

You can also learn from the positive situations. Take time at the end of the day to think though what went right. Note procedures or strategies that worked well for future use.

Explain the Situation

When dealing with customers, explain issues or points clearly and fully. Do not assume the customer already has all the information related to the issue or problem.

Have you ever been in a situation in which you spoke clearly, articulated well, and gave details and yet the individual to whom you were talking still did not understand you? For most people, the answer is "yes." Why did the person not understand your meaning? Perhaps the person is not using the same frame of reference that you are. Consider this story. You are talking with your friend and say, "My new car is a lemon." Your friend responds, "I didn't know that you bought a yellow car." You almost laugh out loud, because you are so surprised. However, you restrain yourself and explain that you have had one mechanical problem after another with the car. That is why you call it a lemon.

People @ Work

CUSTOMER SERVICE REPRESENTATIVE

Customer service representatives are responsible for providing outstanding customer service and technical support to both internal and external customers. These customer exchanges may take place through telephone, e-mail, web, letter, or fax interactions.

The job responsibilities for a customer service representative may include answering questions, taking payments, filling orders, or handling other customer concerns. Because computers are often used to track these events, customer service representatives need excellent computer skills.

Many companies employ customer service representatives who work with customers in person in a traditional office setting. Other organizations provide access to customer service representatives by telephone, e-mail, or Internet.

As an administrative professional, you may provide information on products or services to a customer service representative in your company. You may communicate with a customer service representative from another company when you order products or report problems with products or services which your company uses.

What you thought was a simple statement turned into a communication problem. However, at least the person let you know how the message was interpreted. Often, you do not know; thus, it is important to explain clearly what you mean. Then give the person a chance to let you know if she or he understands by asking, "Does this make sense to you?" With such a statement, you are giving the individual a chance to tell you whether or not you have been clear in your communication.

Follow Up on the Issue

Once a problem has been solved, it is imperative to follow up with the customer. Follow up is checking back to determine whether or not the solutions have been implemented. The most effective problem solving has little or no value if the solution was never put in place.

A customer remembers the end result. Customers who have had excellent service throughout the process do not remember that if their problem does not get resolved. If you need more time to implement a solution, a phone call to let the customer know that you have not forgotten the issue will go a long way toward maintaining customer satisfaction.

Keep a Positive Attitude

A positive customer service encounter starts and ends with a positive attitude. The attitude you display is often as important as the answers you give and the actions you take. Show your positive attitude by attempting to help customers even when you do not have all the answers. People will come to you for help and be more eager to help you with issues or problems if you have a positive attitude.

Customer Service Skills

Whether you are dealing with customers in a face-to-face situation or by telephone, e-mail, or websites, you can develop skills that will help you have

Serving Internal Customers

Administrative professionals should be committed to serving internal customers effectively. Follow these guidelines to show your commitment to internal customers:

↗ Come to work on time. Arriving to work on time demonstrates your commitment to the company and fellow employees.

↗ Be polite and courteous. Say *please* when asking for assistance and *thank you* when someone has helped you. Whether your interactions are face-to-face or by e-mail or telephone, politeness goes a long way toward maintaining a successful relationship.

↗ Answer questions or calls quickly. Get back to your colleagues with answers to their questions in a timely manner. Do not wait for them to contact you again.

↗ Be professional at all times. Offer to help someone if you see she or he needs assistance and you have time to provide it.

↗ Go the extra mile and exceed the expectations of others. When you go out of your way to help others, they will often do the same for you when you are in a similar situation.

successful interactions. Several skills you will need when working with customers are discussed in this section.

Problem-Solving Skills

Regardless of your effectiveness as an administrative professional, problems will arise. What is important, however, is how you choose to handle the problems that occur. Although there are some customers who are difficult to please, most of them are not interested in making your job more stressful. Most customers simply want you to provide information or help them solve a problem.

Satisfied customers may or may not tell anyone about you or your organization, but unhappy customers will likely share their frustrations and experiences with others. Keep your customer focus and take care of any issues that arise promptly and with a smile.

After determining that a problem exists, follow a systematic method to solve it. Steps for solving problems, which were introduced in Chapter 2, are discussed in more detail in this section.

Identify the Problem
Attempt to understand the problem. This is often the most difficult step in the process. When defining the problem, ask yourself: What problem am I trying to solve? What will be the outcome of this problem? Sometimes the true problem will be difficult to identify. You may need to complete part of the next step, collecting information, before you can correctly identify the problem.

Collect and Analyze Information
Collect and analyze information related to the problem. To do this, you must ask a series of questions related to the problem you have identified. The more information you can collect that is related to the problem, the more likely you can solve the problem in a timely manner.

Look for patterns, trends, or relationships in the data you have collected. Your goal is to develop a clear understanding of the problem and related issues before trying to determine a solution.

When solving a problem, talk with people who can provide information about the issues.

Determine Options
The next step in solving a problem is to generate options or possible solutions. Sometimes the problem will be unique, and it will be challenging to develop a solution. Other times, it will be a problem you have seen before; and you may rely on past solutions when determining your course of action.

If a problem has occurred frequently, your company may have collected information or developed specific policies related to the problem. This information can be helpful in finding a solution.

Evaluate and Implement
Effective problem solving requires that you evaluate each of the options you have defined as possible solutions. Sometimes the best alternative will be obvious, and other times it will be difficult to make that determination.

The positive and negative results of a particular solution should be considered from both the company's perspective and the customer's perspective. You should consider both when making your decision. Once your evaluation is complete, implement the best option.

Evaluate the Solution
After a solution has been implemented, it should be evaluated. Evaluation helps you decide whether you have made the right decision for the immediate situation. It also helps you improve your problem-solving skills for the future.

Communicating @ Work

Interpersonal space boundaries (the area of space separating you from others) can affect your communication with others. These boundaries can be based on both cultural and individual preferences.

In some cultures, people tend to have small interpersonal space zones. People get close together to talk, and little personal space is preferred. People in other cultures, however, place a different emphasis on personal space. These people may prefer to have more distance from others.

When you are working with customers, respect their personal space preferences. If you get too close, you will notice that the customer feels uncomfortable. He or she may back away from you. Honor the customer's personal space zone by standing a comfortable distance away.

Nonverbal Communication Skills

Nonverbal communication consists of messages you convey without words. These messages can be as important as the words you speak. Nonverbal communication can occur through eye contact, facial expressions, and other means. You can develop effective nonverbal communication skills to aid you in communicating with customers.

Eye contact is a powerful form of nonverbal communication. It lets customers know that you are interested and attentive to what they are saying. It may also convey compassion and caring. Avoiding eye contact may suggest a lack of concern or lack of honesty. When dealing with customers, you should make eye contact frequently. Customers may perceive that you are not interested in what they are saying if you do not periodically make eye contact with them.

Facial expressions, such as a warm smile, can be valuable in communicating with customers. A smile signals that you care about the customer and are eager to help. Typically, a smile shows the emotion of happiness. However, if the customer is extremely upset, a smile can signal that you are laughing at the individual, suggesting to the customer that you are not taking his or her issue seriously.

If a customer is angry or upset, maintain a facial expression that shows interest but will not be perceived as mocking. Facial expressions that show interest and attention will increase your credibility with customers and make them feel important.

Effective Listening Skills

The importance of listening effectively when dealing with customers cannot be overemphasized. Listening shows that you care about your customers and respect their questions and concerns. Listening says to the customer that you believe he or she is important.

Listening is more than hearing what the speaker is saying. Effective listening requires that you be focused on what the other person is saying and not on what is happening around you.

When listening to someone, allow the person to complete a thought before you begin to respond. Do not interrupt the speaker. Listen for pauses that may indicate the speaker is finished talking before you respond. Chapter 7 presents more information about listening skills.

Human Relations Skills

Human relations skills are abilities that allow one to interact with others effectively. These abilities are sometimes called *people skills*. Showing respect for others, having empathy for others, and showing support for the skills and ideas of others are demonstrations of human relations skills.

Customer service is more than saying the words the customer wants to hear. It involves both the words you say and the way you say them. When talking with internal or external customers, your tone of voice is very important. Your voice can convey concern, respect, and compassion. Most importantly, your words must sound sincere.

Empathy is understanding or concern for someone's feelings or position. It is the ability to imagine yourself in the other person's situation. Empathy does not involve agreeing or disagreeing; it involves attempting to understand the other's person's point of view.

Being able to show genuine empathy for a customer who is describing a problem will help you gain or keep the customer's trust. An empathy statement such as "I can imagine it is frustrating when equipment does not operate as expected" acknowledges how the customer is feeling without admitting or denying fault. Using empathy statements can help defuse a customer's feelings of anger or frustration.

E-mail Customer Service Skills

As an administrative professional, you will probably communicate with internal and external customers through e-mail. Handling e-mail effectively is an important part of developing a customer focus. Steps for writing effective e-mail messages are presented in Chapter 7.

Designate specific times during the day to check and answer your e-mail messages. Determine the scheduled times based on the volume of messages you receive. For example, if much of your job requires handling e-mail customers, you may need to check your e-mail every hour or every half hour. However, if a small part of your job requires handling e-mail questions, you may want to check your e-mail only three or four times a day. Keep in mind that the customer should be served in a timely, caring, and efficient manner.

Telephone Customer Service Skills

The telephone is an important workplace tool. As an administrative professional you must be effective in your telephone communications. Without appropriate telephone customer service skills, you may make customers angry or lose customers for your organization.

A telephone conversation is sometimes challenging because you cannot see the person with whom you are speaking. You must put a "smile" in your voice by using a friendly tone. Speak at an appropriate volume, pitch, and speed. Ask questions tactfully, and respond calmly even when the caller is loud or angry.

Follow these guidelines for effective telephone communications:

- Listen for facts
- Search for subtle meanings
- Be patient
- Repeat back to the customer what you believe the customer said
- Act to handle the problem or issue

Always assist the customer to the best of your ability. Ask questions about anything that is not

Writing @ Work

Using positive words will create a positive environment when dealing with customers. Evaluate the words you use in your written interactions with customers. Examples of words to use and words to avoid are shown below.

Words to Use	Words to Avoid
Can	Can't
Please	Never
Yes	You have to
Do	Not my job
Will	Won't
Thank you	Sorry
Appreciate	I don't know

clear to you. Let the customer know what will happen next, especially if you cannot solve the problem or answer the questions right away.

Conclude every telephone call in a positive manner. At the end of every conversation, thank the caller and ask if there is anything else you can do to help. Effective telephone communication skills are discussed in Chapter 9.

Web Customer Service Skills

Millions of people in countries all over the world use the Internet. People use the web for activities such as booking travel reservations, banking, and shopping for products. Businesses see the web as an avenue for sales and customer service. Some companies offer customers the option of searching for answers to their questions on the company website. This option, called web self-service, may be in addition to or as an alternative to contacting customer service representatives by telephone. Typically this service allows customers to use the same tools and knowledge databases that customer service agents within the organization use to help customers find answers to their questions.

As an administrative professional, your work may not directly involve customer service via the web. However, the organization for which you work may offer web self-service or **live chat** (exchanging text messages in real time) as an option for customers.

©iStock

Dear Savvy Admin

Dear Savvy Admin:

One of my coworkers has a very sharp wit. Although this is fine in social settings, she sometimes comes across as very sarcastic when dealing with customers. Recently our unit has had several complaints from customers who felt they were not treated appropriately. We have been issued warnings as a group, but it really is one person who is causing most of the problems. What can we do?

Taking the Heat

Dear Taking the Heat:

A little bit of humor certainly has its place in the workplace, but not everyone thinks the same things are funny. If your company has specific guidelines about appropriate ways to treat a customer, you might suggest to your coworker that "we all need a refresher" due to the warnings your unit has received.

If no such guidelines exist, you might consider creating some and asking your coworkers, especially the one you feel is causing the most problems, for input in creating this document. This will require that each person evaluate how he or she interacts with customers. In the end, however, requesting a meeting with your supervisor to discuss what you are observing within your work group may be best solution to the problem.

Savvy Admin

Familiarize yourself with web self-service if your organization offers this option so you can be knowledgeable about it when talking with customers. You may also use the database to find answers to questions you have.

Handling Difficult Situations

As you work with organizations that value customer service, treat each customer with respect, and follow the suggestions that have been given in this chapter in regard to working with customers. However, there are times when you encounter individuals who behave inappropriately. You need to understand how to respond when difficult situations arise.

Handling Conflict

One of the best customer service techniques is avoiding problems. This can be accomplished by being proactive with customers. Learn to anticipate customers' needs and provide solutions to their concerns before they ask. Sometimes it is not possible to anticipate concerns or avoid problems. When that happens, conflict may occur.

Effective customer service involves learning how to handle conflict. When dealing with customer conflict, listen carefully to customers' problems or concerns. Work hard to make your customers happy, even if it means fixing something that you do not think is a major concern.

Accept the blame on behalf of your company or department, even if the problem or mistake is not your fault (and certainly if it is your fault). When possible, offer more than one solution from which the customer may choose to give the customer some feeling of being in control.

Handling Difficult Customers

Some people are going to be difficult no matter how helpful and professional you are. When a customer is angry, take a deep breath and tell yourself to stay calm and do your best. Use positive self-talk. Here are some statements you can make to yourself:

- I will not get angry.
- I have been successful in situations such as this one in the past, and I will be successful again.
- I care about people, and I know that most people are not difficult.

Although you can control your own behavior, you cannot control the actions of others. Sometimes a customer will get angry. When that happens, do not take it personally. Usually the customer is not angry at you, but rather at something that has happened. Try to defuse the anger as quickly as possible by listening to the customer's concern.

Acknowledge the situation and ask what you can do to solve the problem or make the situation better. Sometimes just asking the question will get the situation back under control. At other times, making an apology is the best approach. If you (or your company) has made a mistake, apologize for the error and then correct it, if possible. If correcting the error is not possible, perhaps you can offer some form of compensation to keep the customer's goodwill. Remember to stay within company guidelines in such a situation.

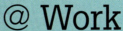

Technology @ Work

Some companies offer a live chat feature as part of their web–based customer service. Customers can exchange text messages with a staff member in real time. This option offers a personalized service that may be less expensive for the company than telephone support. Customers appreciate getting answers to their questions quickly.

Some companies make live chat available during the order process as well as after a sale. Allowing customers to ask questions while ordering may result in fewer returned products because customers are better informed when placing orders.

Dealing with Abusive Customers

Some customers go beyond simply being angry or frustrated and become abusive. Usually, you cannot help an abusive customer until she or he calms down. Do not let yourself become angry, as this behavior would merely escalate the situation.

Look for points of agreement with the customer and voice those points. This technique generally works well, and you can then begin to help solve the problem with the customer. If the customer continues to be abusive, you may have to ask the customer to call back later when he or she can discuss the issue calmly.

Many organizations have a policy concerning difficult or abusive telephone situations. Find out what the policy is and observe it. Some companies have a recorded announcement telling customers that the call may be recorded for customer service quality or training purposes. Customers may be less likely to make threats or inappropriate comments if they know the call might be recorded.

Key Terms

customer

customer focus

customer service

empathy

external customers

human relations skills

internal customers

live chat

strategy

Summary

- Providing excellent customer service is important for success in businesses and other organizations.

- An organization that has a customer focus demonstrates effective customer service in interactions with internal and external customers.

- Strategies that you can use to develop a customer focus include showing respect for customers, seeking customer input, going the extra mile, maintaining effective relationships, taking responsibility, explaining the situation, following up on issues, and keeping a positive attitude.

- You can develop skills that will help you have successful interactions with customers. These skills include problem-solving, nonverbal communication, effective listening, and human relations skills.

- E-mail, telephone, and web customer service skills are also important.

- Understanding how to respond to difficult or abusive customers will help you provide effective customer service even in difficult situations.

Bookmark It. *For convenient access to activities, links, and valuable career resources for administrative professionals, visit the companion website for this text:*

www.cengage.com/officetech/fultoncalkins

Discussion Questions

1. What is customer focus and why is it so important for the success of businesses and other organizations?

2. What is the difference between internal and external customers? Give an example of internal and external customers.

3. Describe three strategies you can use to develop a customer focus.

4. What are the steps you should take to solve a customer service problem?

5. Describe four skills that will help you serve customers effectively.

6. Give four examples of how an administrative professional can demonstrate commitment to serving internal customers.

7. Define empathy and explain why it is important for effective customer service.

8. How should you handle an abusive customer?

Critical Thinking

Unreasonable customer   Leslie Page works as an administrative assistant at the Palms dinner theater. She handles records for sales of season tickets. Today, Mr. Bronson and his wife came in with two guests for the matinee performance. When the Bronsons and their guests found two of their seats occupied, they went to Leslie for assistance.

Mr. Bronson indicated that he had purchased four season tickets. After checking on the computer, Leslie noticed that two of the tickets were returned in January and a credit was issued. When she tells Mr. Bronson this, he indicates that the tickets that were returned were for a show two months ago, not today's performance. Although Leslie wants to be helpful, there is not a lot she can do. Once the original tickets were released (and the credit issued) the tickets were resold. In addition, the table seating for today's matinee performance is sold out. All Leslie can do is offer the Bronsons and their guests four seats in the gallery at the back of the theater.

Mrs. Bronson is angry and insists on sitting in their original seats. She insists that Leslie remove the individuals from her seats. How should Leslie handle the situation? (Learning Objective 4)

Build Workplace Skills

1. **Excellent customer service**   Write a description of a situation where you received excellent customer service. Evaluate your experience according to the customer service skills described in the chapter. Give specific examples of why the experience was positive. Explain why you continue to do business with this company or organization. (Learning Objective 2)

2. **Poor customer service**   Write a description of a situation in which you received poor customer service. Indicate whether you were an internal customer

or an external customer. Give at least three suggestions for ways the situation could have been handled better. (Learning Objectives 1, 2)

3. **Internal customer service problem**   You work as an administrative assistant for three executives. Mr. Rogers wants you to complete a long report by the end of the day. Ms. Park needs a *PowerPoint* presentation, which requires research, by tomorrow morning. Ms. Gomez needs a spreadsheet analysis of sales figure completed by noon. Since you cannot complete all this work by the time requested, you have a big internal customer service problem. How will you solve this problem so that none of the executives are disappointed? How can you avoid a similar problem in the future? Open the *Word* file CH06 CS Problem. Use this document to record your notes as you follow the problem-solving steps you learned in this chapter. (Learning Objective 3)

Communicate Clearly

4. **Customer service message**   Open the *Word* file CH06 E-mail from the data files. Edit the message to correct errors in grammar, spelling, word usage, and punctuation. Revise the paragraph structure, remove any text that should not be part of the body of an e-mail, and reword sentences as needed to make the message more clear and concise. (Learning Objective 3)

5. **Customer service newsletter**   Create a newsletter that includes tips and strategies for providing effective customer service. The newsletter must be at least two pages. Review newsletters you have received or examples you find online to help you format the document. Create an appropriate masthead and include at least two graphics and one bulleted list. (Learning Objectives 2, 3)

6. **Customer service call**   Locate the sound file CH06 Customer Call from the data files. The file is a recording of a conversation in which a customer, Nina, calls Atkins Computers to talk with a customer service representative about a problem with a printer. Listen to the entire conversation. What did Roberto, the customer service representative, do correctly? What could he have done better? Give examples. What could the customer have done differently to make the experience more positive? (Learning Objectives 3, 4)

Develop Relationships

7. **Appropriate language**   Emily Connor was hired two weeks ago and works in the office next to yours. You can hear Emily working with customers on the phone. Although she is courteous, she often uses slang and inappropriate grammar. You have heard her greet clients by saying "Hey" or "What's up?" and she often fails to identify herself. You are Emily's coworker, not her supervisor; but you want to help her succeed. What advice can you give Emily to improve her customer service skills? (Learning Objectives 1, 2)

8. **Handling an angry customer**   Shawn Cornock purchased a new Star-1 model TL10G refrigerator from Steve Wu at Home Sweet Home Appliances. On Tuesday, the new refrigerator was delivered, and the old one was removed. The next morning, Shawn noticed that all his frozen foods were thawed because the freezer section of the refrigerator was not getting cold. Shawn called Steve, who said he would send somebody right over.

The repairperson determined that the refrigerator's compressor was not working. He told Shawn it would take at least two weeks to get another TL10G refrigerator delivered.

Shawn called Steve and demanded that a new refrigerator be delivered today. Steve called around and located another TL10G refrigerator in a company warehouse in a neighboring state. However, the soonest Steve can get this refrigerator delivered is Friday. Shawn is furious and threatening to take his business to another store. What strategies can you give Steve for dealing with this angry customer? (Learning Objective 4)

> *Use Technology*

9. **Customer focus survey**   You are an administrative assistant at E & C Kitchen Sales. Seven salespersons work for the organization. After discussing effective customer service skills with the staff, your supervisor, Mr. Mendoza, wants to determine whether the salespeople are putting these skills into practice. He has asked you to create a survey so customers can provide feedback on their experiences. The survey should include questions on the customer service skills and strategies discussed in the chapter including nonverbal communication, friendliness, positive attitude, effective listening, and empathy. (Learning Objectives 2, 3)

10. **Nonverbal communication presentation**   Your company plans to begin working with similar companies in Spain, Germany, and France. Over the next few months, all employees will work with employees from the partnering businesses. Since nonverbal communication is an important part of internal customer service, your supervisor has asked you to research the differences and similarities in nonverbal communication in those countries. Include information on handshakes, personal space, facial expressions, and two other types of nonverbal communication that you identify. Prepare a *PowerPoint* presentation that your supervisor can share in your monthly staff meeting. (Learning Objective 3)

> *Above and Beyond*

Customer focus interview   Interview an administrative professional who works in an organization that sells a product directly to customers. If possible, interview someone whose organization sells by telephone, e-mail, and/or the web. Discuss the types of customer service the company provides. Ask what advice this person would give to a new administrative assistant to help develop a customer focus. (Learning Objectives 1, 2)

Planning Notes

Part 3

Professional Profile

Cathy Brockelbank

Senior Client Associate
D'Meza & Suplee Wealth Management Group
Wells Fargo Advisors
Alpharetta, Georgia

Cathy Brockelbank is senior client associate for the D'Meza & Suplee Wealth Management Group of Wells Fargo Advisors. Cathy handles all operational functions for the group—based in Atlanta, Georgia—including opening new accounts, transferring funds, processing trade corrections, handling correspondence, managing office expenses and supplies, and scheduling appointments. She also sends birthday cards and flowers to clients on special occasions.

"Communication plays a key role in our business," says Cathy, "and the phone is our main source of communication." Cathy answers all incoming calls and directs each caller to the appropriate person. "We answer all calls personally whenever possible, rather than letting them go to voicemail." Another key medium is e-mail. "Clients forward questions and schedule appointments by e-mail. We make it a point to answer all incoming e-mails within 24 hours."

"We answer all calls personally whenever possible. . . . With the current economy, clients want to hear an upbeat voice on the line."

Good communication with clients requires sensitivity to the changing financial climate and to clients' individual needs. "For example," notes Cathy, "with the current economy, clients want to hear an upbeat voice on the line." Cathy always speaks on the phone with a cheerful, courteous, and confident tone. She advises that ending a phone call properly is as important as a friendly greeting. "Let the caller know that someone will be back in touch shortly and to enjoy their day."

When you know your colleagues well, excellent communication and productivity often go hand in hand. Cathy recalls, "I've worked with Jay D'Meza, our managing director and investment officer, for over twenty years." Once Cathy is assigned to a project, she knows what Jay expects from her and can rely on him to answer any questions. "I feel that the keys to our working relationship are respect and accountability. Jay has always made me feel like a big part of his business success, which encourages me to work harder."

Communication—
The Key to Success

Ready, Set, Plan

Use this space to plan your work in this section. Record the due dates for reading assignments and other activities for each chapter. If you are working with a team or partner, record the schedule for team meetings. Do you need a list of phone numbers or e-mail addresses? Don't forget your other commitments: work, other classes, and family.

Administrative Assistant

Small manufacturing company seeks candidate with good organization and communication skills to assist management team. Candidate must

- Demonstrate effective oral and written communication skills
- Work independently with minimal supervision
- Complete word processing tasks (correspondence, reports, memos, proposals, charts, agreements, etc.)
- Record, key, and distribute minutes with supervision
- Be able to conduct effective Internet searches

©MARK WRAGG, ISTOCK

Do I qualify?

CHAPTER

7

Learning Objectives

1. Describe the communication process and its elements.

2. Identify communication barriers and ways to overcome them.

3. Describe types of listening and ways to improve listening skills.

4. Describe factors related to effective verbal communication.

5. Prepare effective written messages.

Improving Communication Skills

The Communication Process

Communication occurs when a message is sent by one person and received and understood by another person. Communicating effectively is essential to successful business operations. Company personnel must communicate with coworkers, clients, and vendors to achieve the company's goals. Advertisements and product information on websites must be current, correct, and sensitive to the needs and attitudes of customers of different cultures, interests, and abilities. Customer requests and questions must be answered clearly and promptly to maintain goodwill.

As an administrative professional, you will communicate with coworkers and company managers. You will probably also communicate with clients or customers and the public. Improving your communication skills will help you create messages that are clear and effective. Good communication skills may also help you get and keep a job. Employers understand the importance of these skills. When discussing job candidates, "By far, the one skill mentioned most often by employers is the ability to listen, write, and speak effectively."[1]

The communication process involves a message, a sender, a channel, a receiver, and feedback.

- A message is a symbol or group of symbols that conveys meaning, such as a thought or idea. For example, a letter contains words that are written symbols. These words convey a message to the reader.

- The sender is the person who creates the message and transmits it via a channel. In the previous example, the sender is the person who writes the letter.

- A channel is a means by which a message is sent, such as a letter, speaking in person or by telephones, or electronically by e-mail.

- The receiver is the person who receives the message, such as the recipient of a letter or an e-mail message.

Gestures and other nonverbal behaviors can also send messages. When a person (the sender) says "Hello," smiles, and extends a hand toward you (the receiver), that person is sending a message that he or she is glad to meet you. Feedback is a return message sent by the receiver. When you smile and say "Pleased to meet you," you are giving feedback. Feedback helps the sender know whether the message was understood correctly, as illustrated in Figure 7-1.

Communication Barriers

For effective communication to take place, the message must be understood as the speaker or writer intends. If the listener or reader interprets the message differently, problems may occur. For example, suppose you receive an e-mail message from your manager on Thursday morning telling you that you need to finish a project by next Friday. To your manager, the term "next Friday" means

1 Randall S. Hansen and Katharine Hansen, "What Do Employers *Really* Want? Top Skills and Values Employers Seek from Job-Seekers." Quintessential Careers, http://www.quintcareers.com/job_skills_values.html (accessed March 11, 2009).

Figure 7-1 The Communication Process

the following day. However, you interpret the message as meaning that the project is due several days later on Friday of next week. Your manager will be disappointed when the project is not completed the next day, and you will be disappointed to learn that you did not understand the message as intended. You are both the victims of a communication barrier. A **communication barrier** is anything that interferes with successful communication. Communication barriers can be internal or external.

Internal Communication Barriers   In the exchange with your manager described above, an internal barrier prevented the message from being understood. In your previous experience, the term "next Friday" has meant Friday of the following week—not the next Friday to occur. Because of your previous experience, you interpreted the message to have a different meaning than the sender intended.

Mental or emotions distractions, biases, and l___ motivation are other examples of internal c___ nication barriers.

- When you are worried about somethi___ tionally distressed, you may have tr___ on a message. As your mind wan___ part of the message.

- If you have a negative bias toward the topic, it may be hard to accept positive comments. For example, if you had a bad experience with two printers of the same brand, you probably have a negative bias toward that brand. Claims of glowing performance for that printer will be difficult for you to believe.

- Lack of motivation means that you have no reason to be interested in or to try to understand a message. If you think, for example, that a new company policy being discussed will not apply to your department, you may not pay close attention to the discussion. You may miss part of the message or misunderstand a point of the message because you are not listening carefully.

External Communication Barriers   External communication barriers are things such as noise, poor lighting, heat or cold, or uncomfortable seating. Noise may make it difficult to hear or read and focus on a message. Poor lighting, a room that is too cold or warm, and an uncomfortable chair are examples of physical barriers that can distract a sender or receiver and hinder communication. Language can also be an external communication

barrier. When the sender and receiver do not speak the same language, it is difficult for communication to take place.

Overcoming Communication Barriers

Senders and receivers should make an effort to recognize and overcome communication barriers. External barriers are often easier to overcome than internal barriers. For example, you may be able to move to a quiet location to read a message if noise is a problem. You may be able to adjust lighting, seating, or room temperature to prevent these physical conditions from being a distraction.

Some internal barriers can be difficult to overcome. If you are ill, you may need to postpone taking part in the communication until a later time. If you have trouble focusing on a message because you are sleepy, you might take a break to walk about the room or open a window to get some fresh air. These actions may help you feel refreshed and ready to read or listen to the message.

When speaking or writing to someone, be aware of how well the person knows the language you are using. For example, suppose English is your first language and you are writing to someone whose first language is German. You should use standard English in your message. Avoid using acronyms, informal terms, or expressions that the reader might not understand.

Listening Skills

Listening is essential to effective communication. In the words of author Robert Louis Stevenson, "All speech, written or spoken, is a dead language, until it finds a willing and prepared listener."[2] **Listening** is hearing and trying to understand a message using the sounds you hear. Listening is the communication skill that many people use the most. Being an effective listener can help you be more productive and improve your relationships with others. A first step toward becoming an effective listener is understanding the type of listening that is appropriate for particular situations. Listening can be categorized as casual listening or active listening.

2 Robert Louis Stevenson, "On Listening & Writing," Quotations, the International Listening Association, http://www.listen.org (accessed March 11, 2009).

People @Work

TRAINING SPECIALIST

Training specialists direct training activities in response to company and employee requests. They may conduct orientation sessions and arrange on-the-job training. They ... training for using new equip-
... are.

... have ongoing training
... ployees improve their
... topics such as writing
... service, and work-
train... periodically.

... help from
... ts when
... ecialist
... who
... help
... ogram.

Casual Listening

Casual listening is hearing and trying to understand what is being said with the objective of relating to others. For example, when you chat during lunch with a colleague, you use casual listening to understand what is being said and to help you respond appropriately. You typically do not focus on analyzing what is said or trying to remember every detail of the conversation.

Active Listening

Active listening is more goal-oriented than casual listening. When listening actively, you have a definite purpose in mind. The four types of active listening are described below.

- **Informative listening** is used when you wish to hear, understand, and remember the information being presented. For example, when you listen to a manager or coworker give instructions for completing a task, you are using informative listening.

- **Evaluative listening** is used to hear, understand, and judge what is being said. You may evaluate whether the information is useful, accurate, or interesting. For example, suppose you listen to a salesperson describe a product. As you listen, you will evaluate the message to decide whether you accept or reject it.

- **Emphatic listening** is used to hear, understand, and offer feedback that shows you have understood the message. Understanding the message does not necessarily mean that you agree with the speaker. The feedback you offer indicates only that you understand the message. Customer service associates often used emphatic listening to let a caller know that his or her complaint is understood. Consider this response to a customer who called to complain about a printer: "I'm sorry you are having trouble getting the printer to work properly." This statement lets the caller know that the message has been understood. The associate can then ask questions and offer advice to try to solve the problem.

- **Reflective listening** is used to hear, understand, and offer feedback that helps the speaker think about her or his feelings or objectives. The feedback should not be judgmental; rather it should prompt the speaker to think or question further. Prompts, open-ended questions, and restatements of what the speaker has said are useful in giving feedback with reflective listening. Suppose a coworker says to you, "I am at a loss about how to tackle this project." A response that shows reflective listening might be, "So you're not sure where to begin. Tell me more. What's your understanding of the goals of the project?" This feedback reflects what the speaker has said and prompts the speaker to think further about the project and his or her objectives.

Listening Effectively

An effective listener prepares to listen by removing internal and external listening barriers. When someone approaches you at your desk or in a meeting, stop talking or doing tasks. Clear your mind of distracting thoughts and give the speaker your full attention. As the speaker begins talking, quickly determine the type of active listening that will be appropriate. Is the speaker giving you instructions? If so, informative listening is appropriate. Does the speaker seem worried or upset? Emphatic listening may help you communicate effectively in this situation.

Do not let biases or previous experiences keep you from listening with an open mind. Perhaps you have heard a speaker present ideas at several meetings and have found none of the ideas helpful.

Communicating @Work

Follow these tips for effective listening:

- ↗ Focus on the speaker and the message.

- ↗ Use the appropriate type of casual or active listening for the situation.

- ↗ Keep an open mind and do not prejudge the speaker or the message.

- ↗ Keep your emotions in check. Do not let an emotional response to a message distract you from listening.

- ↗ Wait until the speaker pauses to begin framing your response.

- ↗ At an appropriate time, ask questions to clarify the message you heard.

- ↗ Offer feedback to the speaker.

This meeting might be different. Do not miss important information because you prejudge a speaker or a topic. When receiving instructions from someone or listening to someone speak in a meeting, quickly note questions that you will ask later to help clarify points you do not understand.

When talking with someone, do not begin thinking about your response while the other person is still speaking. Doing so might cause you to miss part of the message. A nod or an encouraging smile can show the speaker that you are interested in his or her message. Restating important points of the message at an appropriate time can verify that you have understood the message.

Verbal Communication Skills

The way you speak—not just what you say—makes an impression on listeners. Always use proper grammar when speaking with coworkers, clients, and others in the workplace. Using improper grammar and slang expressions detracts from your professional image. Factors such as pitch, tone, volume, and rate of speech can affect your verbal communications. Using the proper degree of formality when talking with coworkers and clients is also important. These factors are discussed in this chapter. Verbal skills used in giving a presentation are discussed in Chapter 8.

Pitch

Pitch is an attribute of sound that can be described as high or low. Someone who is nervous or frightened may speak in a high-pitched voice as her or his throat tightens. Listeners may be less likely to believe your message if you speak in a high-pitched voice.

On the other hand, people who speak in a low-pitched voice project calmness and control. Listeners are more likely to have confidence in a speaker using a low-pitched voice. If you are nervous or tense as you prepare to speak at a meeting or with a client, make a conscious effort to relax your body. Drinking something warm will help relax your vocal cords so you can speak in a low-pitched voice.

Show Respect for Others

Using the proper degree of formality for different communication situations will make listeners more open to receiving your message. The degree of formality that is considered appropriate when speaking with coworkers, managers, and clients will vary from company to company. In some companies, coworkers (and managers in particular) are addressed by their titles and last names: "Good morning, Mr. Luongo." In other companies, coworkers and clients are addressed more informally by their first names.

Observe the custom followed at your company. However, do not be overly friendly or informal with coworkers or clients you do not know well even if you address them by their first names. Be especially sensitive to the degree of formality you use when talking with coworkers or clients from

ANDREW WAKEFORD/PHOTODISC/GETTY IMAGES

other cultures. In many parts of the United States, direct and concise communications are considered appropriate.

For example, you might say to a coworker, "Great. Call me when you have the final results." To a client or coworker from another culture, this message may seem abrupt or rude. A more appropriate message might be, "That's great news, Mr. Haddad. Will you please call me when you have the final results?"

Tone

Tone is an attribute of voice that conveys the attitude or emotional state of the speaker. The same words spoken in different tones can convey different meanings. For example, the words "that's great" spoken in a friendly and enthusiastic tone convey a positive message. The same words spoken in a sarcastic or frustrated tone convey quite a different meaning. Be aware of your tone of voice to be sure you are sending the message you want to send.

Pace and Volume

If you speak too quickly or softly, the listener may miss part of your message. If you speak too slowly, the listener may become frustrated and lose interest in your message. Listening to someone who is speaking too loudly can also be frustrating for a listener. Control your voice to speak at a medium pace and volume so that your message can be received and understood.

DIGITAL VISION/GETTY IMAGES

Do you think these coworkers are having a friendly chat?

Nonverbal Communication Skills

Nonverbal communication is sending a message without spoken or written words. Facial expressions, gestures, and body language are examples of nonverbal communication. Nonverbal symbols can affect or even alter a message. A job candidate in an interview who sits up straight, makes eye contact with the interviewer, and looks interested in the conversation reinforces the message that he or she is interested in the job and company. A candidate who slumps in the chair, does not make eye contact, and is not focused on the discussion sends the nonverbal message that he or she is not interested in the company or job. Even though the candidate may express interest, nonverbal cues contradict the spoken words. When nonverbal cues do not support a verbal message, the listener is more likely to accept the nonverbal message. Be aware of your facial expressions, gestures, and body language so that your nonverbal messages reinforce your verbal messages.

Nonverbal communication symbols have different meanings from culture to culture. For example, the "okay" sign made by placing the forefinger and thumb into a circle and raising the remaining fingers has a positive meaning in North American cultures. However, in some other cultures, this gesture is considered offensive. People in different cultures feel differently about the use of personal space. Standing one foot away when talking with someone is a comfortable distance for people in some cultures. In other cultures, this distance is too close and will make the listener feel uncomfortable, as if her or his space is being invaded. A listener in this situation may keep backing away from the speaker and have difficulty focusing on the message. Learn about the nonverbal cues of people from other cultures with whom you communicate so that you can send the appropriate nonverbal messages.

Written Communication Skills

Is written communication as important in the workplace today as it was ten years ago? The answer is a resounding *yes*. In fact, because e-mail is so widely used in today's offices, administrative professionals probably write more than in the past. Written communication in all of its forms remains extremely important. Ineffective written communication costs the organization greatly, often resulting in misunderstandings and thus increased time on tasks, loss of customers, and resultant loss of profits.

Writing is a process that involves planning, composing, editing, proofreading, and publishing messages. Each stage of the process is important in creating an effective message.

Planning

Planning is important for all types of written messages from a simple e-mail message to a long report. The first step in planning a message is identifying the objective of the message. The objective is what you want to achieve with the message. You may want to inform the reader, request information, establish a record of facts, persuade the reader to take or forego an action, or simply promote goodwill. Once you have identified the objective, list the main ideas you will include in the message. Identify supporting details to explain or reinforce the main ideas.

Adjust the Message for the Receiver   Your message will be more effective if you adjust the message for the reader. Consider the reader's needs, wants, and interests as they relate to the message. Then state your message in a way that addresses these needs or interests. To help you identify the reader's needs or wants, ask questions such as these: What are the ages, genders, backgrounds, and biases of the readers? What knowledge or experience related to the message topic do the readers have? Will the readers consider the message to be positive, neutral, or negative news?

Writing with the reader's needs and interests in mind is called the *you* approach. The first example shown here is not written with the you approach. The second example uses the you approach and will be

more appealing to the reader. When using the you approach for e-mail messages, memos, and letters, the first paragraph of the message typically begins with *you, your,* or the person's name.

EXAMPLE 1

We have decided to approve the loan application for a mortgage on the home at 234 Michigan Avenue.

EXAMPLE 2

Your loan application has been approved for a mortgage on your new home at 234 Michigan Avenue.

Select a Message Order   After considering the reader, you should select an order for the message that will help achieve your objectives. Messages can be organized in direct or indirect order.

With direct order, the main idea of the message is presented first and followed with supporting details if needed. Direct order is appropriate for positive or neutral messages that deliver good news or make a routine request. Direct order would be appropriate for an e-mail message to a coworker confirming that you can complete a task. Figure 7-2 below is an e-mail message written in direct order. The memo in Figure 7-6 on page 115 is also written in direct order.

Figure 7-2 **E-mail Message in Direct Order**

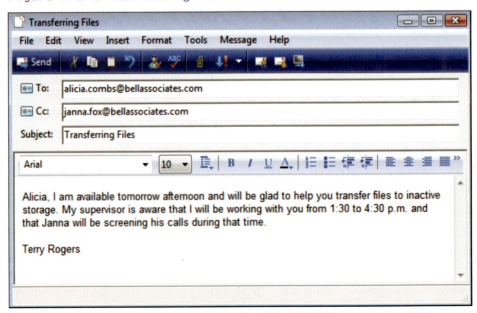

Indirect order is used for messages that give negative news or that attempt to persuade the reader. Supporting details are presented first to prepare the reader for the main idea that comes later in the message. A letter that refuses a request is a typical document for which the indirect order is appropriate. An example letter is shown in Figure 7-3 on page 112. The first paragraph of the letter identifies the subject of the letter without giving the negative news. The second paragraph gives reasons that support a refusal and then states or implies the refusal. The closing paragraph builds goodwill or offers an alternative solution.

©ISTOCK

Composing and Editing

Composing is writing a message based on the objectives and plan developed for the message. A complete business message typically has an opening, one or more developmental paragraphs, and a closing.

- The opening paragraph identifies the subject of the message. If the message is written in direct order, this paragraph also gives the main idea of the message.

- The developmental paragraphs supply supporting details and the main idea if the message is written in indirect order.

- The closing paragraph ends a message. This paragraph may summarize earlier points of the message, ask the reader to take some action, or try to build goodwill.

For reports, you may need to do research to find information needed to write the report. Conducting research is discussed later in the section on reports.

Dear Savvy Admin

Dear Savvy Admin:

One of my coworkers stops by my office several times a day to chat. These conversations are usually about unimportant matters. I like talking with him, but he simply takes too much of my time. How do I get him to leave?

Talk Is Cheap

Dear Talk Is Cheap:

Try physical cues as well as verbal ones. Sometimes just standing up will cue a person that you're ending the conversation. You could even pick up some papers and start out of your office or cubicle to "deliver" them. Or pick up the phone to make a call.

You could say, "I'd love to talk with you later, John, but Sophie wants this report on her desk by the end of day, and I really need to focus on it." Or "May I stop by your office when I have some free time?" Or "Why don't we talk over lunch next week?"

When you're on a tight deadline, try posting a "do not disturb" sign on your door.

Savvy Admin

Editing is reviewing and revising a message to improve its form and content. Effective written communications have certain characteristics in common. They are courteous, correct, concise, clear, and complete. Figure 7-4 on page 113 describes messages with each of these characteristics. Review your messages with these characteristics in mind.

Proofreading

Proofreading

is reviewing and correcting the final draft of a message. While the purpose of editing is to improve writing style and content, the purpose of proofreading mainly involves looking for errors or omissions. Allow ample time for proofreading so you can produce error-free messages. Errors reflect badly on you and your organization. Errors may also cause confusion for readers. Messages can contain many types of errors. The spelling and grammar checking features of word processing software can help you find some but not all errors. When you proofread, look for only one or two types of errors at a time. When proofreading printed documents, use proofreaders' marks to indicate changes or corrections. Commonly used proofreaders' marks are shown in Figure 7-5 on page 114. When proofreading a document on screen, use the program's track changes feature to indicate changes or corrections.

© DANIEL MACKLESTONE PHOTOGRAPHY

Publishing

Publishing is sending a message to the receiver (as with a letter or e-mail message) or making the message available to the receiver (as with posting information on a

Figure 7-3 Letter in Indirect Order

Bell and Associates

304 West Columbia Street | Somerset, KY 42501-0304 | 606-555-0147 | www.bellassociates.com

October 24, 20--

Dr. Alan Mossavi
State College
1800 College Street
Somerset, KY 42501-1800

Dear Alan

Your invitation to speak at the seminar on December 15 is an honor. I know that your students will benefit from hearing professionals in the marketing field discuss the latest trends in marketing products.

Unfortunately, the demands on my time are currently very heavy. Our company is introducing a new product line next year, and I am developing a marketing campaign to be launched on January 1. Handling this campaign along with my other duties leaves me no time for speaking engagements this fall, so I must refuse your request.

Have you met Harmony Ming, one of our marketing assistants? Ms. Ming is very knowledgeable about our company's marketing efforts and the latest trends in product marketing. I have not spoken to her about your request, but I think she may be available. Her telephone number is 606-555-0157. You might wish to invite her to take part in the seminar.

Sincerely

Alexander Ramon

Alexander Ramon
Vice President of Marketing

xx

Figure 7-4 Effective Written Communication

Courteous	A courteous message has a positive tone and is considerate of the reader. Saying *please* and *thank you* and using the proper degree of formality help create a courteous message.
Correct	A correct message does not contain errors or imply information that is not accurate. The mechanics of the message (spelling and grammar) as well as the information itself should be correct.
Concise	A concise message expresses ideas in as few words as possible without being abrupt or incomplete. It does not contain unnecessary elements, redundancies, or empty phrases.
Clear	A clear message gives precise information that cannot be easily misunderstood. It does not contain contradictory information.
Complete	A complete message contains all the information needed to achieve the objectives of the sender. It does not omit dates, times, locations, amounts, or other details that the reader needs to know.

website). Selecting an appropriate method for publishing a message is important. For example, a message to a coworker that contains sensitive or confidential information should not be sent in an e-mail message. A personal conversation or a printed memo should be used instead. When choosing an appropriate communication channel, consider factors such as the following:

- The purpose/objective of the message
- The target audience
- The length of the message
- How quickly the information needs to be delivered
- The cost of distribution, along with the budget available

E-mail Messages

Although e-mail is an informal means of communication, business e-mails should be created following the same effective writing steps as other messages.

- Plan the message by identifying the objective of the message and considering the receiver.
- Make your message courteous, correct, concise, clear, and complete.
- Always fill in the subject line on the form. The subject should be concise yet give enough information so that the receiver knows the purpose of the message at a glance.

- Review and edit the message to be sure it will achieve your objectives for writing.
- Proofread the message carefully and correct all errors.

A sample e-mail message is shown in Figure 7-2 on page 110.

E-mails are often used to transmit memos or reports as attachments. If you plan to send a large file as an e-mail attachment, contact the receiver and ask whether sending a large attachment is acceptable. Some e-mail systems do not handle large file attachments.

Because e-mail messages are not private, never send confidential or sensitive information in an e-mail or as an e-mail attachment. Even if you and the receiver delete the message, it may not be deleted everywhere the message was stored. The receiver can also forward your e-mail to others. Think carefully about what you say when you write an e-mail, and remember to proofread the message and correct errors before you click Send.

Memorandums

Although e-mail is widely used in most organizations, memorandums continue to have a place in the work environment. The hard-copy memorandum (memo for short) generally is written when the message is fairly long (more than one screen) or the information is confidential or sensitive.

Figure 7-5 Proofreaders' Marks

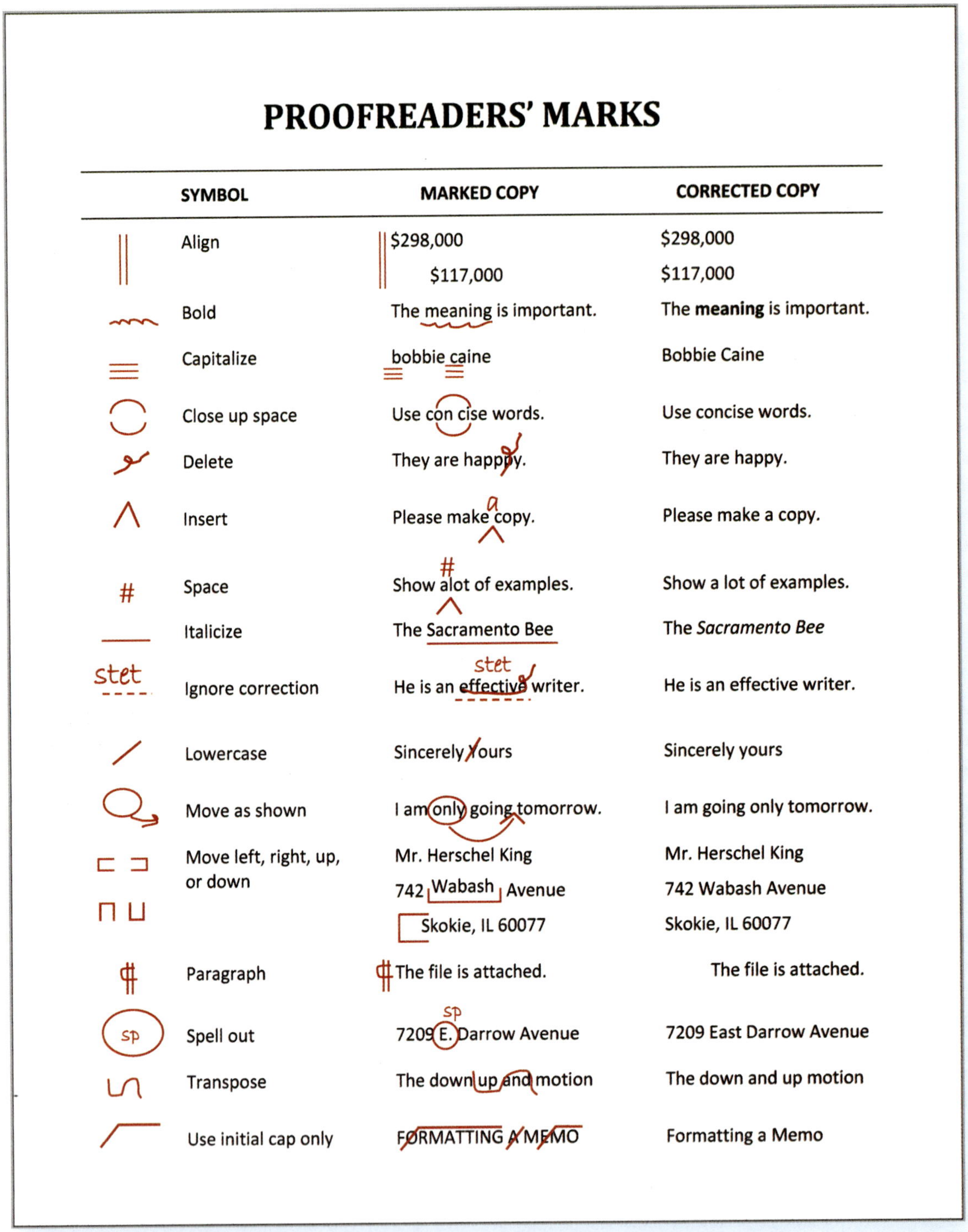

PROOFREADERS' MARKS

SYMBOL		MARKED COPY	CORRECTED COPY
‖	Align	‖$298,000 ‖ $117,000	$298,000 $117,000
∼	Bold	The meaning is important.	The **meaning** is important.
≡	Capitalize	bobbie caine	Bobbie Caine
◡	Close up space	Use con cise words.	Use concise words.
✗	Delete	They are happpy.	They are happy.
∧	Insert	Please make copy.	Please make a copy.
#	Space	Show alot of examples.	Show a lot of examples.
___	Italicize	The Sacramento Bee	The *Sacramento Bee*
stet	Ignore correction	He is an effective writer.	He is an effective writer.
/	Lowercase	Sincerely Yours	Sincerely yours
↻	Move as shown	I am only going tomorrow.	I am going only tomorrow.
⌐ ¬ ⊓ ⊔	Move left, right, up, or down	Mr. Herschel King 742 Wabash Avenue Skokie, IL 60077	Mr. Herschel King 742 Wabash Avenue Skokie, IL 60077
⁋	Paragraph	The file is attached.	The file is attached.
(SP)	Spell out	7209 E. Darrow Avenue	7209 East Darrow Avenue
⌣	Transpose	The down up and motion	The down and up motion
⟋	Use initial cap only	FORMATTING A MEMO	Formatting a Memo

A memorandum usually is written in the same format throughout the organization, with a common format including these elements: To line, From line, Date line, and Subject line. In addition to the name of the individual in the To line, a job title may also be used. However, writers in many organizations do not use titles in memorandums. Figure 7-6 above illustrates an appropriate format. When sending memorandums, specially designed envelopes are often used. These envelopes are reusable and are generally large enough that standard-size stationery can be inserted without folding. Memorandums may also be sent as e-mail attachments if they do not contain confidential information.

If you are sending a memorandum to more than one individual, list the names in alphabetical order or by hierarchical order within the company. If you are addressing a memo to a large group of people (generally six or more), use a generic classification, such as Budget Committee, in the To line. Include a distribution list at the end of the memo giving the names of the recipients. An example of a distribution list for a memo is shown in the Reference Guide.

As with all messages, before writing a memo, plan and gather information. Why are you writing? What is the objective of the message? Who is your audience? What do you want your audience to do after reading the memo? Should the message be organized in direct or indirect order? Memorandums should be complete, clear, accurate, prompt, concise, courteous, and positive. In style, they are slightly more formal than an e-mail, but less formal than a letter. Consider your audience when setting the tone (informal or formal) of the memo. Memos to coworkers may be informal while memos to managers or clients may be more formal.

If a memo is more than one page long, a heading should be placed on the second and following pages. The heading should include the recipient's name, Page 2 (or appropriate page number), and the date. An example of a second-page heading is shown in the Reference Guide.

Letters

Although organizations communicate extensively with their customers, clients, and employees via telephone, memo, and e-mail, letters remain an important method of publishing a message. Letters are more formal than memos and e-mail and are the preferred document when writing to current and prospective clients and customers.

Figure 7-6 Memorandum

Bell and Associates

304 West Columbia Street | Somerset, KY 42501-0304 | 606-555-0147 | www.bellassociates.com

TO: Andrea Wilson, Administrative Assistant

FROM: Karl Leinsdorf, Human Resources Manager

DATE: June 2, 20--

SUBJECT: Leave of Absence

Andrea, your family medical leave of absence request has been approved. Your leave will begin on July 1, 20--, and continue for six weeks as indicated on your leave of absence request form. The approved form is attached. The reasons for your leave of absence will be shared with your supervisor but not with other employees as you requested.

You seemed to have a good understanding of the conditions of a family medical leave when we talked last week. However, if you have any questions regarding your leave, please let me know.

Attachment: Leave of Absence Form

A letter represents the company to the outside public—vendors, customers, clients, and prospective customers and clients. A well-written letter can win friends and customers. Conversely, a poorly written letter can lose customers. One of your tasks as an administrative professional will be assisting your employer with writing effective letters or writing letters yourself for her or his signature. You may also write letters for your signature.

As with all messages, begin by determining the purpose for writing. Why are you writing? Next, consider the audience. Will the reader consider the message as positive, neutral, or negative? Do you want to persuade the reader? Select a direct or indirect approach based on the answers to these questions. Use the you approach, stating the message in a way that will appeal to the reader.

When your planning is complete, write a first draft of the letter. Evaluate the letter to see whether you think it will accomplish your objective. Also consider whether the letter is courteous, correct, concise, clear, and complete. Edit the letter as needed to improve it.

If a letter is more than one page long, a heading should be placed on the second and following pages. The heading should include the recipient's name, the page number, and the date. An example of a second-page heading is shown in the Reference Guide.

The envelope used to mail a letter also makes an impression on the reader. The envelope should match the stationery used for the letter and should be free of errors or smudges. The format for business envelopes is presented in Chapter 12, along with other information about mailing correspondence.

Proofread the revised letter for content and format. For very important letters, you also might ask someone else to proofread the document; it is sometimes difficult to see your own mistakes. Use a letter format approved by your company. Block and modified block formats are commonly used for business letters. Figure 7-3 on page 112 shows a letter formatted in block style with open punctuation. Figure 7-7 on page 117 shows a letter formatted in modified block style with mixed punctuation. Both punctuation styles can be used with either letter format.

Reports

Many types of reports are prepared in the workplace. Some reports are informal and contain only two or three pages. Other reports may be formal reports with a table of contents, bibliography, and appendices in addition to the body of the report.

A summary of a report may be presented orally, in addition to distributing the report electronically or in print. Creating oral presentations and visual aids is discussed in Chapter 8.

The writing process for reports is the same as for other written messages—plan, compose, edit, proofread, and publish—with one exception. The writer may need to do research to find the information needed to compose the report.

The administrative assistant's role in preparing reports varies:

- ■ You may have the responsibility of keying and formatting the report, producing the final copies, and distributing the report.

Writing @Work

When proofreading, look for these common errors in written messages:

- ↗ Missing or repeated words
- ↗ Transposed words
- ↗ Incorrect amounts or dates
- ↗ Misspelled names or other words
- ↗ Incorrect use of words
- ↗ Incorrect or missing punctuation
- ↗ Incorrect capitalization
- ↗ Incorrect grammar
- ↗ Incorrect spacing or placement of document parts

©ISTOCK

Figure 7-7 Modified Block Letter in Indirect Order

Office Solutions

4540 Eastgate Boulevard, Cincinnati, OH 45245-4540   513-555-0125

May 12, 20--

Ms. Janet Waldon
Johnson Company
3574 Kennedy Avenue
Cincinnati, OH 45213-3574

Dear Ms. Waldon:

Thank you for inviting me to make a presentation on document printers. We have several models of ink jet and laser printers for sale, and I will be happy to present information about them to your company. A brochure describing our most popular printer is enclosed.

Your suggested time for the presentation, 3 p.m. on May 20, is convenient for me. I will provide information on several printers. I will also bring three printers that I think would be good choices for your company based on the information you have given to me. You will be able to see these printers in action and judge the quality of the printouts. I will also provide the information on the cost of refill cartridges that you requested.

Please call me if your company has any special printing needs that we have not discussed so I can address those needs in my presentation. I will call you on May 19 to reconfirm our meeting at your company location.

Sincerely,

Anita Diaz

Anita Diaz
Sales Representative

tr

Enclosure

c   Scott Marlin, Account Manager
         Alicia Stokes, Buyer

- You may help with the research.
- You may draft some or all portions of the report.

Since formal or long reports often require much time and effort to prepare, it is especially important that the writer identify the objective of the report clearly and consider the audience for the report. For a long or complicated report, a timeline should be developed to set deadlines for completing stages of the research and report composition.

Research for Reports

Most reports involve some type of research. The research may be primary research—the collecting of information through surveys, observations, or reviewing and analyzing data. For example, suppose your manager asks you to create a report on the use of company sick days. You might need to review the attendance records for all employees for the past five years to determine whether use of sick days has been increasing or decreasing. Your report might include

a graph that shows total sick days used for each of the last five years. The report might include other information that you calculate such as the percent of increase or decrease in the use of sick days and the time of year when the most sick days are used.

The research also may be secondary research—finding data or material that other people have discovered and reported via the Internet, books, periodicals, and various other publications. Suppose you are asked to help do research for a marketing plan for a new product your company plans to sell. You could do research on the demographics of the target market area to find the number of people living in the area. You could also find information about the ages, races, gender, education, and income levels of the residents of the area. Using this information, the report writer can make recommendations for marketing strategies that will appeal to the target buyers. When using information discovered from secondary research, be sure to give proper credit to the source of the information by using

workplace wisdom

With the number of e-mails continually growing, it is important that they be well written. Have you ever not opened an e-mail because the subject did not seem important or you didn't recognize the sender's name? Many people receive dozens of e-mails every day. If you expect your e-mails to be read, you must take care to write them effectively, paying attention to all details, including the subject line.

Follow these guidelines for writing effective e-mails:

- Assign a high priority to the message only when truly needed.
- Ask for approval before sending a large attachment.
- Do not send confidential or sensitive information via e-mail.
- Keep the message short.
- Do not use all capital letters.
- Do not send flames—angry or insulting messages.
- Do not send or forward spam (electronic junk mail).
- Use correct grammar, spelling, and punctuation.

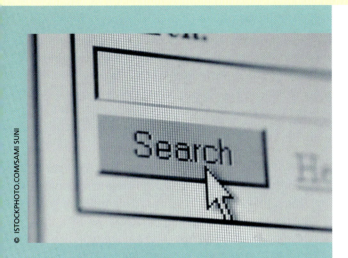

Technology @Work

Knowing how to use search terms effectively is key to getting relevant results when using Internet search engines and the search tools on websites and in electronic databases.

Searchers can use Boolean operators to create more effective searches. Boolean operators are words used to connect words or phrases for a search. Three commonly used Boolean operators are AND, OR, and NOT.

↗ The AND operator can be used to narrow search results. For example, using the search term *cars AND trucks* will return results that have both of these words. An article that only contains *trucks* would not be included.

↗ The OR operator can be used to broaden a search. For example, you could use the search term *cars OR trucks*. A larger list of sources will result because only one of the terms needs to be in a source for it to make the hits list.

↗ NOT can be used to eliminate a specific term from the hits list. For example, you could search using *automobiles NOT trucks* to find articles about all types of automobiles except trucks.

Various Internet search engines may have other advanced features you can use to fine-tune your search. Review the instructions at each site to see the rules that apply.

footnotes or endnotes. Do not reprint copyrighted material without the consent of the copyright holder.

When searching for information on the Internet, using the appropriate search terms will help you find the information you need. Suppose you want to find information related to ethics in the medical profession. If your search term is too broad (*ethics*, for instance), the search will return thousands of hits (search results) that do not relate to the specific research topic. If your search terms are too narrow (*ethics for nurses*, for instance), the results may exclude articles that would be relevant to your research topic. The search term *ethics medical profession* would be more effective in returning results that meet your needs.

Determining the credibility of the company or individual providing the information that you find when doing research is very important. Noting the date of the article or study is also important. All information found in print or on the Internet is not necessarily reliable or current. Ask yourself these questions to help you evaluate the credibility of sources: Who wrote the information? What education or expertise does the person have? Is the person representing a respected organization? Is the information current? Is the information biased toward a particular viewpoint?

Formats for Reports

An informal report may be formatted as a memo. The name of the person requesting the report appears in the To line. The name of the report writer appears in the From line. The title of the report appears in the Subject line. Side headings similar to those used in a formal report may be used to identify sections of the report if the report contains more than one page.

Formal reports are typically formatted in manuscript style. If you are asked to prepare a report that will be submitted for publication or to a scholarly journal, you may need to use a particular report format. MLA (Modern Language Association) style is often used for reports related to the liberal arts and humanities. APA (American Psychological Association) style is commonly used to prepare reports related to the social sciences. You should refer to a style guide published by the

RYAN MCVAY/DIGITAL VISION/GETTY IMAGES

Proofread documents carefully before sending them.

particular organization if you are asked to prepare a report in a special format.

Formal business reports usually contain several parts. These parts may include an executive summary, title page, table of contents, body, bibliography or reference section, and appendix. Not all reports will contain all these parts.

Your company may have a particular format that you will be expected to use for formal reports.

Refer to the company's style guide for documents if one is available. If a style guide is not available, look for reports in the company files to see the formats that have been used for other reports.

Formal business reports usually follow these guidelines:

- Formal business reports are typically prepared in manuscript style. The body of the report includes a main title and side headings to identify parts of the report. Software features such as the Title and Heading styles in *Microsoft® Word* are typically used to format titles and headings.

- The report paragraphs are formatted using 1 or 1.15 line spacing with 10 or 12 points of blank space between paragraphs. The paragraphs are not indented.

- Tables, charts, or other visual aids may be included in the report body or an appendix.

- Footnotes or endnotes are used to cite sources of material used in the report.

- A bibliography or references page lists sources at the end of the report.

- An appendix may be used to provide additional details or related information mentioned in the report.

A sample business report appears in the Reference Guide on page 217.

Key Terms

communication

communication barrier

editing

emphatic listening

evaluative listening

informative listening

listening

nonverbal communication

pitch

proofreading

publishing

reflective listening

tone

Summary

- Communicating effectively is essential to successful business operations. The communication process involves a message, a sender, a channel, a receiver, and feedback.

- For effective communication to take place, the message must be understood as the speaker or writer intends. A communication barrier is anything that interferes with successful communication. Senders and receivers can try to overcome internal barriers and external barriers to improve communications.

- Listening is essential to effective communication. Being an effective listener can help you be more productive and improve your relationships with others.

- Factors such as pitch, tone, volume, rate of speech, and nonverbal cues can affect your verbal communications.

- Writing is a process that involves planning, composing, editing, proofreading, and publishing messages. Each stage of the process is important in creating an effective message.

- Administrative assistants may be expected to write memos and letters for a manager's signature or their own. They may format and distribute reports, write informal reports, or help with research for reports.

Bookmark It. *For convenient access to activities, links, and valuable career resources for administrative professionals, visit the companion website for this text:*

www.cengage.com/officetech/fultoncalkins

Planning Notes

Learning Objectives

1. Describe the communication process and its elements.

2. Identify communication barriers and ways to overcome them.

3. Describe types of listening and ways to improve listening skills.

4. Describe factors related to effective verbal communication.

5. Prepare effective written messages.

 Critical Thinking; Activities 1, 2, 3, 4, 5, 6

 Activities 9, 10; Above & Beyond

 Activities 7, 8

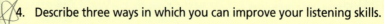

Discussion Questions

1. What elements are involved in the communication process, and what is the role of each element?

2. What is a communication barrier? Give examples of internal and external communication barriers.

3. List four types of active listening and tell the purpose of each type.

4. Describe three ways in which you can improve your listening skills.

5. Describe how pitch, tone, volume, and rate of speech can affect your verbal communications.

6. Why is planning an important first step in the writing process for all types of messages?

7. What is secondary research? Give some examples of sources you could use to find secondary research material.

Critical Thinking

Is the sky falling?   Your manager, Mr. Roberts, stopped by your desk on his way out of the office at 2 p.m. on Friday afternoon. He handed you three letters he had signed and asked you to prepare envelopes and place the letters in the mail today. "Don't call me unless the sky is falling," he said on his way out the door. "I promised to spend some uninterrupted time with my wife and son this weekend." You prepared the envelopes and are looking over the letters when you notice what you think is a huge error. An amount in one of the letters is $1,000,500. You are pretty sure the amount should be $10,500.00.

What do you think Mr. Roberts means by "unless the sky is falling"? Should you mail the letter even though you think the amount is wrong? How should you handle this situation?

Build Workplace Skills

1. **Communication process**   Melissa called her coworker, Jonas, to tell him that the department meeting scheduled for tomorrow afternoon has been moved to next Tuesday at 1 p.m. Jonas indicated that he would note the change on his calendar. Identify each element of the communication process in this situation. (Learning Objective 1)

2. **Communication barriers**   Recently you attended a seminar on improving writing skills. The speaker arrived late and seemed flustered and disorganized. You wondered whether his presentation would also be disorganized. At first the room was quite comfortable. However, as the room filled with people, it became uncomfortably warm. When the speaker turned down the lights to show his presentation, you had to fight to stay awake. Maybe you should not have had such a large lunch. The speaker faced the screen at the front of the room as he discussed points on the slides. The portable microphone he was wearing occasionally omitted a shrill squeak as he moved about the front of

the room. You learned a couple of new ideas for improving your writing, but on the whole, the seminar was not a very enjoyable experience.

What are the internal communication barriers in this scenario? What could you do to help overcome these barriers? What are the external communication barriers in this scenario? What could the speaker do to help overcome these barriers? (Learning Objective 2)

3. **Listening skills**   Test your informative listening skills. Locate the sound file CH07 Assignments from the data files. Play the file to hear some assignments from your supervisor. Play the file only once. Take notes as you listen, but do not pause the recording or replay the file. Working from memory and your notes, list everything you can remember from listening to the instructions. List any questions you would ask your supervisor about the assignments if you were given the opportunity. Now play the sound file again. Were you able to list all parts of the assignments? Were any of your questions answered as you heard the instructions again? (Learning Objective 3)

4. **Verbal communication**   A coworker stops by your desk and says, "Have you heard? I have been assigned to work on the Lane report. I can't wait to get started." Work with a classmate to complete this activity. Take turns role-playing the coworker.

   - First, assume the coworker is genuinely pleased about this assignment. What posture, gestures, or facial expressions would the coworker use? Think about the pitch, volume, tone, and rate of speech the coworker would use. Then make the statements to your partner as you think the coworker would.

   - Next, assume that the coworker is not pleased about the assignment. Again, think about the pitch, volume, tone, rate of speech, and body language the coworker would use. Then make the statements to your partner as you think the coworker would. (Learning Objective 4)

5. **Green practices report**   At a recent department meeting, someone mentioned the attention that Earth Week and "going green" are getting in the media. Another person noted that green initiatives can save money as well as enhance the reputation of a company. Your manager, Ms. Adderley, asked you to do some research and write a short report (two or three pages) about ways an office can implement green practices. The report should also recommend at least three ways that your office can "go green." The changes you recommend should be both practical and cost-effective for the company. Use footnotes or endnotes to document the sources of information you use in the report. Include a title page and a references page. Use the format shown for a business report in the Reference Guide of this textbook. (Learning Objective 5)

> *Communicate Clearly*

6. **Retreat memo**   Your supervisor, Emma Wong, has drafted a memo to the company's department heads regarding a weekend management retreat. She has asked you to edit the memo and print copies for distribution. Open the Word file CH07 Retreat Memo from the data files. Edit the memo to correct errors in grammar, spelling, punctuation, capitalization, number usage, and word usage. (Learning Objective 5)

7. **Acceptance letter**   You have been asked to speak on "Ethics in the Office" at the next meeting of IAAP. Write a letter to the president of the local chapter of IAAP, Ms. Janet Wolfly, Griffin Corporation, 4832 Gold Mountain Road, Hurst, TX 76053-4832, accepting

Planning Notes

the invitation. Use the direct approach for this good news letter. Give her the title of your presentation and mention any special equipment you will need, the number of minutes you will speak (no more than 30 minutes), and any special room setup. You will be using PowerPoint slides in your presentation. (Learning Objective 5)

8. **Persuasive letter** You work for Compton Memorial Hospital, which specializes in research and treatment for illnesses and disabilities of children. Write a letter to be sent to someone who has donated money to the hospital in the past. Use the indirect approach for this persuasive letter. Thank the person for giving in the past and helping to make treatment of ill children possible. Point out that a large part of the hospital's operating funds comes from donations. Ask the person to send a donation of $25, $50, $100, or more as part of a matching funds campaign. A wealthy patron will match all the funds donated by individuals up to $50,000. The donation must be received by (give a date one month from today). Indicate that a reply envelope is enclosed with the letter. Make up an address for the hospital and create a letterhead. You are writing to Mrs. Alma Chaney. Make up an address for her from your local area. (Learning Objective 5)

Develop Relationships

9. **Confidential information** You work as an administrative assistant in the human resources department of your company. In the course of keying documents and taking messages for your supervisor, you have learned that the company is planning to downsize 15 employees. As you are having lunch with two coworkers, the conversation turns to rumors that the company is considering laying off employees.

"Surely you must know what's going on," says your friend, Marsha. "Won't you give us a hint?"

"Come on," says Tim when you hesitate to answer. "You know you can trust us not to say anything."

What is your responsibility to the company in this situation? To your coworkers? What would you say in this situation? You want to do the right thing and stay on good terms with your coworkers.

10. **Sensitive topic** You are relatively new at your position as an administrative assistant at TKO Manufacturing. You work with the controller, Mr. Sakimoto, and the staff of the accounting department. Mr. Sakimoto speaks and writes English as a second language. He seems sensitive regarding his command of the language, and everyone on his staff is careful not to correct his minor speech errors.

You have noticed that Mr. Sakimoto sometimes makes errors in grammar or in stating common expressions in the letters he writes. You would be happy to review his letters and correct these errors for him. How can you approach this subject with Mr. Sakimoto in a way that will not cause him embarrassment?

Use Technology

11. **Mail merge letters** Key the names and addresses shown in the following table in *Excel*. This table will be the data source for a mail merge. Use the letter you wrote soliciting donations for Compton Memorial Hospital as the main document for the mail merge

(Communicate Clearly, activity 8). Replace the appropriate parts of the letter with the related field codes from the table. Merge the letters to create a new document. Look over the letters to make sure they are correct before printing them. (Learning Objective 5)

Title	First Name	Last Name	Street	City	State	ZIP Code
Mrs.	Anita	Boaz	88 Dennis Street	Houston	TX	77006-0088
Mr.	Ralph	Colter	656 King Street	Seattle	WA	98104-0656
Mr.	Shane	Correa	2209 Bayshore Drive	Waldport	OR	97394-2209
Mr.	Hans	Dortmann	2910 E Harcourt Street	Compton	CA	90221-2910
Mr.	Joe	Park	1501 Solano Avenue	Berkeley	CA	94707-1501
Ms.	Alicia	Rhodes	7715 Balboa Avenue	San Diego	CA	92111-7715
Mrs.	Lora	Roberts	1040 Florin Street	Sacramento	CA	95831-1040
Mrs.	Elena	Vega	5850 Craig Road	Las Vegas	NV	89103-5850
Ms.	Tami	Wong	2879 Lancaster Drive	Salem	OR	97305-2879
Mr.	Ed	Woo	39508 Mountain Drive	Phoenix	AZ	85086-0015

12. **Donations spreadsheet**   All the people to whom you sent letters have sent donations to Compton Memorial Hospital. Open the table you created in *Excel* and add three columns to the right of the ZIP Code column. Name the first column *Donation*. Name the second column *Matching Funds*. Name the third column *Total*. Enter the amount shown below for each person in the Donation column. Copy the amounts into the Matching Funds column. Enter a formula in the Total column to add the donation and the matching funds. Sum the Total column to find the total donations from these patrons.

Mrs. Anita Boaz	$ 50.00	Ms. Alicia Rhodes	$ 25.00
Mr. Ralph Colter	50.00	Mrs. Lora Roberts	75.00
Mr. Shane Correa	25.00	Mrs. Elena Vega	100.00
Mr. Hans Dortmann	125.00	Ms. Tami Wong	250.00
Mr. Joe Park	50.00	Mr. Ed Woo	300.00

> *Above & Beyond*

Donations web page   Your supervisor at Compton Memorial Hospital complimented you on the donation request letter that you wrote and the great response the hospital received in donations. She asked you to create a web page related to donations that can be placed on the hospital's website. Search the Internet using the search term *hospital donations*. View the websites of some real hospitals to see the type of information they have about donations. Create an attractive and informative web page, making up details as needed. Save the file as a single-file web page. (Learning Objective 5)

Administrative Assistant

Marketing agency needs an administrative assistant to provide support for three account executives. Good human relations and organizational skills are essential in this position. The job involves:

- Handling verbal and written communications
- Managing customer records and other files
- Developing electronic slide presentations using *PowerPoint*
- Other duties as assigned

Do I qualify?

©MARK WRAGG, ISTOCK

CHAPTER

8

Learning Objectives

1. Plan, research, and write presentations.

2. Develop visual aids for presentations and meetings.

3. Practice and deliver effective presentations.

Developing Presentation Skills

Need for Presentation Skills

As an administrative professional, you will have many opportunities to speak before small groups. Your job may include working with small teams and presenting the teams' reports to groups in your organization. You may be asked to develop electronic slides to use as discussion aids for meetings or for someone else to use in a presentation.

As you become active in professional organizations such as IAAP, you may have the chance to assume leadership roles, giving you opportunities to present to small groups in your local IAAP chapter or larger groups at national conventions. Developing your presentation skills is important for your professional growth.

Planning Presentations

Many people experience presentation anxiety, commonly called stage fright. Presenters often lack the confidence and skill to make effective presentations. With proper planning and practice, you can develop effective presentation skills and overcome presentation anxiety. You can also learn techniques for developing effective slides to use as visuals for meetings and presentations. The planning steps in this section are important when you give a presentation and when you help develop a speech that someone else will present.

Identify the Objective

Planning a presentation involves the same steps you studied for planning a written message. First, you should identify the objective or goal of the presentation. Once you have identified the goal, write it in one clear, concise statement. As you prepare the presentation, review the statement frequently to stay on track.

Most of the time as an administrative professional, your goal in giving a presentation is to inform your audience. For example, if you have chaired a committee in your organization, you might give a presentation to managers on the activities of the committee. Other goals of a presentation might be to persuade or entertain. For example, you might give a presentation to other administrative assistants about the benefits of the company's new flextime schedule and encourage them to sign up for the program. You might speak at a luncheon for a retiring coworker. Your purpose would be to entertain the audience by recounting anecdotes or describing the accomplishments of the retiring colleague.

Consider the Audience

After identifying the goal of the presentation, consider the audience for the presentation. As an administrative professional, you will generally give presentations to coworkers in your organization. The coworkers might be a team or department or a group of people from many areas in the company. If you belong to a professional organization such as IAAP, you might give a presentation to your colleagues in the organization.

When considering the audience, ask and answer questions such as these:

- Why are they attending the presentation?
- What do they want to learn or how can they benefit from your presentation?
- What are the **demographics** (characteristics such as age, gender, race, education, and income level) of the audience?
- What are their interests?
- What knowledge do they have about the topic that you plan to present?

Consider the Time and Length

Ask the meeting organizer when you will present and the desired length of the presentation. Plan a presentation that you can give effectively within the allotted time.

workplace wisdom

Employees who are required to attend a presentation may not be very interested in hearing the presentation. You have to convince them early in your presentation that the time they spend listening to you will be worthwhile. What relevance does the topic have for their jobs? How can they use the information you give them to make their work life easier or more productive? Addressing these questions will help you gain—and keep—the audience's attention.

Select a room that is appropriate for the expected size of the audience.

You may have a choice of when to speak:

- Mid morning, when listeners are alert, is often a good time to speak.

- If you will use slides that require the lights to be low, right after lunch may not be a good time. Listeners may become drowsy in the low light.

- If you are speaking at a breakfast meeting, keep the talk brief. The audience probably has a full day ahead and will appreciate a short presentation.

As a general rule, presentations should be no longer than 20 minutes, with 30 to 40 minutes being the maximum time to speak. When a speaker talks longer than 30 minutes, the audience tends to become bored and restless. An exception to this rule exists if the audience will be actively involved in the presentation. For example, you may be a workshop presenter, with several activities for small groups. You may present for 20 minutes, give groups a task, get their feedback, and then present for another 15 or 20 minutes. You might end with another small group activity, or the entire group might share what they learned from the earlier activities.

Consider the Location

The location of the presentation and related activities are important to know. Ask these questions about the setting:

- Where will the presentation be given? In the workplace? A hotel? A conference center? A school?

How much time do you need to allow for travel to the location?

- Are other activities scheduled before or after the presentation? You need this information so you will know when the room can be set up and when you must remove any material or equipment after the presentation.

- What is the size of the room? What is the configuration of the seating? If the audience is small, should the audience sit around a table? As the presenter, you may be able to determine the seating arrangements.

If possible, check the room well before the presentation. Be certain the size of the room is appropriate. You do not want to give a presentation to 12 people in a room designed for 100 people. The too-large room will make it seem that you expected many more people. Nor do you want to give a presentation to 50 people crowded into a room designed for 25.

Talk with the person responsible for the room arrangements. Ask him or her to check the room on the morning of the presentation to ensure that the equipment is present, the room is clean, the temperature is pleasant, and the lighting is appropriate.

Research the Topic

One key to overcoming stage fright is knowing the topic of your presentation well. When you know the topic well, you will feel more confident and less nervous during the presentation.

Research your topic to find the information you need. You may be able to find the information in company records or by talking with employees or customers. For example, if you give a presentation about sales trends for three products your company sells, the information you need is probably in the company's sales records. If your presentation is on employee satisfaction with the company's benefits plan, you could interview employees about their thoughts on the plan.

When the topic is more general or not specific to your company, conduct research on the Internet or in a library. Be sure to record complete source information for each source you use. You may want to give the audience these details in a handout. Do not reprint copyrighted information without permission from the copyright holder.

Writing Presentations

Once you have planned and researched adequately, you are ready to begin the writing process. Your writing tasks include organizing the material, developing an opening, developing a strong body, and preparing an appropriate conclusion. As you write, continue to think of ways to make your presentation interesting to your audience.

Organize the Material

Organize your message before you start writing. First, record the main points you want to make in the body of the presentation. Next, decide on the order for presenting the main points. Use direct order for the body of the message if the presentation delivers good news or neutral news. If the presentation delivers negative news or seeks to persuade the audience, use indirect order.

Put the main points in logical order to create an outline. This can be a formal outline or a simple list of the points you will cover. If you will create slides in *Microsoft PowerPoint,* you can also create the outline there, as shown in Figure 8-1. Record the details you want to discuss under the main points.

Develop an Opening

The opening should immediately get the audience's attention and preview your message. Be creative in developing your opening. You might ask a question, refer to a current event, use a quotation, or tell a brief story. If you are good at telling jokes, you might open with a joke. If you use a joke or story, be sure it is in good taste and appropriate for the occasion. If you decide to tell a story, ask and answer these questions for yourself:

- How is the story relevant to the presentation? (Do not use a story that is not related to the presentation.)

- Is the story new ? Will the audience members be bored because they have already heard this story?

- Are you telling the story as succinctly as possible? You do not want to spend one-third of your time on your opening story.

However you decide to begin, remember that your purpose is to set the stage for your message. Write a strong opening that relates to the message.

Figure 8-1 Outline for a Presentation in PowerPoint

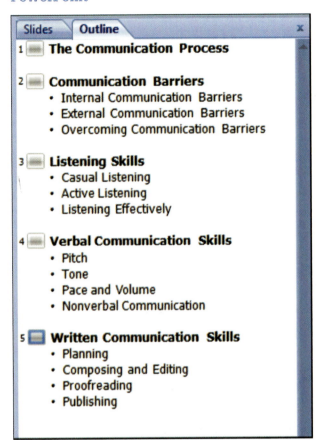

Develop a Strong Message

Start with your strongest points. Get to your major points quickly; do not spend time on irrelevant facts. As you develop the message, keep your focus on the audience. Keep asking these questions as you write:

- What is your message?

- Are you developing the right message for your audience?

- Are you using current examples to illustrate concepts? Do you have current facts and figures?

- Do the quotations relate to points you make? Do not use too many quotes; they can distract from the main message.

- Are you using direct language? Do not try to impress your audience with multisyllable words or little-used terminology.

- Are you using active voice rather than passive voice? For example, say "I believe . . ." instead of "It is believed . . ."

- Is your message sincere, relevant, and credible?

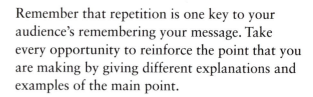

Writing @Work

Using a positive tone gives the audience a favorable impression of you and your organization. A positive tone is set by the words you choose. Use words that evoke positive feelings. People like to hear the word *yes* rather than the word *no*. A person is likely to be more eager to "discuss a concern" than to "listen to a complaint."

Effective communicators present their messages in positive tones. For example, instead of the negative statement "Do not litter" use a positive statement such as "Please deposit all trash in the nearest receptacle." Examples of positive and negative words and phrases are shown below.

Positive	Negative
Glad	Sorry
Pleasure	Displeasure
Satisfactory	Unsatisfactory
Please let us know	You failed to let us know
Please send your check	Because we did not receive your check
Your order will be shipped no later than October 30, 20--.	We regret to inform you that the item is out of stock.

Remember that repetition is one key to your audience's remembering your message. Take every opportunity to reinforce the point that you are making by giving different explanations and examples of the main point.

Develop a Strong Closing

The final impression you make on the audience is the one they will remember the most. You must plan your last few sentences with care. You want to leave your audience energized to reach the goal you established in the beginning of your presentation.

A strong closing gets the audience's attention. It helps them see the relationship between each part of your presentation—the opening, the body, and the closing. The conclusion can be a moving statement, a story, a call to action, or a challenge. Let the audience know you are ready to conclude by stating simply, "In conclusion . . ." or "My final point is . . ."

Make the conclusion powerful but short (about 5 to 10 percent of your talk). For example, you can urge listeners to action, make them think about new possibilities, or even make them laugh. You want the audience to leave thinking you have helped them learn and/or have motivated them to take some action.

Using Visual Aids

A **visual aid** is an object or image that your audience can see and that will help them understand your message. When used properly, visual aids can be very effective.

William Glasser, a well-known author and psychiatrist, determined that people retain about 20 percent of what they hear, 30 percent of what they see, and 50 percent of what they both hear and see.[1] Visual aids can increase the amount of information your audience remembers. Various types of objects or images can be used. Select visual aids that reinforce your message and that are appropriate for the presentation or meeting.

1 De Young Consulting Services, "Presentation Pointers," http://www.deyoung consultingservices.com/pointers.htm (accessed March 31, 2010).

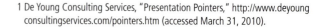

©ISTOCK

Objects

Natural objects (a plant), pieces of equipment (a flash drive), and products (a book) are examples of objects that can be used as visual aids. For example, at a meeting of company sales representatives, a new product the sales reps will sell is an effective visual aid. If the audience is small, the object can be displayed or passed around so everyone can see it.

If the audience is large, you can place small objects on an optical projector for remote viewing. The object is placed on the bed of the projector. A large image of the object is projected onto a screen.

Transparencies, Posters, and Flipcharts

Overhead transparencies, posters, and flipcharts are the most traditional types of visual aids. Although some people may consider these aids to be outdated or low-tech, they are effective in many situations.

Transparencies   A transparency is a thin sheet of clear or colored acetate that can be placed on an overhead projector. The text or images that are drawn or printed on the sheet are projected onto a large screen. The use of transparences and overhead projectors is declining for business presentations as electronic slides and computer projection systems are more commonly used.

Posters   A poster is an effective visual aid in meetings and presentations to small groups. The poster might show an image related to the discussion or list the key points you want the audience to remember. Posters that give the session title and presenter's name are often used at the doors to meeting rooms at seminars and conferences.

You can use software, such as *Microsoft Publisher*, to create posters. If you have a printer that can handle large sheets of paper, you can achieve professional-looking results. If you have a printer that uses standard sheets (8½ by 11 inches), you

Handling Questions in a Presentation

IMAGE SOURCE/GETTY IMAGE

Determine whether you are going to invite the audience to ask questions during or at the end of the presentation. If so, identify the ten most likely questions that you may be asked. Prepare answers to these questions. When you open up the session for questions, typically after the closing, use these guidelines:

↗ Be sure you understand the question before answering. Repeat the question or paraphrase it. This confirms that you understood correctly and ensures that everyone in the audience can hear the question.

↗ Be honest; if you cannot answer the question, say so.

↗ Control interchanges: if a questioner becomes a heckler, try to enlist the audience in moving

on to other comments. If a questioner digresses, gently remind the questioner of the presentation goal.

↗ After you answer the last question, briefly restate the main point of the presentation closing. Remind listeners of what they have learned or what action you want them to take.

SMART TECHNOLOGIES

Figure 8-2 *Microsoft Publisher* can be used to create effective posters.

can print the poster on several sheets and tape them together. The resulting poster would be appropriate for informal, in-house meetings.

When you need a poster with a more professional look, you can hire an outside printer. Several Internet sites offer full-color poster printing on high-quality paper or vinyl with a quick turnaround. You upload a file with the images and text for the poster, review a proof of the poster, and receive the printed poster in as little as two days.

Flipcharts   Flipcharts are tablets of large paper for drawing pictures or recording notes during a presentation or meeting. The pages can be removed from the tablet and displayed on the meeting room walls as reminders of the discussion as a meeting progresses. This low-tech method for creating visual aids can be effective in small group meetings where listeners are asked to participate by generating questions or ideas.

Whiteboards

An electronic whiteboard can also be used to draw images or record notes during a presentation or meeting. An **electronic whiteboard** scans images drawn or written on it. The images can be uploaded to a computer, edited, printed, or e-mailed. Not

only can the audience see the text or images as they are created, they can also have access to the notes after the presentation or meeting. An electronic whiteboard works well for small group meetings with a lot of interaction by participants.

An **interactive whiteboard** (IBW) is a large display board connected to a computer. In addition to capturing images and notes as with an electronic whiteboard, an IBW works with a projector to display a computer's desktop. The user can access the computer's programs, including using browser software to surf the Internet. The user touches the IBW to move the mouse and taps the screen (as you would click a mouse) to activate commands. Some IBWs can translate cursive writing on the board into text that can be saved or edited.

Electronic Slides

Electronic slides are an effective type of visual aid commonly used in presentations and business meetings. Computer programs, such as *PowerPoint*, make creating slides quick and easy. Slides should be easy to read from all locations in the meeting room. Before your presentation, display the slides in the room where you will present,

A whiteboard can be an effective visual aid.

or a room of similar size, to be sure that viewers in the back of the room can read the slides.

The text should highlight the main points about the topic. They should not include everything you intend to say in the presentation. Follow these guidelines for creating slides:

- Develop one slide for every two or three minutes of your presentation. This number keeps the audience interested and does not overwhelm the listeners with visuals.

- Include a title on each slide and two to four short words or phrases as bullet points.

- Do not crowd the text or images on the slides.

- Use graphics (charts, photos, clip art) on some slides to help illustrate points and add interest.

- Use contrasting colors for the slide background and the text. For example, use a light background with dark text or a dark background with white text.

- Limit the number of fonts used—perhaps one font for the title and a different font or size for the bullet points. Do not use all capital letters, which are hard to read, for bullet points.

- Strive for a professional look. Use design themes or templates in the software (as shown in Figure 8-3 on page 134) to ensure a consistent look. You may wish to include the company or organization logo on the title slide.

- Be creative. Use animated bullet points and slide transitions to add interest to the slides. Use special effects, sound, and video sparingly and only if appropriate for the presentation. Special effects

should not divert the listeners' focus from the content of the presentation.

Slides are often used to facilitate discussions during meetings. You may be asked to prepare slides for a meeting on two or three topics that may or may not be related. Follow the same design guidelines listed earlier for presentation slides.

©iStock

Dear Savvy Admin

Dear Savvy Admin:

I work for the superintendent of parks in a large city. She has asked me to prepare *PowerPoint* slides about a pest called the emerald ash borer for a presentation she will give to the city council.

I know she it is expecting me to do a good job, but I know so little about this pest. I'm planning to research it online and at the library. I want the slides to look professional, so I want to include photographs or drawings. Where can I get some appropriate ones?

Can't Be Boring

Dear Can't Be Boring:

You can find lots of photographs and drawings that you can use without paying a fee. Search for phrases such as *free images* and *public domain images*.

The U.S. government is also a terrific source for information and images. Go to the websites of the U.S. Department of Agriculture and the U.S. Forest Service. You will find a wealth of information and images there.

Savvy Admin

Handouts

Handouts can be an important part of a presentation. The simplest handouts are copies of the slides. Handouts that list the main points you will discuss and provide space for notes can be passed out at the beginning of a speech or meeting. Handouts with additional information about a topic are often distributed when the topic is introduced or near the close of the session. For example, if the presentation is about a new health insurance plan, a handout with details about the plan would be helpful.

Handouts should be attractive, easy to read, and free of errors. If you have a complex handout that may distract the audience, pass it out just before you discuss the topic or at the end of the presentation.

Practicing Presentations

Nervousness or anxiety is a normal reaction for many people when they think about presenting before an audience. Knowing that you are well prepared and well rehearsed can decrease your nervousness and help you give an effective presentation.

Figure 8-3 *PowerPoint* provides design themes to help users create effective slides.

Rehearse

Make arrangements, if at all possible, to rehearse in the room where you will give the presentation. If this is not possible, try to rehearse the presentation in a room of similar size to the one in which you will speak. Learn whom to contact for help if the equipment malfunctions during your presentation.

Rehearse the presentation just as you are going to give it. For example, if you will stand at a lectern during the presentation, stand at a lectern during rehearsal. If you will use a microphone, use one during the rehearsal.

Find out what type of microphone you will use. With a stationary microphone, you do not have to be concerned about holding it or worry that it is positioned on your jacket correctly. Unfortunately, a stationary mic has a major disadvantage—it ties you to the lectern. In most presentations, you will want to be free to walk across the front of the room and even into the audience.

If you are using an unfamiliar laptop, bring your presentation on a flash drive, even if you e-mailed it ahead of time. A backup copy of the presentation and handouts on a flash drive is *always* a good idea.

Practice giving the presentation three or four times. Then ask a colleague to listen to you and give you constructive criticism. With repeated rehearsals, the content becomes part of your memory; you will be more at ease because you are not likely to forget important points during your presentation.

Memorize your opening line, question, quotation, or story. Doing so will help you feel confident as you begin to speak. However, do not try to memorize the entire presentation. Use your slides or an outline to help you move smoothly from point to point as you speak in a conversational tone. Put details that you want to be sure to include in the notes section of the slides. You can view these notes on your monitor or a printout, but they will not be visible to the audience.

Use Visual Aids Effectively

As you rehearse, display the visual aids you plan to use in the presentation. Stand where you will not block the view of listeners. Look at the audience, not at the visual aids, as you speak. If the lights will be dimmed, try to keep the light at a level that lets the audience see both you and the slides and other visual aids. The room should have enough light for the audience to take notes.

Know how to operate the equipment, such as the laptop, remote mouse, and IWB. If you are uncomfortable showing the slides while you talk, ask someone to assist you. If you choose this approach, the person should rehearse with you so he or she knows when each slide is displayed. Give the person an outline that indicates when to advance the slides, when to show a visual aid, and when to pass out the handouts.

Plan Your Attire

Determine what you will wear several days before the presentation. The usual attire for a woman is a suit or dress; for a man, it is a suit and tie. Wear something that you are comfortable in and that looks good on you. Bright colors are perfectly okay.

Avoid necklaces and earrings that are large and distracting. Rings and bracelets are okay, but avoid large, noisy bracelets. Your hair should be well groomed. This is not the time to try a new hairstyle.

Delivering Presentations

Arrive early enough to check the layout of the room, the equipment, and the microphone. Have the name and telephone number of the contact person at the location where you are giving your presentation in case you have last-minute changes. In the 10 or 15 minutes before your presentation starts, find a private place where you can relax.

Respond to Your Introduction

Your introduction should help establish that you are a credible speaker. **Credible** means believable or trustworthy.

Use nonverbal cues to establish credibility from the start. Pay attention to your body language as you are being introduced. Stand or sit up straight in a relaxed posture. Look at the speaker and then look at members of the audience.

Walk to the lectern confidently. Respond briefly to the introduction. For example, you might say, "Thank you, Ms. Perez" and exchange a firm handshake. If you are not being introduced, you will need to introduce yourself.

Pause for a moment before beginning your presentation. Let your eyes sweep the room. Making eye contact with listeners gives an impression of openness and honesty. If you are in a small group, look briefly at each person. When you are in a large group, make eye contact with one person, then another, and another as you speak.

As you speak, demonstrate your competence. Let the audience know you are experienced in your field. Make a few relevant comments about your past experiences.

Focus on the Message

As you speak, do not think about being nervous or wonder whether your talk is being well received. Simply focus on sharing your message with the listeners. Begin with the opening line, question, quotation, or story you memorized earlier. Then follow your slides and notes to move through the points of the presentation.

Be animated in your speech as well as in your expression. Speak in a normal tone of voice—not too loudly, too softly, or too quickly.

In conversations with others, your facial expressions reinforce what you are saying; the same is true when delivering a presentation. Use natural gestures. It's fine to use your arms and hands to emphasize points, but too many gestures can distract the audience. Act naturally; do not perform.

During the presentation, observe the nonverbal feedback from the audience. Puzzled looks or blank stares are cues that the audience does not understand what you are saying. You may need to speak more slowly and give more examples to clarify what you mean. Smiles and nodding heads are positive reactions.

Watch your time. If you have been asked to deliver a 20-minute presentation, do so. Do not go over the time limit. Because you rehearsed your

Your Introduction

One way to build credibility with the audience is to present your **credentials**. Your credentials are evidence of your qualifications, competence, skills, or knowledge. How do you do this?

First, find out who will introduce you. Write a brief introduction of yourself—one that will take no more than two minutes to deliver. Highlight your major accomplishments.

Do not send a packet of information about yourself and leave it up to the person introducing you to determine the highlights. They may skip important information that you want the audience to know.

You should take a copy of your introduction to the presentation in case the speaker has misplaced the copy you sent. If you are not being introduced by another person, introduce yourself as you begin.

presentation several times before giving it, you know how long it will take. It is essential that you watch the time during your presentation; however, do not be obvious about it. Such behavior would be distracting for the audience. Some speakers place their watch on the lectern where they can refer to it discreetly. Determine a plan that works for you, with no audience distraction.

Deliver a Strong Closing

Use the closing to summarize what you want the audience to remember or to ask them to take some action appropriate for the goal of the presentation. Your conclusion, summary, or call to action should clearly tie in with your opening statements and the points you made in the body of the message.

If the presentation includes a question-and-answer session, be sure to repeat questions so that everyone in the audience can hear the question you are answering. Answer questions briefly since time for this part of the presentation is usually limited.

Do not get frustrated if someone asks a question about a point you covered earlier; the questioner may have been distracted or may not have fully understood what you said. Answer the question patiently, and try to use different statements or examples than you used earlier. If you do not know the answer, say so. Take the person's name and get back to him or her with the answer if that is appropriate for the situation.

Watch the time and do not let the session run longer than the time allotted. Use the last few minutes of the session to repeat the main points or action you want the audience to remember.

Seek Feedback

Within a day after the presentation, critique your performance. In evaluating yourself, be kind but honest. List the good points along with the not-so-good points. Identify one or two areas to improve before you deliver your next presentation. After that presentation, identify one or two more things to improve. Evaluation is an ongoing process. Give yourself credit for the improvements you make.

You or the individuals who asked you to speak may provide evaluation forms for the people in the

Communicating @ Work

When you speak during a meeting or a presentation, avoid using clichés. A **cliché** is a trite expression or phrase that has been overused to the point of no longer being effective. Using clichés can make your message seem boring or insincere. Notice the following clichés and the improved wording.

Cliché	Improved
At the present time	Now
By return mail	Mail today
Your kind letter	Your letter. (Omit *kind*. People, not letters, are kind.)
Among those present	Here or present
Perfect in every detail	Perfect
Cool as a cucumber	Calm
Powers that be	Managers, senators, or whomever you are referring to
Words are inadequate to express how I feel about this honor.	Thank you for the invitation to speak here today.

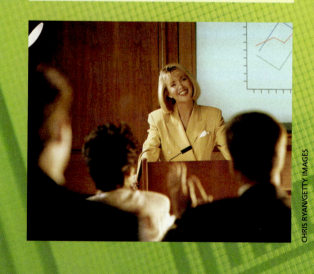

audience. Ask to see copies of the completed forms; review them carefully. Do not let yourself become upset over a few negative comments. Know that there will always be some negatives. However, take seriously the points that are made in the critique. Before you speak again, concentrate on how you might improve your presentation techniques.

ISTOCKPHOTO/KOHLERPHOTO

Technology @ Work

In addition to being used as visual aids in presentations and meetings, slides can be formatted for presentation on the Internet or a company intranet. (An **intranet** is a private computer network that looks and performs much like sites on the World Wide Web. An intranet is for access and use by employees or members of an organization and is not open to the public.)

Many organizations use slideshows to present information and training over an intranet. Suppose a company is modifying its benefits plan. Rather than posting several pages of text, the company could post slides that highlight the key parts of the new plan. Printed documents with more details might also be made available to employees.

As with slides that are developed for an oral presentation, effective slides for an intranet have a unifying design or theme; a title; short bullet points of text; and animation, pictures, or other graphics to present a message. Recorded speech giving more information related to each slide may be part of the file as well.

Giving Team Presentations

Teams are used extensively in businesses and other organizations. Team presentations require certain different skills and offer some benefits that a single presenter does not have. Some of these benefits include the following:

- Having two or more people deliver parts of the presentation can increase and hold the attention of the audience.

- Having more than one speaker brings greater experience and expertise to the presentation.

- If the audience works in small groups on a particular assignment, team members are available to mingle with the groups and provide expertise and leadership.

- One presenter can record comments or questions from the audience while another speaks.

Select the Team

Having the right combination of people on a team can make the team more effective. In some cases, you may be assigned to the team and have no input on who the other members will be. In other cases, you may be able to choose the people on the team. What should you consider when assembling a team? Here are a few suggestions to consider:

- What are the strengths and weaknesses of each person?

- What does the strength of each person add to the strength of the team?

- Do the team members collectively have a breadth of knowledge about the topic?

- What particular knowledge does each individual have? Do individual team members have the technical knowledge needed for the presentation?

- What people skills does each presenter possess? For example, is the person a team player? An effective communicator? A good listener?

A presentation team needs a strong leader who can make decisions and motivate the team. In some cases, the team may select its leader after a team discussion about the strengths and weaknesses of the group. Team members need to be willing to engage in this discussion non defensively. If the team is going to work together for a longer period of time, management may appoint the leader. If the

People @ Work

MARKETING MANAGER

A marketing manager develops plans and strategies for how a company will promote and sell its products or services. Marketing managers may direct or do research on competing products, the target market (consumers or other businesses), and current and predicted business conditions. They may plan or conduct surveys of customers to determine customer satisfaction with current products and customer wants or needs for future products. They may help estimate the expected demand for a product so that the company can produce the right amount of the product.

Marketing managers typically develop and give presentations to company managers, business partners, and customers. If you are an administrative professional who works with a marketing team, you may be asked to help do research and develop these presentations. If you work in another area of the company, you may be asked to provide information on products or services to the marketing team.

presentation will be delivered to an external group, the person who was initially contacted by the external group may be the leader. That person can assemble a team with members she or he chooses.

Work Together for Success

Each team member and the team collectively should know exactly what the purpose of the presentation(s) will be. The team leader should facilitate this session. Questions that need to be asked and answered are: What do you want the audience to know or do as a result of the presentation? What is the best way to convey the message?

Identify duties for each team member related to planning, research, writing, developing visual aids, and presenting. Set deadlines for when each task should be completed and times for when the team will meet to work or rehearse the presentation. When deciding who will be responsible for various duties, consider each team member's area of expertise, presentation style and skill, and understanding of the audience.

Not all team members need to speak during the presentation, but everyone should be present and available to answer questions and help during small group activities. All members should review the feedback and discuss ways to improve.

IMAGE COPYRIGHT MARCIN BALCERZAK 2009. USED UNDER LICENSE FROM SHUTTERSTOCK.COM

RYAN MCVAY/GETTY IMAGES

Be aware of nonverbal cues during a presentation.

Key Terms

cliché

credentials

credible

demographics

electronic whiteboard

interactive whiteboard

intranet

visual aid

Summary

■ As an administrative professional, your job may include helping to develop or deliver presentations. Developing your presentation skills is important for your professional growth.

■ Many people experience presentation anxiety, commonly called stage fright. With proper planning and practice, you can develop effective presentation skills and overcome presentation anxiety.

■ When planning a presentation, identify the goal of the presentation; consider the audience, the time and length of the presentation, and the location; and research the topic if needed.

■ When writing a presentation, organize the material using a list or outline, develop an opening, create a strong message for the body, and write an effective closing.

■ Using visual aids, such as posters, whiteboards, and electronic slides, can increase the amount of information the listeners remember from the presentation.

■ Rehearse your presentation several times using your visual aids and in the room where you will present if possible.

■ When delivering a presentation, focus on sharing your message with the listeners. Use the last couple of minutes of the session to repeat the main points or action you want the audience to remember as they leave the presentation.

■ Teams are used extensively in businesses and other organizations. Team members should agree on the purpose of the presentation and work together to plan, research, write, and deliver the presentation.

Bookmark It. *For convenient access to activities, links, and valuable career resources for administrative professionals, visit the companion website for this text:*

www.cengage.com/officetech/fultoncalkins

Planning Notes

Learning Objectives

1. Plan, research, and write presentations.

2. Develop visual aids for presentations and meetings.

3. Practice and deliver effective presentations.

21st Century Skills
INNOVATION

Activities 1, 3, 4, 5, 6, 7

21st Century Skills
TECHNOLOGY

Activities 2, 10, 11

21st Century Skills
CAREER

Activities 8, 9

Discussion Questions

1. Why does an administrative professional need to develop presentation skills?

2. What steps are involved in planning a presentation?

3. Describe ways to organize information for a presentation.

4. What are some options you might use as an opening for a presentation? What points should you consider when selecting one of these options?

5. What two important points should you keep in mind when writing the body of a presentation?

6. During the question-and-answer part of a presentation, why should you repeat the question before answering it?

7. Is memorizing an entire 20-minute presentation and reciting it from memory a good way to present? Why or why not?

8. What are two benefits of giving a team presentation rather than an individual presentation?

Critical Thinking

Presentation objective   You are a member of a local chapter of IAAP. You have been asked to speak at the national meeting of IAAP, which will be held in Boston this year. Your speech is not a keynote; you will be presenting at a session on the first afternoon of the conference from 2:00 p.m. to 2:40 p.m. You have been given the prerogative of choosing your own topic and whether or not you will present as an individual or make it a team effort. The theme of the conference is Promoting Professional Growth. You decide you will do a team presentation; there are two additional people within your chapter who have agreed to present with you. (Work with two of your classmates on this project.)

As a team, list the steps that you will need to take to select a topic and prepare the presentation. Select a topic and write an objective statement for the presentation. Develop an introduction for each person on the team.

Build Workplace Skills

1. **Team presentation**   Do further planning, including needed research, to develop the team presentation on the topic you selected in the Critical Thinking activity. As a team, develop a strong opening for the presentation. Create an outline for the presentation body and write the body and closing for the presentation. Develop a list of five questions that might be asked during a question-and-answer session and write answers for each question. (Learning Objective 1)

2. **Visual aids**   Continue to develop your team presentation. Identify visual aids that will be helpful in giving the presentation. As a team, create the visual aids. Create a handout to accompany the presentation. The handout can be a printout of slides with space for taking notes or a sheet with additional details or related information. (Learning Objective 2)

3. **Deliver a presentation**   Identify which part of the presentation will be delivered by each team member. Rehearse the team presentation, using the visual aids you created earlier. Deliver the presentation to your class or a group of classmates. As a team, write an evaluation of the presentation and the team's delivery, noting strong points and weak points that you should try to improve for future presentations. (Learning Objective 3)

4. **Individual presentation**   Now that you have gained confidence from taking part in a team presentation, you will give an individual presentation. Your goal is to inform the audience (your classmates) or persuade them to take some action. Select a topic related to business or a current event. Write a goal statement and plan the presentation. The presentation should last about 15 minutes, including a few minutes for questions and answers. Develop a creative opening, write a strong message for the presentation body, and create an effective closing. Write questions that you think the audience members might ask and answers to the questions. Create appropriate visual aids. Rehearse the presentation several times and deliver it to the class or a group of classmates. Evaluate the presentation and your delivery, noting strong points and weak points that you should try to improve for future presentations. (Learning Objectives 1, 2, 3)

Communicate Clearly

5. **Editing exercise**   Open the *Word* file CH08 Bank E-mail from the data files. Edit the message to correct errors in grammar, spelling, punctuation, capitalization, number usage, and word usage.

6. **IAAP Presentation**   You recently gave a presentation on "Ethics in the Office" at a local meeting of IAAP. The goals of the presentation were to inform listeners about this important topic and to persuade them to use ethical practices. The president of the IAAP chapter has asked you to provide the main points of your talk in an electronic slide show that can be posted online for IAAP members who were not able to attend your presentation.

   • Do research on the topic using the Internet and other resources.

   • Write an outline of the main points and the details you will include in the slides.

   • Create a *PowerPoint* slide show to include a title slide and at least nine additional slides. Use appropriate photos, pictures, or graphics and animation for the slides. For each slide except the title slide, record a voice file and attach it to the slide so users can hear your comments. The voice file for each slide should be about one to two minutes in length. (Learning Objectives 1 and 2)

7. **Feedback form**   As you waited for your dentist appointment recently, you wrote a few notes about developing a form to request feedback from the listeners at your next presentation. Open the *Word* file CH08 Feedback from the data files. Review the notes in this file. Think of additional questions or information you might want to include on the form. Create and print an attractive form that you can use to get feedback from the audience when you give a presentation.

Develop Relationships

8. **Unappreciative coworker**   You work as an administrative assistant for the marketing team. You create the visual aids, such as posters and slides, for most of the presentations. Three team members appreciate your work and give you credit for creating the visual aids. Gloria, however, never acknowledges your contributions. This situation makes you feel a bit resentful toward Gloria. You think that your work should be acknowledged. Sometimes Gloria seems to notice that you are upset, but she does not seem to connect her actions

Planning Notes

Planning Notes

with your negative feelings. Should you discuss your feelings with Gloria? What would you say to her about this situation? You want to improve your working relationship with her and be able to feel good about being part of the team.

9. **Incorrect data**   You work as an administrative assistant at Jackson Industries. One of your duties is reporting production numbers for the company's major products to Mr. Lui every Friday. He uses the information in a report to managers on the following Monday afternoon. Last Friday, you almost forgot to send the data to Mr. Lui because you were busy preparing slides that your supervisor requested. Just before you left for the day, you sent an e-mail message to Mr. Lui with the data in an attached file. All weekend, you had a nagging feeling that you forgot something. Now, back at work on Monday morning, you decide to verify that your e-mail message to Mr. Lui was sent from your outbox. When you view the message, you realize what has been bothering you. The file you attached contains data for two weeks ago, not the numbers for last week. How should you handle this situation? What steps should you take to correct your error? What will you say to Mr. Lui?

Use Technology

10. **Green practices presentation**   In an activity in Chapter 7, your manager, Ms. Adderley, asked you to do some research and write a short report about ways an office can implement green practices. The report also recommends ways that your office can "go green." Ms. Adderley is pleased with your report and has asked you to present your recommendations at the next staff meeting. Create slides that you can use when presenting the information from the report. Include a slide that gives a title for the presentation and your name. Include at least five slides that emphasize points from the report. Include photos, clip art, or other graphics on at least two of the slides. Use animation for the bullet items on the slides. Select a design theme or template that is appropriate for the topic and use it for all the slides. (Learning Objective 2)

11. **Intranet pages**   Ms. Adderley wants staff members who cannot attend a staff meeting to be able to view your "go green" recommendations on the company intranet. Revise the slideshow in activity 10 for the intranet. Viewers will not have your comments about the slides as did the people attending the meeting. Be creative in editing the slides to tell a complete message while still using brief bullet points and graphics. You may need to add slides to present all the information without having too much text on any slides. Save your edited file as a single-file web page. View the file in a browser program, such as *Internet Explorer*. Revise the slides again, if needed, to adjust them for viewing in the browser.

Above and Beyond

IAAP membership   As an administrative professional, you may want to join a professional organization such as IAAP. Belonging to a professional organization can help you stay abreast of changes in your career field and can offer other opportunities for professional growth. Use an Internet search engine to find the website for IAAP. Access and review the site; then answer the following questions:

1. What is the mission of IAAP?

2. How many members and chapters does IAAP have?

3. What types of membership are available in IAAP?

4. What are some of the benefits of membership in IAAP?

Administrative Assistant

Seeking an administrative assistant with excellent communication and technology skills. Job duties include:

- Handling telephone and e-mail communications
- Working collaboratively with coworkers and managers
- Processing and sharing data via a company intranet and an extranet
- Doing research using the Internet

Do I qualify?

© MARK WRAGG, ISTOCK

CHAPTER

9

Handling Telecommunications

Telecommunication Tools

Telecommunications is the transmission of electronic information (text, data, voice, video, and images) from one location to another. Having accurate and timely information—about sales, expenses, products, suppliers, customers, employees, investors, and so forth—is essential for businesses that want to stay competitive in today's global economy.

Telecommunication tools make sharing this information fast and affordable. As an administrative professional, many of your daily tasks will involve gathering data, processing data into usable information, and then sharing the information with your supervisor, coworkers, suppliers, and customers. You will use telecommunication tools, such as a telephone, a computer, a local area network, and the Internet, to help you complete these tasks.

Learning Objectives

1. Explain the value of telecommunication tools.

2. Describe types of networks used for telecommunications.

3. Describe equipment and effective techniques for telephone communication.

4. Use workplace collaboration tools.

5. Identify security threats and solutions for protecting computer data.

Networks for Telecommunications

Changes continue to take place in telecommunication technologies. A major change has been the movement from traditional telephone networks developed to transmit only voice messages to converged networks capable of both voice and data transmissions. Converged networks use Internet protocols to transmit data and allow multiple users to share the same path or connection. For this reason, they are also called IP (Internet protocol) networks.

When you place a telephone call, send an e-mail message, or do research on the Internet, you are using a telecommunication network. A network is two or more telephones, computers, or other devices connected for purposes of communicating and sharing resources. Sometimes these communications occur within an organization's private network; other times they occur globally over the Internet or through standard phone lines. Networks facilitate sharing information. When using a network, any authorized user can access data stored on other computers connected to the network. For example, many businesses store product information on an internal network so that employees in different departments can access the information.

Local Area Networks

A **local area network (LAN)** covers a small geographical area and links computers, printers, and other devices within an office, a building, or several nearby buildings. LANs are common in the workplace. One benefit of a LAN is that employees can share resources, such as a printer. The network administrator can manage the installation of software for all employees and the backup of files stored on the file servers (network storage). Fast electronic messages can be sent between users on the network.

Metropolitan and Wide Area Networks

A network that links computers and other devices across a city or region is called a **metropolitan area network (MAN)**. A college or university network that links several city or regional campuses is an example of a MAN. A network that connects

LAN users can share network resources, such as a printer.

computers and other devices over the largest geographical area—perhaps hundreds of thousands of miles—is a **wide area network (WAN)**. International businesses can link their offices around the world with private WANs. The largest public WAN is the Internet.

The Internet

The Internet is a worldwide public computer network that connects private networks. The Internet has revolutionized the way people communicate and the way business is conducted. Organizations around the world use the Internet to communicate with vendors and customers, to sell their products and services, and to provide customer support after the sale. According to the Internet World Stats website, more than 1.5 billion people worldwide use the Internet.[1]

The World Wide Web (web) is a part of the Internet that consists of computers called web servers. Web servers store multimedia documents called web pages that can contain text, graphics, video, audio, and links to other web pages. The application software used to access and view web pages is called a web browser. *Internet Explorer®* and *Firefox®* are popular web browsers.

Telecommunication Pipelines

The information transmitted by telecommunication systems travels through a variety of electronic

---

1 Internet World Stats, "World Internet Usage and Population Statistics," September 30, 2009, http://www.internetworldstats.com/stats.htm (accessed April 1, 2010).

channels called pipelines. Telecommunication pipelines connect people and machines through traditional telephone lines as well as through analog dial-up connections, cables, digital subscriber lines, satellites, wireless communications, and fiber-optic cables. Depending on whom you call, the location of the website you visit, or the address to which you send an e-mail message, the route that the information travels can vary widely. You should be aware of the pipeline you use for communications at work and how the type of pipeline may affect communication speeds.

Analog Dial-Up   Early telecommunications were transmitted via analog dial-up connections using modems. A **modem** is a device that converts the digital signal from a computer to an analog signal that can

Intranets and Extranets

An intranet is a private network that uses web pages and other web technologies. It looks and operates much like pages on the World Wide Web. An intranet is accessible only by an organization's employees through their LAN. Intranets are used to share information that needs to be quickly and easily disseminated, such as company policies and in-house newsletters. Individual departments and groups use the intranet to share and revise documents.

An extranet also uses web technologies but is available to certain individuals, companies, and others outside an organization. Access to an extranet is controlled by usernames and passwords. These same usernames and passwords also control what users can see and do on the extranet. An extranet may be used by financial institutions to provide clients with account information and performance reports; by health institutions to access medical records; or by businesses to allow stockholders to view financial information.

be transmitted through an ordinary phone line. This type of connection can be used to access the Internet. However, of the pipelines available for transmitting information, analog dial-up is the slowest. Some people continue to use this pipeline because it is less expensive or because faster connection methods are not available in the area at a reasonable cost.

Cable   Cable is a pipeline that connects computers to a coaxial cable to provide voice and data transmission. You are probably familiar with the coaxial cable that provides access to hundreds of channels on a television set. Because the data-carrying capacity on this network is much higher than required for a television signal, the excess capacity is commonly used to provide Internet access. The Internet service provided via coaxial cable is often referred to as broadband access. **Broadband** is a form of digital data transmission that uses a wide range of frequencies to achieve high-speed and high-capacity transmissions.

When compared to dial-up connections, cable provides faster access to data. Another advantage is that a cable modem provides a continuous connection. The greatest drawback to a cable connection is a limited amount of bandwidth that is provided by each cable line. If large numbers of users are accessing the cable at the same time, Internet connection speeds can be slow. Also, cable services are not available in some rural areas.

Digital Subscriber Line (DSL)   A digital subscriber line (DSL) is a technology that transmits and receives digital data over existing telephone lines. Because DSL systems use broadband access, the download and access times are similar to those of cable access. DSL connections are typically much faster than analog dial-up connections. With DSL the user can access the Internet and make voice calls at the same time with a continuous connection. Because DSL subscribers do not share bandwidth, access speed remains constant and is not affected by the number of users. As with cable systems, DSL is not available in some areas.

Satellite   Much of today's communication is transmitted around the globe by satellite. A satellite is a device that orbits the Earth and relays signals between telecommunication stations. Satellite

Fiber Optic Cable

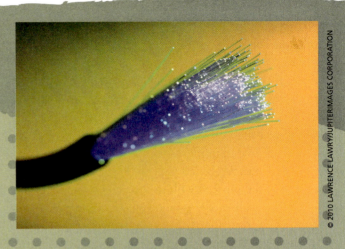

© 2010 LAWRENCE LAWRY/JUPITERIMAGES CORPORATION

Many newly installed telephone lines are equipped with fiber optic cables. A fiber optic cable consists of hundreds or thousands of glass threads or fibers. Each fiber, about the diameter of a human hair, is capable of transmitting large amounts of information.

Fiber optic technology has several advantages over other transmission methods. Fiber optic cables are thinner and lighter than metal wires and are less susceptible to signal interference. Fiber optic cables have a much greater bandwidth than cable, DSL, or satellite can provide. Also, data can be transmitted digitally (the natural form for computer data), which makes it a perfect technology for telecommunications. Although it will take time before fiber optic cables are available everywhere, telephone companies are steadily replacing traditional telephone lines with fiber optic cables.

modems are used to transmit and receive data through a satellite dish. Satellite communication has been around for many years and has recently become a high-speed Internet solution available to nearly everyone in the United States.

One of the disadvantages of cable and DSL is that broadband pipelines are not available in certain areas of the country, particularly in rural areas. Satellite connections have the advantage of being available for use in rural areas. Broadband by satellite allows users to access the Internet, download files in seconds, enjoy web music and video, and receive voice calls. However, because dish installation in North America requires an unobstructed view of the southern sky, performance might degrade or stop during very heavy rain or snowstorms.

Wireless Connections Wireless communication is a transfer of information via radio waves or microwaves without the use of a physical connection. Wireless technology allows users to eliminate the cords associated with keyboards or other computer peripherals, connect a smartphone to an earpiece, or send a print job from a notebook computer to a printer.

Bluetooth is the name given to a technology that uses short-range radio signals to connect and exchange information between devices such as mobile phones, computers, printers, and digital cameras. Bluetooth technology has a limited transmission range of 3 to 300 feet, but because the devices use radio signals, they do not have to be in line of sight of each other.

Wi-Fi, or wireless fidelity, is a medium-range radio transmission technology. It can be used to create an entirely wireless network in a home or office as well as to add wireless capabilities to an existing wired network. Wi-Fi is designed for medium-range data transfers, which typically are described as 300 to 1,000 feet.

If you have recently been in an airport, a coffee shop, a library, or a hotel, you probably have been in the middle of a Wi-Fi hotspot. A **hotspot** is a public location that offers network access via Wi-Fi. For example, some hotels offer wireless capabilities through hotspots in common areas of the hotel. Colleges typically have hotspots on campus to allow students to connect wirelessly to the campus network. Some public hotspots can be accessed for free. Others charge a fee by the minute or the hour. WeFi is a website that helps users find and connect to Wi-Fi hotspots. Some cities provide maps of hotspots in the area.

Wireless technologies continue to be developed and enhanced. For example, cities are developing

Many public locations provide network access through hotspots.

municipal wireless networks to enable fire and police departments to do parts of their jobs remotely. Other technologies, including WiMax (long-range wireless broadband), have been designed to provide faster speeds and services for distances of up to 30 miles.

Telephone Communication

You will find a variety of telephone equipment in the workplace, including standard phone sets, cordless sets, conference call speakers, and headsets to use with computers and software. Common features on business phone sets include buttons for answering multiple phone lines, built-in speaker phones, displays to view caller identification information, and programmable buttons for setting up call management features. Popular call management features include call forwarding, call waiting, holding, conferencing, redialing, transferring, and speed dialing.

Call Management Skills

As an administrative professional, you will communicate by phone daily with many people without ever seeing or meeting them. Regardless of the calling technology you use, remember that good human relations skills are crucial to making a positive impression of you and your company. Never answer the phone in a curt or rude manner. Instead, use a pleasant tone and let the caller know you are interested in her or him. Be careful to use correct English (not slang) and word pronunciation.

Callers appreciate being recognized and called by name. Responding with "Yes, Mr. Bradshaw. I will be happy to get the information" indicates to the caller that you know who he is and that you care about him.

Handle Problem Calls Carefully   Most callers are pleasant, especially if you are courteous to them. Occasionally you may have a caller who has had a difficult day or for some other reason is unhappy. Sometimes you can diffuse a caller's anger simply by taking the time to listen to his or her story. Remember that the caller is not angry with you, but rather with a situation or an event. Do not become emotionally involved in the situation.

Once you have listened to the caller's story, try to help the person solve the problem. This approach may mean that you suggest a solution or that you tell the person you will have someone who can solve the problem return the call. Do not put the person on hold or mishandle the call by transferring it to an individual who cannot help. Such actions merely make the caller angrier.

From time to time, you may answer a call for your supervisor and the caller may refuse to give you her or his name. You should discuss this possibility with your supervisor and understand exactly what you are expected to do in such a situation. However, if you are unsure what to do, put the caller on hold and explain the situation to your supervisor. He or she can then decide whether or not to speak to the caller.

Do Not Discriminate   Have you ever found yourself being nicer over the telephone to the president of your company than to a caller you do not know? If the answer is yes, make a point of being friendly before you know who is on the other end of the line. Try saying to yourself, "A friend is calling" before answering the phone. Remember that all assistants are not female and all executives are not male. If you answer the telephone and hear a woman's voice, do not assume she is an assistant and ask to speak to her supervisor. When addressing anyone, use terms that show respect. Do not refer to a woman as a girl or a young lady or use any other term that can sound gender-biased. Do not refer to a man as a boy or a guy.

Incoming Calls

When your telephone rings, answer promptly—on the first ring if possible and certainly by the third ring. You may lose a potential customer if you are slow in answering the telephone.

Most businesses and supervisors have specific procedures for answering the telephone. In large businesses, calls are often routed first to a person whose job it is to greet telephone or in-person visitors. This person identifies the company and then routes the incoming call to the appropriate party, which may be a supervisor's administrative professional. For example, if the target of the call is Ms. Diaz, you might answer her line as "Ms. Diaz's office, Dana Wilson." If you are the target of the call, you might answer, "Good morning. Dana Wilson. How may I help you?" You can include the company name before your name if you answer outside calls that are not forwarded by a receptionist.

Transfer Calls Carefully
Make certain you know how to transfer calls on your telephone system. Callers dislike being told they are going to be transferred and then getting disconnected. Before you transfer a call, explain to the caller why it must be transferred. Make sure the caller is willing to be transferred. For example, you may say, "Ms. Wong is out, but James Gonzales can give you the information. May I transfer you to Mr. Gonzales?"

If it is not against company policy, you may also want to give the caller the complete number or the extension of the person the caller is trying to reach in case the transfer is not completed. The caller can then call the person without having to call you again. (Some organizations have a policy against giving company phone numbers or extensions to outside callers. If your job involves taking outside calls, ask your supervisor what the policy is.)

Place Calls on Hold
A caller may sometimes request information that you do not have at hand. You may need to check with someone else or go to your files to get the information. You may be answering your supervisor's line because she or he is not available to take a call. If you must place the caller on hold until your supervisor is available or until you retrieve the necessary information, do so only with the caller's permission.

Do not assume that a caller is willing to be placed on hold. You may say, "I need to pull the information from my files. Would you like to hold for a moment while I get it, or shall I call you back?" or "Mr. O'Malley is on another call. Would you like to hold?"

If the caller agrees to hold, try to get back to him or her as soon as possible. When you return to the line, let the caller know you are back by saying, "Thank you for waiting." If there is a delay in responding to the call, return to the line and ask whether the caller wants to continue to hold or leave a message. Apologize for the length of time it is taking to complete the call. If the caller leaves a message, make certain that the message is delivered promptly.

Communicating @Work

Be discreet when you must tell a caller that your supervisor is unavailable. Explain that your supervisor cannot answer her or his phone—but do not say too much. You may say, "Ms. Portosky is away from the office now. I expect her back in approximately an hour. May I have her call you when she returns?"

Never say, "Ms. Portosky is not here yet" (at 10 a.m.), "She's gone for the day" (at 2 p.m.), or "She's out sick" (at any time of day). A good rule to remember is to be helpful about when your supervisor is returning without specifying where the supervisor is or what he or she may be doing.

Writing @Work

When answering the telephone for another person, write complete and accurate messages. Messages may be created in word processing software and printed or attached to an e-mail for the recipient. Messages may also be recorded manually using paper message pads. When writing a message, be careful to include all the needed information as listed below. Repeat the message to the caller so you can be certain it is accurate.

↗ The caller's name spelled correctly (Ask the caller to spell her or his name if you are not certain how it is spelled.)

↗ Company name

↗ Telephone number (with area code)

↗ Time of call

↗ Exact message text

©ISTOCK

Handle Multiple Calls   You may be responsible for answering more than one phone line. If so, at times you will be answering a call on one line when another line rings. When this happens, you must remember that the caller on the second line does not know you are already on the phone. The caller is expecting to get an answer immediately. Excuse yourself politely by saying to the first caller, "May I place you on hold for a moment? I must answer another line." If the second call is going to take a while, ask the caller for a number so you can call back as soon as you finish the first call. Then go back to the first caller with "Thank you for wait-

ing." Your responsibility is to handle all calls as quickly and efficiently as possible.

Screen Calls as Instructed   Some supervisors have one telephone number that is published for callers and another private number that is not published. The unpublished number is often used to make outgoing calls or may be given out to close friends or family members.

An administrative professional is usually expected to screen incoming calls from the published number. For example, when the supervisor receives a call, an administrative professional is expected to determine who is calling and why and then route to others those calls that the supervisor will not take, such as unsolicited sales calls. If someone else in your company can handle the call, transfer it to that person after requesting permission from the caller. If no one is available to take the call, let the person know courteously that your employer is not interested. One response might be, "I appreciate the information; however, Ms. Tikhonov is not interested in pursuing the matter at the present time."

Be tactful when asking a caller questions. Avoid blunt questions such as "Who is calling?" that may offend the caller. Instead, say, "May I tell Ms. Tikhonov who is calling?" or "When Ms. Tikhonov returns, may I tell her who called?"

If your supervisor is not in or cannot take the call for some reason, ask about the nature of the call so you can handle it or refer it to someone else. For example, you may say, "If you tell me the nature of your call, perhaps I can help you or refer you to someone who can."

Outgoing Calls

As an administrative professional, you may be responsible for placing calls for your supervisor; certainly you will make your own business calls. Professional handling of outgoing calls is just as important as for incoming calls.

Plan Your Call   Having a list of frequently called numbers can save time when placing calls. Store the numbers on your phone system or your personal information management software. If you use your cell phone for work, store the numbers there too.

Answer incoming calls promptly, using a friendly tone of voice.

Take a few minutes to plan a call before you make it. Know the purpose of the call and what you intend to say. Be prepared to speak with someone—and also be prepared to leave a voice message. Your call may be answered first by a receptionist or administrative assistant. Always identify yourself and your company and be prepared to state the purpose of your call clearly and concisely. For example, you may say, "This is Tom Lange of Alvarez Associates. I'm calling to verify Mr. Poinar's attendance at the breakfast meeting tomorrow at 7 a.m. at the Executive Club."

If you are transferred to someone else, be prepared to restate the purpose of your call. Although you may exchange pleasantries, don't forget that the

main purpose is to get your message across without wasting the recipient's time.

Note the Time Zone   Be aware of time zone differences when planning calls. You may place business calls to places all around the country or the world. In the United States, the time zones are Eastern, Central, Mountain, and Pacific.

The Official U.S. Time website, shown in Figure 9-1, gives quick access to the current time in U.S. time zones. The World Clock website gives times for locations around the world. The companion website for the textbook has links to these sites.

Voice Mail

Voice mail or voice messaging is an efficient method of managing incoming calls when the call recipients are unavailable. The voice mail feature plays a recorded announcement and records voice messages. Most workplace telephone systems today use voice mail for inside calls between employees and for calls from outside the company.

Voice messages are delivered to a call recipient's voice mail box, from which they can be retrieved, forwarded, and erased. A voice mail box is generally set up with a private access code that permits the owner to retrieve recorded messages. This

Figure 9-1 The Official U.S. Time Website

prevents anyone else from listening to and forwarding or erasing messages.

A voice mail box owner usually accesses her or his voice mail box from a phone inside the workplace. Many voice mail systems also permit mail box access from a phone outside the workplace. Some voice mail systems provide automatic notification that messages are waiting for the mail box owner via his or her PDA, cell phone, or pager. Many voice mail systems also support message broadcasting, or sending the same message to multiple voice mail boxes. Because some callers may not want to leave voice mail messages, some voice mail systems provide a return-to-operator feature that allows callers to talk with a person.

The proper use of voice mail in the workplace increases productivity and saves time and money. For example:

- Workers can leave a voice message instead of placing repeated calls to someone who is not available.

- Voice messages are to the point, eliminating extraneous conversation.

- Business travelers can communicate with the workplace at any time.

- Message delivery speed can be increased even between different time zones because a voice message can be left at any time of the day or night.

Caller Instructions
As an administrative professional, you may be assigned the task of setting up your telephone system's voice mail announcement—the first message a caller may hear when calling your company.

- Begin by identifying the company.

- If your voice mail system has multiple levels of call routing, give callers no more than four options. Callers strongly dislike trying to follow a maze of instructions to record their messages.

- Keep caller instructions short—under 15 seconds if possible.

- Provide the most important information or answer the most frequently asked questions first.

- When recording step-by-step instructions, tell callers exactly what you want them to do first—then explain what action to take. For example, you may say, "To transfer your call to our receptionist, press zero."

- Be certain your instructions tell the caller how to reach a person. Callers dislike getting lost in a voice message system that never allows them to speak to a person.

Your individual voice mail outgoing message is very important as it can create either a favorable or an unfavorable impression on the caller. A well-crafted announcement succinctly provides key information, such as your name, in-office or out-of-office information, and whom to contact if the call is urgent. The sound and tone of your voice message greeting should make a favorable impression. When recording your outgoing message, vary your vocal tone; do not talk in a monotone. When recording your message, try to eliminate background noise that could interfere with your message.

Leaving a Message
When leaving a voice message, make the message short and to the point. Include your name and company, a number where you can be reached, and a brief statement of the purpose of the call. Ask for a return call if that is what you want. Do not include sensitive or confidential information in a voice message.

IP Telephony

Voice over Internet Protocol (VoIP), also called IP telephony (te-LEF-uh-nee), is changing voice communication drastically. **IP telephony** is transmitting voice over a private IP network or a public IP network such as the Internet. The primary advantage of IP telephony is reduced cost. Sending and receiving voice messages over the Internet or a private network eliminates long-distance phone charges. Businesses can also reduce service and maintenance costs by supporting just one network—the IP network—instead of operating separate networks for data and voice. Other IP telephony advantages include the following:

- Users are not tied to one area code and may even be given a choice of area codes by their service provider.

- There is no need to transfer phone service when moving to new office space or a new city.

- Voice mail can be routed to a computer's electronic mailbox.

■ Phone numbers kept in a user's personal information management (PIM) software can be dialed from a computer.

There are some disadvantages to IP telephony. While IP telephony voice quality is continuing to improve, in some circumstances it may not be equal to voice quality on a standard phone line. A high-speed Internet connection is required, and connection reliability depends on an Internet service provider's reliability.

Mobile Phones

Mobile phones, also called cell phones, are popular as business and personal tools because they allow communications in many places outside the office or home. Many mobile phones also support the use of instant messaging and voice message services. Smartphones provide users with even more capabilities than regular mobile phones.

Smartphones A **smartphone** is a full-featured mobile phone that has many of the functions of a handheld computer, including a keyboard (on-screen or physical). In addition to the typical telephone features, smartphones may include a digital camera, e-mail software, Internet access, scheduling software, and contact management software. Additional features such as navigation software and the ability to read document files may be included. Some smartphones allow users to record video and download electronic music files. Many accessories are available for smartphones, including detachable speakers, printers, and headphones.

Mobile Phone Etiquette Cell phones are used by many businesspeople. Interrupting your interaction with others—clients, vendors, or coworkers—to answer your cell phone is discourteous. Taking these calls gives the impression that you have something more important to do than what you are currently doing. Be courteous by turning your business cell phone to silent mode when working with others. If you are expecting an urgent call on your business cell phone, be sure the client, vendor, or coworker with whom you are working understands this before you answer the call. You may say, "We may be interrupted by a call I must take, but I promise to be as quick as possible." If the call comes through, excuse yourself and keep the conversation as brief as possible.

Do not make or accept personal cell phone calls during business hours unless you have permission from your supervisor. When you are in a meeting, do not use your phone to read or send e-mail or text messages or play games. The people in the room with you deserve your full attention. They will notice and probably be offended if your eyes stray to your phone.

Consider privacy issues and the needs of others when using your phone in a public place or an open work area. Follow these guidelines to show your respect for others:

■ Use discretion when discussing private matters or sensitive topics that may be overheard by others.

■ Keep your voice low so as not to disturb others around you.

■ Turn off your cell phone or use the silent alert setting in one-on-one interactions and during meetings, classes, and other public events.

Smartphones combine the features of a mobile phone and a handheld computer.

© COURTESY RESEARCH IN MOTION

People @Work

COMPUTER SUPPORT SPECIALIST

Companies rely on their computers and networks to provide and store data for company operations. A computer support specialist helps keep the company's computers and networks running smoothly. This person may install software on a network, troubleshoot problems with users' computers, and run security checks. Upgrading the network and installing new equipment are also part of a computer support specialist's duties. As an administrative professional, you may need to ask for help from a computer support specialist to solve problems you are having with your computer or network.

IMAGE COPYRIGHT AMY WALTERS 2009. USED UNDER LICENSE FROM SHUTTERSTOCK.COM

- Make and answer calls only when absolutely necessary in public places such as restaurants and elevators. Whenever possible, move to a more private area before you make or answer a call.

- Be aware of your surroundings when walking and talking on your phone.

Workplace Collaboration Tools

As an administrative professional, you will spend many hours collaborating with others to accomplish a variety of tasks, such as creating and revising documents. Software productivity suites contain basic collaboration tools that allow you to schedule, host, and participate in electronic meetings and send and receive e-mail. Productivity suites also contain features to route documents across an IP network to coworkers who can then review, revise, and return them.

IP networks enable several other useful electronic collaboration tools—e-mail, shared workspaces, weblogs, wikis, and web conferencing—that are becoming essential for collaboration in the modern workplace. (You can read about weblogs and wikis on page 156.) Network and web-based software used for workplace collaboration is commonly called groupware. Groupware examples include *IBM Lotus Notes®, Microsoft SharePoint® Services, Novell GroupWise®,* and *EMC Documentum eRoom®.*

Electronic Mail

The most popular workplace collaboration tool is e-mail—electronic text messages sent from one computer to another over an IP network. E-mail is an indispensable tool for workplace communication because e-mail messages:

- Can be composed, sent, and delivered in minutes no matter the destination.

- Are sent when convenient to the sender and read when convenient to the recipient.

- Can be used to transfer files across the network as e-mail attachments.

- Can be accessed from a number of locations and devices.

- Are a low-cost method of communicating.

- Can be saved as a permanent record of a business activity.

IMAGE COPYRIGHT PERKUS 2009. USED UNDER LICENSE FROM SHUTTERSTOCK.COM

Technology @Work

Employees sometimes believe it is acceptable to use a workplace computer after the workday has ended for personal use or even to take a few minutes during the day to send an e-mail to a friend or shop on the Internet. It is not okay to do so without permission. Many businesses publish computer and Internet use policies. However, never assume that the absence of a policy regarding acceptable computer and Internet usage gives you the right to do as you please. It is unethical to use your workplace computer to:

↗ Access your company's data for non–work-related purposes.

↗ Log into the network using a coworker's username and password without the person's permission.

↗ Allow someone else to use your password and username to access data without authorization.

↗ Access a coworker's electronic files to read, edit, or delete them.

↗ Send racist, sexist, or offensive messages and attachments to anyone.

Unless you have permission to do so, you should not send personal e-mail, use the web for personal shopping or entertainment, or download non–work-related files.

To receive e-mail, you must have an e-mail address, an electronic mailbox, and a computer to access the network. An e-mail address has three parts: a name or nickname that identifies the recipient, the @ sign, and a host name. The host name is the identifying name of the account that hosts the electronic mailbox. Mark.Jenkins@hostname.net is an example of an e-mail address. To access the e-mail messages in an electronic mailbox, you can use e-mail software or web mail.

Web Mail Another way to access e-mail is with a web browser. Popular web-based e-mail services include Yahoo!® Mail, EarthLink® Web Mail, and MSN Hotmail®. An advantage of web-based e-mail is its portability. You can access a web-based e-mail account from any computer that has a web browser and Internet connection.

E-mail Use Policies E-mail is a powerful business tool for increased collaboration between coworkers and for communicating with clients, vendors, investors, and others. But e-mail abuse also poses potential problems for a business.

Sending personal e-mails from workplace computers reduces employee productivity. Forwarding jokes, junk mail, and chain letters to others stresses the e-mail system and reduces productivity. Offensive e-mail content can place a company at risk for charges of workplace harassment. Many businesses protect themselves from these risks by using network software to monitor their employees' e-mail.

Another way to protect against e-mail abuse is a clearly stated and strongly enforced company-wide e-mail policy. Every business should have a formal e-mail policy that each employee agrees to follow. The policy should outline rules for e-mail use, tell employees what types of e-mails to save and file as company records, and remind employees that e-mail is not private and may be reviewed by company personnel.

Instant Messaging

An **instant message** is an electronic message sent and received by two or more people who are connected to a network at the same time. The instant message opens in a small window on the recipient's computer screen. Instant messaging services support text, video, and audio messaging. Participating in instant messaging that includes video and audio requires a microphone, speakers, video camera, and application software, such as *Windows Media®* *Player* or *RealPlayer®*.

As with e-mail, you can use instant messaging to transfer electronic files as attachments. Some examples of instant message programs are *AOL Instant Messenger®, Yahoo! Messenger,* and *MSN® Messenger.*

As a workplace collaboration tool, instant messaging has some real advantages. It is easy to use, gets a faster response than e-mail, and can be quicker than making a phone call. However, the use of instant messaging does raise concerns, including the possible unauthorized interception of messages or sending viruses with instant message attachments.

Some workers find instant messages popping up on their screens a distraction. Also, productivity can be lost by exchanging personal instant messages during work hours. Businesses are increasingly establishing company-wide procedures for using instant messaging in the workplace. Some businesses are installing network software to monitor and secure employees' instant messages.

Instant messaging is quick and easy to use, but just as with e-mail messages, you must always be careful about what you say and how you say it. Keep your instant messages short and to the point. Send instant messages only when you must get a prompt reply to a question or send urgent information. Remember that you must not disclose private or confidential information or spread office gossip via instant messaging. To do so is both embarrassing and unethical. Being too casual with coworkers and supervisors in your instant messages may be viewed as unprofessional.

As is true with e-mail, instant message users are at risk for unwanted and unsolicited messages. These messages are referred to as *spam via IM* or *spim.*

Shared Workspaces

An IP network allows team members to collaborate in a shared workspace, a virtual work area hosted by a web server and accessed via a web browser. Team members can work together in the shared workspace to create and revise documents, view the status of projects, and share project calendars. Features of a shared workspace include:

- Names and contact information for each team member.
- Links to other web-based information needed by the team members.

workplace wisdom

With today's ease of Internet access, millions of web pages, along with the data and images they contain, are at your fingertips. You must be vigilant in your ethical use of the data and images you find on the web. Remember that web page content is protected by U.S. copyright law. Do not copy web page data and use it as your own work; cite the source of web page data that you use in documents and reports. Do not download web page images without permission from the copyright holder. As an administrative professional, it is your responsibility to use your workplace computer, private networks, and the Internet ethically.

- Document libraries containing stored documents related to the specific project.

- Tasks assigned to each team member and the tasks' status.

The application software in some productivity suites can be used as an interface to a shared workspace. The software works in combination with web server technologies.

Discussion Groups

A discussion group is an online forum in which participants discuss or monitor information on a specific topic. Discussion groups include newsgroups (virtual bulletin boards), mailing lists (e-mail newsletters), and web-based forums (messages posted via a web browser). Businesses use mailing lists and web-based forums to provide customer service and make customers aware of products and services. Professionals can use discussion groups to connect with peers and stay updated with the latest information in their field.

Wikis

A **wiki** is a website or group of web pages on which anyone can add, edit, or delete content. An example of a wiki is Wikipedia®, a popular web-based free encyclopedia to which anyone can contribute. In the workplace, businesses host wikis on their secure intranets to enable work groups to build knowledge bases on specific work-related topics.

Blogs

Blogs, also called *weblogs*, are web-based journals in which participants express their opinions, thoughts, and feelings. Posting to a blog is called *blogging*. Although a wiki and a blog are both web-based, they are used differently. Unlike a wiki, postings to a weblog are added chronologically and generally follow conversational threads or ideas. Postings to a blog may be monitored by a moderator and edited to remove inappropriate content. Examples of public blogs include those hosted by reporters and columnists at online news sites such as MSNBC or CNN.com.

Businesses are increasingly using public blogs to create forums for exchanging product information.

An example of this type of blog is one hosted by an application software manufacturer for its users. Users can share ways to use and troubleshoot the software and make suggestions for software updates and new features. Users testing a manufacturer's latest software version can share their testing results with other testers. A business may encourage its executives to host public blogs that present a "human face" to customers. Small business owners can use blogs to connect with other entrepreneurs. Private business blogs hosted on an intranet can help work groups manage their projects.

Video, Internet, and Web Conferencing

A video conference is a live, interactive conference between two or more people in separate geographical areas. Video conferencing uses telephony and video technologies to connect participants. The equipment and facilities to host or participate in a video conference can be expensive.

A lower-cost alternative to a video conference is an Internet or web conference. Internet and web conferencing allows businesses to save time and money by eliminating travel time and costs and by reducing the need for expensive equipment and facilities.

An Internet conference is hosted over an IP network and may include video, audio, and other resources shared by two or more users. You can use application software, such as *Windows® Meeting Space*, to participate in an Internet conference.

A web conference also uses an IP network, such as the Internet, to bring people in different geographic areas together using a website interface. Skype is a popular program used to communicate via the web. Both businesses and individuals use Skype to make video and voice calls. Skype users can also send instant messages and share files. Skype-to-Skype calls are free. Skype users can make calls to landlines or mobile phones at a low cost.[2] To learn more about Skype, visit the company's website. A link to the website is provided on the website for this product.

---

2 Skype, "About Skype," http://about.skype.com (accessed May 13, 2010).

Interacting during an Internet or web conference with sound and video requires a microphone, speakers, and a video camera, called a webcam, connected to the computer. Participants in a web conference may need special software downloaded from the conference service provider, or they may need only a browser and a connection to the network. Web conferencing can be hosted on a business's own LAN or intranet. Alternatively, a web conference can be hosted by a web conferencing service provider.

©ISTOCK

Fax Communications

Workplace collaboration tools have forever changed the way tasks get done in the workplace and how team members communicate with each other. But another more traditional workplace communication tool—a fax machine—still plays an important role.

The facsimile or fax machine is a standard piece of telecommunication equipment in the workplace. You can communicate with other people within the same building, in the same city, across the nation, or across the world by sending them a fax message.

Fax Machines A fax machine copies or scans a document containing text or pictures, treating both as an image. The fax machine then sends the image over telephone lines to a destination telephone number assigned to another fax machine, printer, or computer. Two fax modems are involved: one to convert the outgoing signals so that they can be sent over the phone lines and one to convert the incoming signals back into a format the receiving device can read. The ability to attach documents to e-mail messages has eliminated much of the need for sending faxes.

Multifunction Machines

Fax machines are often multifunction machines, combining printing, faxing, copying, and scanning capabilities into one machine. The multifunction machines are inexpensive and particularly useful in a small office in which cost and space are considerations. When considering purchasing a multifunction machine, be aware of:

- Space available—One multifunction device takes up far less space than the machines it replaces and can be installed more easily because only one connection to a computer is needed.

- Capability and cost—Multifunction machines are available with various speeds, print resolutions, and capabilities. The cost of the machine increases with more capabilities.

- Downtime—When a multifunction device malfunctions, you may lose all features—the copier, printer, scanner, and fax. This is an important factor to consider, especially in a small business or home office in which there are no backup machines.

Securing Messages Securing fax messages is important for protecting sensitive or confidential data. Fax messages are generally automatically printed at their destination. They can remain unsecured and available to anyone who walks by the fax

---

Dear Savvy Admin

Dear Savvy Admin:

I'm an administrative assistant for a busy cotton mill. We get dozens of fax messages every day, and I'm responsible for routing them to the right department or person. So much of what we receive is just plain junk advertising. This not only takes a lot of my time . . . it also wastes paper printing documents we don't even want. What can I do?

Buried in Faxes

Dear Buried in Faxes:

There are regulations against junk faxes under the Telephone Consumer Protection Act and the Federal Communications Commission (FCC) rules. However, if you have an established business relationship with the companies sending the faxes, and if you have given them your fax number, it is legal for them to send you faxes. You do have a right to opt out of such situations. Visit the FCC website to learn how to do this. There is also computer software that allows you to display faxes on your monitor, printing only those you want to print.

Savvy Admin

machine. Always take the appropriate measures to secure any fax transmissions—both outgoing and incoming messages. Follow these guidelines to secure fax messages:

- Place the fax machine in a private area and limit access to it.

- Use a fax cover sheet that includes the recipient's name, fax number, and phone number and the receiver's name, fax number, and phone number. Also indicate the number of pages in the fax and the date.

- Check the page count on incoming fax messages to ensure no pages are missing.

- For a fax containing urgent or sensitive information, request a confirmation that the fax has been received.

- Double-check the entered fax number before sending the fax.

- If a fax is received in error, notify the sender.

Security Issues

It is important to make the information on your computer and network secure. There are a variety of ways you can accomplish this. The first step is to recognize security threats that exist. Then you can take steps to protect your hardware and software.

Security Risks

Spam is the term used to describe unwanted and unsolicited electronic messages. Spam messages are more than unsolicited advertising. Spam brings the risk of a **computer virus** (a program designed to infect, destroy, or interfere with computer operation), financial fraud, or identity theft.

Online criminals send spam that looks as though it is from a legitimate financial institution or business, such as a bank, requesting credit card numbers or Social Security numbers or other personal information. The e-mail may be dressed up with company logos and contact information to make it look legitimate. It may contain a link that appears to be to the institution's website. This type of online scam is called **phishing**.

Spyware is another security threat. **Spyware** is a program that runs on a computer without the permission of the user to gather personal information, often through an Internet connection. The information gathered by the spyware, such as e-mail addresses or credit card numbers, is transmitted in the background to someone who may use it for illegal purposes.

Security Solutions

You must remain constantly vigilant to protect yourself and your company from security risks. A legitimate business should never ask you to provide personal and sensitive information via e-mail. Be suspicious of every message from an unknown source. Do not click any links in a suspect message! Clicking a link can expose your computer or network to threats, such as viruses or spyware. A link in a phishing message may jump to a fraudulent copy of an actual business website created to collect personal information from unsuspecting users.

Spam-blocking or filtering software can be installed on servers and individual computers in an attempt to block spam. E-mail software generally contains some features for managing unwanted messages. Antivirus software can be used to scan a computer and identify and remove viruses and other security threats. *Norton™ Internet Security*, shown in Figure 9-2, is an example of software designed to control security risks. Anti-spyware software can be used to find and remove spyware.

Figure 9-2 **Norton Internet Security Software**

Others steps can be taken to keep computer data secure. Some of them are as follows:

- Back up and carefully store important information so that a copy exists if the data are lost or corrupted.

- Protect hardware and data by assigning effective passwords. Tips for creating effective passwords are shown below.

- Log off the computer or network before you leave your desk to prevent unauthorized users from accessing information.

- Do not open e-mail attachments from people you do not know.

- Update and run your antivirus and anti-spyware software regularly.

- Use a **firewall** (a software program that monitors information as it enters and leaves a computer) to shield your computer from unauthorized users.

Creating Effective Passwords

© ISTOCKPHOTO.COM/DANIEL NORMAN

Creating effective passwords will help ensure that computer access and data remain secure. Follow these guidelines:

- Create passwords that are at least eight characters in length.

- Use both lowercase and capital letters.

- Use a combination of letters, numbers, and special characters.

- Use different passwords on different systems.

- Do not use passwords that are based on personal information that can be easily accessed or guessed.

- Do not use words that can be found in a dictionary.

- Develop a mnemonic (a memory aid) for remembering complex passwords.

Source: Mindi McDowell, Jason Rafail, and Shawn Hernan, "Choosing and Protecting Passwords," Cyber Security Tip ST04-002, US-CERT, http://www.us-cert.gov/cas/tips/ST04-002.html (accessed June 9, 2009).

Key Terms

blog

broadband

computer virus

firewall

hotspot

instant message

IP telephony

local area network (LAN)

metropolitan area network (MAN)

modem

phishing

smartphone

spam

spyware

telecommunications

voice mail

wide area network (WAN)

wiki

Summary

- Telecommunication tools, such as telephones, computers, and networks make sharing information fast and affordable.

- LANs, MANs, WANs, and the Internet are telecommunication networks that allow users to share many types of data.

- The information transmitted by telecommunication systems travels through a variety of electronic channels called pipelines, such as analog dial-up connections, cable, digital subscriber lines, satellites, and wireless connections.

- Using good human relations skills leaves a positive impression of you and your company with the caller.

- Voice mail is an efficient method of managing incoming calls when the call recipients are unavailable.

- IP telephony has the advantage of reduced cost compared to other methods for long-distance calls.

- Smartphones are a popular type of mobile phone that includes many of the functions of a handheld computer.

- Groupware, e-mail, shared workspaces, weblogs, wikis, and web conferencing are examples of tools used for collaboration in the workplace.

- Users should be aware of security risks for computers and data and take steps to reduce those risks.

Bookmark It. *For convenient access to activities, links, and valuable career resources for administrative professionals, visit the companion website for this text:*

www.cengage.com/officetech/fultoncalkins

Discussion Questions

1. Why are telecommunication tools valuable to businesses?

2. How does a converged telecommunication network differ from a traditional telephone network?

3. How do LANs, MANs, and WANs differ? How are they the same?

4. What are some types of telecommunication pipelines through which a voice message or an e-mail might travel?

5. What are some popular call management features of telephone systems?

6. Why is considering time zones important when planning a call?

7. What is a major advantage of using IP telephony as compared to a traditional phone system?

8. How does a smartphone differ from a regular mobile phone?

9. What are some tools that you might use for workplace collaboration?

10. What are some steps you can take to combat security risks and keep computer data secure?

Critical Thinking

Impatient coworker   Anna Chilingarov works as computer support specialist at a small manufacturing company. Yesterday, she received a call from Kent Sieber, an administrative assistant. Kent demanded that Anna help him right away with a computer problem. Anna explained that she was currently helping another employee and would be with Kent as soon as she could. When Anna arrived at Kent's workstation, Kent said, "It's about time you got here. My monitor is not working, and I have an important report to prepare for my supervisor." Anna apologized for the delay and said, "Let's see what the problem is."

Anna checked that the monitor was connected to the computer and that the power cord was plugged in. She then pressed the on button for the monitor. In a few seconds, the monitor came on. Kent said, "Well, that beats all. Why can't you fix this thing so that it works for me?" Anna explained that the monitor takes a few seconds to come on. She suggested that perhaps in his haste Kent had pressed the on button twice, thus turning the monitor on and then off again. Kent said, "I don't think I did that. Please leave now so I can prepare my report."

Does this situation reflect a good working relationship between Anna and Kent? What problems do you see with Kent's behavior? What could Kent do to improve their relationship? What could Anna do to improve their relationship?

Building Workplace Skills

1. **Telecommunication tools interview**   Select a company or other organization in your local area. Interview (by phone or in person) an administrative professional or other employee at the organization regarding the organization's use of telecommunication tools. You may wish to select one or two tools, such as

Planning Notes

Learning Objectives

1. Explain the value of telecommunication tools.

2. Describe types of networks used for telecommunications.

3. Describe equipment and effective techniques for telephone communication.

4. Use workplace collaboration tools.

5. Identify security threats and solutions for protecting computer data.

 Activities 11, 12, Above & Beyond

 Activities 1, 2, 3, 4, 5, 6, 8

 Activities 7, 9, 10

telephone and e-mail, to keep the interview brief. Ask how the tools are used and what their values are to the organization. Write a summary of the interview. (Learning Objective 1)

2. **Telecommunication networks**   Open the *Word* file CH09 Networks from the data files. For each situation described, indicate the type of network (LAN, WAN, MAN, the Internet, or converged telephone network) that would be appropriate. (Learning Objective 2)

3. **Compare smartphones**   Identify three current-model smartphones. Do research on the Internet or at local service providers to find the features of each phone. Prepare a table (in word processing or spreadsheet software) that compares the three phones. Include the phone maker or brand, model, price, and features. Write an e-mail telling your instructor which phone you think would be the best value for a businessperson and why. Also explain which phone would be best for you and why. Attach the phone comparison table to the e-mail. (Learning Objective 3)

4. **Telephone techniques web page**   Create a web page that can be posted on your company's intranet. The topic of the page is "Effective Telephone Techniques." Using the information you learned in this chapter and other information you gather from research, write a brief introductory paragraph about the importance of using the telephone effectively. Follow the paragraph with a list of guidelines for effective telephone use. Include an appropriate photo or other graphic on the page. Save the file as a single-file web page. (Learning Objective 3)

5. **Critique web pages**   Work with two classmates to complete this activity. Send an e-mail to your two teammates asking them to review and critique the web page you created in the previous activity. Attach the web page file to the e-mail. Review the web pages your teammates send you. Open the web pages in *Word* and use the Track Changes feature to indicate suggested changes, additions, or comments. E-mail the web page files back to your teammates. Update your web page based on the comments and corrections you received. View the page in a web browser to check for attractive format. (Learning Objective 4)

Communicate Clearly

6. **Edit recycling article**   Open the *Word* file CH09 Recycling from the data files. Edit the article to correct errors in grammar, spelling, punctuation, capitalization, and word usage. E-mail the corrected file to your instructor.

7. **Identity theft slides**   Do research to learn about identity theft. The companion website for this book has a link to the Federal Trade Commission's advice on identity theft protection. You will also find other useful sources online. Create an electronic slide show using the information you learn from your research. Include a title slide with the topic name and your name. Include a concise definition of identity theft. List ways that criminals may get your private information. Tell what steps you should take if your information is stolen and used by an identity thief. Give suggestions for protecting your private information online. Deliver the presentation to a group of your classmates. (Learning Objective 5)

8. **Voice mail greeting**   You work as an administrative assistant at Park Associates. The company has a voice mail system and encourages employees to change their voice mail greetings as needed to fit their current work status. You will be on vacation next Monday through Friday. In your absence, a coworker, Tomas Perez, will handle any urgent business your callers may have. Before you leave for your vacation, write a new greeting for your voice mail. Include all the appropriate information, making up details as needed. If possible, record your message. (Learning Objective 3)

Develop Relationships

9. **Inconsiderate behavior**   Your supervisor, Mr. Kim, often has you e-mail coworkers and clients to set up conference calls. You correspond with the participants to find a time when everyone can take part in the call. When you have everyone's input, you send a message with the date and time for the call. You also tell participants the number to call and a pass code to enter to access the call. Mr. Kim, who will be the host for conference call, also receives this information. However, Mr. Kim often does not dial in to the call until five or ten minutes after the time set for the call to begin. The other call participants must wait on hold several minutes for Mr. Kim. Coworkers and clients complain to you, wondering if you gave them the wrong time for the call. What messages does Mr. Kim's behavior give to coworkers and clients? What should you say when you talk to him about this situation?

10. **Shareware use**   Shareware is software that is typically distributed free of charge, sometimes on a trial basis. Your supervisor, Ms. Lee, recommended that you download and use a shareware program that lets you easily back up, synchronize, and restore computer files. The program information states that the software is free for personal and trial use. Continued use by a business requires a payment of $30 for a single user. You tried the software and found it very helpful. You sent a message to Ms. Lee asking that she approve purchase of the program for continued use. Ms. Lee responded, "Oh, we don't have to pay the fee. The company will never know it is for business rather than personal use." Would doing as Ms. Lee suggests be ethical? What would you say in response to Ms. Lee?

Use Technology

11. **Wiki entry**   Wikis are available on many subjects. Locate a wiki of interest to you by keying *wiki directory* as the search term in an Internet search engine. As an alternative, you can locate a topic of interest to you on the Wikipedia website. Create a new wiki entry or update an existing wiki entry. For example, you might visit the Wikitravel website and update or create an entry about your hometown or a favorite vacation spot. Save and print a copy of your new or updated entry. (Learning Objective 4)

12. **Hotspots**   Using public Wi-Fi hotspots makes computing and accessing messages easy from many locations. Some cities publish online directories or maps that show hotspots in the area. WeFi is a website that helps users locate hotspots. Use one of these or other resources to find a list or map of Wi-Fi hotspots on your campus or in your local community or city.

Above & Beyond

Create a blog   Several sites on the Internet offer free blog services. Locate such a site by keying *free blog* in an Internet search engine. Review several sites from the results list. Follow the instructions on one site to create your own blog. Select a blog topic you care about and about which you are knowledgeable. It could relate to your education or career, a hobby, a civic topic, or a charitable interest. Post your comments every day for at least two weeks. Allow readers to comment on your posts. Write a summary of the experience to include:

- Your blog topic.

- The blog service you used.

- What was easy and challenging about creating and maintaining the blog.

- The number and types of comments you received from readers.

Planning Notes

Administrative Assistant

Growing company seeks an administrative assistant with good planning and organizational skills. Job duties include:

- Handling telephone and written communications
- Working collaboratively with coworkers and managers
- Planning meetings and handling related tasks
- Doing research and creating documents and presentations

©MARK WRAGG, ISTOCK

Do I qualify?

CHAPTER

10

Learning Objectives

1. Identify types of business meetings and appropriate formats for various situations.

2. Describe meeting responsibilities of executives, leaders, administrative assistants, and other participants.

3. Complete duties for an administrative assistant that are related to meetings.

4. Develop conflict resolution skills.

Planning Meetings and Events

Meetings in the Workplace

Meetings are a way of life in the workplace. In an environment where many businesses are downsizing, you might expect fewer meetings. However, business is increasingly multinational and technology-driven. Although e-mail, telephones, and faxes allow quick communication both nationally and globally, the need for meetings is actually increasing.

According to one study, the average CEO in the United States spends 17 hours a week in meetings, with senior executives spending 23 hours a week and middle managers spending 11 hours per week in meetings.[1] Another study details the cost of meetings to United States corporations as more than $37 billion annually. This study also gives the following information:

1 Jon Jenkins and Gerrit Visser, "Meetings Bloody Meetings," Imaginal Training, http://www.imaginal.nl/mgtonlinemeetings1.htm (accessed March 19, 2010).

- Business managers spend nearly 80 percent of their time in meetings.
- U.S. corporations hold 15 million meetings per day.
- The average business trip consumes $1,400 in hard costs and more than $3,000 in total costs, including personnel time.
- Business professionals rate at least 40 percent of meetings as unproductive.
- Meetings are responsible for more than $30 billion in productivity losses each year.[2]

As you can readily see, meetings are costly to organizations. With teams increasingly becoming a standard method of operation, it is imperative that meetings be effective. This chapter will help you develop the knowledge and skills you need to assist your supervisor in holding meetings that are productive for all participants. This chapter will also help you develop the skills to be a productive team member and to run an effective meeting.

Board of Directors Meetings

Most large corporations and organizations operate with a board of directors. There are usually **bylaws**, written policies and procedures that clearly define how meetings are to be conducted. Boards may meet once a month or less. The chairperson of the board conducts the meeting, and strict procedures are usually followed. An agenda is distributed before the meeting, indicating the items to be discussed. If the organization is a public entity required by law to hold open meetings, notice of the meeting is posted according to legal procedures. Participants generally follow parliamentary procedures as set forth in *Robert's Rules of Order.*

Staff Meetings

Staff meetings are common within organizations. Such meetings may be scheduled on a regular basis or arranged as needed. For example, an executive may meet with the six people who report to him or her as a group every week. The purpose of staff meetings may be to review directions, plans, or assignments or to handle routine problems.

2 "Smarter Decisions.Faster," http://www.groupsystems.com/site/statis/pdfs/gs-sales-sheet.pdf-Microsoft (accessed July 1, 2005).

Committee/Task Force Meetings

In most organizations, committees or task forces are created. A **task force** is a work group formed to deal with a specific issue or problem. Once the problem has been handled or solved, the task force is disbanded. In other words, the task force has a specific beginning and ending. It is organized for a purpose; once the purpose is accomplished, it no longer exists. A **committee** is generally established for an ongoing purpose. For example, your workplace may have a safety committee that meets regularly (perhaps every month) to identify and address safety concerns. Since safety is an ongoing concern, the committee usually functions from year to year.

Project Team Meetings

Project teams are frequently used in organizations. For example, a project team might be formed to plan, produce, and market a new product. The team may include people in product research and design who will create a new product, people in manufacturing who will oversee production of the product, and people in sales and marketing who will plan or oversee the advertising and sales of the product. Although team members are from different departments, they work together on the project.

Customer/Client Meetings

Some employers hold meetings with customers or clients. These meetings are generally small, including only two or three people. For example, a lawyer may meet with a client to discuss the evidence in a case. An engineer may meet with a customer to discuss the design of a product.

Staff meetings are held regularly in many companies.

International Meetings

For international organizations, meetings with staff in locations outside the United States are common for upper-level managers. Also, as organizations within the United States continue to broaden their international scope, meetings to pursue international opportunities are held with business leaders in many other countries.

You may be involved in setting up and/or participating in electronic meetings with individuals from or even in other countries. Remember that cultural differences exist; these differences must be understood and respected. Otherwise, you may be dealing with an international misunderstanding rather than getting a resolution on an important contract or issue. It is important for you and your employer to do your homework before the meeting.

Find out as much as you can about the culture or cultures that will be represented. Then, be sensitive to the needs of the individuals in the meeting. Remember to consider the differences in time zones. For example, when it is noon in Chicago, it is the following day in Tokyo. There are good time zones calculators on the Internet to help you find a time when everyone can meet electronically. International meetings are typically more formal in nature than local meetings. Learn and use proper greetings. Follow accepted practices for exchanging business cards and giving (or not giving) gifts or other amenities.

Meeting Formats

The meeting format is most often face to face. Organizations will continue to have numerous face-to-face meetings because of the increase in teamwork within organizations and the need for these teams to share information in person. Audio conferencing (although an older technology) remains a viable type of meeting format. The use of video conferencing and web conferencing is growing.

Etiquette for International Meetings

Follow these suggestions for what to do and not to do in international meetings:

- Greet each person properly in all meetings.

- Do not use first names of participants. Even though using first names is common in U.S. meetings, it may be an inappropriate practice in other countries.

- Recognize the leader of the other group(s). For example, if the presidents of companies are involved, they should be recognized first and speak first.

- Disagree agreeably; some cultures consider it offensive to be contradictory.

- Avoid gesturing with your hands. Such gestures may mean something you do not intend in

another cultural context. Also, some people are put off by gestures.

- Watch your body language; remember that body language has different meanings in different cultures.

- Show respect for everyone but especially for people in positions of authority.

Face-to-Face Meetings

Even though we live in a technological world, the traditional face-to-face meeting is still common. These meetings are ones where people gather to discuss issues or problems in person. Advantages of face-to-face meetings include the following:

- A creative, interactive group discussion is more likely to take place when people are together in the same room; the participants can see and hear all group members.

- People can observe and respond to body language of participants.

- People generally feel more relaxed in this type of session because its format is more familiar.

- The atmosphere generally allows people to deal more effectively with difficult items.

- More group members are likely to participate in a face-to-face meeting.

Although face-to-face meetings can be effective, they have some disadvantages. Travel to and from the meeting can be costly, particularly to another city, state, or country. Cost includes not only transportation and possibly overnight hotel rooms but also the productive work time lost in travel. The meeting room may be costly. If the meeting is held at the company, finding a vacant room or tying up a room that is used for multiple purposes can be a problem. Socializing can consume part of the meeting time if it is not controlled by the leader. People (particularly those who work together daily) may tend to rely on their colleagues' suggestions or solutions reducing creative contributions.

Audio Conferences

An **audio conference** is a meeting in which a number of people can participate via telephone or some other device. An audio conference differs from other telephone conversations in that it involves more than two people in at least two locations. The communication device may be as simple as a speakerphone or as elaborate as a meeting room with microphones, speakers, and bridging technology. Bridging services, supplied by telephone and communication service companies, allow participants in multiple locations to dial in to a single phone number to talk with each other.

Video Conferences

A **video conference** is a meeting in which two or more people at different locations use equipment such as computers, video cameras, and microphones to see and hear each other. A web camera, a microphone, and speakers may be connected to computers and used to transmit video and audio to other computers. On a larger scale, a videoconferencing room may be used to provide audio and video communication for several people at different locations.

Web Conferences

Three types of web conferencing are introduced here—the web meeting, the webinar, and the webcast.

Web Meeting   A **web meeting** is a meeting in which two or more people at different locations communicate and share information via computers and a network connection, such as the Internet or a local area network. Some web meetings are fully interactive, allowing participants to see video of one another, talk in real time, and exchange information via computers. *Microsoft Windows Live Meeting* can be used for such a web meeting. For other web meetings, participants may speak with one another via a traditional telephone conference while using meeting software to share information. *Windows Meeting Space* (Figure 10-1) is a program that allows you to set up a meeting and share documents, programs, or your computer desktop with several other people who have the same program.

Webinar   A **webinar** is a seminar presented over the World Wide Web. It enables the presenter to conduct question-and-answer sessions with participants, but it does not provide the same degree of interaction as a web meeting.

Webcast   A **webcast** is a type of broadcast that is similar in nature to a television broadcast, except it takes place over the World Wide Web. However, the one-way nature of this type of conferencing means that there is little opportunity for the presenter and the audience members to interact. A webcast is primarily a presenting tool, which can be broadcast simultaneously to hundreds of recipients.

Advantages and Disadvantages of Remote Conferences

Remote conferences (audio, video, and web conferences) have both advantages and disadvantages just as face-to-face meetings have.

Advantages include:

- Savings in travel time and costs, including meals and hotel rooms.

- Bringing people together who have expertise in a number of different areas with a minimum of effort.

Disadvantages include:

- Less chance for effective brainstorming on issues.

- Less spontaneity among individuals because of a structured environment.

- No chance for the interaction before or after the meeting that is often so effective in face-to-face meetings.

Meeting Responsibilities

As you help plan and organize a meeting, remember that several people play an important part in ensuring that the meeting is effective. These people include the executive who calls the meeting, the person who makes the arrangements for the meeting, the leader who facilitates the meeting, the meeting participants, and the administrative assistant who assists in planning and preparing materials for the meeting. Each individual or group has specific roles and responsibilities that help ensure an effective meeting.

Executive's Responsibilities

The executive (an individual who has managerial authority in an organization) has a variety of responsibilities when planning meetings. She or he must determine the purpose of the meeting, set

Figure 10-1 Windows Meeting Space

the objectives, determine who should attend, plan the agenda, and establish the time and place. The executive may work closely with the administrative professional in accomplishing these tasks.

Determine the Purpose of the Meeting   Every meeting must have a purpose; without it, there is no need for a meeting. Generally, the executive calls the meeting, so it is his or her role to state the purpose. When meeting notices are sent out, the purpose should be clearly stated. All participants must understand why the meeting is occurring. Although the administrative assistant is not responsible for determining the purpose, she or he must understand the purpose so that appropriate arrangements can be made. Without this understanding, things can go wrong.

Set the Objectives   Every meeting should have specific written objectives. Objectives should clearly define the purpose and state what is to be accomplished. For example, if the purpose is to establish a strategic plan for the next year, the objectives might be:

- Evaluate the accomplishment of objectives for the current year.

- Establish objectives and timelines for the next year based on the organization's three-year strategic plan.

- Determine the resources needed to meet these objectives.

- Determine responsibility for carrying out all objectives.

Meeting objectives should be shared with the participants before the meeting. The attendees may be a group of executives, a group of nonmanagerial employees, or a mixed group of managers and other employees.

Sharing the objectives with the participants will not only provide them with an understanding of the purpose of the meeting, but will also allow them to be prepared for the meeting. If they have questions about the purpose, they will have a chance to ask them before the meeting.

Determine Who Should Attend   People invited to the meeting should be those who can contribute to the objectives, who will be responsible for implementing the decisions made, or who represent a group affected by the decisions. In the previous situation where the purpose is to establish a strategic plan for the next year, all managers in the department should be invited to the meeting.

Now, assume that another meeting is being called. The objective is to brainstorm ideas for international expansion in three or four new countries. The people who should attend are the officers of the company. This decision is a top-level one that will, after consideration by the officers, be presented to the board of directors for approval.

In determining who should attend a meeting, consideration should always be given to the purpose of the meeting and who is most affected by the issue or problem that is to be discussed. Consideration should be given to the background of each individual being asked to attend. For example, a **heterogeneous group** (a group with dissimilar backgrounds and experiences) can often solve problems more satisfactorily than a **homogeneous group** (a group with similar backgrounds and experiences). Since a heterogeneous group will usually bring varying views to the problem, creative thinking is more likely to occur than in a homogeneous group.

workplace wisdom

Meetings can be very useful; however, there are situations when a meeting is not the best choice. Schedule meetings only when necessary. A meeting with no purpose, or an ill-defined purpose, can result in wasted time, frustration for meeting participants, and unnecessary costs for the organization. To determine whether a meeting is needed, ask the following questions:

- Is a meeting the most effective way to communicate the necessary information?

- Have alternatives to a meeting been considered? Would an e-mail or a phone call be just as effective?

- Does the meeting leader have the necessary facilitation skills? Is the leader capable of handling a challenging group?

- Are the right people going to attend? Is the agenda clear and complete? What supporting materials, such as facts and figures, are needed?

- Is computer or audiovisual equipment needed?

© ISTOCKPHOTO.COM/JACOB WACKERHAUSEN

A heterogeneous group of people bring different experiences and ideas to a meeting.

In the two examples given previously, the participants have been determined by their expertise in the matter being discussed. Now, assume a very different type of meeting. This meeting is one in which the group is to determine new product lines for the company to pursue. An extremely creative group is needed to brainstorm ideas. One way to accomplish the goal is to include individuals from a cross section of the company with different backgrounds, education, and experiences. Generally, a heterogeneous group will bring varying views to an issue or problem.

The ideal number of participants is based on the purpose of the meeting, with the number of people invited who can best achieve the purpose. A good size for a problem-solving and decision-making group is from 7 to 15 people. This size group allows for creative synergy. **Synergy** is the interaction of people or things that can accomplish more than the sum of the individual parts. With this group size, there are enough people to generate divergent points of view and to challenge each other's thinking.

Small groups of seven people or fewer may be necessary at times. For example, if the purpose of the meeting is to discuss a personnel matter, the human resources director and the supervisor may be the only ones in attendance. If the purpose of the meeting is to discuss a faulty product design, the product engineer, the manager of the department, and the technician may attend.

Advantages to having only a few people in a meeting are:

- Participants may be assembled more quickly since there are fewer.

- A smaller group can provide a more informal setting to encourage more spontaneity.

- Group dynamics are easier to manage.

The disadvantages of a small group include:

- Points of view are limited.

- There may not be enough ideas to create the best solution to the problem.

- Participants may not be willing to challenge each other's point of view if they are a close-knit group.

Plan the Agenda   The executive's role is to plan the agenda. The **agenda**, which should be distributed before the meeting, is a document that lists the topics to be discussed at a meeting. The agenda should include the following information:

- Name of the group, department, or committee

- Date and time of the meeting

- Location of the meeting

- The items to be discussed, in order of presentation

- The individual responsible for presenting each agenda item

- Background materials (if needed)

A well-planned agenda saves time and increases productivity in a meeting. Be realistic in planning times to discuss each agenda item. Send the agenda to the people invited to attend the meeting at least two days before the meeting. By providing participants with the proper information before a meeting, the leader can use time in the meeting effectively and decisions can be made in a timely manner. A sample agenda is shown in Figure 10-2 on the next page.

Establish the Time and Place   The executive is responsible for establishing the approximate time of the meeting and the general location for the meeting. For example, the executive may tell the administrative assistant that the meeting will take place in-house on Thursday morning, but not give a specific time. The administrative assistant has the

Figure 10-2 Agenda

MEETING AGENDA

Telephone System Task Force

Conference Room C
10 a.m., June 15, 20--

1. Telephone Systems Needs and Wants (20 minutes).. All Managers

2. Vendor Research Reports (30 minutes) .... Stanislaw Jawor
Alice Sumphi
Paul Alciere

3. Funding and Return on Investment
for Telephone System (20 minutes) .... Maria Menendez, Controller

4. Assignments for Preparing an Action Plan .... Tim Fowler

responsibility of checking with other participants (or their administrative assistants) to determine the most appropriate time for the meeting.

The administrative assistant finds an appropriate conference room available at the particular time needed. If the meeting is a routine meeting that occurs each month, a time and place is usually established when the first meeting is held. Such an approach eliminates work for the administrative assistant and also keeps the participants from having schedule conflicts.

Leader's Responsibilities

The leader, the individual who is in charge of the meeting, is generally your supervisor. Since teams are used extensively in organizations today, you as an administrative professional may be the team leader (individual who heads a team that is charged with getting some type of task accomplished) in a meeting. You may also be a co-leader (one member of a team of two members who are in charge) with another administrative assistant in the organization. Leaders have several responsibilities when conducting a meeting.

Follow the Agenda When the meeting begins, the leader should state the purpose of the meeting. The leader should also let the participants know what

outcomes are expected. For example, if the purpose of a meeting is to establish a direction for the unit for the next year, the expected outcomes of the meeting may be to determine at least four unit objectives. The leader may want to remind participants tactfully to turn off cell phones and pagers for the duration of the meeting. If participants stray from the agenda, the leader is responsible for tactfully, but firmly, bringing them back to the topic at hand. The leader might say, for example, "Thank you for your comments concerning this issue. We can put it on the agenda for a later meeting. Now, let's continue discussing the unit's objectives for this next year."

Manage Time Meetings should begin on time, even if several people are late in arriving. Waiting for others is not fair to the individuals who have made an effort to be on time. Timeframes (both beginning and approximate ending times) should be established when the meeting notice is sent out.

In addition to beginning on time, the leader is responsible for ending on time. Have you ever been in a meeting that was planned to last for one hour and you were still sitting there two hours later? Allowing a meeting to run over significantly from the time scheduled is poor management on the part of the leader, in addition to being insensitive to the needs of the participants. With our fast-paced business world,

A meeting leader should encourage individuals to participate in the meeting.

calendars are generally tightly scheduled. To allow one meeting to go longer than scheduled may make participants late for other commitments.

If a meeting goes longer than scheduled, it is perfectly acceptable to excuse yourself by making the following statement to the leader: "I am so sorry, Jim or Gloria (the leader of the group). As you will recall, I mentioned to you when I agreed to be at this meeting that I had another meeting today. Unfortunately, that meeting is starting in ten minutes, and I must leave. I promise to read the minutes carefully so I will know what I have missed." A statement like this shows the group that you care and that you told the leader you had another meeting when you accepted the invitation. It demonstrates your desire to fulfill your commitments and lets the other participants know you are being responsible, not inconsiderate or rude—you are fulfilling another obligation.

Encourage Participation   The leader is responsible for seeing that everyone participates and that no one dominates the discussion to the exclusion of others. The leader should help individuals feel secure enough to say what they think. If, as the meeting gets under way, several people have not spoken, the leader may make statements similar to these:

- "Elena, what direction do you think we should take?"
- "Yoshi, we haven't heard from you on this issue. What are your thoughts?"

Let each participant know that you and the group value her or his opinion. Encourage everyone to

contribute. Respect participants and the comments they make. You might make statements such as these:

- "Thank you for that contribution."
- "That's an excellent idea."
- "Your idea definitely has possibilities. Can you explain it more?"

The leader is also responsible for seeing that one or two people do not dominate the conversation, even if their contributions are beneficial. The leader might use the following types of statements:

- "Diana, that is an excellent idea. Eduardo, how could it be implemented in your area?"
- "Thanks, Roger; Michele, what direction do you think we should take?"

The leader needs to keep the participants focused on the agenda, positively reinforce all individuals for their contributions, and keep the discussion moving to accomplish the outcomes desired.

Facilitate Reaching Decisions   The leader is responsible for helping the participants reach a decision about an issue, problem, or direction. A leader should carefully assess all alternatives that have been discussed. Next, the leader needs to push for a decision on the issue. For example, the leader might say, "We seem to have identified each issue and the possible solutions. Does anyone else have anything to add? Are we overlooking anything? Are there problems we haven't seen?"

If the group seems to be comfortable with the alternatives that have been discussed, the leader can move to resolution by saying, "Now, of the two solutions that have been proposed, let's determine which solution will work better for our group. Let's take a quick vote to help clarify which alternative the group thinks is better." In this situation, the leader has been supportive of the group members by listening carefully to alternatives that were presented and then has helped the group make a decision by calling for a vote on the alternative considered the better of the two presented.

Evaluate the Meeting   Generally, with informal meetings within an organization, no formal evaluation is necessary. However, an informal evaluation by the leader (and possibly the participants) should be done. Participants are usually forthright; they may tell the leader that the meeting was not as successful as they had hoped. When participants make this type of statement, the leader should seek clarification on exactly what was meant. The leader may want to ask two or three individual participants how the meeting went. The leader will also want to consider the following questions to help evaluate the meeting:

- Did everyone in attendance take part in the meeting?
- Was the nonverbal behavior positive?
- Were the participants creative problem solvers?
- Did the participants exhibit a high energy level?
- Was the purpose of the meeting satisfied?
- Were appropriate decisions made?
- Can I improve the ways I handled the issues, the people, or the meeting?

Participants' Responsibilities

Just as a leader has responsibilities, so do the participants. Their role is much broader than attending the meeting. Their responsibilities begin before the meeting and continue after the meeting.

Before the Meeting   Participants are responsible for reading the meeting notice, responding to it promptly, and reading the agenda and any related materials received before the meeting. Participants are also responsible for understanding the purpose of the meeting. Each participant must take her or his responsibility to contribute to the success of the meeting seriously, which means that the participant must be prepared. No one appreciates an unprepared person who arrives at a meeting late.

During the Meeting   The participants are responsible for being on time to the meeting and for contributing thoughtful, well-considered, or well-researched comments. Other responsibilities include these: listening nonjudgmentally to others, respecting the leader's role, and being courteous to each individual.

Although making these types of contributions sounds simple, it is not always so. Your mind tends to wander, focusing on other work-related tasks or on personal issues. However, your contributions can be the very

ones that get the meeting back on track if individuals stray or help the leader keep the meeting focused. Your obligation is always to contribute in a positive manner to the success of the meeting. Participants should give their full attention to the meeting and not answer text messages, e-mails, or cell phone calls during the meeting. Cell phones and pagers should be turned off.

After the Meeting   A participant's responsibilities do not necessarily end when the meeting is over. The participant may have been asked to research a topic or work with a group of individuals to bring back a recommendation on a particular item for the next meeting. Although after-meeting assignments may be time-consuming, the assumption is that the contribution made from the assignments will positively affect the organization.

Administrative Professional's Responsibilities

In planning meetings (whether they are face-to-face or some type of electronic meeting), you, as the administrative professional, have a number of responsibilities. You must communicate with the supervisor to determine the purpose of the meeting and the duties you are expected to perform. When you first join an organization or begin to work with a different supervisor, you should take time before each meeting to understand his or her needs and preferences. As you learn the supervisor's preferences, you will need to spend less time in discussing the details of preparing for a meeting. However, you

Using a laptop computer is an efficient way to take notes during a meeting.

Technology @Work

The administrative assistant may have access to an online calendar of meetings scheduled in the organization. Such a calendar saves time and effort if it is kept up-to-date because you can see times when people are already committed to other meetings.

Employees may make their online calendars accessible to members of their work group or to their supervisors and the group's administrative assistant.

Before sending a meeting notice, you can check the online calendar of each person you plan to invite to find a time when everyone can attend.

should always discuss the purpose of the meeting. Otherwise, you may make decisions about details that cause problems.

Confirm the Date and Time

At times, the executive will direct that a meeting be held on a specific date and at a specific time. At other times, only a general timeframe will be given. The specific date and time of the meeting will be left up to the administrative assistant to arrange and may depend on when participants are available. You will probably want to avoid scheduling meetings on Monday mornings and Friday afternoons. Employees often use Monday mornings to get an overview of the week and handle any pressing items that may have occurred over the weekend. Friday afternoons are often used to complete projects. When determining the time of a meeting, avoid selecting a time immediately after lunch or near the end of the day.

Meetings generally should last no longer than two hours because people can get restless. However, if a long meeting cannot be avoided, schedule five- or ten-minute breaks for participants.

Select and Prepare the Room   Room arrangements should be made immediately after you know the date and time of the meeting. Organizations generally do not have a large number of conference rooms, and these rooms are usually booked quickly for meetings. If conference rooms of various sizes are available, you will want to book one that meets your seating needs. For example, if you have 12 people coming to the meeting and you schedule a conference room that seats 30, participants may feel lost in the room. Conversely, if you choose a room that is too small, participants will feel crowded.

Check the temperature controls before the meeting. Remember that bodies give off heat, so the room will be warmer with people in it. A standard rule is to aim for a room temperature of approximately 68°F. A hot, stuffy room or a room that is icy cold is a distraction for people who are trying to make important decisions. Be certain you understand how to change the thermostat if the room becomes too hot or cold. Although maintenance personnel may be available, it may take them a while to get to the room, and usually the task is a simple one.

Determine the Seating Arrangement   The seating arrangement you should choose for the room depends on the objectives of the meeting.

Schedule short breaks for meetings that last more than two hours.

The five basic seating arrangements are rectangular, circular, oval, semicircular, and U-shaped. Figure 10-3 shows these arrangements.

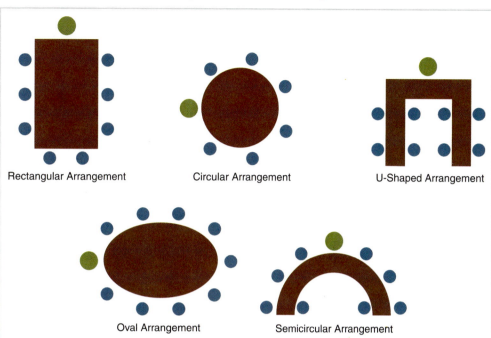

Figure 10-3 Seating Arrangements for Meetings

Rectangular Arrangement

Circular Arrangement

U-Shaped Arrangement

Oval Arrangement

Semicircular Arrangement

The rectangular arrangement allows the leader to maintain control because she or he sits at the head of the table. This arrangement is also effective when participants will be talking in groups of two or three. Individuals seated next to or opposite each other have a chance to discuss issues as they arise.

However, if discussion is important, the table should not be too long. A long table may make communication difficult because people cannot hear clearly or see the nonverbal behavior of other participants. A long table may also prevent the leader from taking part in discussions if she or he is seated away from other participants. The rectangular arrangement is most effective in formal meetings.

The circular and oval arrangements work best when the purpose of the meeting is to generate ideas and discussion in a relatively informal meeting. These arrangements encourage interaction and participation. Participants can make direct eye contact with everyone else in the group. Communication channels are considered equal among all participants because no one person is in a dominant position.

The semicircular and U-shaped arrangements work well for small groups of six to eight people. The leader retains moderate control because she or he is in a dominant position. These two arrangements are also good for showing visuals because the visual can be positioned at the front of the configuration.

Make certain you have enough chairs for the number of participants who are scheduled to attend. You do not want to have several extra chairs; they just get in the way, and it appears as though some people failed to attend. You also do not want to have too few chairs.

Prepare the Meeting Agenda All meeting participants should know the purpose of a meeting before coming to the meeting. As discussed earlier, an agenda is an outline of what will occur at the meeting. Participants should receive the agenda at least two days and preferably a week before the meeting. For some meetings, such as a staff meeting, participants may suggest additional agenda items, which you can add if your supervisor agrees.

Ask the meeting leader whether you should allocate a particular time for the presentation of each agenda item. Although this process is not essential, it does remind people of the importance of time and adherence to a schedule. The order of the agenda items can vary. Some people think that the most difficult items should be presented first so participants can deal with them while they are fresh. Others think the difficult items should be presented last. Check with your supervisor to find out which order she or he prefers.

The word *Action* may be listed after certain agenda items. This word indicates that a decision should be made. This approach helps participants know that they should come to the meeting prepared to make a decision.

Prepare the Meeting Notice

If the meeting is scheduled within the organization, notify participants by e-mail, with the meeting agenda sent as an attachment. If you have access to employees' online calendars, you can check the schedules of meeting participants to determine whether they are free at the time of the meeting. The meeting notification should include the following information:

- Purpose and objectives of the meeting
- Location, date, and time
- Meeting agenda
- Names of participants
- Background information or other needed materials

You may be responsible for following up on meeting notices. Although you have asked people to let you know whether they can attend, everyone may not respond. Send an e-mail message to the people who have not responded to determine whether they will be present. You also need to let your supervisor know who will be attending the meeting and who will not be. If a number of people are unable to attend, your supervisor may choose to change the meeting time and/or date.

Prepare Materials for the Leader

Materials that you should prepare for the leader include:

- The meeting notice and agenda with a list of the people who will attend.
- Related materials, such as reports or handouts, needed for the meeting.

If the leader is a participant in an off-site meeting, you may need to include directions to the meeting. Using a website such as MapQuest®, you can get maps and driving directions.

Prepare Materials for Participants

Background materials (if needed) should be sent to participants with the meeting notice and agenda. If handouts are to be distributed during the meeting, prepare them well in advance. If handouts are made up of several pages, place them in individual folders. Sometimes participants may need to take notes. You might put a pad of paper in the folder, along with a pen.

Order Equipment

Determine what equipment, if any, is needed for the meeting. For example, if electronic slides are going to be shown, you will need to have a computer available, along with a projection unit and a screen. Follow through to make sure the equipment is available. It is a good idea to make a list of the necessary equipment and to note on the list the arrangements that have been made. List the person responsible for obtaining each item. If it is your responsibility, note that. Before the meeting begins, check the room to verify that the equipment is there and in working order.

Order Food and Beverages

For a morning meeting, coffee, tea, and juice may be provided for the participants. Water should also be available. For an afternoon meeting, you may want to provide soft drinks, juice, coffee, and tea. Providing beverages is not mandatory, however. Check with your supervisor to see what she or he prefers.

For a luncheon meeting, you may have the responsibility of selecting the menu, calling the caterer, and arranging for the meal to be served. Avoid a heavy lunch if you are expecting people to work afterward. A salad or light entrée is more appropriate for a working lunch. For a dinner meeting, you may have the responsibility of working with an

An administrative professional may organize the details of a dinner meeting.

outside caterer. Sometimes there are health issues to consider. If you know the participants, provide food that meets their needs. If you do not know the participants, ask the caterer what dishes other clients order in this circumstance (vegetarian, non-dairy, etc.). Be certain to ask your supervisor what the budget allocation is for the meal.

For a dinner meeting at a hotel, you can expect assistance from the hotel staff. You will usually be responsible for selecting the menu. If the event is formal, you might wish to have table decorations and place cards. You should consider the group when selecting the seating arrangement; your supervisor can advise you.

©ISTOCK

Handle Duties During the Meeting

The administrative professional's responsibilities during the meeting are varied. You may be expected to greet the participants and to introduce individuals if they do not know each other. Your courteousness, warmth, and friendliness can go a long way toward making people feel comfortable and getting the meeting off to a good start.

Your main responsibility during the meeting will probably be to take notes for the **minutes** (a record of a meeting). Sit near the leader so you can clearly hear what he or she says. You may want to use a laptop computer to take notes. Minutes should contain a record of the important matters that were presented in the meeting. You do not need to record the meeting discussions **verbatim** (word for word) with the exception of motions. For motions, include the name of the person who made the motion, the name of the person who seconded it, the exact wording of the

motion, and whether the motion passed or failed. For discussions, summarize and record all pertinent information.

Follow Up After the Meeting

Your duties after the meeting include seeing that the meeting room is left in order, preparing the minutes, and handling other details. These routine tasks are essential after a meeting.

- Return all equipment. See that additional tables and chairs are removed from the room. Clean up any food or beverage leftovers, or notify the cleaning staff if the room needs a general cleaning.

- Write items that require future attention by you or your employer on your calendar.

- Send out any necessary follow-up messages.

- Evaluate the meeting. Review what happened; consider how you might improve the arrangements for the next meeting.

- Keep files on meetings long enough to refer to them when planning the next similar meeting. Your notes will help ensure future success. You might also keep names and telephone numbers of contact people.

If minutes are necessary, they should be prepared and distributed within 24 to 48 hours of a meeting. Prompt preparation and distribution of minutes reminds participants of what they must do before the next meeting. Ask your supervisor if any nonparticipants should get copies of the minutes. For example, minutes from a company board meeting may be made available to all

Dear Savvy Admin

Dear Savvy Admin:

Andrea, the interior designer I work for, is out of the country, and I can't reach her. She asked me to make arrangements for a catered lunch meeting in her office on the day she returns. Andrea is really, really fussy, and I'm afraid I'll choose the wrong entrée or the wrong dessert. The client and her husband are very important to Andrea. What can I do?

I'm No Foodie

Dear I'm No Foodie:

Perhaps you could call the client to ask if she or her husband has any dietary restrictions. That would give you an opening to ask, "Would you prefer the roast lamb or the crab salad as an entrée?" Then you could ask, "Would you like to hear the dessert choices?" I'm guessing that the caterer might be able to help, too, since Andrea has apparently done business with him or her before. The caterer may even know which entrée Andrea might like.

Savvy Admin

executives within a company. Sample minutes from a meeting are shown in Figure 10-4 on page 179.

Although there is no set format for writing minutes, general guidelines are given here.

- The title *Minutes*, the type of meeting, the group's name, and the date should appear at the top of the document.

- Minutes should use 1 or 1.15 spacing. The side margins should be at least 1 inch. If the minutes are to be placed in a bound book, the left margin should be 1 1/2 inches.

- Subject captions should be used as side headings. Subject captions usually correspond to the agenda topics.

- Minutes may or may not be signed. Minutes of board meetings and professional organizations are generally signed. If minutes are to be signed, a signature line should be provided.

Minutes should be stored for future reference. In addition to keeping a copy of the electronic file, you will probably want to store the minutes in hard-copy form in a notebook. The agenda and all pertinent materials presented in the meeting should be stored with the minutes.

Organization—The Key

Regardless of what your meeting responsibilities are, the key is organization. Know what you have to do, and stay organized in doing it. As you plan a meeting, continue through the process of the meeting, and oversee the follow-up activities, ask yourself these questions:

- How can I best organize my time and efforts?
- When should each task be completed?
- Who is responsible for each activity?
- What should I discuss with my supervisor?
- What can I do on my own?

Conferences

A conference is much larger in scope and has more participants than a meeting. Executives may belong to a professional organization in a particular field of expertise, such as accounting, engineering, or human resources. Many of these organizations hold at least one major conference each year. Most companies encourage their executives to participate in conferences as a means of broadening their knowledge. If you are a member of a professional organization such as IAAP, you may attend and help plan some of the organization's conferences.

Before the Conference

Preparing for a regional or national conference takes months of work. Good planning ensures

Writing @Work

You may be asked to record notes for minutes during a meeting and to write the minutes after the meeting. Minutes should include the following information:

↗ Name of the group

↗ Date, time, and place of the meeting

↗ Name of the presiding officer

↗ Members present and absent

↗ Approval or correction of the minutes from the previous meeting

↗ Reports of committees, officers, or individuals

↗ Complete information for motions made

↗ Items on which action needs to be taken and the person responsible for taking the action

↗ A concise summary of the important points of discussion

↗ The date and time of the next meeting (if one is scheduled)

↗ The name and title of the person who will be signing the minutes, along with space to sign his or her name

©ISTOCK

Figure 10-4 Minutes of a Meeting

MINUTES

Board of Directors Meeting
Management Association, Dallas Chapter
December 14, 20--

Time and Place of Meeting

The regular monthly meeting of the Board of Directors of the Management Association was held on December 14 at the Regent Hotel at 6:30 p.m. The meeting was called to order by the president, Marjorie Martin. All 12 board members were present.

Minutes

The minutes of the November meeting were approved without reading because each member received a copy prior to the meeting.

Financial Review

Edwardo Rejuan gave a summary of the financial transactions for the past month and the ending cash balance. He also reviewed major points of the financial plan for the year and compared them to the actual balances.

New Business

Membership Committee: The application of Phelire Nkhoma for membership was unanimously approved.

Service Committee: It was suggested that the merit award qualifications be included in the chapter bulletin for the first week of February.

Program Committee: Richard Wong, chairperson of the speakers bureau, reported that he and the committee are planning to increase the number of programs at the winter seminar. He also reported that the committee agreed on "Ethics in International Business" as the theme for the seminar.

Adjournment

The meeting was adjourned at 8:30 p.m.

Respectfully submitted,

Patricia McIntosh

Patricia McIntosh
Secretary, Dallas Chapter

a smooth, successful conference. Poor planning results in a disorganized, ineffective conference. One of the major responsibilities of planning is to determine the location and meeting facilities for the conference. You may wish to contact the chamber of commerce in the city being considered to ask for information about the city and appropriate conference facilities. You may also request conference planning guides from the hotels and conference centers that you are considering. These guides usually give floor plans of the facilities, dining and catering services, price lists for rooms and services, and the layout of meeting rooms.

Your task will not be to invite someone to speak unless you are working on a conference where you are a member and assisting with the planning (an IAAP conference, for example). However, you may contact presenters to make travel and lodging arrangements. If you are responsible for making hotel arrangements for a presenter, you should determine the types of accommodations the presenter would like to have—within the cost limitations of the budget—because presenters' expenses are usually covered, at least in part, by the host organization. For example, does the presenter need a handicap accessible room? If the conference is not at a hotel, you might give the presenter a choice of two or three hotels (within your price range) in the area. If you are making flight reservations, you need to know the person's desired arrival and departure times and rental car needs.

Preregistration is typically held before the conference; you may be involved in setting up the preregistration in addition to actually registering individuals. Most registration is now done online, and your role may be to design the online registration process and put the appropriate information online. Also, you may be involved in preparing packets of information for the registrants. Often, program information, a list of participants, and a small gift or two are included in the registration packet.

During the Conference

Your responsibilities during the conference may include running errands, delivering messages to participants, and solving problems that may occur. Other responsibilities may include checking room arrangements, equipment needs, meal

People @Work

MEETING PLANNER

Meeting planners coordinate the details of a meeting or conference as requested by a client. The client may be a business, an organization, or an individual. A meeting planner typically handles tasks such as these:

- ↗ Arrange for the meeting location at a hotel or convention center

- ↗ Handle lodging arrangements and set up transportation to the meeting site from hotels for participants

- ↗ Plan meal functions in conjunction with a caterer

- ↗ Arrange for telecommunication services and audiovisual equipment for meetings

- ↗ Assign exhibit space and work with exhibitors to resolve any issues related to the exhibits

Your company may hire a meeting planner to coordinate the details of a large meeting or conference. As an administrative assistant, you may work with the planner to explore ways to meet your company's needs and stay within your budget.

GETTY IMAGES/RED CHOPSTICKS

Communicating @Work

When trying to resolve a conflict, listen with empathy to what others are saying. Express your concern and support for the other person's opinions. Express your empathy by stating, in your own words, what you understand the other person is saying.

You might even say, "This is what I heard you say" and repeat what you believe the person said. Then you might ask, "Did I hear you correctly?"

Do not be closed to the opinions of others. Be willing to change your position if others present appropriate reasons for doing so.

You may be responsible for mailing the CDs to the appropriate individuals.

Conference Evaluation

A post-conference evaluation session should be held with all individuals who worked on the conference. At this meeting, you will need to review what was successful and what was not. A formal evaluation of the conference may have been filled out by participants. If so, evaluations need to be tallied and presented in the post-conference evaluation session. Notes of all issues and/or problems need to be taken and passed on to the appropriate organization or company personnel so that people involved in the next conference will have the benefit of your experiences. No one ever wants to make the same mistake twice. A record of the problems or issues and their solutions or outcomes will help the next group avoid some mistakes.

arrangements, and a multitude of other last-minute details that always occur. Since you are a representative of the company for which you work or the organization of which you are a member, it is imperative that you present a positive image at all times. You also need to keep a smile on your face and handle even the most difficult situations, which may even involve resolving conflicts with the hotel, the caterers, or the participants. The last section of this chapter on conflict resolution will help you be successful at these difficult tasks.

After the Conference

After the conference, your basic duties involve cleaning up and following up. These responsibilities include seeing that all equipment is returned, presenters are assisted with transportation to the airport, letters of appreciation are sent to presenters and others as appropriate, expense reports are filled out, and bills are paid. You may also be responsible for seeing that the proceedings of the conference are published and mailed to participants. Many times, presentations are recorded on CDs, with the participants given the option of buying the CDs.

Conflict Resolution

Conflict resolution is so needed in our world that seminars and entire books are written on the subject. Numerous companies have personnel in the human resources offices or in other parts of the organization that specialize in resolving workplace conflicts.

As a successful administrative professional, you will find that you must possess conflict resolution skills and use them frequently. You must use these skills with executives and other administrative assistants, in internal meetings with people working in the same organization, on the telephone, or on the Internet as you communicate with customers or prospective customers. You will also use these skills in your written correspondence with both internal and external audiences. Conflict cannot always be avoided, but you can learn to deal with it in a positive manner.

If you are to be successful in conflict resolution, you need to develop an attitude of openness and empathy with others. Additionally, you must treat all people equally, never showing favoritism even if the person is your friend. You must continually practice effective conflict resolution skills. Commit to becoming an administrative professional who resolves rather than encourages conflict.

Openness

Be open to what others think and feel. State your feelings and thoughts openly without being negative. In other words, use "I" statements about how you feel and what you think should happen. For example, if a conflict erupts about the type of meeting that should be held, you might say, "I suggest we try an online conference rather than a face-to-face meeting. It will save both money and time." You should not say, "You're not thinking! A face-to-face meeting would not be productive in this situation. Twenty people would have to travel from all over the United States, costing both time and money."

Do you see the difference between these two statements?

- In the first one, you use an "I" statement, and you state your reason for suggesting an online conference in a very straightforward but nonthreatening manner.

- In the second statement, you begin by accusing the others involved of not thinking. Such a statement immediately puts the individuals on the defensive.

Give other people time to express their feelings. Evaluate all ideas equally. Do not base your opinion of an idea on whether the person is a friend of yours or whether you like or dislike the individual.

Practice Your Skills

This section has given you several suggestions for successfully solving conflicts that may occur in your organization. However, reading by itself will not make a difference; you must practice your skills daily if you are to become a truly effective administrative professional—one who not only cares about others but also constantly seeks ways to make the workplace environment more productive.

Commit to practicing these ideas daily in your work and school environment. Start by taking one of the suggestions and practicing that suggestion for one week until it becomes part of your method of operation. Then, move to the next suggestion and practice it for one week, along with continuing to practice the first suggestion. Move through the list in this manner until the suggestions have become a part of how you respond each day to your workplace and school environment.

Conflict Resolution

Follow these guidelines to help resolve conflicts:

- Do not react too quickly. Many times individuals act too quickly when a conflict occurs. Step back, collect your thoughts, and try to see the situation as objectively as possible.

- Identify what is causing the conflict. Is it power, resources, recognition, or acceptance? Many times our needs for these items are at the heart of the conflict.

- Create a safe environment. Establish a neutral location and a tone that is accepting of the other person's view and feelings.

- Ask questions to determine what the other person needs or wants. Be willing to listen to the other person. If you do not understand what the other person is saying, paraphrase what you think you hear and ask for clarification.

- Identify points of agreement. Work from these points first. Then identify the points of disagreement.

- Actively listen. Watch the individual's eyes; notice his or her body language.

- Separate people from the issue. When the people and the problem are considered together, the problem becomes difficult to solve. Talk in specifics rather than general terms.

- Do not seek to win during a confrontation. Negotiate the issues, and translate the negotiation into a lasting agreement that is positive for all parties.

Key Terms

agenda

audio conference

bylaws

committee

heterogeneous group

homogeneous group

minutes

synergy

task force

verbatim

video conference

webcast

webinar

web meeting

Summary

- Meetings are held extensively in businesses and other organizations. Because meetings use the time of employees and other resources, it is important that meetings be productive.

- A meeting may be held in one of various formats, such as face to face, audio conference, video conference, or web conference.

- Executives, meeting leaders, meeting participants, and administrative professionals all have particular duties related to meetings.

- An agenda is a document that lists the topics to be discussed at a meeting. The agenda should be distributed to meeting participants before the meeting.

- The appropriate seating arrangement (rectangular, circular, oval, semicircular, or U-shaped) for a meeting depends on the objectives of the meeting.

- The administrative professional may be asked to take notes during a meeting and to prepare the minutes (a record of a meeting) after the meeting.

- A conference is much larger in scope and has more participants than a meeting.

- A successful administrative professional uses conflict resolution skills to interact with managers, coworkers, and clients in a productive manner.

Bookmark It. *For convenient access to activities, links, and valuable career resources for administrative professionals, visit the companion website for this text:*

www.cengage.com/officetech/fultoncalkins

Planning Notes

Learning Objectives

1. Identify types of business meetings and appropriate formats for various situations.

2. Describe meeting responsibilities of executives, leaders, administrative assistants, and other participants.

3. Complete duties for an administrative assistant that are related to meetings.

4. Develop conflict resolution skills.

 Activities 3, 4, 5, 7; Critical Thinking

 Activities 9, 10; Above & Beyond

 Activities 1, 8

Discussion Questions

1. How does the work of a task force differ from the work of a committee?

2. What are three types of remote meetings or conferences? What are some advantages to remote meetings?

3. What are the meeting responsibilities of an executive?

4. What are the responsibilities of a meeting leader?

5. Why should the administrative professional always discuss the purpose of the meeting with the executive who calls the meeting?

6. When taking notes to be used in preparing meeting minutes, why should the wording of motions be recorded exactly, word for word, as stated?

7. When might a company or organization use the services of a meeting planner?

8. Give three guidelines for resolving conflicts that you think are the most important ones to follow.

Critical Thinking

Brainstorming or just storming? The members of the marketing team of your company meet regularly to discuss sales initiatives and other matters. These comments were made at a recent meeting led by Mr. Park:

Mr. Park: As you know, sales for last quarter were down significantly. Let's brainstorm some ideas for increasing sales.

Ms. Diaz: We could do a customer satisfaction survey that might give us some insight into why customers are not buying.

Mr. Pottier: We could design a new advertising campaign to increase customer interest in our products.

Ms. Hevelius: We could make some deep price cuts. That would mean selling below our costs in some cases, but we would make it up on volume.

Mr. Barcott: That's the worst idea I've ever heard! Obviously, you can't add, or you wouldn't make such a ridiculous statement.

Ms. Hevelius: Oh, yeah? Well, I don't hear you coming up with any bright ideas!

Are these meeting participants following the guidelines for a successful brainstorming session? Explain your response. What do you think Mr. Park should say at this point in the conversation?

Build Workplace Skills

1. **Types of meetings** From the board of directors to the office staff, meetings are commonplace in companies and other organizations. For each situation below, identify the type of meeting described and the format(s) that could be used for the meeting. (Learning Objective 1)

a. The persons responsible for the overall direction of a company are meeting to discuss long-range plans and policies.

b. A group of employees from one location are meeting to discuss the ongoing issue of office safety.

c. A group of employees from locations around the country are meeting to write a recommendation for a new flextime work policy for the company.

d. The manager of the human resources department is meeting with people who work in that department to discuss the progress of work assignments.

e. Company representatives and customers from the United States, Germany, and India are meeting to learn about new products the company will introduce next quarter.

2. **Meetings interview**   Interview (in person, by phone, or by e-mail) an administrative assistant. Ask him or her to describe a meeting that is conducted regularly in the organization and the duties he or she has related to the meeting. Write a summary of your interview and send it to your instructor. (Learning Objective 2)

3. **Meeting minutes**   Attend or view on television a meeting of a local club, governmental body, or civic organization. For example, city council meetings are often broadcast on local television channels. Take notes as the meeting is conducted. Write minutes of the meeting, using the minutes in Figure 10-4 as an example. Write a short report that describes the behavior and comments of the meeting leader and the participants. Evaluate the success of the meeting and the effectiveness of the leader and the participants. (Learning Objectives 2 and 3)

Communicate Clearly

4. **Seminar announcement**   Your supervisor has asked you to create a final copy from a draft of a seminar announcement. Open the *Microsoft Word* file CH10 Seminar from the data files. Make the changes indicated and edit the announcement to correct errors in grammar, spelling, punctuation, capitalization, number usage, and word usage. (Learning Objective 3)

5. **Green meetings presentation**   As with other aspects of business, using green (environmentally friendly) practices is important when planning meetings and conferences. Search the Internet or other sources to find tips and advice on ways to incorporate green principles into aspects of conference and meeting planning. Create an electronic slide presentation on this topic that can be placed on your company intranet. Include appropriate photos or other graphics and cite the sources of your information. The Green Meetings section of the U.S. Environmental Protection Agency website is a good place to begin your research.

6. **Business introductions**   As an administrative professional, you may be expected to introduce individuals attending a meeting at your company to company employees, clients, or others. Review the information you learned about making introductions in Chapter 2. Do research to find additional guidelines for making business introductions. Create a bulleted list of the guidelines and give the list an appropriate title. Save the list as a single-file web page that could be posted on your company intranet.

Planning Notes > ## Develop Relationships

7. **Conference room conflicts**   The use of your company's four conference rooms has become a growing point of tension among the office staff. You have been asked to lead a task force of other administrative assistants to work out a plan for assigning use of conference rooms that will resolve some of the conflicts. You open the meeting on time and ask for comments on how to begin creating a plan.

   "First," says Janna, "I think we need to identify all the problems we are having. For example, my team went to Conference Room A yesterday to have a meeting at 2 p.m.—the time at which I reserved the room. Another meeting was still in progress, so we had to find another place to meet."

   "The whole reservation system is a problem," says Kindra. "I reserved a room last Wednesday. By Thursday, someone had marked my name off the reservation book and scheduled another meeting there at that time."

   "I think we need a system that gives priority to some types of meetings that are more important than others," comments Miguel. "I can't go the vice president of operations and tell her that no conference rooms are available for an important meeting she wants me to schedule."

   What general steps can you ask the group to follow to resolve some of these conflicts? What specific recommendations can you make for resolving each type of conflict? (Learning Objective 4)

8. **Sharing accommodations**   You are good friends with Marion, another administrative assistant at your company. You, Marion, and several other company employees will attend a conference in another city next month. As a cost-saving measure, your department manager, Ms. Lui, has asked for volunteers who would be willing to share a hotel room at the conference with a coworker. Marion has suggested that the two of you volunteer to share a room. You are not comfortable with the idea of sharing a hotel room with a coworker. What can you say to Marion to decline the suggestion without causing hurt feelings? What are some reasons you could give for not wanting to share a room? (Learning Objective 4)

> ## Use Technology

9. **Conference call**   You need to schedule a telephone conference call with participants in Atlanta, Georgia; Las Vegas, Nevada; Mexico City, Mexico; and Paris, France. The participants have indicated that a Tuesday is the best day of the week for the call. About one hour is needed for the call. The call can begin as early as 8 a.m. local time and should be completed by about 6 p.m. local time. At what time should you schedule the call to begin? Give the local time for each city. Websites such as the World Clock Meeting Planner and the World Time Server can help you find the best time. Links are provided on the website for this book. (Learning Objective 3)

10. **Online map**   Your supervisor will drive to a conference in Washington, D.C., from the company location in Arlington, Virginia. Use the Internet or other sources to find a map and driving directions from the company to the conference site. The company address is 5328 Lee Hwy., Arlington, VA 22207. The conference is at the Walter E. Washington Convention Center in Washington, D.C. (Learning Objective 3)

> *Above & Beyond*

Meeting evaluation form   Your company managers have announced an initiative to improve the quality of meetings held in the company. For the next six weeks, everyone who attends a meeting will be asked to complete and submit an evaluation of the meeting. You have been asked to create an online evaluation form that can be completed in *Microsoft Word*. Open the file CH10 Form from the data files. Use the information in the file to create the evaluation form. (If you are not familiar with creating online forms in *Word*, search the *Word* Help information using the phrase *create forms that users complete in Word*.) Protect the form and save it. Test the form by completing it and saving the completed form under a new name. (Learning Objective 3)

Planning Notes

Part 4

Professional Profile

Tere Richard

Senior Administrative Assistant
College of Nursing
University of Central Florida
Orlando, Florida

Tere Richard is senior administrative assistant in the College of Nursing at the University of Central Florida. For the last two years, her primary job has been to assist the dean of the College of Nursing with her business affairs within and outside the college.

Though Tere has one official job title, she wears several hats. "My specific activities are wide-ranging, since we have a small staff. Examples of my tasks include planning and supervising a graduation ceremony for more than a thousand guests, preparing drafts of presentations and speeches for the dean, gathering data and drafting reports, helping faculty with computer needs, and attending meetings."

"Establishing a logical organizational framework is essential, especially with electronic files.... Once that structure is in place, it is well worth the effort."

Tere manages both electronic and paper files. "Most of our business files are maintained electronically on a shared drive," explains Tere. "This shared drive is divided into private and public files. Public files, such as college forms and student handbooks, are accessible by all employees in our college." Private files are saved in a special portion of the drive with limited accessibility. Examples of private files include evaluations, correspondence, and faculty data.

Managing the dean's travel schedule is also a challenge, given the university's complex procedures. "The provost's office needs to approve travel requests. As a result, I need adequate lead time to prepare the internal paperwork, get approval from the finance office, and receive final approval before reservations can be made." To help plan ahead, Tere marks conference dates on her calendar many months in advance.

Tere, an organizational wizard, shares her secret to well-maintained files and records: "Establishing a logical organizational framework is essential, especially with electronic files. It may take some time to determine the most effective organizational system, but once that structure is in place, it is well worth the effort."

Records Management, Travel, and Finances

Ready, Set, Plan

Use this space to plan your work in this section. Record the due dates for reading assignments and other activities for each chapter. If you are working with a team or partner, record the schedule for team meetings. Do you need a list of phone numbers or email addresses? Don't forget your other commitments: work, other classes, and family.

©ANTHONY STRACK, GALLO IMAGES/GETTY IMAGES

Do I qualify?

Administrative Assistant

Fast-paced law firm is looking for a hard-working and reliable administrative assistant to perform the following duties:

- Coordinate, store, and retrieve files at the request of attorneys and paralegals
- Coordinate case transfers, including creating inventory lists for files
- Copy and ship files to other sites
- Independently review and process correspondence on a daily basis
- Communicate filing backlog and any other file-room issues to the team leader

Dependability, attention to details, and ability to follow/interpret procedures are required for success in this job.

©MARK WRAGG, ISTOCK

CHAPTER

11

Learning Objectives

1. Identify reasons that records are valuable.

2. Describe supplies, equipment, and media for filing electronic and physical records.

3. Describe types of records storage systems.

4. Apply filing procedures for physical and electronic records.

Managing Records

Value of Records

Businesses need current, accurate, and relevant information to be successful. Information is received and created by businesses in many ways. Letters are sent and received from clients and customers. Governments provide regulations on filing taxes and reports. Marketing campaigns tell customers about the company's products or services. A business executive may receive dozens of e-mail messages each day about various business matters. The amount of information a business handles can be overwhelming unless it is managed effectively. Managing information is an important part of an administrative professional's duties.

Business Records

A **record** is information stored on any medium that is received or created by an organization and that provides evidence of an event, activity, or business transaction. A record may be a printed document, such as a letter or report, or an electronic file, such as an e-mail message or spreadsheet table. Sound recordings, movies, photographs, and images on microfilm may also be records.

Records are assets that have value to a business or organization depending on their content and purpose. Figure 11-1 lists four areas in which records have value.

Records Life Cycle

Records are important because they provide a history of a business or organization. Successful organizations use the information in records to make decisions, handle daily operations, and plan for the future.

Because records are so valuable, they must be properly managed. **Records management** is the systematic control of records, from the creation or receipt of the record to its final disposition.

After records are created or received by an organization, they have value for a period of time. During this time period, records are stored and may be retrieved for use. Eventually, most records are destroyed because they are no longer useful. The records life cycle has five phases:

1. Creation or receipt of the record
2. Distribution of the record to people inside or outside the company who use the information
3. Use of the record (for making decisions, locating information, and so on)
4. Maintenance of the record (filing and retrieving as needed)
5. Disposition of the record (retaining the record or destroying the record)

Documents or messages that have no continuing value to the organization are not considered records and should not be kept. These documents should be discarded after they are read. For example, an e-mail message that states the time for

meeting will have no value after the meeting has taken place and can be discarded. Records retention is discussed further in Chapter 12.

Storage Supplies, Equipment, and Media

The selection and arrangement of records storage supplies, equipment, and electronic media depend on whether the organization's records management system contains physical records, electronic records, or both.

Physical records include items such as traditional paper documents (forms, correspondence, contracts, reports, and hard-copy printouts of e-mail or web pages), microfilm rolls or sheets, films, videos, recordings, and photographs.

Electronic records are files stored on personal computers, network file servers, DVDs, and other electronic media. Selection of systems and equipment to manage this wide array of business records is best achieved when personnel are knowledgeable about the available systems, equipment, and supplies.

Basic Filing Supplies

Basic filing supplies for physical records include file folders, hanging or suspension folders, file guides, and labels.

Figure 11-1 Value of Records

AREA	EXAMPLES
Legal	Articles of incorporation, contracts, deeds
Financial	Budgets, balance sheets, income statements, receipts for travel and equipment purchases, bank statements
Historical	Employee evaluations, payroll records, job termination records
Daily Operations	Policy and procedures manuals, organization charts, minutes of meetings, sales reports, production reports

File Folders   A file folder is generally a manila folder either 8 ½ by 11 inches or 8 ½ by 14 inches. Colored folders are also available. The filing designation for the paper document(s) that are placed in the folder is keyed on a label and then affixed to the tab of the folder. The tab may be at the top of the folder for traditional drawer files or on the side of the folder for open-shelf filing (a type of filing in which files are placed on shelves similar to books on a shelf).

Folders are made with tabs of various widths, called cuts. The cuts are straight cut, one-half cut, one-third cut, and one-fifth cut. File folders may be purchased with these cuts in various positions. For example, if you are buying folders with one-third cuts, you may want to have all the tabs in first position. Or you may want to have the tabs in first, second, and third positions. With folders that have tabs in three positions, you can see the file captions on three folders at once. Figure 11-2 illustrates the cuts in various positions.

Suspension folders for storing records are also available. These folders are also called hanging file folders because small metal rods attached to the folders allow them to hang on the sides of the file drawer. Plastic tabs and insertable labels are used with the folders. These tabs and labels can be placed in any position using the precut slots on the folder. Standard file folders are often placed in hanging folders. The standard folders can be easily removed when working with the files.

File Guides   A file guide is usually made of heavy pressboard and is used to separate the file drawer into sections. Each guide has a printed tab with a name, number, or letter representing a section of the file drawer in accordance with the filing system. Guides with hollow tabs in which labels are inserted are also available. The filing designation is keyed on the label and inserted in the tab. Guides are always placed in front of the file folders.

File Folder Labels   File folder labels may be purchased in various configurations, including continuous folder strips, separate strips, rolls in boxes, and pressure-sensitive adhesive labels. Different colored labels can speed up the process of filing and finding records and can eliminate much misfiling. It is easy to spot a colored label that has been misfiled because that color stands out from the other colors that surround it.

Be consistent when you key labels for files. Follow these suggestions:

- Key label captions in all capital letters with no punctuation.

- Begin the caption about 1/4 inch from the left edge of the label; key any additional information about 1/2 inch to the right.

- Always key the name on the label in correct indexing order. (Indexing order is covered later in the chapter.)

- Use the same style of labels on all folders. For example, if you decide to use labels with color strips, use them on all folders. If you decide to use colored labels, be consistent in using them on all folders.

- Key wraparound side-tab labels for lateral file cabinets both above and below the color bar separator so the information is readable from both sides.

Some computer software programs have features to format standard label sizes. Using the software features makes creating and printing labels easy.

Figure 11-2 **Folder Cuts**

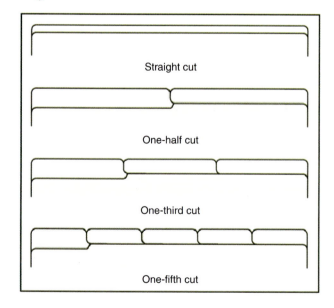

Straight cut

One-half cut

One-third cut

One-fifth cut

Equipment for Physical Records

Vertical drawer cabinets are the traditional storage cabinet for physical records, with the most common vertical file having four drawers. Lateral files are similar to vertical files except the drawer rolls out sideways, exposing the entire contents of the file drawer at once. Lateral files require less aisle space than vertical files.

Movable-aisle systems consist of modular units of open-shelf files mounted on tracks in the floor. Files are placed directly against each other. Wheels or rails permit the individual units to be moved apart for access. The movable racks may be electrically powered or moved manually. Because these movable systems take up less space than standard files, they are being used more and more today.

Equipment and Media for Electronic Records

The personal computer is a major electronic filing equipment component. With database and document management software, the personal computer that is networked with other PCs can:

- Provide electronic document storage and retrieval.
- Serve as an access device for scanned and electronically generated documents.
- Maintain records inventories.
- Retrieve documents stored electronically.
- Store records retention and destruction data.

In addition to being stored on the hard drive of a computer, electronic records may be stored on a variety of external storage media. External hard drives, CDs, DVDs, and flash drives are examples of external storage devices.

An external hard drive connects to a computer using a USB port, making the device easily portable. An external hard drive stores data like an internal hard drive of a computer. Files can be saved, retrieved, copied, and deleted. External hard drives are useful for backing up files from a computer or for long-term storage of files. A typical hard drive can hold several hundred gigabytes of data. Hard drives with larger storage capacity are being developed.

Communicating @Work

As you manage records, you may see confidential information contained in the records. Confidential information is data that should be kept private or secret from those who are not authorized to have access to this information. Discuss confidential information with coworkers or others only if you are sure they are authorized to know the information and only for business purposes.

Reasonable protection must also be exercised to keep records that contain confidential information secure. Users should follow company policies for handling confidential information.

↗ In some offices, a written request bearing the signature of a designated person is required for release of classified or confidential records.

↗ In an electronic system, access to confidential records is limited to those users who know the password or have been given access through a security system.

↗ In other instances, confidentiality of records may preclude users from removing the records from the storage room.

CD (compact disc) technology has become popular in digital archiving because information stored in this format cannot be modified or erased but can be read any number of times. If the information stored on the CD needs to be revised, then CD-RW (CD-rewritable) technology is used. CDs provide 700 megabytes of storage.

DVD (digital versatile disc) technology is a popular choice for file storage. A DVD can contain video and sound files as well as data files, such as a word processing document. The disc may have one or two sides and one or two layers of data per side.

Microfilm and Microfiche

There are two common types of microforms:

↗ Microfilm is a roll of film that contains a series of frames or images.

↗ Microfiche is a sheet of film that contains a series of images arranged in a grid pattern.

Microfiche is easier to handle than rolls of microfilm because each fiche has a title that can be read without magnification. Each fiche holds approximately 90 pages of information. Additional microfiche can be added to the file as needed, making updates easier than with microfilm.

© GRAMPER | DREAMSTIME.COM

© ISTOCKPHOTO.COM/TREVOR NORMAN

The number of sides and layers determines the disc capacity. A typical double-sided disc can store 9.4 gigabytes of data.

A flash drive is a storage device that contains a memory chip for storing data. It connects to a computer via a USB port. Once files are saved on the device, no power source is required for the device to continue to store files. Users can save, retrieve, copy, and delete files just as they would on a hard drive. A flash drive is useful for backing up files or transferring files between computers. Flash drives can hold anywhere from several megabytes to several gigabytes of data. They are also called by names such as jump drives, thumb drives, keychain drives, pen drives, and memory sticks.

Microform Media

In addition to the storage of records in paper and electronic form, microforms may be used to store records. **Microform** is a general term for microimage media such as microfilm and microfiche.

Most applications of microform storage are for records that are inactive or infrequently accessed. For example, personnel departments store personnel records of former employees on microforms, and libraries store newspapers on microforms. Little space is required to store microform records compared to the space required for paper records.

Records stored on microfilm remain complete and in their original order. Magnification equipment is required to read microimages.

Records Storage Systems

Records may be organized in alphabetical order, numerical order, or a combination of both. Records in a physical or electronic system may be stored by either of these methods.

Alphabetic Storage Methods

The **alphabetic storage method** uses the letters of the alphabet to determine the order in which a record is filed. This is the most common method used for storing records.

Figure 11-3 illustrates an alphabetic file for physical records. Records are filed according to alphabetic filing rules, which are given in a later section of this chapter. In Figure 11-3, the primary guides are placed in first position. Special guides, used to lead the eye quickly to a specific area of the file, are in second position. A general folder holds records for names that do not have enough records (usually three to five records) to warrant an individual folder.

Records in the folder are arranged alphabetically. If there are two or more records for the same name, the records are arranged by date with the most recent date in front. Individual folders, such as ARNOUX GERALD in Figure 11-3, hold only records related to that company. Records in the folder are arranged by date with the most recent date in front.

Advantages of an alphabetic system include:

- It is a direct access system. There is no need to refer to anything except the file to find the record.

- The dictionary arrangement is simple to understand.

- Misfiling is easily checked by alphabetic sequence.

Variations of the alphabetic storage method include the **subject storage method** (arranging records by their subject) and the **geographic storage method** (arranging records by geographic location).

Subject Storage Method   The subject storage method is widely used in organizations. Filing by subject requires that each record be read completely to determine the subject—a time-consuming process. This method is difficult to control because one person may read a record and determine the subject to be one thing, and another person may read the record and decide the subject is something entirely different. For example, one person who classifies records about advertising promotions may determine that the subject is *advertising*, while another person may determine that the subject is *promotions*.

Figure 11-3 Alphabetic File

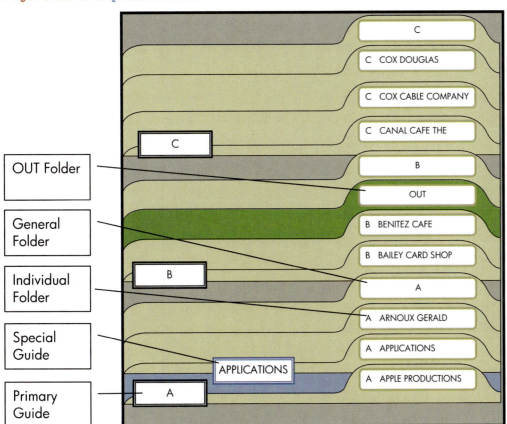

Figure 11-4 shows a subject file. The main subjects are indicated by the primary guides in first position. Secondary guides indicate subdivisions of the main subjects. A subject folder holds records for each secondary guide. A general folder holds other records for that subject that do not have enough records for a separate subject folder. For example, records for customer services that are not related to discount cards would be in the Customer Services general folder.

A permanent cross-reference guide directs filers to look for records related to *advertising* under *promotions*. Preparing cross-references is discussed later in this chapter.

A subject system can be a direct or indirect access system. When the system is direct, the subject file is a simple one (with only a few subjects) and access can be obtained directly through its alphabetic title. Keeping the subjects in alphabetical order is necessary.

Most subject systems are more complex and require some type of index. An **index** is a listing of the names or titles used in a filing system. Without an index, it is almost impossible for the subject storage method to work well. This index may include several levels.

Figure 11-5 on page 197 illustrates two- and three-level subject indexes. The index should be kept up-to-date as new subjects are added and old ones eliminated. When new subjects are added, the index provides guidance to avoid the duplication of subjects.

Geographic Storage Method Another variation of an alphabetic system is the geographic storage method, in which related records are grouped by location. Geographic filing is considered a direct method if you know the location of the file needed. If you do not, it is an indirect system and requires a separate geographic index file in a physical system or the appropriate keywords

Figure 11-4 Subject File

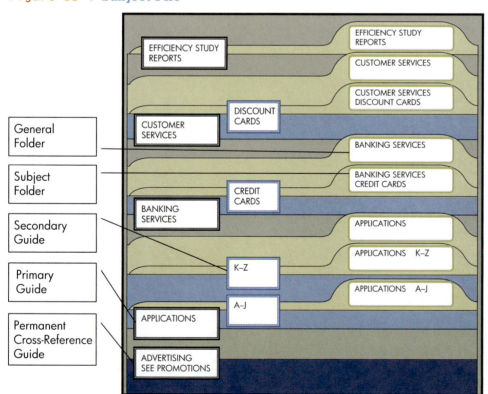

Figure 11-5 Three-Level Subject Index

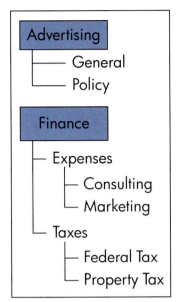

folders: individual folders, city folders, and general state folders. Individual folders hold records for one person or company. City folders hold other records for that city. General state folders hold records for that state that do not relate to one of the individual or city folders.

Numeric Storage Methods

Under the **numeric storage method**, records are given numbers and are arranged in a numeric sequence when stored. The numeric method is particularly useful to organizations such as these:

- Insurance companies that keep records according to policy numbers

- Law firms that assign numbers to cases and/or clients

- Real estate agencies that list properties by code numbers

(unique identifiers) set up for an electronic system so you can query the system in a variety of ways.

Figure 11-6 shows a geographic file. Geographic filing is particularly useful for these types of organizations:

- Utility companies, for which street names and numbers are of primary importance in troubleshooting

- Real estate firms that track listings by area

- Sales organizations that are concerned with the geographic location of their customers

- Government agencies that file records by state, county, or other geographic division

In Figure 11-6, the primary guide in first position shows the main division of the file, state names. The secondary guides in second position show cities names. Folders captions are in fourth and fifth positions. There are three types of

Figure 11-6 Geographic File

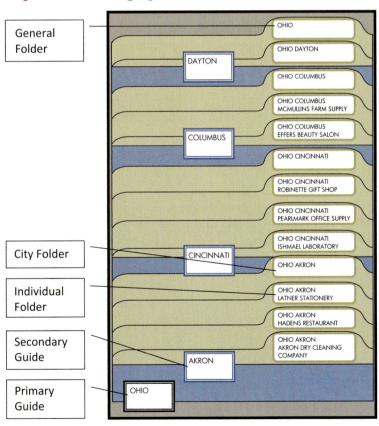

Figure 11-7 Numeric File

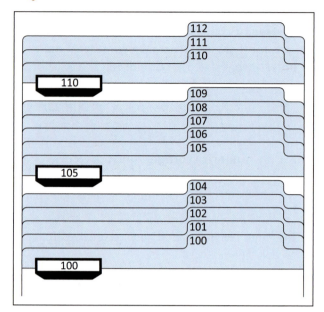

A physical numeric file has four basic parts:

1. Numeric file

2. Alphabetic general file

3. Alphabetic index (a file containing the names of individuals, organizations, and companies with the number that has been assigned to each one)

4. **Accession log** (a file containing a list of the numbers that have been used)

In practice, here is how the numeric method works:

1. When a document is ready to be filed, the alphabetic index is consulted to get the number that corresponds to the name by which the record is to be filed.

2. The number established is placed on the document; the document is placed in the numeric file.

3. If the filing name is new and no number is established, the document may be placed in the alphabetic file until there are enough records for this name to open an individual numeric file.

4. If it is necessary to establish a new numeric file, the accession log is consulted to determine the next number to be used.

Consecutive Storage Method   In the consecutive storage method, also called *serial* or *straight-number* filing, each digit is an indexing unit. The first digits of a number are compared to determine filing order. When the first digits are the same, the second digits are compared, and so on. The numbers used may be part of the record itself, such as a number on an invoice, or the number may be written on the record. As each new record is added to the system, the number assigned becomes higher.

Figure 11-7 illustrates a numeric file in which consecutive numbers are used. Primary guides in first position divide the file drawer into sections. Folder labels show individual numbers. Folders can also show the names of the correspondents to the right of the number if privacy or security is not a factor.

Terminal-Digit Storage Method   The terminal-digit storage method is another variation of numeric filing. In the basic numeric method, as the files increase, the numbers assigned become higher. Each new file needs to be placed behind all the lower-numbered files, which means that the file arrangement expands at the back.

This arrangement can be inconvenient. One alternative is the use of terminal-digit filing, in which a number is divided into three groups of digits. For example, 129845 becomes 12-98-45. By adding zeros to the left of a smaller number, three groups are created. The number 68559 becomes 06-85-59. The purpose is to indicate primary (first), secondary, and tertiary (final) groupings of numbers. These primary, secondary, and tertiary numbers tell the location of the record.

Figure 11-8 illustrates how the record 06 85 59 would be located. You would go to the 59 shelf and look behind the 85 guide to locate the 06 folder.

Note that you are reading the numbers from right to left in terminal digit filing. The next number (folder) to be assigned would be 07 85 59. After 99 85 59, a new guide, 86, would be created. The first new number behind Guide 86 would be 01 86 59.

Figure 11-8 Terminal Digit Storage Method

06	85	59
Tertiary (Folder number)	Secondary (Guide number)	Primary (File Section, Shelf, or Drawer number)

Filing Procedures for Physical Records

When filing physical records, such as paper documents, CD-ROMs, and microfilm, certain procedures should be followed before placing the record in the file. Physical records should be inspected, indexed, coded, and sorted in preparation for storing the records. Each step is described below. A cross-reference may also be required. That procedure is described later in this chapter.

1. **Inspecting** is checking to see that the record is ready to be filed. A release mark (such as a supervisor's initials, a "File" stamp, or some other agreed-upon designation) lets you know the record is ready to be filed.

2. **Indexing** is determining the filing segment by which the record is to be filed—the name, the subject, the number, or the geographic location—according to the procedures defined for the filing system.

3. **Coding** is marking the record with the filing segment (the name, subject, location, or number that was determined in the indexing process). For example, in an alphabetic filing system, an incoming letter would typically be filed under the name of the company in the letterhead.

Figure 11-9 on page 200 shows a letterhead in which the filing segment has been coded. The first unit of the filing segment is underlined. The remaining units are divided by diagonal marks and numbered.

4. **Sorting** is placing the records (paper, microfilm, or other physical records) in order for storage. Sorting records before going to the file cabinet or other container speeds the storage process.

5. **Storing** is placing records in storage containers, such as file cabinets, in the proper location.

Alphabetic Indexing Rules

Alphabetic indexing rules are used for indexing and coding physical records in an alphabetic filing system. Following a systematic set of rules for storing and retrieving records results in an accurate, efficient records management system.

The rules for filing may vary among organizations based on specific needs of the organization. Many organizations base their systems on the rules published by ARMA International, an association for information management professionals. The rules in this chapter are compatible with ARMA International filing rules. The companion website to this textbook has a link to ARMA International's website.

Chronological Filing

Chronological filing is a variation of numeric filing. The physical records are arranged by reverse date order within a file folder. This arrangement places the oldest records at the back of the file and the newest records at the front. The files may be divided by year or month, depending on the number of records.

Chronological filing is also used for tickler files (files used to tickle your memory and remind you to take certain actions). For example, in a task list on a calendar program, the items are arranged by the date the item should be completed. Once the items have been added to the program, you can readily call up the list of tasks you plan to accomplish each day.

Figure 11-9 **Letter Coded for Filing**

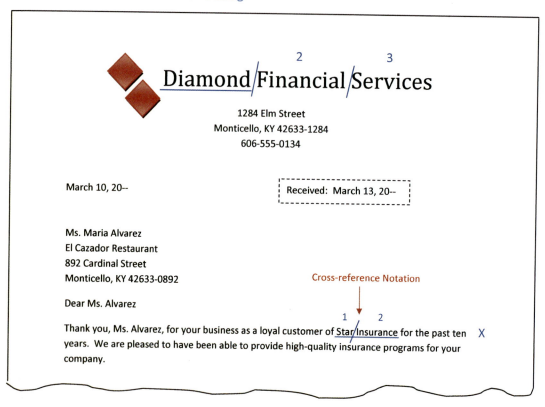

Rule 1: Indexing Order of Units

A. Personal Names

A personal name is indexed in this order: (1) the surname (last name) is the first unit, (2) the given name (first name) or initial is the second unit, and (3) the middle name or initial is the third unit. If it is difficult to determine the surname, consider the last name written as the surname. An initial precedes a complete name beginning with the same letter—nothing before something. When indexing, punctuation is omitted.

Rule 1 Personal Names

Name	Unit 1	Unit 2	Unit 3
Russ Evans	Evans	Russ	
Ruth T. Evans	Evans	Ruth	T
Sam Thomas Evans	Evans	Sam	Thomas

B. Business Names

Business names are indexed as written using letterheads or trademarks as guides. Each word in a business name is considered a separate unit. Business names containing personal names are indexed as written.

Rule 1 Business Names

Name	Unit 1	Unit 2	Unit 3
Juan Juarez Foods	Juan	Juarez	Foods
Milford Auto Repair	Milford	Auto	Repair
Virginia Street Cleaners	Virginia	Street	Cleaners

Rule 2: Minor Words and Symbols in Business Names

Articles, prepositions, conjunctions, and symbols are considered separate indexing units. Symbols are considered as spelled in full. When the word The *appears as the first word of a business name, it is considered the last indexing unit. Examples:*

Articles: *a, an, the*

Prepositions: *at, in, out, on, off, by, to, with, for, of, over*

Conjunctions: *and, but, or, nor*

Symbols: *&, ¢, $, #, % (and, cent or cents, dollar or dollars, number or pound, percent)*

Rule 2 Minor Words and Symbols

Name	Unit 1	Unit 2	Unit 3	Unit 4
B & B Atlanta	B	and	B	Atlanta
Dollar and Cents Store	Dollar	and	Cents	Store
The $ Tree	Dollar	Tree	The	
The Gingerbread House	Gingerbread	House	The	
Lawton & Lawton Shoes	Lawton	and	Lawton	Shoes

Rule 3: Punctuation and Possessives

All punctuation is disregarded when indexing personal and business names. Commas, periods, hyphens, apostrophes, dashes, exclamation points, question marks, quotation marks, underscores, and diagonals (/) are disregarded, and names are indexed as written.

Rule 3 Punctuation and Possessives

Name	Unit 1	Unit 2	Unit 3
A-Z Filing System	AZ	Filing	System
Iris B. Mills-Peters	MillsPeters	Iris	B
North/South Basketball League	NorthSouth	Basketball	League
Smith-Jones Corporation	SmithJones	Corporation	
Tom's Foods	Toms	Foods	

Rule 4: Single Letters and Abbreviations

A. Personal Names

Initials in personal names are considered separate indexing units. Abbreviations of personal names (Wm., Jas., Jos., Thos.) and nicknames (Liz, Bill) are indexed as written.

Rule 4 Single Letters and Abbreviations, Personal Names

Name	Unit 1	Unit 2	Unit 3
J. T. Park	Park	J	T
Jas. T. Park	Park	Jas	T
L. Pauline Park	Park	L	Pauline
Liz P. Park	Park	Liz	P

B. Business Names

Single letters in business and organization names are indexed as written. If single letters are separated by spaces, index each letter as a separate unit. Index acronyms (words formed from the first few letters of several words, such as ARCO and NASDAQ) as one unit regardless of punctuation or spacing. Abbreviated words (Corp., Inc.) and names (IBM, GE) are indexed as one unit regardless of punctuation or spacing. Radio and television station call letters are indexed as one unit.

Rule 4 Single Letters and Abbreviations, Business Names

Name	Unit 1	Unit 2	Unit 3	Unit 4
E K M Inc.	E	K	M	Inc
EG Environmental	EG	Environmental		
F A D Mfgs.	F	A	D	Mfgs
KBER Radio	KBER	Radio		
L & M Enterprises	L	and	M	Enterprises

Has Anybody Seen . . .?

As information flows in and out of an organization at an ever-increasing rate, it can be difficult to find essential information when it is needed. The administrative assistant is the person most often asked to locate a record and is expected to do so in a timely manner.

Understanding records management procedures and techniques can help you locate needed materials quickly—a skill that can make you invaluable to your supervisor and the organization.

Rule 5: Titles and Suffixes

A. Personal Names

A title before a name (Dr., Miss, Mr., Mrs., Ms., Professor, Sir, Sister), a seniority suffix (II, III, Jr., Sr.) or a professional suffix (CRM, D.D.S., Mayor, M.D., Ph.D., Senator) after a name is the last indexing unit. Numeric suffixes (II, III) are filed before alphabetic suffixes (Jr., Mayor, Senator, Sr.). If a name contains a title and a suffix (Ms. Emily Pagel, Ph.D.), the title (Ms.), is the last unit. Royal and religious titles followed by either a given name or a surname only (Princess Anne, Father Mark) are indexed and filed as written.

Rule 5 Titles and Suffixes, Personal Names

Name	Unit 1	Unit 2	Unit 3	Unit 4
Father Ryan	Father	Ryan		
Alberto J. Fernandez	Fernandez	Alberto	J	
Alberto J. Fernandez, II	Fernandez	Alberto	J	II
Alberto J. Fernandez, Jr.	Fernandez	Alberto	J	Jr
Mr. Alberto J. Fernandez	Fernandez	Alberto	J	Mr
Maria D. Perez, M.D.	Perez	Maria	D	MD
Miss Maria D. Perez	Perez	Maria	D	Miss
Sister Maria Perez	Perez	Maria	Sister	
Sister Maria	Sister	Maria		

B. Business Names

Titles in business names are indexed as written. Exception: The word The *that begins a business name is considered the last indexing unit.*

Rule 5 Titles and Suffixes, Business Names

Name	Unit 1	Unit 2	Unit 3	Unit 4
Aunt Elena's Fudge	Aunt	Elenas	Fudge	
Doctor Joe's Greenhouse	Doctor	Joes	Greenhouse	
Dr. Kim's Counseling	Dr	Kims	Counseling	
The Dr. Store	Dr	Store	The	
Mr. Aiken's Bait Shop	Mr	Aikens	Bait	Shop
Sister Susan's Donut Shack	Sister	Susans	Donut	Shack

Rule 6: Prefixes, Articles, and Particles

A foreign article or particle in a name is combined with the part of the name following it to form a single indexing unit. The indexing order is not affected by a space between a prefix and the rest of the name (Amber De La Cruz), and the space is disregarded when indexing.

Rule 6 Prefixes, Articles, and Particles

Name	Unit 1	Unit 2	Unit 3	Unit 4
Mrs. Gloria R. De Gabriele	DeGabriele	Gloria	R	Mrs
LeMay's Fine Foods	LeMays	Fine	Foods	
Dr. Mark P. O'Connell	OConnell	Mark	P	Dr
St. Germain and McDougal CPAs	StGermain	and	McDougal	CPAs
Mr. Alexis P. Von der Grieff	VonderGrieff	Alexis	P	Mr

Rule 7: Numbers in Business Names

Numbers spelled out in a business name (Sixth Street Grocery) are considered as written and filed alphabetically. Numbers written in digits are filed before alphabetic letters or words (1 Day Cleaner is filed before Adams Cleaners). Names with numbers written in digits in the first units are filed in ascending order (lowest to highest number) before alphabetic names (229 Boutique, 534 Grocers, First National Bank of Marquette). Arabic numerals (2, 3) are filed before Roman numerals (II, III).

Names with inclusive numbers (33-37 Fence Court) are arranged by the first digit(s) only (33). Names with numbers appearing in places other than the first position (Pier 36 Cafe) are filed immediately before a similar name without a number (Pier 36 Cafe comes before Pier and Port Cafe).

When indexing names with numbers written in digit form that contain st, d, and th (1st Mortgage Co., 2d Avenue Cinemas), ignore the letter endings and consider only the digits (1, 2, 3). When indexing names with a number (in figures or words) linked by a hyphen to a letter or word (A-1 Laundry, Fifty-Eight Auto Body, 10-Minute Photo), ignore the hyphen and treat it as a single unit (A1, FiftyEight, 10Minute). When indexing names with a number plus a symbol (55+ Social Center), treat it as a single unit (55Plus).

Rule 7 Numbers in Business Names

Name	Unit 1	Unit 2	Unit 3	Unit 4
5 Step Cleaners	5	Step	Cleaners	
5th Street Bakery	5	Street	Bakery	
50% Discounters	50Percent	Discounters		
65+ Senior Center	65Plus	Senior	Center	
400-700 Rustic Way	400	Rustic	Way	
The 500 Princess Shop	500	Princess	Shop	The
XXI Club	XXI	Club		
Fifth Street News Shoppe	Fifth	Street	News	Shoppe
Finally 21 Club	Finally	21	Club	
Finally Free Club	Finally	Free	Club	
I-275 Garage	I275	Garage		
#1 TV Deals	Number1	TV	Deals	
Sixty-Six Highway Deli	SixtySix	Highway	Deli	

Rule 8: Organizations and Institutions

Banks and other financial institutions, clubs, colleges, hospitals, hotels, lodges, magazines, motels, museums, newspapers, religious institutions, schools, unions, universities, and other organizations and institutions are indexed and filed according to the names written on their letterheads. Exception: The word The that begins an organization name is considered the last indexing unit.

Rule 8 Organizations and Institutions

Name	Unit 1	Unit 2	Unit 3	Unit 4
1st National Bank	1	National	Bank	
Assembly of God Church	Assembly	of	God	Church
University of Michigan	University	of	Michigan	
Western High School	Western	High	School	

Rule 9: Identical Names

When personal names and names of businesses, institutions, and organizations are identical, filing order is determined by the addresses. Compare the addresses in the following order:

1. City names
2. State or province names (if city names are identical)
3. Street names, including *Avenue*, *Boulevard*, *Drive*, and *Street* (if city and state names are identical)
4. House or building numbers (if city, state, and street names are identical)

Rule 9 Identical Names

Name	Unit 1	Unit 2	Unit 3	Unit 4	Unit 5	Unit 6
Stop-N-Shop 5185 Texas Ave. Abilene, Texas	StopNShop	Abilene				
Stop-N-Shop 1903 Hwy. 192 London, Kentucky	StopNShop	London	Kentucky			
Stop-N-Shop 6490 6th St. London, Ohio	StopNShop	London	Ohio	6	St	
Stop-N-Shop 1692 Birch Ave. London, Ohio	StopNShop	London	Ohio	Birch	Ave	
Stop-N-Shop 21500 Birch St. London, Ohio	StopNShop	London	Ohio	Birch	St	21500
Stop-N-Shop 32890 Birch St. London, Ohio	StopNShop	London	Ohio	Birch	St	32890

Rule 10: Government Names

Government names are indexed first by the name of the governmental unit—city, county, state, or country. Next, the distinctive name of the department, bureau, office, or board is indexed.

A. Federal Government Names

Use three indexing "levels" (rather than units) for United States federal government names. Use **United States Government** *as the first level. The second level is the name of a department; for example,* **Department of Agriculture.** *Level 3 is the next most distinctive name; for example,* **Forest Service.** *If necessary, invert the names to file by the distinctive name. (Change* **Department of Commerce** *to* **Commerce Department.**) *The words* **of** *and* **of the** *are extraneous and should* <u>not</u> *be considered when indexing. They may be placed in parentheses for clarity.*

Rule 10 Federal Government Names

Name	Level 1	Level 2	Level 3
1. National Weather Service, Department of Commerce	United States Government	Commerce Department (of)	National Weather Service
2. Office of Civil Rights, Department of Education	United States Government	Education Department (of)	Civil Rights Office (of)
3. Federal Emergency Management Agency, Department of Homeland Security	United States Government	Homeland Security Department (of)	Federal Emergency Management Agency
4. Bureau of Reclamation, Department of the Interior	United States Government	Interior Department (of the)	Reclamation Bureau (of)
5. Federal Bureau of Investigation, Department of Justice	United States Government	Justice Department (of)	Investigation Federal Bureau (of)

Following the Rules

Following filing rules ensures that records are stored properly and can be retrieved quickly. For filing physical records, many organizations use rules based on those published by ARMA International. However, these rules may be adapted to the special needs of the organization.

The filing rules and procedures for your organization should be documented and followed consistently by all office employees. New employees should become familiar with them and any special procedures that are in place. Changes to the rules or procedures should be approved by the appropriate managers before being implemented.

B. State and Local Government Names

The first indexing unit is the name of the state, province, county, city, town, township, or village. The next unit is the most distinctive name of the department, board, bureau, office, or government/political division. The words State of, Province of, Department of, *etc., are retained for clarity and are considered separate indexing units. If* of *is not a part of the official name as written, it is not added as an indexing unit.*

Rule 10 State and Local Government Names

Name	Unit 1	Unit 2	Unit 3	Unit 4	Unit 5
Alabama Department of Education	Alabama	Education	Department	of	
Alabama State Attorney General	Alabama	State	Attorney	General	
City of Arlington Public Library	Arlington	City	of	Public	Library
City of Arlington Senior Center	Arlington	City	of	Senior	Center
Ashley County Department of Elections	Ashley	County	Elections	Department	of
Baker County Bureau of Licenses	Baker	County	Licenses	Bureau	of
Barstow Municipal Court	Barstow	Municipal	Court		
Benton City Hall	Benton	City	Hall		
Benton Mayor's Office	Benton	Mayors	Office		

C. Foreign Government Names

The names of a foreign government and its agencies are often written in a foreign language. When indexing foreign names, begin by writing the English translation of the government name on the document. The English translation is used for indexing. The most distinctive part of the English name is the first unit. Then index the balance of the formal name of the government, if needed, or if it is in the official name (China Republic of). Branches, departments, and divisions follow in order by their distinctive names. States, colonies, provinces, cities, and other divisions of foreign governments are followed by their distinctive or official names as spelled in English.

Rule 10 Foreign Government Names

Name	Unit 1	Unit 2	Unit 3	Unit 4
Govern d'Andorra	Andorra	Government		
Republik Osterreich	Austria	Republic	of	
Druk Yul	Bhutan	Kingdom	of	
Bundesrepublik Deutschland	Germany	Federal	Republic	of
Jamhuri ya Kenya	Kenya	Republic	of	

Cross-Referencing Records

A record can be requested by a name that is different from the one by which it was stored. This is particularly true if the first unit of the name is difficult to determine. When a record is likely to be requested by more than one name, a cross-reference is prepared. A **cross-reference** shows an alternate name or subject by which a record might be requested and indicates the storage location of the original record. Cross-referencing saves time when there may be confusion about where a record is stored.

On the original document, the name for the cross-reference should be underlined and the filing segments numbered. An *X* should be placed in the margin of the document near the cross-reference name as shown in Figure 11-9 on page 200. The cross-reference may be prepared using a cross-reference sheet. The cross-reference sheet shows the name under which the item is cross-referenced, and the sheet is filed under that name. The sheet also shows the name under which the record is filed. As an alternative to preparing a cross-reference sheet, a copy of the document may be made and filed under the cross-reference name.

Use cross-referencing for personal names and business or organization names that may be requested under a different name. Similar names that sound the same but have different spellings should also be cross-referenced. Figure 11-10 on page 209 shows examples of names that should be cross-referenced.

Filing Procedures for Electronic Records

Electronic records may be part of an electronic database or automated system. For example, customer names, addresses, and telephone numbers may be recorded in a database.

Electronic records may also be contained in individual files. Letters, reports, and contracts may be stored as word processing files. Budgets and cost analysis reports may be stored as spreadsheet files. Technical drawings and photos may be stored as graphic files.

Whatever the format, electronic records should be managed through the five steps of the records life cycle: creation or receipt, distribution, use, maintenance, and disposition.

Writing @Work

If you work for a large organization, filing procedures may be standardized across your department or the organization.

In some organizations, especially small companies, procedures used for filing records may vary by department or even by employee. If you work in such a situation, you should write a list of procedures that you or your department uses for filing records.

The procedures should contain enough details so that a temporary employee or someone from another department can easily follow them to file and retrieve records in your absence.

©ISTOCK

Automated Records

Electronic records may be created automatically by a system, such as an automated order system. For example, when a customer enters an order online, a record of the order is created and stored electronically. The customer's contact and payment information are added to a customer database. (When the customer orders from the company again, that information can be accessed by the

Figure 11-10 **Cross-Reference Examples**

Name Type	Original	Cross-Reference
Easily confused name	Andrew / <u>Scott</u>	Scott / <u>Andrew</u> SEE Andrew / <u>Scott</u>
Hyphenated personal name	Francine / <u>Haslitt-Higgins</u>	Francine / <u>Higgins</u> SEE Francine / <u>Haslitt-Higgins</u>
Hyphenated business name	<u>Trenton-Harding</u> / Excavating	<u>Harding-Trenton</u> / Excavating SEE <u>Trenton-Harding</u> / Excavating
Compound name	<u>Kendricks</u> / and / Adamini / Cleaners	<u>Adamini</u> / and / Kendricks / Cleaners SEE <u>Kendricks</u> / and / Adamini / Cleaners
Alternate name	Isabel / <u>Rodriguez</u>	Isabel / <u>Perez</u> SEE Isabel / <u>Rodriguez</u>
Popular or coined name	<u>Tom</u> / Chung's / Asian / Garden	<u>Tommy's</u> SEE <u>Tom</u> Chung's Asian Garden
Name with acronym	<u>MADD</u>	<u>Mothers</u> / Against / Drunk / Driving SEE <u>MADD</u>
Changed name	<u>Harris</u> / Distribution / Inc.	<u>Harris</u> / Supply SEE <u>Harris</u> / Distribution / Inc.
Similar name	<u>Allstate</u> / Insurance / Co.	<u>All</u> / State Insurance Co. SEE <u>Allstate</u> Insurance Co.

workplace wisdom

Whether records are in paper, microfilm, or electronic form, the ability to find records in a timely manner is crucial. *Findability* is a measure of how quickly and easily a record can be located.

Think of file folders and electronic folders as places to find records, not just places to store records. Before determining where to file an item, consider how the record will be requested.

Prepare cross-references when the record may be requested under more than one name or subject.

order system so that the customer does not have to enter it again.) Typically, an e-mail message is automatically sent to the customer confirming the order. In the distribution phase, the order information is automatically ⊙ISTOCK sent to the warehouse. Once the items have been shipped, tracking information may be available from the company's records or the delivery company's records.

Although these types of records are created and distributed automatically, employees use and maintain the records. Knowing how to access the records is important. For example, an electronic order record might be retrieved by entering the order number, the customer's name, or the customer's phone number. Once the record has been retrieved, it can be used, for example, to answer a customer's question about the order. You may have little or no involvement with the disposition of these kinds of records. However, someone in the company will be responsible for transferring the records to offline storage and eventually destroying them or placing them in permanent storage as company policy dictates. Chapter 12 has more information about records retention.

Individual Records

Creation and receipt of electronic records is a routine process for a typical administrative assistant. For example, you will key letters and reports and receive many e-mail messages. Not all

Dear Savvy Admin

Dear Savvy Admin:

I work for an obstetrician and part of my job is to create and maintain medical records.

Federal law protects the privacy of patients, and we are very careful in restricting access. Today an angry man came in demanding copies of his wife's medical records. I tried to explain patiently that a written release signed by his wife is required before I can release her records. What can I do to help avoid situations like this in the future?

Frazzled

Dear Frazzled:

As you know, the federal Health Insurance Portability and Accountability Act (HIPAA) safeguards patients' privacy. There are exceptions, though. For example, insurance companies, government agencies, and other health professionals providing treatment for the patient may have some information about patients. You might consider posting a sign in the office that highlights the main rules and restrictions so that patients' relatives are aware of the rules. You could also propose that staff members who explain the policy to patients suggest that patients share the information with their relatives.

Savvy Admin

electronic information that you create or receive should be treated as a record.

Only those items that have continuing value for the organization should be considered records. An e-mail from a coworker reminding you about tomorrow's brown-bag lunch does not have continuing value and is not considered a record.

Distribution of electronic records may be accomplished in several ways. For example, the record could be sent as an e-mail attachment, saved on a network where it is accessible to those who need it, posted on a website, shared in a web meeting, or saved on a CD and mailed or given to recipients. Use of electronic records is as varied as use of physical records. You or the recipients of the record may use the information it contains to answer questions, make decisions, compile data, or complete other activities.

For maintenance (storing and retrieving) of electronic records, using consistent procedures to code (name) and organize the records is very important. Record files can be named and stored using an alphabetic, subject, geographic, or numeric arrangement.

You may wish to organize records on your computer into folders in the same way that folders are organized in the company's physical records system (or in a similar way). As with physical records, think about how the record will

Technology @Work

Document management systems allow users to store and manage electronic documents and images of paper documents. Document management systems enable fast access to an organization's documents via a computer system or network.

The database of a document management system contains information, called **metadata**, about each record. Metadata typically includes the name of the author(s), date of the record, key words or terms that indicate the subject of the record, and the structure of the data (letter, spreadsheet, photo). Using this metadata, a record can be located quickly.

The system may provide security by limiting the access to a record to approved users. The system may include components or equipment for creating digital images or versions of paper documents, managing the workflow of records, and saving records to DVDs or microfilm for offline storage.

queries and filters to find particular subsets of information and to create reports using the information. An electronic database may be available to many users in an organization via a network or intranet or it may be stored on a single computer for use by a few people. *Microsoft Access* is an example of a popular database program.

When creating a database to store records, group data into tables of related information. For example, an automobile dealership might place customer contact information (name, address, e-mail address, and telephone number) in one table. The brand, model, year, and date of purchase of vehicles bought by each customer might be placed in another table. The tables can be related using a common field in each table, such as a customer name or customer number.

Storing data in related tables eliminates redundant data and allows you to create queries and reports that show data from several related tables at once. Figure 11-12 on page 212 shows an *Access* database table.

Figure 11-11 Document Properties

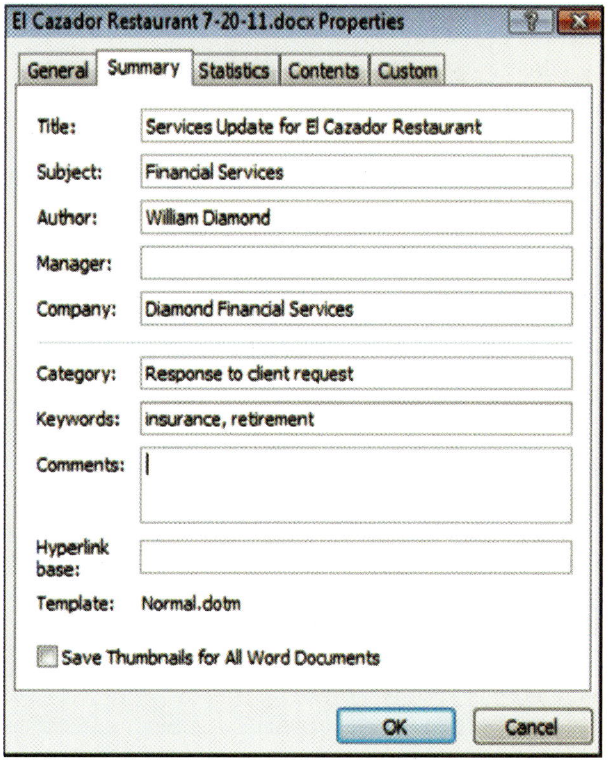

be requested when selecting a name for the file. In addition to using a consistent naming procedure, many programs allow you to enter metadata for records you create. For example, for a *Microsoft Word* document, you can enter details such as title, author name, subject, and keywords that identify the document's topics or contents. These properties can be used to search for the document if you cannot locate it by name. Document properties for a *Word* letter are shown in Figure 11-11.

Disposition of records you create or receive will be at your discretion for some records and according to company policies for other records. Information about creating backup copies of electronic records and records retention is provided in Chapter 12.

Database Records

A **database** is a collection of records about one topic or related topics. The records can be updated, copied, or deleted as needed. You can use database

When deciding which fields to use in a database table, consider the smallest unit of information you might use separately from the other information. For example, when creating personalized letters using mail merge, you might want to include a person's last name in the salutation of a letter. This field will not be available if you create only one field in the database for the customer name. If you create separate fields for the customer title, customer first name, and customer last name, you can easily create personalized salutations that include the customer's title and last name.

A database is often used to create an index or an accession log for a physical records system. If you want records in the database and the physical system to be sorted in the same way, experiment or read the program documentation to see how text and numbers are sorted in the program. You might need to make adjustments to the way you enter data or file records so that both systems work in the same way. For example, some programs require the use of leading zeros to make all numbers to be sorted the same length.

People @Work

RECORDS CLERK

A records clerk (also called a file clerk) classifies, stores, retrieves, and updates records. He or she inspects, indexes, and codes records for alphabetic or numeric filing systems. Records clerks handle both physical records (paper and microfilm) and electronic records stored in computer files. They may operate mechanized filing cabinets or shelves that rotate to make physical files accessible.

When a record is requested, the records clerk locates it and gives the record or a copy of the record to the person requesting it. The clerk keeps track of materials removed from the files to ensure that borrowed files are returned. Records clerks may also convert paper documents to electronic or microform files for storage. If you work in a company in which records are stored in a central location, you may need to request records from a records clerk.

Figure 11-12 Database Table

Customer #	Title	First Name	Last Name	Address	City	State
24671	Mr.	David	Morad	100 Bent Tree	Fairfield	OH
25567	Mr.	David	Sujak	2400 Greenview	Naperville	IL
25788	Mrs.	Dineen	Ebert	27 Main	Indianapolis	IN
29807	Ms.	Jenna	Ericksen	34 Emerson	Covington	KY
32679	Ms.	Sue	Chang	691 Meadow Lane	Cincinnati	OH
34788	Ms.	Patti	Jachowicz	302 North Lake	Cincinnati	OH
35228	Mrs.	Barbara	Johnson	764 Prairie	Henderson	KY
35447	Mrs.	Dorothy	Kutemeier	115 Wesley	Evanston	IL
35789	Mr.	Alfredo	Morales	5773 Beech Grove	Covington	KY
35801	Mr.	Mike	Goldstein	321 Asbury Dr.	Cincinnati	OH
36778	Ms.	Jackie	Kaufman	505 Pennsylvania	Carbondale	IL
36788	Ms.	Dorothy	Wiese	28 South Water	Elgin	IL
42631	Mr.	Chris	Wong	3115 Dunne Rd.	Alexandria	KY

Record: 13 of 35   No Filter   Search

Key Terms

accession log

alphabetic storage method

coding

cross-reference

database

geographic storage method

index

indexing

metadata

microform

numeric storage method

record

records management

subject storage method

Summary

- Businesses need current, accurate, and relevant information to be successful. A record is information stored on any medium that is received or created by an organization and provides evidence of an event, activity, or business transaction.

- Records management is the systematic control of records from the creation or receipt of the record to its final disposition.

- The records life cycle has five phases: creation or receipt, distribution, use, maintenance, and disposition.

- Basic filing supplies for physical records include file folders, file guides, and labels. Vertical and lateral drawer cabinets are the traditional storage equipment for physical records.

- The personal computer is the major electronic filing equipment component. Electronic records may also be stored on a variety of external storage media, such as external hard drives, CDs, DVDs, and flash drives.

- Records in a physical or electronic system may be organized in alphabetical order, numerical order, or a combination of both.

- Procedures for filing physical records include inspecting, indexing, coding, sorting, storing, and preparing cross-references as needed.

- Alphabetic indexing rules are used for indexing and coding physical records in an alphabetic filing system.

- Electronic records may be part of an electronic database, generated by an automated system, or created individually. Electronic records should be managed through the five steps of the records life cycle.

Bookmark It. *For convenient access to activities, links, and valuable career resources for administrative professionals, visit the companion website for this text:*

www.cengage.com/officetech/fultoncalkins

Planning Notes

Learning Objectives

1. Identify reasons that records are valuable.

2. Describe supplies, equipment, and media for filing electronic and physical records.

3. Describe types of records storage systems.

4. Apply filing procedures for physical and electronic records.

 Critical Thinking; Activity 5

 Activities 1, 2, 3, 4, 6, 10, 11

 Activities 7, 8, 9

Discussion Questions

1. In what four areas may a record have value for an organization?

2. In which phase of the records life cycle are indexing and coding most important?

3. Which microform, microfilm or microfiche, is easier to handle and why?

4. What is the most common storage method for physical records?

5. How does the terminal-digit numeric storage method differ from the consecutive numeric storage method?

6. What is the difference between the indexing and coding filing procedures?

7. What is the purpose of a cross-reference?

8. What is the advantage of entering metadata for electronic records that you create?

Critical Thinking

Improve records management   You began work at the Todd Real Estate Agency five months ago. You have found working with the company records challenging as you provide support for six real estate agents. The company has no standardized procedures for filing records. Each real estate agent and administrative assistant has his or her own system for handling records. There is a central file managed by another administrative assistant. The alphabetic storage method is used for these files, which are often duplicates of files kept by the agents.

What changes would you recommend to the agency manager to improve records management at the company?

Build Workplace Skills

1. **Value of records**   For each record described below, identify the area (legal, financial, historical, or daily operations) in which it has value to an organization. (Learning Objective 1)

   a. Filing procedures manual

   b. Employee termination records

   c. Contract to supply services to a customer

   d. Bank statements and canceled checks

   e. Tax payment records

2. **Records in the real world**   Visit a local business or other organization that maintains records. Observe the supplies, equipment, media, and storage method used for filing electronic and physical records. Write a short report that describes the filing procedures, equipment, and supplies used by the organization. Describe how you think the organization could improve its filing procedures or equipment. (Learning Objective 2)

3. **Terminal-digit filing**   Physical records that you are to store in a terminal-digit numeric filing system are coded with the numbers listed below. Sort the numbers in preparation for placing the records in the files. (Learning Objective 4)

06 24 79	06 75 23
06 25 79	06 75 22
08 19 45	06 24 78
07 02 98	08 92 15
08 54 79	08 93 15
08 19 23	07 01 14

4. **Alphabetic filing**   Open the *Word* file CH11 Names from the data files. This file contains names of individuals, companies, organizations, and government agencies that appear on paper records. Index and code each name. Place the names in order for storage in an alphabetic filing system. (Learning Objective 4)

Communicate Clearly

5. **Records follow-up message**   Open the Word file CH11 E-mail from the data files. This file contains the body of an e-mail message sent to remind an employee to return borrowed files. Edit the message to make it courteous and professional, using the *you* approach. Also correct errors in grammar, spelling, punctuation, capitalization, number usage, and word usage.

6. **Personal records**   Business records have value in one or more of four areas: legal, financial, historical, and daily operations. Personal records also have value in these areas. For each area, write a paragraph that describes your personal records and how you use them. (Learning Objective 1)

7. **Records storage systems**   Create an electronic slide presentation that describes alphabetic, subject, geographic, consecutive numeric, chronological, and terminal-digit numeric records storage systems. Include the main features of each system and give examples to illustrate how the system works. (Learning Objective 3)

Develop Relationships

8. **Maintaining goodwill**   You and three other administrative assistants are the primary users of an alphabetic storage system for physical files. Two of your coworkers are very prompt in filing new records and returning records to the filing cabinets after using them. One of your coworkers, Clarice Woo, is not. She often waits weeks to file new records. Stack of folders that she has taken from the files and not returned cover the desk and table in her office. Clarice is a good friend and an effective worker in other aspects of her job. You want to keep Clarice's goodwill, but her filing habits make finding records that you need difficult. What should you say to Clarice in an effort to resolve this problem? If Clarice is not cooperative in working toward a solution, what should you do?

9. **Confidential information**   You are good friends with Mario Diaz, another administrative assistant at your company. At lunch yesterday, Mario asked if you had heard about the

new bonus plan the company is going to implement. You have heard about the plan, but you know the information is confidential until the company is ready to announce details of the plan. Instead of answering directly, you said, "How did you learn about the plan, Mario?" "Oh, I happened to come across the information when I was filing a report this morning," Mario answered. What should you say to Mario in this situation? What is your responsibility regarding the company's confidential information?

Use Technology

10. **Client records**   You need to send correspondence to everyone on a client list several times a year. In addition, you are often asked to find addresses for individual clients or information about groups of clients. To make these tasks easier, you will create a new electronic database to contain records for each client. Open and print the *Word* file CH11 Clients from the data files. This file contains the client information. (Learning Objective 4)

    a. In a new database file, create a table named Clients. Enter the names and contact information for the clients.

    b. Create a query to show records for all the male clients that live in Illinois. Include the clients' first names, last names, and the state in the query results. Sort the records by last name. Print the query table.

    c. Create a report that includes all fields except the home phone number for clients in Cincinnati, Ohio. Sort the names in the report by last name. Print the report.

11. **Online storage**   Several companies provide file hosting and backup services for personal or business files via the Internet. Search the Internet using a search term such as *online storage*. Access several links on the search results list and read the information provided. Write a short report about the services provided by one company.

Above and Beyond

Research scanning services   You work as an administrative assistant for a small company in your town or city. The company owner has decided to move from a paper records system to an electronic system. All paper records are to be scanned into computer files for electronic storage. Since the company has thousands of documents to be converted, you will need help from a company that specializes in scanning documents for records management. It is your task to find a company to complete this task. Use your local Yellow Pages and the Internet to find a company that you will recommend for this job. Send an e-mail message to your instructor giving the name of the company and why you recommend this company for the job. Include the company's website address if one is available.

Administrative Assistant

Opportunity for a responsible worker to help with preparing and managing correspondence. Duties include:

- Prepare outgoing mail
- Pick up mail daily from the USPS and deliver mail to departments
- Conduct transactions with USPS and private carriers
- Print postage and labels
- Operate copier, paper shredder, and sorter
- Assist with records management
- Complete a variety of other administrative duties as assigned

Do I qualify?

©MARK WRAGG, ISTOCK

CHAPTER 12

Handling Mail and Retaining Records

Preparing Outgoing Mail

In Chapter 11, you learned about the value records have for an organization. Many documents that are created in an organization are mailed to clients, customers, vendors, government agencies, or other people or organizations. Copies of those documents become records to be used and maintained according to the organization's records storage procedures. In this chapter, you will learn effective ways to create and handle correspondence and about short- and long-term storage of records.

Your duties as an administrative assistant for handling outgoing mail will vary depending on the organization where you work. You will prepare and mail items such as individual letters, contracts, reports, and packages. You may also prepare bulk mailings, such as advertising brochures, flyers, or letters going to dozens or hundreds of recipients.

Learning Objectives

1. Prepare outgoing mail effectively.

2. Identify methods for sending outgoing mail.

3. Describe ways to handle incoming mail effectively.

4. Describe office copier types and features.

5. Describe procedures for records retention.

In Chapter 7, you learned to write and format effective letters, memos, and reports. You can increase your productivity when creating documents by using formatting features of your word processing software such as templates, macros, and building blocks. Other features, such as mail merge and envelope options, will speed up the process of addressing and mailing documents.

Templates

A **template** is a model for creating similar items. In the case of documents, templates can be used to create documents quickly and consistently. Word processing programs, such as *Microsoft Word*, provide templates for letters, memos, invitations, brochures, announcements, and other documents as shown in Figure 12-1.

A template file contains settings for margins, line spacing, formatting, and page layout that are appropriate for the type of document you will create. The template may also contain text and design elements, such as tables, borders, shading, or graphics.

Using a template file with these settings already in place saves time in creating a document and helps ensure that formats will be consistent. To use a template, open the template file and save it as a document (rather than a template file) using a different name. Key text, change document settings, and insert pictures or graphics as you normally would.

Figure 12-1 Templates for *Microsoft Word*

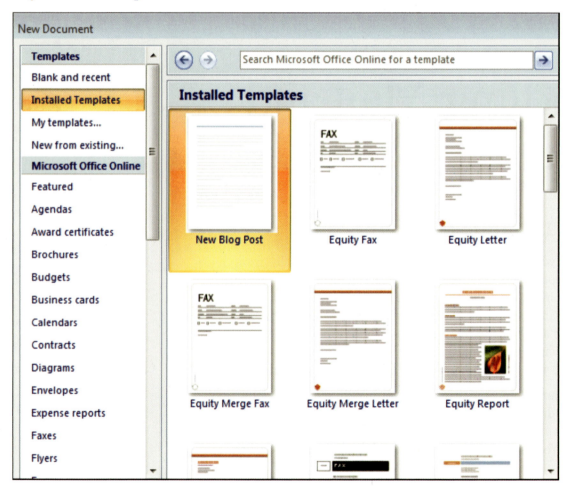

Once you have created a document or modified a template, you can create a new template based on the document. For example, you might start with a template for a product brochure. You could modify the template to add data, such as a company logo, name, address, web address, and e-mail address. Saving this document as a template and using it the next time you want to create a similar brochure will save time in creating the new document.

Building Blocks

Building blocks are parts of a document or text that are often used in a particular type of document. For example, every letter that you create will have a signature block that includes a name and title for the sender. The complimentary close for the letter might also be included in the signature block file. Another building block might include the company logo, name, and contact information, formatted as a letterhead. The cover or title page for a report could be in a building block.

Design elements, such as a text box, clip art, or formatted table, can also be placed in building blocks. Programs such as *Microsoft Word* contain galleries of building blocks that you can select and use in a document. Figure 12-2 shows *Word's* Cover Page gallery. You can also create a document part or **boilerplate text** (standard text used in documents) and add it to a gallery. The building blocks available in *Word* are listed in one place in the Building Blocks Organizer.

Figure 12-2 *Microsoft Word's* Cover Page Gallery

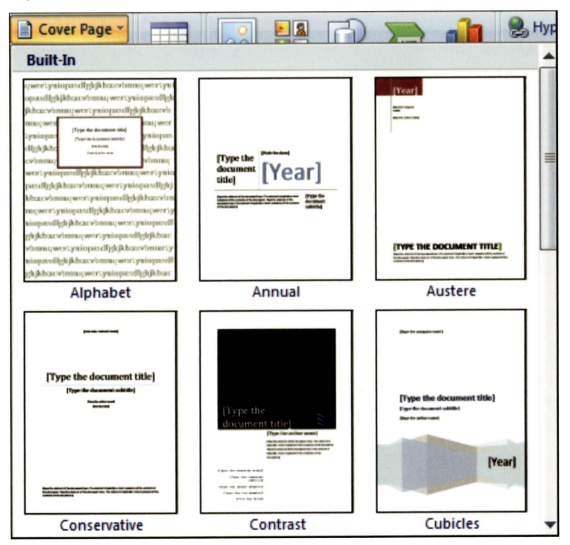

Mail Merge

Mail merge is a feature of word processing programs that allows you to create personalized letters, labels, or envelopes for large mailings. The text of the letter or other document is stored in the main file. A list of recipients (names, addresses, and other needed information) is stored in a data file. The list could be in a word processing table, a spreadsheet table, or a database table. In the main file, codes are placed in the document at places where personalized data should appear, such as the name and address of the recipient and the salutation, which will be individualized to the letter that person receives. The codes match the names of columns or fields in the data file.

The mail merge operation creates new documents that contain the text of the main file and data from the data file. Using mail merge is an efficient way to create letters for several recipients when only a small amount of data specific to each recipient changes with each letter.

Microsoft Word provides a mail merge wizard, as shown in Figure 12-3, that walks users through the steps of completing a mail merge operation.

Envelopes and Labels

Envelopes and labels can be created automatically for letters or other documents that contain a recipient's address. Creating an envelope automatically saves times and ensures that exactly the same name and address appear on the letter and the envelope. To create an envelope, follow the specific steps that are appropriate for your word processing software. For example, for *Microsoft Word*, open the file that contains the letter or other document. Select Mailings, Envelopes. *Word* displays the dialog box shown in Figure 12-4 on page 221, with the letter address and your return address (entered earlier as a default). You can print the envelope or add it to the document for later printing.

Similar procedures can be followed to create a mailing label. You will be given options to select the label size and to print a full page of the same label or a single label.

Figure 12-3 *Microsoft Word's* Mail Merge Wizard

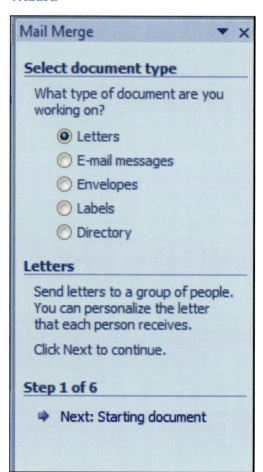

The address on an envelope should be located in an area that can be read by the U.S. Postal Service's automated equipment, such as an optical character reader. An optical character reader (OCR) is a machine that can "read" printed text and convert it to an electronic form that can be used by a computer, in this case to sort mail.

Figure 12-5 on page 222 shows the OCR area for a letter-sized envelope.* When automatically creating an envelope with word processing software, the address will be placed properly. When you place a label on an envelope or create an envelope address manually, be sure the address is placed in the OCR read zone.

---

* U.S. Postal Service, *Domestic Mail Manual*, "Address Placement," http://pe.usps.com/text/dmm300/202.htm#wp1047150 (accessed July 27, 2009).

Sending Outgoing Mail

Outgoing mail may be picked up and delivered by the U.S. Postal Service or by private mail carriers or delivery companies. When deciding which service to use, you should consider when the envelope or package should reach its destination, the cost of sending (and sometimes of insuring) the item, possible safety precautions for the contents, proof of delivery, or other services needed.

U.S. Postal Service

The U.S. Postal Service is a popular choice for mailing envelopes and packages. You should be familiar with USPS recommendations and restrictions for items that you send by U.S. Mail. The Postal Service identifies letters and cards in these categories: machinable, nonmachinable, and automation. Machinable items have a correct address and can be processed by Postal Service equipment. In most cases, you want individual envelopes you mail to be in the machinable category.

For large mailings, you may be able to save money by meeting the requirements for items in the automation category. Mail in the automation category contains barcodes and can be processed by high-speed equipment. Other requirements, such as a minimum number of pieces, may be required for automation mail. Consult the U.S. Postal Service website to learn about current requirements and costs for mailing items.

Figure 12-4 *Microsoft Word's* Envelopes and Labels Dialog Box

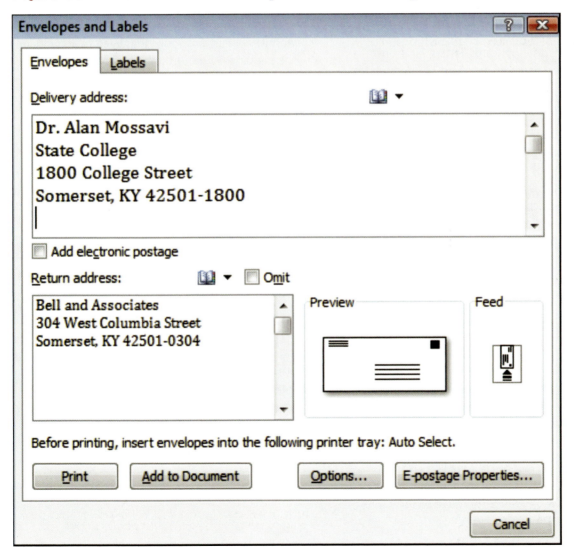

Figure 12-5 OCR Read Area for Letter Envelope

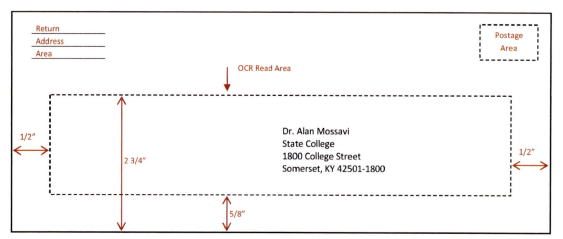

Classes of U.S. Mail   Some popular classes of U.S. Mail services are listed below. When selecting a service, consider the mailing cost and the time when the envelope or package should reach the recipient.

- First-Class Mail is for postcards, letters, large envelopes, and small packages weighing 13 ounces or less.

- Priority Mail is for envelopes and packages that weigh less than 70 pounds and fit in Priority Mail packaging.

- Express Mail is the fastest way to send envelopes and packages with guaranteed overnight delivery to many locations.

- Parcel Post is an option for envelopes and packages that weigh up to 70 pounds and measure up to 130 inches in combined length and width. Parcel Post is less expensive than Priority Mail, but it may take longer for the item to reach its destination.

- International Mail is available for envelopes and small packages going to most foreign destinations with various prices depending upon the weight and delivery time. When sending packages to other countries, be sure to check the Postal Service website for customs forms that need to accompany the package. Without these forms, the package may not clear customs in the country in question.

Special Services   The Postal Service offers several special services related to mail delivery. Some of these services are described in the following list:

- A Certificate of Mailing is a receipt that provides proof of the date when an item was mailed as well as the name and address of the recipient.

- Certified Mail provides a receipt stamped with the date and delivery information for the mailing that can be tracked online.

workplace wisdom

The letter, brochure, or other document that you prepare and mail may be the recipient's first contact with your organization. To make a good impression, documents must be written effectively, formatted in an attractive style that is easy to read, and free of errors. Documents that have smudges, errors, or omissions may make a bad impression on the reader.

- Delivery Confirmation provides access to the date and time an item was delivered via an online tracking system or by telephone.

- Insured Mail and Registered Mail provide insurance for mailed items. Items can be insured for their actual value up to $25,000.

- Return Receipt provides proof of delivery in the form of a card that shows the signature or stamp of the receiver and the delivery address and date. The card may be returned to your mailbox or as an e-mail attachment.

- Signature Confirmation provides the date, time, and location of the delivery of an item and a copy of the signature of the recipient. If you want to require that a specific person sign for mail, use Restricted Delivery service.

People @Work

MAIL CLERK

A mail clerk typically works in the mail room for a large organization. This person performs duties related to preparing outgoing mail and delivering mail to departments of the organization. The mail clerk may operate equipment such as a postage meter, copier, paper shredder, sealer, and sorter. She or he may seal envelopes or packages and apply correct postage from a postage meter or labels printed from a computer printer.

The mail clerk may conduct transactions with the U.S. Postal Service, private mail carriers, or online mail vendors such as Stamps.com. In some companies, the mail clerk keeps a log of all outgoing and incoming packages. Sorting and applying barcodes and postage for bulk mailing items is another duty typically performed by a mail clerk. If you work in a large company with a mail room, you may need to request services from a mail clerk.

You may want to combine services for a mailing. For example, purchasing Return Receipt service along with Certified Mail service provides proof of mailing and proof of delivery for an item. Fees vary by service.

Private Delivery Companies

Private delivery companies are used by organizations to mail envelopes and packages to recipients locally, around the country, or worldwide. The cost of services from private companies can be lower or higher than the U.S. Postal Service, depending on the delivery time, distance to the recipient, and size or weight of the envelope or package.

Many companies offer guaranteed overnight or second-day delivery of items. Private delivery services, such as FedEx and UPS, typically have websites where users can track packages from mailing to delivery. Some private carriers make scheduled daily pickups and deliveries to businesses. Drop-off locations are also available where packages can be mailed.

Handling Incoming Mail

Just as outgoing mail responsibilities depend largely on the size of the company, so do incoming mail responsibilities. One of your responsibilities as an administrative professional in a small firm may be to receive and process mail. In large companies, a big percentage of mail functions may be outsourced to independent companies. If mail is not outsourced, however, large companies usually have centralized mail departments that receive and distribute mail.

Mail is generally delivered by mail-room employees at set times during the day. In small organizations, a Postal Service carrier may deliver the mail directly to the organization. If the small organization maintains a post office box, you may be responsible for picking up the mail.

Sorting Mail

Once you receive the mail in your office or department, you must do a preliminary mail sort. If several individuals work in the department, sort the mail according to the addressee. An alphabetical sorter is handy if you are sorting mail for a number of individuals. Once the mail is sorted, place the mail for each individual into separate stacks.

When this preliminary sort is completed, sort each person's mail in this order:

1. Personal and confidential items. The administrative professional should not open mail marked "Personal" or "Confidential." Place this mail to one side so you do not inadvertently open it.

2. Special Delivery, Registered Mail, or Certified Mail. This mail is important and should be placed so the individual to whom it is addressed sees it first.

3. Regular business mail (First-Class Mail) from customers, clients, and suppliers. This mail is also considered important and should be sorted so it receives priority.

4. Interoffice communications. Although many interoffice messages are sent by e-mail, there are still times when the interoffice memorandum is more appropriate, particularly when the correspondence is relatively long or the information is confidential. Interoffice memorandums are generally sent in a distinctive interoffice envelope that can be readdressed and reused.

5. Advertisements and circulars. Advertisements and circulars are considered relatively unimportant and can be handled after other mail is answered.

6. Newspapers, magazines, and catalogs. These materials should be placed at the bottom of the correspondence stack since they may be read at the executive's convenience.

Opening Mail

Mail may be opened in the mail room or in the individual's office. Mail opened in an individual's office is usually opened by hand, using an envelope opener. When opening mail, follow these procedures:

- Have necessary supplies available, such as a date and time stamp, routing and action slips, a stapler, paper clips, and a pen or pencil.

- Before opening an envelope, tap the lower edge of the envelope on the desk so the contents fall to the bottom and are not cut when the envelope is opened.

- Check the envelope carefully to be certain all items have been removed.

- Fasten any enclosures to the correspondence. Attach smaller enclosures to the front of the correspondence. Attach larger enclosures to the back.

Communicating @ Work

Listen carefully when being given instructions for preparing mailings. The executive may not tell you whether to use U.S. Mail or a private carrier or which class of mail service to use. Instead you may simply be told, "This is routine" or "Be sure this contract gets to Ms. Martinez tomorrow."

You will be expected to make mailing decisions based on when the letter or package should arrive, the cost of delivery, and any special services that are needed. If you are not sure about the required delivery time or other special needs for mailing a letter or package, ask the executive for more details.

- Mend any torn paper with tape.

- If a personal or confidential letter is opened by mistake, do not remove it from the envelope. Write "Opened by Mistake" on the front of the envelope, add your initials, and reseal the envelope with tape.

Stack the envelopes on the desk in the same order as the opened mail in case it becomes necessary to refer to the envelopes. A good practice is to save all envelopes for at least one day in case they are needed for reference. Then they may be thrown away. Envelopes should be retained when one or more of the following situations exist:

- An incorrectly addressed envelope—You or your supervisor may want to call attention to this fact when answering the correspondence.

- A letter with no return address—The envelope usually will have the return address.

- An envelope that has a significantly different postmark from the date on the document—The document date may be compared with the postmark date to determine the delay in receiving the document.

- A letter specifying an enclosure that is not enclosed—Write *No Enclosure* on the letter and attach the envelope. Contact the sender if the enclosure is an important item.

- A letter containing a bid, an offer, or an acceptance of a contract—the postmark date may be needed as legal evidence.

- An envelope that appears to contain any suspicious substance or materials. Proper procedures for handling suspicious mail should be in place.

In many organizations, all incoming mail is stamped with the date and time of receipt. This procedure furnishes a record of when the correspondence was received. For example, a letter may arrive too late to handle the matter referred to in the letter. The stamped date of receipt on the envelope is a record showing that it arrived too late to complete a response.

Sometimes the correspondence is not dated; the date stamped on the letter shows the approximate date it was mailed. Date and time stamping may be done with a hand stamp or a small machine that prints the date and time.

Reviewing Mail

Busy executives need help with the large amount of mail that crosses their desks each day. As an administrative professional, you can help by reviewing the mail for the executive.

You may be asked to read the correspondence, underline or highlight important words and phrases, and check any calculations or dates that appear in the correspondence. Follow the executive's preferences.

If an enclosure is missing from the letter, make a note of this information. If a bill is received, check the computations. Indicate any discrepancies in a note. If the correspondence refers to a previous piece of correspondence, pull a copy of that correspondence and attach it to the reply letter with a note indicating that there is an attachment.

Presenting Mail

After you have completed the preliminary mail sorts and have opened, dated, time-stamped, read, and annotated, you are ready to do a final sort before distributing the mail. Sort items in this order: items that need immediate action, routine correspondence, and informational mail. Items that require immediate action must be handled on the

day of receipt or shortly thereafter. You will also have routine correspondence, such as memorandums and other types of non-urgent mail, as well as informational mail, which includes magazines, journals, newspapers, advertisements, and other types of mail that do not require replies but are for the executive's review.

The executive may ask you to distribute the mail two times a day. For example, if external mail is received in the morning and afternoon, the executive may ask that you organize and deliver it approximately 30 minutes after you receive the mail.

If you have been with the executive for a period of time, he or she may not want to see all mail. For example, you may be authorized to answer routine requests for information. The executive may not wish to see certain types of advertisements or catalogs.

At times, more than one person may need to read a piece of correspondence. In that case, make

Writing @Work

In addition to reviewing correspondence received in the mail, you may be asked to annotate it (write notes about previous action taken or facts that will assist the reader). You can annotate by writing notes in the margin of the correspondence or by attaching sticky notes. The advantage of sticky notes is that they can be peeled off and destroyed when you and the executive are finished with them.

Annotations may also be used to remind the executive of a previous commitment. For example, the executive might have agreed to have lunch with the person who signed the correspondence. When answering the letter, the executive may want to refer to their lunch plans.

©ISTOCK

photocopies of the correspondence and send a copy to each person on the list or route the correspondence to everyone, using a routing slip.

When determining whether to make photocopies, ask yourself if it is urgent that all individuals receive the information contained in the correspondence immediately. If so, it is best to photocopy the document. If not, it generally is best to use a routing slip, particularly if the correspondence is lengthy.

Handling E-mail

Some executives expect the administrative professional to assist with their e-mails. If so, be certain that you understand how she or he wants you to handle them. You might be expected to answer routine e-mail; if so, your employer needs to know that you have done so. Here are some suggestions for handling your employer's e-mail:

- Check the e-mail three or four times per day, depending on your employer's instructions. For example, you may check it at 9 a.m., 11 a.m., 2 p.m., and 4 p.m.

- Do not open e-mail marked "Confidential" unless your employer instructs you to do so.

- Read the e-mail, reply to the e-mail (if appropriate), and forward it, if necessary, to appropriate individuals.

- If the individual does not know that you routinely handle the e-mail of your employer, be explicit in the e-mail when you answer it. Say, for example, "Mr. Lui has asked that I respond to your e-mail."

- If you cannot handle the e-mail, send a note to your employer informing him or her of the e-mail you have not been able to handle. If your employer needs to handle it immediately, mark your e-mail as urgent.

When your employer is out of town, handle the e-mail as usual assuming you have been authorized to do so. If not, forward the e-mail to the appropriate person who is in charge during your employer's absence.

Handling Mail During the Executive's Absence

You may be expected to handle the executive's mail while he or she is away from the office. Talk with the executive before she or he leaves concerning your responsibilities in handling the mail. Ask specific questions so you have a clear understanding of

Technology @ Work

The U.S. Postal Service and some companies provide online options for printing postage and shipping labels from a computer. Using an online service to print labels and postage can be more convenient than making trips to the Post Office and less expensive than using a postage meter.

Click-N-Ship from the Postal Service allows users to download and print shipping labels with postage for packages. Free Delivery Confirmation is included for Priority Mail packages. There is no monthly fee for using Click-N-Ship.

Approved vendors, such as Stamps.com, Pitney Bowes, and Endicia, offer additional mailing services for those who need to ship higher volumes. These vendors charge a monthly fee for using the service.

what to do. Mistakes in handling mail can be costly or embarrassing to the company. Follow these general guidelines:

- When urgent mail (any mail, including e-mail, containing a matter to be handled immediately) is received, respond to the correspondence the same day. If you cannot answer the mail, send it to the appropriate person in your organization who can answer the correspondence. Usually your employer will have designated someone who is in charge in his or her absence. Make sure that person receives the urgent correspondence quickly.

- Answer mail that falls within your area of responsibility in a timely manner.

- Keep a copy of mail as well as a copy of your reply in a folder. The executive may want to review it when she or he returns.

- Keep mail that can wait for the executive's return in a separate folder along with any previous correspondence the executive may need when reviewing the mail.

Office Copiers

As an administrative professional, you will use office copiers extensively. You will make file copies of outgoing mail. You will make copies of some incoming mail to route to others or to use as working copies. Depending on the filing procedures used in your organization, you may also make copies of documents for cross-references. It is important that you know the capabilities of copiers and also that you avoid wasting resources by making unnecessary copies.

Copier Classifications

Copiers are classified into four basic categories, depending on their speed.

Low-Volume Copiers	Produce copies in the range of 18 to 30 cpm (copies per minute) and 5,000 to 10,000 ppm (pages per month)
Mid-Volume Copiers	Produce approximately 25 to 60 cpm and 80,000 ppm
High-Volume Copiers	Produce approximately 50 to 140 cpm and 500,000 ppm
Copy/ Duplicators	High-performance machines generally found in specialized copy/duplication centers or in print shops

If you work for a small company, you may be asked to research and recommend a copier for purchase by the company. Consider the number of copies that are typically made each week or month. This number will indicate whether you need a low-, mid-, or high-volume copier. Think carefully about features you may need, such as automatic sorting or collating. Also consider the cost of the copier, the cost of toner or ink cartridges, and the availability and cost of maintenance and repairs.

Copier Features

Office copiers have several features that can be helpful in your work. Learn to use the features of your particular copier by reading the product manual, viewing videos provided by the manufacturer, or attending training sessions. Some common copier features are mentioned here:

- **Reduction and enlargement.** This feature allows you to make the copy larger or smaller than the original. For example, reduced copies can be made of large documents so all filed copies are uniform in size. An enlargement feature also allows an original document to be magnified. Fine details on an original can be made more legible by using this feature.

- **Automatic document feeding.** The automatic document feeder (ADF) allows you to copy multi-page documents without having to lift and lower the platen cover for every sheet.

Postage Meters

COURTESY FP MAILING SOLUTIONS

A postage meter is a device that prints prepaid postage on an envelope or label. Postage meters are used extensively by businesses. The company pays for a certain amount of postage, which is credited to the postage meter. The postage is then printed and applied as needed until the prepaid amount has been used. Additional postage for the meter can be obtained by telephone or online.

Postage meters range from ones that simply apply postage and process at a relatively slow rate to those that can track dozens of accounts and process at speeds up to 140 letters per minute. Some meters allow users to print images, such as a company logo, on items in addition to printing postage.

- **Duplexing.** Copying on both sides of a sheet of paper is known as **duplexing**. On this setting, the copier automatically prints on both sides of the page, saving paper.

- **Editing.** A number of copiers have built-in editing features. These features include border erasing, centering, color adjusting, marker editing, and masking. Marker editing lets you change the color of specific sections of a document to highlight these areas. Masking allows you to block out areas of sensitive or confidential information.

©ISTOCK

Cost Control

Many organizations monitor the use of copiers in an effort to avoid the waste created by making more copies than needed. For example, employees may make ten copies of a document when only six are required. The additional copies are made "just in case." More often than not, the extra copies are thrown away.

Some organizations use copy control devices. For example, the user may enter an account number on a keypad or swipe a card through a card reader to gain access to the copier. With such systems, the number of copies made and the person (or his or her department) who made the copies are recorded. Costs may be charged to departments based upon these counts. This system allows managers to review the number of copies made by each person or department. If the copy count seems too high, appropriate action can be taken to investigate whether unneeded copies are being made.

Dear Savvy Admin

Dear Savvy Admin:

As the executive assistant to the director of human resources, I have access to confidential information about salaries, bonuses, commissions, and severance packages. My cubicle is in a high-traffic area and my monitor faces the aisle. I get distracted when anyone walks by, and I worry that some of my coworkers who stop by to chat are looking at my screen. It's distracting to keep closing my files, and rearranging my cubicle is not an option. What can I do?

On Display

Dear On Display:

Even if no one is peeking at your work, this potentially serious issue is obviously affecting your peace of mind. I assume that your system is password-protected and that you use a screen saver, but I suggest that you talk to the director about other solutions. Can you move to a cubicle in a more out-of-the-way location? At the very least, research the cost of a privacy shield for your monitor. It sounds like a wise investment.

Savvy Admin

Selecting the proper supplies for the copying job and recycling used paper are additional ways to control costs. Paper for in-house documents such as a department meeting agenda can be printed on less expensive paper, while documents going outside the organization may require higher-quality paper. Specialty papers, such as colored paper, card stock, or glossy stock, may be used to copy advertising brochures and flyers. These papers are more expensive than standard copy paper and should be used only when needed.

Many companies keep bins for used paper near the copier area. Pages that have smudges or do not copy properly for some reason can be put in the bins for recycling. Paper documents that are no longer needed can also be recycled. This paper may be sent to a recycling center or shredded to use as packaging material for shipping items. This is one way that an office can "go green." If your company does not have a recycling program, you can see suggestions for how to start a program by visiting the PaperRecycles.org website hosted by the Paper Industry Association Council.

Ethical and Legal Considerations

Unfortunately, some employees use the office copier to copy materials for personal use without approval of the company. Such behavior is clearly an ethical violation. Behave ethically by using the office copier for approved uses only.

Employees should also be aware of the legal restrictions on the copying of certain documents. You should not copy materials, such as portions of books or magazines, that are protected by copyright laws without the permission of the copyright holder. You should not copy certain documents, such as paper money, passports, and postage stamps. If you have questions about what is legal to copy, check with your organization's attorney or review regulations on the U.S. Copyright Office website, as shown in Figure 12-6 below. The FAQs section will answer many of your questions about copyright.

Copier Courtesy

As with all shared equipment, observing basic courtesies is important. If the machine malfunctions while you are copying, try to fix the problem. If you cannot do so, call the **key operator** (a person who has been trained to operate and handle

problems that may occur with the equipment). Do not walk away, leaving the problem for the next person to handle. If you are the key operator or your company has not designated a key operator and you cannot fix the problem, ask permission to call a service repairperson.

When sharing a copier with several people, be considerate of their time. Observe the courtesies listed here:

- If you are involved in an extensive copying job, let your colleagues interrupt when they have only a few pages to copy.

- When the toner or ink runs out, refill it.

- When paper gets low, add more.

- When paper jams or other problems occur, fix the problem or call the key operator.

- If you are using additional supplies such as paper clips, scissors, and so on, put them back where they belong before leaving the copier.

Figure 12-6 U.S. Copyright Office Website

Source: U.S. Copyright Office, http://www.copyright.gov (accessed March 2, 2010).

- If you run copies that are not usable, destroy them in a shredder and/or put them in a recycle bin. Do not leave a messy work area for the next person to clean up.

- When you finish your project, return the copier to its standard settings.

- Check the copier before you leave to make sure you have your originals.

Retaining Records

As you learned in Chapter 11, records are documents that have value to the organization. Records may be valuable for legal, financial, or historical reference or for use in daily operations. Much of the mail you receive or prepare may become records to be stored according to the company's records storage procedures.

Classifications of Records

Records can be classified as to their importance or usefulness to the organization as vital records, important records, useful records, or nonessential records. The record classification will determine, in part, how long the records should be retained.

Vital Records   Records that cannot be replaced and should never be destroyed are called **vital records.** These records are essential to the effective continued operation of the organization and/or are required by law to be retained. Some examples of vital records are corporate charters, deeds, tax returns, constitutions and bylaws, insurance policies, procedures manuals, audited financial statements, patents, and copyrights.

Important Records   Records that are necessary to an orderly continuation of the business and are replaceable only at considerable cost of time and money are known as **important records.** Such records may be transferred to inactive storage but are not destroyed. Examples of important records are financial statements, operating and statistical records, physical inventories, electronic business records, and board minutes.

Useful Records   **Useful records** are those needed for the smooth, effective operation of the organization.

Such records are replaceable, but their loss involves delay or inconvenience to the organization. These records may be transferred to inactive files or destroyed after a certain period of time. Examples include letters, memorandums, reports, and bank records.

Nonessential Records   Documents that have no future value to the organization are considered **nonessential records.** Once the purpose for which they were created has been fulfilled, they may be destroyed. For example, a memorandum that is written to arrange a meeting generally has no value once the meeting has occurred.

Retention Schedules

In both electronic and manual systems, it is important to know how long records should be retained by the organization. The cost of maintaining documents that are no longer of any use can be significant, particularly in manual systems, because of the floor space necessary for the files. Even though electronic storage takes up less space, there is some cost to maintaining unneeded documents.

To avoid keeping records longer than needed, organizations use a records retention schedule. A **records retention schedule** is a document that specifies how long various types of records should be kept. The first page of a records retention schedule is shown on page 231. Retention times

Knowing how to properly classify the paperwork that crosses your desk will help ensure that vital records are stored and retained properly.

Figure 12-7 Retention Schedule

Records Retention Schedule

RECORD	RETENTION PERIOD
Accident reports and claims	7 years
Accounts payable ledgers	7 years
Accounts receivable ledgers	7 years
Audit reports of accounts	Permanent
Bank reconciliations	3 years
Capital stock and bond records	Permanent
Cash books	Permanent
Charts of accounts	Permanent
Checks (canceled)	7 years
Contracts and leases (expired)	7 years
Correspondence (general)	3 years
Correspondence (legal and important matters only)	Permanent
Deeds, mortgages, and bills of sale	Permanent
Depreciation schedules	Permanent
Employee personnel records (after termination)	7 years
Employment applications	3 years
Expense analysis and expense distribution schedules	7 years
Financial statements (end-of-year)	Permanent
General and private ledgers	Permanent
Insurance policies (expired)	3 years
Insurance records, claims, policies	Permanent
Internal audit reports	3 years
Inventories of products, materials, and supplies	7 years
Invoices	7 years
Journals	Permanent

Records Retention Schedule   Page 1

for some records will vary by state because they are based on state laws. The retention schedule may also identify how long records are needed in the active storage area and how long records should be retained in inactive storage.

Some benefits of using a records retention schedule include the following:

- Vital legal, financial, compliance, regulatory, or administrative records will not be disposed of prematurely.

- Valuable historical records will be preserved.

- Records that are no longer needed can be disposed of systematically.

- Clear procedures for when to transfer records from active to inactive storage and whether to convert to microform or digital format will be established.

As an administrative professional, you generally will not create a retention schedule. Typically, company managers will consult with the legal counsel of the organization (or, if it is a small organization, an outside legal firm) and then develop appropriate retention schedules. You will, however, need to follow the retention schedule as you make records management decisions. If the company does not have a records retention schedule, check with your supervisor before making decisions about transferring or destroying documents.

Active to Inactive File Procedures

At some point in the life of a record, based on records retention information, you decide to destroy it, retain it permanently, or transfer it to inactive storage. Two common methods of transfer are perpetual and periodic.

Perpetual Transfer With **perpetual transfer**, records are continuously transferred from the active to the inactive files. The advantage of this method is that all files are kept current because any inactive material is immediately transferred to storage. The perpetual transfer method works well in offices where projects or tasks are completed. For example, when a lawyer finishes a case, the file is complete and probably will not need to be referred to at all or certainly not frequently. Therefore, it can be transferred to the inactive files.

Backing Up Records

Backing up a record involves making a copy of it and storing it in a safe place. As you create electronic records such as documents, spreadsheets, and database files, you should periodically save the files to offline storage using a CD, DVD, flash drive, or external hard drive or network drive. In the event that your computer is damaged and the files are lost or that you delete a file by mistake, you can restore the files from the backup copies. Delete the backup copies when they are no longer needed.

Vital and important records of a business should be backed up, in either physical (paper or microform) or electronic form. This procedure should be part of a larger disaster recovery plan that details how the resources of a business will be handled and restored in case of a disaster such as a fire or flood. Records should be stored off-site at a safe location that has a controlled environment to prevent damage from water, heat, light, and other sources. The records retention schedule will determine how long to store the records.

When distinguishing between active and inactive records, use the following categories:

- Active records used three or more times a month should be kept in an accessible area.

- Inactive records used fewer than 15 times a year may be stored in less accessible areas than active records.

- Archive records with historical value are preserved permanently.

Periodic Transfer With **periodic transfer**, active records are transferred to inactive status at the end of a stated time. For example, you may transfer records that are more than six months old to the inactive file and maintain records that are less than six months old in the active file. Every six months you would follow this procedure.

Key Terms

boilerplate text

duplexing

important records

key operator

mail merge

nonessential records

periodic transfer

perpetual transfer

records retention schedule

template

useful records

vital records

Summary

- ◼ Many documents that are created in an organization are mailed to clients, vendors, government agencies, or others. Copies of those documents become records to be used and maintained according to the organization's records storage procedures.

- ◼ Administrative assistants can increase productivity when creating documents by using efficient procedures and features of word processing software, such as templates, building blocks, mail merge, and envelope options.

- ◼ To make a good impression on the recipient, documents must be written effectively, formatted in an attractive style that is easy to read, and free of errors.

- ◼ Outgoing mail may be sent by the U.S. Postal Service or by private mail carriers or delivery companies.

- ◼ The U.S. Postal Service offers several classes of mail and several special services for mailing items.

- ◼ Sorting, opening, annotating, and presenting incoming mail are typical responsibilities of an administrative professional.

- ◼ Administrative professionals use office copiers extensively to make copies of outgoing mail, incoming mail, and documents for cross-references.

- ◼ Records can be classified by their importance or usefulness to the organization as vital records, important records, useful records, or nonessential records. A records retention schedule specifies how long these types of records should be kept.

- ◼ Perpetual and periodic are two transfer methods used to move files from active to inactive storage.

Bookmark It. *For convenient access to activities, links, and valuable career resources for administrative professionals, visit the companion website for this text:*

www.cengage.com/officetech/fultoncalkins

Planning Notes

Learning Objectives

1. Prepare outgoing mail effectively.

2. Identify methods for sending outgoing mail.

3. Describe ways to handle incoming mail effectively.

4. Describe office copier types and features.

5. Describe procedures for records retention.

Activities 7, 8

Activities 1, 2, 3, 9, 10

Activities 4, 5, 6

Discussion Questions

1. What are three software features you can use to help prepare outgoing mail effectively? Which feature do you think is most helpful and why?

2. What is boilerplate text, and how can it be helpful in preparing documents?

3. Why is it important that the letter address on an envelope be placed within a particular area?

4. Why might you select Parcel Post for mailing a package with the U.S. Postal Service rather than Priority Mail?

5. Why might you choose to use a private delivery company to mail an item rather than the U.S. Postal Service?

6. Why should you sort mail into categories before presenting it to the executive?

7. When reviewing incoming mail, what should you do if a letter lists an enclosure, but nothing is enclosed?

8. What is the purpose of annotating mail?

9. What are two strategies a company might use to reduce copying costs?

10. What do vital, important, and useful records have in common? How do they differ in their importance to the organization?

Critical Thinking

What went wrong? Your employer, Frank Cline, was out of town for two weeks recently. While he was out, you became sick and had to take three days off. You called in and talked with Eden Brumfield, another administrative assistant, who agreed to handle Mr. Cline's mail and other items. You came back two days before Mr. Cline returned. You did not have a chance to talk with Eden about the mail that was received in your absence; however, she left you a note about a few things. Mr. Cline did not understand some of Eden's notes to him and asked you to explain. You could not since you had not talked with Eden. Mr. Cline was upset and asked you to get the information immediately. You did so, but you know that Mr. Cline thinks you did not perform your job well. Explain what you can do now.

Build Workplace Skills

1. **Send outgoing mail** Using your textbook information and websites for the U.S. Postal Service and private mail delivery companies, determine how you would mail each item and any special services you would request. (Learning Objective 2)

    a. A letter that must be delivered to the addressee before noon tomorrow

    b. Valuables that are worth $20,000

    c. A letter that must be received in Thailand in three days

    d. A package that weighs ten pounds and is worth $500

    e. A letter for which you need evidence of delivery

2. **Handle incoming mail**   The following items were received in today's mail. Indicate the order in which the items should be sorted, items for which you should attach the envelope, and items that you would annotate or for which you would attach related materials. (Learning Objective 3)

   a. A letter from a client about a proposal the executive sent last week |

   b. An equipment catalog 7

   c. A newspaper 6

   d. A contract sent by Certified Mail 2

   e. A letter marked "Confidential" 1

   f. An advertising brochure 5

   g. A letter requesting information about a new service your company is offering 3

   h. An interoffice memo about an employee performance evaluation that was submitted by the executive 4

   i. A letter that indicates a bid is enclosed but has no enclosure 3

3. **Records retention**   Open the *Word* file CH12 Schedule from the data files. Use the records retention schedule in this file to determine the retention time for each record below. (Learning Objective 5)

   a. Trademark registrations

   b. Payroll records and summaries

   c. Invoices

   d. Mortgages

   e. Accounts payable ledgers

   f. Tax returns

   g. Minutes of stockholder meetings

   h. Equipment repair records

   i. Expired insurance policies

Communicate Clearly

4. **Sales worksheet**   Open the *Excel* file CH12 Sales Worksheet from the data files. This file contains sales data and a chart for Diamond Industries. Edit the table and chart to correct errors in spelling, capitalization, formulas, and numbers.

5. **Office copiers**   You work as an administrative assistant for a small company with 20 office employees. The office has one low-volume copier that is old and breaks down often. Your supervisor, Mae Chang, has asked you to research and recommend a new copier to be purchased. It should print color as well as black-and-white copies and should have basic features such as reduction/enlargement, duplexing, and automatic document feeding. The copier should print at least 20 pages per minute and handle a volume of at least 25,000 pages per month. Write a memo to your supervisor with your recommendation. Include all relevant details about the copier, its cost, and a source from which the company can purchase it. (Learning Objective 4)

6. **Retention procedures**   You joined Ace Company four months ago as an administrative assistant. The owner, Alicia Ace, started this home decorating business four years ago. Ms. Ace is a talented decorator, but she does not know how to manage business records. All the records are currently in active storage. She has asked for your advice on setting up an inactive file storage area and transferring files from active to inactive storage. Write a memo to Ms. Ace explaining the differences between the periodic transfer method and the perpetual transfer method for moving files. Recommend one of the methods and give reasons for your recommendation. (Learning Objective 5)

Planning Notes

Planning Notes

Develop Relationships

7. **Overnight delivery**   Your supervisor, Margaretta Longoria, asked you to mail the contract for a new project for overnight delivery to Mr. Wheat. Your company uses a private delivery carrier for this type of mailing. You were headed to the mail room with the package when Sue Waters, another administrative assistant, offered to take your package along with several she was taking to the mail room. You thanked Sue and gave her the package. The next afternoon, Ms. Longoria sent you an e-mail saying that Mr. Wheat did not receive the contract. When you checked with Sue, she assured you that she took all the packages to the mail room—and placed them in the bin for regular (second or third day) delivery. What will you say to Sue? What will you say to Ms. Longoria? How can you keep your relationship with each person positive?

8. **Copier etiquette**   You are friends with Josh Roland, another administrative assistant at your company. You have heard three people complain recently about Josh's behavior. In one instance, he refused to let another person who needed to make only two copies interrupt his long copying job. Another time, he left the copier with a paper jam. Today, the copier was completely out of toner and paper when Josh finished using it, and he left it in that state. Since you are Josh's friend, you think you should approach him about his lack of courtesy regarding use of the copier. What can you say to Josh to encourage him to improve his behavior while keeping his goodwill?

Use Technology

9. **Mail merge labels**   Open the *Access* file CH12 Contact Data from the data files. Create a query to contain all fields except Home Phone for clients who live in Ohio or Illinois. Sort the records by the Last Name field. Use mail merge to create mailing labels for these clients. The labels will be attached to advertising brochures to be sent to these clients. (Learning Objective 1)

10. **Building blocks**   You often prepare letters for Mr. Roberto Diaz, Advertising Manager; Ms. Constance DeBoer, Controller; and Ms. Alice Wong, Human Resources Director. All three executives prefer to use *Sincerely* as the complimentary close, block letter style, and open punctuation for their letters. Create three building blocks that you can use to speed the preparation of letters for these executives. Use an appropriate name for each building block. In a blank document, insert each building block to check that it has been created correctly. (Learning Objective 1)

Above & Beyond

Online mailing services   Research a company that provides online postage and mailing solutions. You can find a list of such companies on the U.S. Postal Service website or by using an Internet search engine. Prepare a short report that gives the name and web address of the company, some of the services or products that the company offers, and any monthly or yearly fees for using the service. (Learning Objective 1)

Travel Administrative Assistant

The ideal candidate will have at least three years of office experience and the ability to work in a fast-paced team environment. Duties include:

- Review travel request forms prior to booking travel
- Make travel arrangements for airfare, hotel, and rental cars using approved lists and websites
- Handle revisions to travel arrangements
- Follow company guidelines for getting the best rates
- Handle related phone calls and manage records

Do I qualify?

©MARK WRAGG, ISTOCK

CHAPTER **13**

Coordinating Business Travel

Domestic Travel

Many companies and organizations in the United States have locations in a number of different cities within the country. Having offices or subsidiaries in other cities may require the company's executives to travel. Also, executives are often members of professional organizations that conduct statewide or nationwide conventions at least once each year.

As an administrative assistant, you will probably be responsible for handling travel arrangements for other employees and perhaps for yourself. If you are to handle travel arrangements effectively, you must become familiar with the types of services available. You also need to understand what your responsibilities are while the executive is out of the office.

Learning Objectives

1. Plan domestic and international travel arrangements.

2. Research business customs related to international travel.

3. Discuss and apply organizational travel procedures.

Air Travel

Because time is a valuable resource for business executives, much of their travel is done by air. During a flight, executives can use their time productively by reading mail, newspapers, and professional periodicals. They may also use computers to communicate with coworkers or clients and to complete work tasks.

Flight Classifications

Airlines offer different classes of flights. While different airlines may use slightly different names for their flight classes, there are basically three classes—first class, business class, and coach (also called economy class). First-class accommodations are the most expensive and the most luxurious. The seats are wider and farther apart than in coach. A higher level of services is provided with more flight attendants per passenger. Free beverages and snacks are typically offered, and meals are often served on long flights. First-class flyers are allowed to board and exit before other flyers. Headsets for listening to music or movies may be offered at no additional cost.

Business-class travel is a level between first class and coach or economy class. Designed especially for passengers traveling for business purposes, business class is not available on all aircraft or on all flights. Typically, this class is offered on long-distance flights such as those between New York and cities on the West Coast. Business services, such as laptop power ports and Internet access, may be available. Business class passengers typically board and exit the plane before coach passengers and may enjoy larger seats. Seats that fully recline to sleeping positions may be available. Complimentary beverages are provided, and meals may be available on long flights.

Economy-class accommodations are typically the lowest-priced seats on the airplane. This type of accommodation is also called coach class or tourist class. Seats are closer together than in first class and generally than in business class. Fewer flight attendants are available to serve the needs of the passengers in this section of the plane. Some airlines offer complimentary beverages and snacks in economy class, while others may charge a fee. In-flight entertainment may be available, but customers may be required to buy or rent headsets. With increased emphasis on reducing the expense of air travel, several low-fare airlines offer only economy-class accommodations. Low-fare airlines can typically charge less because they have eliminated many traditional passenger services. In addition, low-fare airlines may offer limited flight schedules, serve only secondary airports, or serve fewer destinations than other airlines.

Ticketing

An **e-ticket** is an electronic ticket that represents the purchase of a seat on a specific flight, usually through a website or by telephone. Rather than receiving paper tickets, the buyer receives a ticket confirmation number or receipt number. This type of ticket has all but replaced paper tickets for domestic flights and is also commonly used for international flights. Information from an e-ticket may be presented at the airport ticket counter to obtain boarding passes. Many airports have self-service kiosks near ticket counters. A customer inserts information from an e-ticket and receives a boarding pass from the machine. This option eliminates standing in line at airline ticket counters. Some airlines or ticketing services offer paper tickets for an added fee. Paper tickets are also used in remote airports where airlines have not invested in extensive computer systems.

Occasionally, it is necessary to change or cancel flight reservations. Travelers may be charged a

People @Work

TRAVEL AGENT

A travel agent is a person who makes travel arrangements, such as airline, hotel, and car reservations, for clients. Travel agents provide information and offer advice on travel destinations as well as information on travel documents (passports, visas, and certificates of vaccination), travel advisories, and currency exchange rates. Most travel agents work for travel agencies or tour operators; some are self-employed. As an administrative assistant, you may provide information on travel needs of executives or coworkers to a travel agent who will make the travel arrangements.

penalty for changing to another flight or cancelling a flight. The policy for cancellations is described at the airline's website. The cancellation policy or penalty may be different for different classes of flights. Passengers are not charged when a flight is cancelled or changed because of mechanical problems or other issues. Since passengers are usually inconvenienced by these changes, the airline tries to make the situation as painless as possible. When the change involves an overnight stay, the airline may pay for a hotel room and provide vouchers for food.

Airline Security Everyone who travels by air must go through airport security checkpoints, and their baggage must go through security checkpoints as well. These checkpoints were developed to help prevent passengers from bringing anything on a plane that would enable them to take over or damage the plane. A variety of security precautions are currently in place at airports across the United States. Being knowledgeable about security measures is important for business travelers. The following suggestions will help business travelers cope with the security procedures at airports:

- Arrive early. Most airlines advise arriving at the airport up to two hours before your scheduled departure. If you have special needs or concerns, you may need to arrive even earlier.

- Bring proper identification. An acceptable government-issued photo identification is required. This identification may include a state-issued driver's license, state ID card, military ID card, or passport.

- When possible, print a boarding pass before arriving at the airport. This will allow you to avoid the ticket counter. Having only a carry-on bag will also allow you to bypass the ticket counter.

- Check your bags and remove prohibited items. A list of prohibited items is available on the airline website. Take the time to make sure you are following the established regulations for baggage.

- Follow the screening guidelines. Keep your identification and boarding pass in a location that is easy to access. Take your laptop computer out of the carrying case for screening, and wear shoes that you can take off easily.

Airline Clubs For the frequent business traveler, membership in an airline club may be a worthwhile investment. Major airlines provide private rooms for club members in large airports, and membership is available through the individual airline. Membership fees vary. A variety of services are available in the clubs, including the following:

- Computer equipment, fax machines, and copy machines

- Conference rooms and lounge space

workplace wisdom

Observe these security measures when traveling by air for personal or business reasons:

- Watch your bags and personal belongings at all times.

- Do not accept packages from strangers.

- Report unattended bags or packages to airport security.

- Report suspicious activities and individuals to airport security.

- Be prepared to take your laptop computer and other electronic devices from their cases so they can be scanned separately.

- Check to be certain you have all your belongings before you leave the security area—wallets, keys, jewelry, cell phones, and so on.

- Reading material
- Free soft drinks, juice, and coffee
- Alcoholic beverages
- Pastries and snacks
- Help with airline reservations

Parking Services   Large airports generally provide free shuttle service from airport parking locations; however, you are charged for parking your car. The fee is based on the location of your car, with parking lots closer to the airport being more expensive, and the time your car is in the lot.

Because parking at an airport for an extended period can become expensive, private shuttle services are available in many large cities. Shuttle buses take you to and from the airport. These buses run frequently, with generally no more than a ten-minute wait between runs. Paying for a shuttle to and from the airport may be cheaper than paying for parking at the airport for an extended time.

Company-Owned and Chartered Planes   Large corporations may lease their own plane or fleet of planes if the amount of travel by company employees makes it advantageous to do so. Some small airlines specialize in privately chartered jet service. In this instance, a business would rent an entire airplane rather than seats on a commercial flight. Chartered planes are generally small, since most private chartering is for small groups of people.

Sometimes called air taxis, charter planes are usually located adjacent to regular airports and use the same runways as the major airlines. Food is often available on these jets for an additional cost; flight attendants are generally not available.

Ground Transportation   Once executives arrive at their destination, they may need some type of ground transportation to their hotel. That transportation may be a taxi or shuttle bus. When making arrangements, you should check taxi costs and the availability of shuttle services. Some hotels provide free shuttle service to and from the airport. Shuttle services from private vendors are less expensive than taxi service.

If executives must attend meetings at several locations during their stay, renting a car may be the most economical and convenient method of ground

© JACK HOLLINGSWORTH/CORBIS

Private shuttle services that take travelers to and from the airport are available in many cities.

transportation. Car rental agencies are available at most airports. Cars may also be rented through airlines or travel agents or on the Internet. When renting a car, specify the make and model preferred, along with the date and time the car will be picked up and returned. Most car rental agencies have age restrictions; the person renting the car must be at least 21 or 25, depending on the agency.

Hotel Reservations

Hotel reservations may be made online or by telephone. Most hotels offer special corporate rates for business travelers. Hotel reservations can also be made through travel agents or travel websites. Always check for booking fees or cancellation restrictions when making reservations. The lowest room rate may require immediate payment and may not be refundable if the reservation must be cancelled.

Many hotels have business centers with computers, copiers, fax machines, and other equipment for use by business travelers. However, cell phones, PDAs, and/or laptop computers are standard equipment for many traveling executives. Travelers can access the Internet using wireless connections in some hotels. Meeting rooms are also available in many hotels. If you are making hotel reservations directly with the hotel, let the reservations clerk know what equipment and/or meeting rooms are needed. If the traveler will arrive late, it is important to give that information to the hotel clerk. Rooms can be released at a certain hour if reservations have not been confirmed for late arrival.

Car Travel

An executive who is traveling only a few hundred miles may prefer to travel by car. Some executives use cars furnished by the company. Other executives are reimbursed on a per-mile basis for job-related car travel. Your responsibilities for a trip by car may include determining the best route to follow, making hotel reservations, and identifying restaurants along the way. The American Automobile Association (AAA) provides map services, along with hotel and restaurant information. However, you must be a member of AAA to get these services. As an alternative, check the Internet for sites with maps, travel information, driving directions, lists of restaurants in particular cities, weather forecasts, and points of interest in specific geographic locations.

Rail Travel

Rail travel is seldom used for business travel because it takes more time than traveling by air. Rail travel is available between major cities in the United States, but few rural locations are served by train. First-class and sleeping accommodations are available, as well as coach accommodations for more economical travel. Reservations can be made online at the Amtrak website. Routes and schedules are also available on the site.

International Travel

Because of the increasingly global nature of business, executives must sometimes make trips abroad. As an administrative professional, you need to know

Hotel Security Considerations

When staying in a hotel, it is important to pay attention to your personal security and safety. To maintain your personal safety, do not discuss your business or travel plans in public areas where they may be overheard. Additional security considerations include the following:

↗ Do not allow strangers in your hotel room. If you need to meet with someone you do not know, meet in a public place such as the hotel lobby or a restaurant.

↗ Never leave exposed or unattended valuables in your hotel room. Keep items such as money, jewelry, tickets, credit cards, and your passport with you or place them in a hotel safety deposit box. Some high-end hotels have room safes.

↗ Become familiar with escape routes in case of fire or another emergency.

↗ Use the door chain or bolt lock whenever you are in your room.

↗ Use the peephole before opening the door to visitors.

↗ Do not discuss your room number when standing in the lobby where you may be overheard.

↗ Keep track of your room key. If you lose your key, immediately asked that your room lock be changed.

↗ Keep your room neat so you will notice disturbed or missing items quickly.

Source: U.S. Department of State, "Personal Security—At Home, On the Street, While Traveling," http://www.state.gov/m/ds/rls/rpt/19773.htm (accessed August 24, 2009).

how to make arrangements for an international trip. You should also know something about the business culture of the country the traveler is visiting.

Flights and Appointments

International flight classifications are the same as those for domestic air travel. Classes of flights are first class and economy/coach, with business class available on many international flights. Weight and size restrictions for luggage may vary slightly from one airline to another. International travelers must arrive at the airport earlier than normal; most airlines suggest arriving at least two hours before the flight.

If you are involved in setting up appointments or meetings for the executive, remember time zone differences. **Jet lag** (the feeling of exhaustion following a flight through several time zones) can limit an executive's effectiveness. Since it takes the body approximately a day to adapt to the new environment for each time zone crossed, try to give the traveler a day to recover from the trip before scheduling the most important meetings.

If executives do not have the luxury of a full day before appointments, they can take advantage of certain techniques to help with jet lag. For example, if they are traveling west, they can postpone the time they usually go to bed by two or three hours for two days before the flight. If they are traveling east, they can retire a couple of hours earlier than usual. They can also start shifting mealtimes to those of the destination city. Their body clock will not be fully adapted to the new time when they land, but they will have made a start in the right direction.

If at all possible, do not schedule appointments for the executive on the day before or after an international trip. The day before a trip is usually a busy one in preparation for the trip. When the executive returns from a trip, she or he must again contend with time zone changes.

Travel Documents and Currency

International travelers need a passport. Travelers may also need a visa, health-related documents, and local currency.

Passports A **passport** is an official government document that certifies the identity and citizenship of an individual and grants the person permission to travel abroad. A passport is required to travel outside the United States. (Mexico and Canada require air passengers to have a passport. At the time of this writing, it is possible to enter these countries by car without a passport; however, requirements can change at any time. To find current requirements, visit the Embassy of Mexico website or the Canadian Border Services Agency website.)

Passports are granted by the U.S. Department of State. You can apply for a passport at many post offices, clerks of court, public libraries, and other state, county, township, and municipal government offices. Applications can also be obtained from the Travel. State.Gov website, hosted by the U.S. Department of State. This site has other helpful information about renewing a passport, changing information on a passport, and reporting a lost or stolen passport.

Technology @Work

An e-passport (U.S. electronic passport) is the same as a traditional passport with the addition of a small electronic chip (integrated circuit) embedded in the back cover. The chip stores the following information:

- ↗ The same data shown on the data page of the passport
- ↗ A digital image of the passport photograph
- ↗ The unique chip identification number
- ↗ A digital signature to protect the stored data from alteration

The digital image of the passport photograph facilitates the use of face recognition technology at ports of entry. Since August 2007, the United States has been issuing only e-passports. Passports without chips can be used until they expire.

Source: U.S. Department of State, "The U.S. Electronic Passport," Travel.State.Gov, http://travel.state.gov/passport/eppt/eppt_2498.html (accessed August 24, 2009).

A passport is valid for ten years from the date of issue. (Passports issued to children 15 and younger are valid for five years.) As soon as the passport is received, it should be signed, rendering it valid. Also, the information in the front pages should be filled out, including the address of the bearer and names of persons to be contacted in case of an emergency. Travelers should always carry passports with them while abroad; they should never be left in hotel rooms. The U.S. Department of State recommends that you renew your passport approximately nine months before it expires.

The U.S. Passport Card is a less expensive alternative to a passport for land and sea travel between the United States and Mexico, Canada, Bermuda, and the Bahamas. The passport card cannot be used for air travel. Figure 13-1 shows the credit-card-sized passport card. The U.S. Department of State's Travel.State.Gov website has information about applying for a passport card.

Visas

A **visa** is a document granted by a government that permits a traveler to enter and travel within that particular country. A visa usually appears as a stamped notation on a passport indicating that the bearer may enter the country for a certain time. Rules and restrictions for visas vary from country to country; check the "International Travel, Country Specific Information" section of the Travel.State.Gov website, which also has links to each country's embassy website.

Health-Related Documents

Some countries require people entering the country to have specific vaccinations or health tests, such as testing for contagious diseases. Records documenting these tests or vaccinations may be required for travel to the country. The entry requirements for a particular country should be checked before every trip in case of changes; for example, many countries have enacted specific practices in response to the worldwide 2009 H1N1 flu outbreak. The "International Travel, Country Specific Information" section of the Travel.State.Gov website is the best starting place for information. A travel agency or the website of the country to be visited can also supply information about required vaccinations or tests.

Travelers who take prescription medicine should order enough medicine to cover their needs while they are away. It is a good idea to take some extra medicine as a backup in case some of the medicine is lost or the trip lasts longer than planned. Do not pack prescription medicine in a bag that will be checked. The traveler should carry written prescriptions for the medicine as well as the names and contact information for the doctors and pharmacists at home.

Currency

Before leaving the United States, the executive can exchange money from certain banks and currency exchange offices for the currency of the country being visited. The rate of exchange for various countries is published in some newspapers and is available online. Several websites provide currency converter utilities that show equivalent amounts in two or more currencies. To find such a website, search the Internet using the term *currency converter*. If the executive prefers, a small amount of money can be exchanged in the United States and more money exchanged upon arrival at the country of destination. Any currency left over at the end of a trip can be exchanged for U.S. currency.

It is always a good idea to be aware of the exchange rates before traveling to another country and to pay attention to the exchange rates once in the country. Exchange rates can vary daily and are not always exactly the same at different

Figure 13-1 U.S. Passport Card

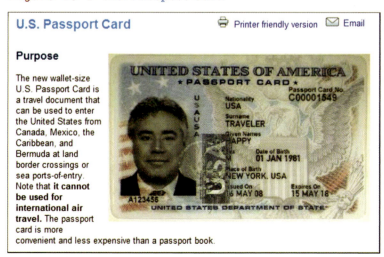

Source: U.S. State Department, "U.S. Passport Card," Travel.State.Gov, http://travel.state.gov/passport/ppt_card/ppt_card_3926.html (accessed March 2, 2010).

locations. For example, the exchange rate at a bank or post office may be more favorable than the exchange rate at an exchange bureau in an airport or train station. When you make purchases quoted in a foreign currency using a credit card or withdraw funds using an ATM, the credit card company or bank will apply the current exchange rate to charge your account in U.S. dollars. The exchange rate for credit card purchases and ATM withdrawals is typically a little better than the rate for exchanging cash or travelers' checks for local currency.

Health Precautions

Before leaving for a foreign country, the traveler should check with a physician concerning any medical issues. Because environmental factors may be different from those in the United States, there is a possibility of developing an illness as a result of the food, water, or climate of the country. A physician can prescribe medications for stomach-related illnesses or colds. Vaccinations may be recommended or required before traveling to certain countries.

If you are staying with a host family in a country where there are health precautions that must be taken or you personally have some health issues that do not allow you to eat certain foods, you should politely explain these issues to your host. For example, if you have an allergy to fruits such as mangos, tell your host of this allergy as soon as you arrive.

Tap water in another country may be safe for local residents; however, it may contain different microbes than water in the United States, thus causing possible digestive problems. To be safe, it is important to use purified water at all times, even when brushing your teeth, washing your hands, or rinsing raw foods. For the same reasons, you may want to avoid consuming ice served in drinks. Many restaurants and markets serve and sell purified water.

International Car Rental

Travel agencies can arrange for car rentals before executives arrive in a country, or the executive can rent a car after arrival. In many countries, a U.S. driver's license is sufficient. You can obtain an International Driver's License from AAA. However, in some countries (for example, China) a driver's

International travelers can exchange U.S. currency for foreign currency.

license issued by that country is required. Getting the driver's license can take several days and may require copies of travel documents such as a passport and visa. Travelers must have appropriate insurance and become familiar with the driving regulations of the country they are visiting.

Driving conditions—and customs—are sometimes quite different from those in the United States. In several countries (the largest being the United Kingdom, Australia, New Zealand, and Japan), you must drive on the left-hand side of the road and pass on the right-hand side. Steering wheels are mounted on the right-hand side of the car.

International Rail Transportation

Many countries have excellent rail service, particularly in Europe. A traveler can go from one city in Europe to another in a short period of time. Trains are generally clean, and the accommodations are comfortable. Underground rail is also available in a number of countries in Europe.

Tips for International Travelers

Follow these tips to interact effectively with others while on an international trip:

↗ Learn the appropriate greeting for the country you will be visiting.

↗ Learn how to say please and thank you in the language of the country.

↗ Have business cards printed with your name and your company name in both English and the language of the country you are visiting.

↗ Do not criticize the people or customs of the country you are visiting. Show appreciation for the music, art, and culture of the country.

↗ Remember that business generally is conducted more formally in other countries than it is in the United States.

↗ Dress appropriately; this generally means business suits for men and conservative dresses or suits for women. Although dress in the United States has become more casual than in the past, do not assume that is true for international organizations. Casual business dress generally does not imply a professional image. It may be seen as sloppy dress.

↗ Eat the food that is offered you; do not ask what you are being served. Show appreciation to your host.

↗ Be courteous and respectful at all times.

GALLO IMAGES/GETTY IMAGES

Cultural Differences

Business practices can differ greatly from country to country. For example, in some countries, business gifts are expected. In others, business gifts are not particularly welcomed. If a business gift is given, it should be a small one, a nice pen or some memento representative of the United States. However, executives must be aware of customs and taboos when giving gifts to avoid offending someone without knowing it. Before an executive takes a business trip abroad, the business practices of that country need to be carefully studied.

A basic understanding of the culture of the people in the country where the executive is traveling will help you make appropriate travel arrangements. This knowledge can also be helpful as you work with people from diverse backgrounds. Information about countries can be obtained from a variety of sources, some of which are listed here.

■ Consulates of the country to be visited. (A **consulate** is an office of a government in a foreign city that acts to assist and protect citizens of the consul's country.) Check the consulate websites of the country.

■ Travel books. Although geared for tourists, many travel books contain information about local customs related to business practices.

■ Seminars and short courses. Colleges and universities often provide short courses or one-day seminars on the culture of various countries, along with tips on doing business with particular countries.

■ The Internet. Numerous articles are available about cultural differences and business etiquette in different countries.

Travel Procedures

How travel arrangements are made depends on the business/organization where you work. Some companies use a travel agency to schedule all travel arrangements. This agency becomes knowledgeable about the needs of the organization and is able to provide services the executives need with limited assistance. Other organizations, particularly small ones, ask that individuals or their assistants make travel arrangements.

Arrangements by Travel Agencies

A **travel agency** is a company that offers travel advice and makes travel arrangements for clients. Travel agencies can make all travel arrangements for the executive. Travel agencies are particularly helpful when the executive is traveling internationally. The agency can schedule the flights, make hotel reservations, and arrange car rental. The agency will also provide an **itinerary**, a document that gives travel information such as flight arrival and departure times, hotel reservations, and car rental arrangements.

©ISTOCK

Arrangements by the Assistant

Regardless of how travel arrangements are made, you as an administrative assistant will have a role. It is a good idea to set up a folder when you learn about an upcoming trip. Place all notes and information relating to the trip in the folder. It is then available for instant referral when needed.

Although you may telephone some airlines or hotels that you use frequently, typically the most efficient method of making reservations is to use the Internet. You can make flight reservations through airline websites or through independent travel websites that give prices for several airlines at the same time. Hotel and car reservations can be made at these sites or through individual hotel and car rental websites.

If an executive is traveling by air, you need to know the name of the preferred airline (if the executive has a preference) as well as his or her frequent flyer program number. A **frequent flyer program** is an incentive program that provides a variety of awards after the accumulation of a certain number of mileage points. Awards may include upgrades from coach to first class and free airline tickets.

If you are making arrangements for more than one top-level executive to travel to the same location at the same time, company policy may dictate that the executives travel on separate flights. In case of a serious accident when both executives are on the same plane, both might be lost to the company.

You may assist executives with travel arrangements by determining passport and visa requirements, checking on currency needs, researching health issues in the country to be visited, making hotel reservations, arranging car rental, and arranging rail transportation. In addition, you may have the following responsibilities:

- Preparing an itinerary
- Obtaining travel funds
- Preparing and organizing materials for the trip
- Checking the executive's appointments
- Determining procedures to follow in the executive's absence

Dear Savvy Admin

Dear Savvy Admin:

When a group of Japanese businesspeople visited our office on a sales call, we went out of our way to be friendly, but they seemed uncomfortable and standoffish. They used our last names, and they didn't make eye contact with anyone. They were very quiet.

Perplexed

Dear Perplexed:

Your visitors were probably not as unhappy as you think they were. The Japanese form of address is the last name with the title of respect *-san* attached. So, for example, if your name is Anne Carey or Andrew Carey, you would be addressed as Carey-san. Making direct eye contact is considered rude in the Japanese culture (look at the person's neck or the knot of his tie). Among the Japanese, respectful silence is a way of being polite. Your Japanese visitors may also have nodded when you didn't expect them to. Nodding indicates listening, it does not indicate agreement.

Savvy Admin

Communicating @Work

The first time you make travel arrangements for an executive or coworker, talk with the person about travel preferences. When making travel arrangements, you will need to know information such as the following:

↗ Destinations, dates, and times of travel

↗ Flight preferences—class of accommodations, seating, meals

↗ Hotel preferences—price range, number of nights, single or double room, bed size, smoking or nonsmoking room, accessible for special needs

↗ Car rental preferences—type of car, size, make and model, number of days of usage, pick-up and drop-off locations

↗ Reimbursement—reimbursement policies of the company (per diem for meals and other travel expenses)

↗ Arrangements for transportation to the airport or train station

↗ Appointments to be made and where and when

↗ Materials—business cards, cell phone, PDA, laptop

↗ Executive's credit card number or company account number for charging tickets, hotel, and car rental

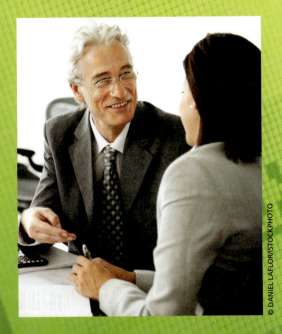
© DANIEL LAFLOR/ISTOCKPHOTO

Prepare an Itinerary   The itinerary is a must for you and your employer. If you are working with a travel agency, the agency will prepare an itinerary that includes flight numbers, departure and arrival times, car rentals, and hotels. However, an agency will not have the specific information on appointments and other meetings you may schedule. Because the executive needs to have an itinerary that reflects all activities on the trip, you should prepare a complete itinerary. Copies of the itinerary should be distributed to the executive and to the person who will be in charge while the executive is away. The executive may request a copy of the itinerary to leave with family members. A file copy should be kept at the office for reference. Figure 13-2 on page 248 shows a sample itinerary.

Obtain Travel Funds   Organizations differ in how they handle funds for trips. Airline tickets may be charged directly to the organization, or the traveler may pay and be reimbursed by the company. Hotel, meals, and car rental may be charged on a credit card provided by the organization. Another practice is for the individual to get a cash advance to cover all expenses of the trip. To do so, the individual fills out a travel form before leaving, indicating how much money she or he will need for lodging, meals, and other expenses. The company advances the money to the employee before the person leaves on the trip. Another practice is for the executive to pay the expenses; she or he is then reimbursed by the company upon returning from the trip. Company policies generally require employees to turn in a receipt for an expense above a certain amount.

Prepare and Organize Materials   Several items may be needed for a trip. If it is an international trip, items such as passports, medications, business cards, and small gifts may be necessary. Whether the trip is domestic or international, several items usually must be prepared, such as proposals, reports for meetings, and presentation materials. Once the materials are prepared, the administrative assistant assembles the appropriate number of copies and gives them to the executive. The traveler needs items such as these:

■ Itinerary

■ E-ticket confirmation

Figure 13-2 Itinerary

Itinerary for Maria Diaz

April 1 to April 3, 20--
Grand Rapids, Michigan

Monday, April 1	**(Fort Worth, Texas, to Grand Rapids, Michigan)**
9:30 a.m. CST	Leave DWF International Airport on Delta Flight 62 (e-ticket confirmation in briefcase)
2:00 p.m. EST	Arrive GRF International Airport
	Take shuttle bus to Amway Grand Plaza Hotel, telephone 616-555-0124 (confirmation 454038)
	Hotel reservations at the Amway Grand Plaza Hotel, 187 Monroe Avenue NW, telephone 616-555-0156 (confirmation 828382)
3:30 p.m. EST	Meeting with Mark Rogers, Room 212, Ranier Building, telephone 616-555-0129, blue folder contains papers for meeting
Tuesday, April 2	**(Grand Rapids, Michigan)**
10:00 a.m. EST	Meeting with Susie Chang, Conference Room A, Temple Building, telephone 616-555-0165, manila folder contains papers for meeting
	Lunch with Susie follows the meeting; she is making arrangements for lunch
3:00 p.m. EST	Meeting with Louis Roberts, Conference Room C, Temple Building, telephone 616-555-0166, red folder contains meeting notes
Wednesday, April 3	**(Grand Rapids, Michigan, to Fort Worth, Texas)**
9:30 a.m. EST	Meeting with Angela Thomas, Room 220, Thurston Building, telephone 616-555-0138, yellow folder contains proposed contract
1:30 p.m. EST	Leave GRF International Airport on Delta Flight 82 (e-ticket confirmation in briefcase)
5:00 p.m. CST	Arrive DFW International Airport

- Passport and visas
- Calendar or appointment schedule
- Credit cards and currency
- Hotel and/or car rental confirmation
- Special materials, reports, or presentation materials
- Business cards
- Cell phone and PDA or laptop
- Reading materials

Check Appointments Check your employer's electronic and desk calendars, along with your calendar, to see if any appointments have been scheduled for the period in which the executive will be gone. If so, find out if these appointments are to be cancelled or if someone else in the company will handle them. Then, notify the people involved. Check other files, such as tickler files or pending files, to see if there are matters that should be handled before the executive leaves. Also, find out who will be in charge during your employer's absence.

E-mail or call people the executive plans to see during the trip to confirm appointments. It is wise to do so before preparing the itinerary. Obtain or verify addresses and directions from the hotel to the location of all meetings. Make a note of these addresses and directions on the itinerary or on a separate appointment schedule as the executive prefers.

Duties During the Executive's Absence

You have the responsibility of making wise decisions within the scope of your responsibility during the executive's absence. You should know which matters to handle yourself, which to refer to someone else in the company, and which to refer directly to the executive through an e-mail, a fax, or a telephone call. You do not want to place an excessive number of calls to the executive while he or she is away, but there may be matters that the executive should be informed of immediately.

Handle Messages Executives may e-mail or call the office on a daily basis while they are away on trips. If the executive prefers to call, determine the approximate time of day the call will be so you can have all messages and items reviewed and be ready to discuss them. Always keep urgent messages and correspondence in an established place on your desk so you can refer to them quickly. You may find it helpful to keep a log of all items that need to be discussed with your employer.

Handle Appointments While the executive is away, you may need to set up appointments for people who want to see her or him after the trip. The executive will probably already have a full day of work to handle on the first day back, so it is not a good idea to schedule appointments for that day. If the trip was international, the executive probably will have some jet lag. If an appointment is absolutely necessary on her or his first day back,

Writing @Work

You may be responsible for answering routine correspondence while the executive is away on a trip. If so, keep a copy of the correspondence and response for your employer to review after he or she returns.

You may also be responsible for seeing that all urgent correspondence that you are not authorized to handle is given to a designated person. You may be required to assist this person in answering the correspondence.

© ISTOCK

Business travelers should keep receipts for expenses to attach to travel expense reports.

set up and the telephone calls, e-mail, and other correspondence you received.

Expense Reports Following a trip, many organizations require employees to prepare an **expense report** and turn in receipts for expenses above a certain amount. The following information is often included on an expense report:

- Employee's name and department
- Date of expense
- Category of expense (meals, lodging, airfare)
- Description of entertainment expenses (lunch with client, Tom Chung)
- Expense amount (converted to U.S. dollars if the expense is from international travel)
- Receipts if required (some organizations do not require receipts if a corporate credit card is used or if the expense is below a certain dollar amount)
- Employee's signature and date
- Supervisor's signature and date

The executive will usually provide you with a list of receipts from the trip, including flight, hotel, and meal receipts. Your task is to complete the expense report carefully, double-checking all figures and totals. Copies of receipts are usually attached to the expense report. Figure 13-3 on page 251 shows a sample expense report.

Post-Trip Activities

When the executive returns, you must brief her or him on what occurred in the office during the trip, providing all necessary information. You should also inform the executive of the appointments you

schedule it in the afternoon rather than the morning. Avoiding early-morning appointments is also a good idea in case of delayed return flights.

Follow-up Correspondence The executive may need to write several follow-up letters after a trip. For example, he or she may want to send thank-you letters to the executives or clients contacted on the trip. Information on products or services may need to be sent to customers or prospective customers. Contracts may be written and mailed. The executive may also need to answer correspondence that accumulated during the trip or ask you to respond to certain items.

Figure 13-3 Expense Report

Oak Industries
Expense Report

For the Week Ending	1/21/--						
Employee Name	Elaine Stanislaw			Destination	Tulsa, Oklahoma		
Department	Marketing			Purpose	IAAP Convention		

	Monday	Tuesday	Wednesday	Thursday	Friday	Saturday	Sunday	Total
Date	1/15/--	1/16/--	1/17/--	1/18/--	1/19/--	1/20/--	1/21/--	Total
Airfare								
Car Rental								
Local Transportation								
Tolls/Parking	12.50	12.50	12.50					37.50
Miles	242.00	5.00	242.00					
Mileage Amount	133.10	2.75	133.10					268.95
Lodging	165.50	165.50						331.00
Subtotal	311.10	180.75	145.60					637.45
Breakfast		13.00	13.00					26.00
Lunch	15.00	16.75	12.00					43.75
Dinner	34.58							34.58
Subtotal	49.58	29.75	25.00					104.33
Business Meals*		175.85						175.85
Other Entertainment								
Subtotal		175.85						175.85
Gifts	25.00							25.00
Other*								
Subtotal	25.00							25.00
Grand Total	385.68	386.35	170.60					942.63

Employee Signature	*Elaine Stanislaw*	Date	1/23/--
Supervisor Signature	*Teresa Williams*	Date	1/24/--

Comments:
*Explanation Required   Dinner on 1/16 with Standards Review Committee members: Joan Roberts, Tom Chung, and Maria Gonzales

Key Terms

consulate

e-ticket

expense report

frequent flyer program

itinerary

jet lag

passport

travel agency

visa

Summary

■ Many companies and organizations in the United States have locations in a number of different cities within the country and abroad. For this and other reasons, some employees travel on business frequently.

■ Because time is a valuable resource for business executives, much of their travel is done by air. Airline flight classifications include first class, business class, and economy or coach class.

■ Once executives arrive at their destination, they may use some type of ground transportation such as a rental car, taxi, or shuttle bus.

■ Hotel reservations may be made online or by telephone; some hotels offer special corporate rates for business travelers.

■ If an executive is traveling only a few hundred miles, she or he may prefer to travel by car. An executive might use a car furnished by the company, a rental car, or a personal car.

■ Because of the increasingly global nature of business, executives often must make trips abroad. Before the trip, the business practices and customs of that country need to be carefully studied.

■ When traveling abroad, the traveler will need a passport. Travelers may also need a visa, health-related documents, and local currency.

■ Some companies use a travel agency to make travel arrangements. Other organizations, particularly small ones, ask that individuals or their assistants make travel arrangements.

■ As an administrative assistant, you will have a role in making travel arrangements, preparing materials for the trip, handling issues while the executive is away, and completing follow-up activities after the trip.

Bookmark It. *For convenient access to activities, links, and valuable career resources for administrative professionals, visit the companion website for this text:*

www.cengage.com/officetech/fultoncalkins

Discussion Questions

1. Why do many business travelers travel by air? What are three common classifications of air flight accommodations?

2. Describe how an e-ticket for air travel works.

3. Give five guidelines that will help business travelers cope with the security procedures at airports.

4. If the traveler will arrive late, why it is important to give that information to the hotel clerk?

5. Why is it important that the business practices of the destination country be carefully studied before an executive takes a business trip abroad?

6. What is the difference between a passport and a visa?

7. What is a U.S. Passport Card?

8. Why is it important for a business traveler to have a complete itinerary?

9. What are typical duties an administrative assistant must handle while the executive is away on a trip?

10. What are typical duties an administrative assistant must handle after the executive returns from a trip?

Critical Thinking

Conflict of interest   You work as an administrative assistant for Ivan Petrov, director of marketing, for whom you often make travel arrangements. Company policy states that employees should select flights with the lowest fares that will meet their needs when traveling on company business. Mr. Petrov has asked you to book a flight for him from Atlanta to Los Angeles. He prefers to travel with one or more stops before reaching his destination because he earns more frequent flyer points than he would with a nonstop flight.

In the past when you have booked flights for Mr. Petrov, the fares have been close to the same amount for nonstop flights and flights with stops. However, for this trip, the fare for flights with stops be will be about $150 more than for a nonstop flight. How should you handle this situation?

Build Workplace Skills

1. **Business customs**   Select a country from the list below or ask your instructor for approval to research a different country. Use the Internet and other resources to research business customs and practices for this country. Write a report that details your findings. The report should address (but not be limited to) issues such as those listed below. Include complete source information for the references used in writing the report. (Learning Objective 2)

   • Attitudes toward time and appointments

   • Formality appropriate for business meetings and related events

Planning Notes

- Language spoken and possible need for an interpreter
- Personal space comfort zones and nonverbal behavior
- Exchanging business cards and gifts
- Appropriate dress for business meetings
- Travel alerts or warnings for this country
- Health-related concerns for travel to this country
- Currency of this country
- Travel documents needed for a U.S. traveler (passport, visa, health documents)

  Countries:

Albania	Iran
Brazil	Italy
China	Japan
Egypt	Russia
France	Spain
Germany	Syria
India	

2. **International travel arrangements**   Your supervisor will be traveling to the country you researched in activity 1 to meet with clients. The trip will begin one month from today. The trip will last for seven days, including travel time.

   a. Select a city to which your supervisor will travel. Research flights to that city.

   b. Select a flight itinerary for the trip and print/record this information.

   c. Select a hotel where your supervisor will stay. Record the hotel name and address, reservation dates, and room rates as you would when booking the hotel.

   d. Research the best way for your supervisor to get from the airport to the hotel and record those arrangements. (Learning Objective 1)

3. **Travel itinerary**   Create an itinerary for your supervisor for the trip you planned in activity 2, using the itinerary in Figure 13-2 as an example. Include the travel arrangements you planned earlier. Schedule three meetings with clients (choose names for the clients and appointment times) to be held at the hotel where your supervisor is staying. (Learning Objective 3)

> Communicate Clearly

4. **Expense report**   Open the *Excel* file CH13 Expense Report from the data files. Edit the expense report to correct errors in spelling, capitalization, formulas, and numbers. Attach a comment about any missing information. (Learning Objective 3)

5. **Follow-up correspondence**   Your supervisor, Ms. Sandra Young, marketing associate, has returned from a trip during which she met with several clients. Ms. Young has asked you to write a follow-up letter to a client, Mr. Frazer.

- Make up a company name and address and create a letterhead for the letter. Use an appropriate letter and punctuation style.

- Writing as Ms. Young, thank Mr. Frazer for meeting with you and indicate that you thought the meeting was very productive. Tell the client that the product information he requested is provided in an enclosed brochure. Invite him to call you if he has any questions about the information. Indicate that you will call next week to discuss payment options and credit terms.

- The client's name and address are shown below. (Learning Objective 3)

  Mr. Donald Frazer
  Frazer Insurance Company
  3228 Eastern Avenue
  Baltimore, MD 21224-3228

6. **Travel safety slides**   Using information in this textbook and additional information you find on the Internet, create electronic slides about travel safety. Create a title slide for the overall presentation. Create three or four additional slides, each with a title and a bullet list of tips for travel safety. Add an appropriate graphic to at least one slide. Save the slides as a single-file web page that could be posted on the company intranet.

Develop Relationships

7. **Travel expenses**   You and a coworker, Steve Palmer, recently took a day trip to a meeting in a nearby city. Sandwiches, chips, and drinks were provided by the meeting host for lunch. This is a common practice that saves time on busy meeting days. As the two of you were driving back to your office late that afternoon, Steve said, "Okay, what amount are we going to say we spent for lunch on our expense reports? We should make them about the same so it will look as if we ate out at the same place."

   What kind of relationship do you think Steve has with his employer? What would you say to Steve?

8. **Travel and time zones**   Two days ago, your supervisor, Ms. Walters, asked you to make travel plans for her to attend a conference today. She was planning to give a presentation for a coworker who had to cancel the trip due to illness. You made the reservations and allowed two hours for Ms. Walters to get from the airport to the meeting. This seemed to be ample time, since the airport is only 20 minutes from the meeting site. Ms. Walters was very busy making last-minute preparations for the presentation and did not pay much attention to the flight itinerary.

   This afternoon, Ms. Walters called you. She was very upset because she barely made it to the meeting on time. It seems you forgot to take time zone differences into account when making the travel plans. What will you say to Ms. Walters? How can you repair the damage this situation has done to your working relationship?

Planning Notes

> ## Use Technology

9. **Domestic travel arrangements** Your supervisor, Mr. Wilson, plans to go to New York City on business. He wants to leave Nashville before 10 a.m. on October 1 and return after 5 p.m. on October 3. Using airline websites, check the times available and the costs. He does not want you to do an itinerary at this point; he merely wants an e-mail with the times and costs. (The e-mail should be sent to your instructor.) (Learning Objective 1)

10. **Currency conversion** You have been asked to find information about currency conversion amounts for three currencies: the euro, the Japanese yen, and the Australian dollar. Use a currency converter from the Internet to find the value of $1 U.S. in each of these three currencies. Send the information to your instructor in an e-mail.

> ## Above and Beyond

Travel alerts and warnings Visit the Travel.State.Gov website (a link is provided on the website for this textbook) to learn about travel alerts and travel warnings issued by the U.S. Department of State. Write a paragraph describing travel alerts and travel warnings and list three countries that currently have travel warnings. Send the information to your instructor in an e-mail.

Administrative Assistant

Small company seeks responsible and motivated worker to assist management and accounting staff. Duties include:

- Answer phone calls and handle records management tasks
- Enter sales and purchase transactions and prepare financial statements using accounting software
- Maintain a petty cash fund and register
- Order office supplies
- Relieve receptionist at the front desk
- Communicate with customers and vendors via phone, e-mail, or mail

Do I qualify?

CHAPTER 14

Understanding Financial Responsibilities

Financial Statements

A goal of businesses is to make more money than is spent in operating the business. The amount of money made in a given time and the financial condition of a business are shown in financial statements such as income statements and balance sheets. Nonprofit organizations also use these statements to show the financial condition of the organization.

As an administrative professional, you may be involved in preparing financial statements and should understand the importance of these statements to company employees, investors, and others interested in the organization.

Learning Objectives

1. Describe financial statements for organizations.
2. Describe common employee benefits.
3. Describe and calculate employee payroll deductions.
4. Describe and prepare financial forms.

Income Statement

An **income statement** is a financial document that shows the income, expenses, and profit or loss of an organization for a given period of time. Typically, an income statement is prepared each month to show income and expenses for the month. A yearly income statement is prepared to show income and expenses for the fiscal year. A **fiscal year** is a 12-month period used for accounting purposes. A fiscal year might be from January 1 through December 31, from July 1 through June 30, or any other continuous 12-month period.

Profit is the amount by which income exceeds expenses. The income statement for a retail company shown in Figure 14-1 below, shows that the business made a profit. If income is too low or expenses are too high, the business may have a loss. **Loss** is the amount by which expenses exceed income. Most businesses cannot continue to operate in the long term if they do not make a profit. Nonprofit organizations often seek to break even, having enough income to pay expenses but not a significant amount more than expenses. The income statement also shows the gross profit, income from operations, income before tax, and income after tax as a percent of sales. The profit or loss amount from the income statement is shown on the organization's balance sheet.

Figure 14-1 Income Statement

Morrison Company
Income Statement
For the Month Ended August 31, 20--

			% of Sales
Sales		$200,000	
Cost of Goods Sold	$100,000		
Gross Profit on Sales		100,000	50%
Operating Expenses			
Advertising Expense	3,500		
Insurance Expense	5,600		
Miscellaneous Expense	459		
Salaries Expense	35,000		
Payroll Taxes Expense	2,800		
Utilities Expense	4,560		
Total Operating Expenses		51,919	
Net Income from Operations		48,081	24%
Other Income and Expenses			
Interest Income		2,000	
Net Income Before Income Tax		50,081	25%
Less Income Tax		14,023	
Net Income After Tax		$36,058	18%

Balance Sheet

A **balance sheet** is a financial document that shows the assets, liabilities, and owner's equity of an organization on a given date. **Assets** are money and anything of material value owned by an organization. **Liabilities** are the debts of an organization that must be paid in the future. Current or short-term liabilities are debts that must be paid within one year. Long-term liabilities are debts that are not due for a longer time (more than one year). **Owner's equity** is the financial claims to the assets of the organization by the owner or stockholders after all debts have been paid. If the company is a corporation, the owners' equity may

Figure 14-2 Balance Sheet

Rose Corporation
Balance Sheet
As of December 31, 20--
(Dollars in Thousands)

Assets

Current Assets	
Cash and Cash Equivalents	$200,012
Account Receivables	276,282
Inventories	399,026
Prepare Expenses	52,380
Total Current Assets	927,700
Property and Equipment, Net	1,409,151
Total Assets	$2,336,851

Liabilities and Stockholders' Equity

Current Liabilities	
Notes Payable, Current	$9,559
Accounts Payable	246,920
Accrued Expenses	225,009
Total Current Liabilities	481,488
Notes Payable, Long Term	658,697
Total Liabilities	$1,140,185
Stockholders' Equity	
Common Stock	$56,587
Additional Paid-in Capital	520,989
Retained Earnings	619,090
Total Stockholders' Equity	$1,196,666
Total Liabilities and Stockholders' Equity	$2,336,851

be called *capital* or *stockholders' equity*. Retained earnings are profits of the business that have not been paid to shareholders. Retained earnings are used to help the business improve operations or expand. A balance sheet is shown in Figure 14-2 on the previous page. As with income statements, balance sheets are typically prepared monthly and yearly.

Cash Flow Statement

A **cash flow statement** is a financial document that shows incoming and outgoing cash for a given period. Keeping track of cash flow is important so that the company has enough cash on hand to fund its payroll and pay other current bills. However, company managers typically do not want to have more cash than is currently needed in accounts that draw no or little interest. Managing the cash flow of a business is an important task that requires balancing current cash needs with investment opportunities. Cash flow statements are typically created monthly or on an as-needed basis. A sample cash flow statement is shown in Figure 14-3 below.

Budget

A **budget** is a plan that includes projected income and expenses for a business for a given time

Figure 14-3 Cash Flow Statement

Morrison Company		
Cash Flow Statement		
For the Month Ended August 31, 20--		
Cash Inflows		
Cash Collections	$5,000	
Credit Collections	75,000	
Investment Income	2,000	
Sale of Equipment	5,000	
Total Cash Inflows	$87,000	
Cash Outflows		
Advertising Expense	$3,500	
Insurance Expense	5,600	
Miscellaneous Expense	459	
Salaries Expense	35,000	
Payroll Taxes Expense	2,800	
Utilities Expense	4,560	
Total Cash Outflows	$51,919	
Net Cash Flow		$35,081
Beginning Cash Balance		125,000
Ending Cash Balance		$160,081

period. Budgets are created for each department or operating unit and for the business as a whole. Businesses typically create yearly budgets and may break down these plans into quarterly or monthly budgets. Budgets affect employees at all levels of the company. If you are an administrative assistant responsible for ordering office supplies, for instance, you may have a budget amount that has been approved for supplies. You may be expected to spend no more than the budgeted amount. If circumstances change and you realize that the budgeted amount will not be enough, you need to seek approval from your supervisor to spend additional money on supplies.

Creating a realistic business plan for a year or longer is an important but challenging task. The company must estimate how much income will be received from sales and other sources. If the projected income is not received, the business may have cash flow problems or suffer a loss for the year. The same is true if expenses prove to be higher than projected. As the fiscal year progresses, the actual income and expenses of the business are compared to those in the budget to see how close to the plan the business is performing. If income is too low or expenses are too high, company managers attempt to make changes to bring the actual numbers in line with the plan numbers.

Types of Business Organizations

As you learned in Chapter 1, a business can be organized in one of three basic forms: a sole proprietorship, a partnership, or a corporation. In a sole proprietorship, the business is owned by one person. This person may operate the business or hire managers and workers to operate the business. The owner receives all the profits from the business and is responsible for debts of the business.

In a partnership, two or more people own the business. They may or may not take part in running the business and may hire managers and other workers. The owners receive all the profits from the business and are responsible for debts of the business.

In a corporation, the business is owned by stockholders who buy shares of stock in the business. Stockholders may or may not be involved in running the business. Stockholders may receive part of the profits of the business in the form of dividends. Stockholders are generally not responsible for the debts of the business. Variations of these three forms also exist as discussed in Chapter 1.

TED ALJIBE/AFP/GETTY IMAGES

Knowing how the business you work for is organized will help you understand operations of the business.

Technology @Work

Many small companies and organizations use accounting software to enter transactions, prepare financial statements, create checks, and perform other accounting tasks. *QuickBooks®* is a popular accounting program for small businesses.

Financial statements can be created automatically by the program using information (beginning balances and transactions) entered earlier. The user simply selects the type of statement, the time period, and other options to customize the statement. If you work in a small company, you may use accounting software to create statements rather than keying them in a spreadsheet program.

Employee Benefits

In addition to salary or wages, many organizations offer benefits to employees. When considering taking a job, you should consider the benefits offered along with other factors about the job. These benefits can be a large part of the overall compensation received. Typical benefits include paid time off (vacation, holidays, and sick days), group insurance plans, retirement plans, and stock option plans. Once employed, you should be aware of the benefits offered by your company and how vacation days and holidays may affect work schedules.

Paid Time Off

Paid time off for business employees typically includes vacation days, holidays, and sick days. Having time away from work for holidays and vacations helps employees relax and return to work with a positive outlook and desire to perform well.

Many U.S. companies give workers ten or more paid vacation days per year. The number of vacation days may depend on the length of time the employee has worked for the company, with more days given as years of service increase. In many companies, workers are allowed to take vacation days at the times they request. Employees within one department may have to take vacation at different times in order to keep the department running smoothly. In some companies, the company closes operations for one or two weeks a year, with all employees taking vacation at that time.

Many companies give employees paid holidays in addition to vacation days. For U.S. companies, the holidays typically include New Year's Day, Martin Luther King, Jr. Day, Presidents' Day, Memorial Day, Independence Day, Labor Day, Columbus Day, Veterans Day, Thanksgiving Day, and Christmas Day. Some companies give employees one or two floating holidays that can be taken whenever the employee wishes. This allows employees to have time off on religious holidays that may not be on the company's holiday list.

Some companies offer paid sick days to allow employees to recover from an illness, to care for a family member who is ill, and to have diagnostic or preventive health care. Paid sick days are a valuable employee benefit. Millions of workers in the United States do not get paid sick days. In some cases, sick days cannot be used to care for a sick child but only for the worker's illness. Full-time workers are more likely to have paid sick days as a benefit than part-time workers.

© ISTOCKPHOTO.COM/JACOMSTEPHENS

Paid vacation days are a valued employee benefit.

Group Insurance

Many companies offer health care insurance plans to employees. Insurance costs for members of a group plan are lower than when individuals purchase health care insurance on their own, making this a valuable employee benefit.

Some companies pay a portion of the insurance plan costs; others require employees to pay the full cost. Employees may have two or more insurance plans (with varying coverage and costs) from which to choose. Eye care and dental plans may be offered. Some companies offer life insurance plans for employees, which may be paid for by the company or by the employee.

In 1968 Congress passed the Consolidated Omnibus Budget Reconciliation Act (COBRA). This act provides employees who leave a company the right to continue getting health care coverage at the company's group rate for 18 months. The former employee generally must pay the entire cost of the insurance, but this may still be less expensive than getting an individual health care plan. COBRA continuation coverage is often a good choice for individuals who are between jobs.

However, not all workers are covered by COBRA. For example, workers in companies with fewer than 20 employees may not be covered. The Department of Labor website provides answers to frequently asked questions about COBRA, as shown in Figure 14-4.

Figure 14-4 FAQS for Employees about COBRA

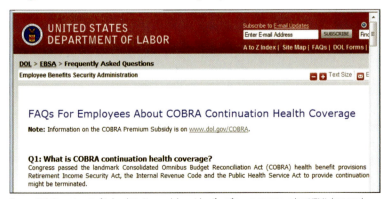

Source: U.S. Department of Labor, http://www.dol.gov/ebsa/faqs/faq_ consumer_cobra.HTML (accessed March 2, 2010).

Retirement Plans

Most workers need to establish a saving and investing plan for their working years that will generate the income needed in retirement. Tax-deferred retirement plans and defined benefit plans are two options offered by some employers that can contribute to an individual's plan.

401(k) and 403(b) Accounts

Many companies and organizations offer employees an option to enroll in a 401(k) or 403(b) plan. A **401(k) account** is a tax-deferred retirement plan for employees of private companies and corporations. The employee sets aside money each month through a pre-tax payroll deduction. The employer may also contribute money to the account. Sometimes employers match a certain percentage of employee contributions. Employees choose investments for their 401(k) accounts based on the willingness to take risks.

A **403(b) account** is a tax-deferred retirement plan for employees of nonprofit organizations or educational institutions. Teachers, nurses, professors, and ministers are examples of people who might qualify for a 403(b) account. If you work as an administrative assistant at a nonprofit organization, such as a charity, you might also quality for a 403(b) account. The employee sets aside money each month through a pre-tax payroll deduction and chooses investments for the account. Contributions may also be made by the employer. Specific rules govern how much employees and employers can contribute, types of investments that can be made, and how funds may be withdrawn. The IRS website provides detailed information about 401(k) and 403(b) accounts.

Defined Benefit Pension Plans   Some
employers offer retirement accounts that are paid for by the employer. These accounts are called defined benefit pension plans or simply pensions. (The plan is called *defined* because there is a set formula for computing the employer's contributions to the plan.) In some plans, the employee can also contribute money to the account. These plans usually

People @Work

EMPLOYEE BENEFITS MANAGER

Organizations want to attract qualified employees. A good employee benefits package helps make this possible. An employee benefits manager is a person who manages the company's employee benefits program, particularly its health insurance and pension plans.

This person must keep up with changes in state and federal rules and regulations that affect employee benefits as well as be familiar with the terms of the various benefits offered, such as health care insurance, life insurance, paid time off, and pension plans. The benefits manager may assist with research for new or changing benefits, answer employee questions, and help employees with procedures for filing claims.

As an employee, you may interact with an employee benefits manager as you select benefit options or request information about benefits.

require that you work for a minimum number of years (typically five) before you qualify for the plan. The amount contributed to the plan on your behalf increases as you continue to work for the company. Your benefits during retirement depend on the number of years worked, your salary, and other factors. When retired employees receive benefits, they must pay taxes on the money.

Defined benefit pension plans are costly for the company and complex to administrate. For these reasons, they are offered by fewer companies than in the past. The March 2008 National Compensation Survey benefits data show that 21 percent of private industry workers had access to a defined benefit plan.[1] Defined contribution plans, such as

1 U.S. Bureau of Labor Statistics, *National Compensation Survey, March 2008,* http://www.bls.gov/ncs/ebs/benefits/2008/ownership/private/table02a.pdf (accessed September 16, 2009).

the 401(k) accounts discussed earlier, have become the primary means of retirement savings.

Stock Purchase Plans

Some corporations offer their employees an opportunity to buy stock in the company through payroll deduction. A **stock** is a share of ownership in a corporation. Such a plan allows employees to have a stake in the company's financial growth. The benefits of buying stock in this manner include the following:

- You can save money with which to buy stock through automatic deduction from your paycheck.

- The company may provide a discount on the price of the stock over what you would pay on the open market. The company may also give bonuses in the form of stock.

- You do not have to pay for the services of a stockbroker.

IRAs

An IRA (individual retirement account) is a plan that permits individuals to save and invest for retirement (as opposed to an employer-sponsored plan). The money deposited is not taxed until you start to withdraw it, usually during retirement.

You decide how to invest the funds; however, the types of investments that can be purchased through an IRA are restricted. Money can be invested in items such as stocks, mutual funds, and certificates of deposit. Money cannot be invested in collectibles such as artwork, antiques, gems, and coins.

Money placed in an IRA can be deducted from gross income if you meet certain requirements. This lowers your income tax. The contribution amount per year is limited with limits changing from year to year. Details about contribution amounts can be found on the IRS website.

Employee Payroll Deductions

Employers may deduct money from your pay for items such as taxes, insurance, retirement plans, or stock purchase plans. You may receive a paycheck or simply a pay stub that documents an automatic payroll deposit. Many companies use automatic deposit for payroll because it saves the company money and is convenient for employees. In either case, you need to understand and check all the deductions from your pay to be sure that they are correct and that the deductions you requested are being made.

Taxes

When you work for an organization or are self-employed, a portion of your salary is deducted for payroll taxes. These taxes include federal income tax, Social Security tax, and Medicare tax. Many states, counties, and cities also

Figure 14-5 **Taxes and Deductions from Pay**

Taxes and Deductions

Description	Current Amount	Year-to-Date Amount
Taxes Withheld		
Social Security Tax	217.00	1,953.00
Medicare Tax	50.75	456.75
Federal Income Tax	420.00	3,780.00
State Tax	122.50	1,102.50
City Tax	87.50	787.50
Total Taxes	897.75	8,079.75
Pre-Tax Deductions		
401(k)	350.00	3,150.00
Medical Insurance	125.00	1,125.00
Total Pre-Tax Deductions	475.00	4,275.00

tax personal income. If so, this tax is also withheld from your pay as shown in Figure 14-5 above.

workplace wisdom

You may be employed by several different organizations during your working years. You may have a 401(k) account or a defined benefit pension plan at one or more of these organizations. Keep careful records of your benefits at each organization.

When you leave an organization, determine whether your retirement investments can be rolled over into another account or whether they will stay in the current pension plan. You should receive statements about your retirement accounts periodically. Review these retirement statements and then file them for future reference.

Income Taxes Federal income tax is a mandatory deduction under federal law. Taxes are withheld from your pay on the basis of information you give on a Form W-4 (Employee's Withholding Allowance Certificate). The number of exemptions claimed on the Form W-4, in addition to the amount of money you earn and current tax rates, determines the amount to be deducted for federal income taxes.

Most states have mandatory state income taxes. Seven states have no state income tax: Alaska, Florida, Nevada, South Dakota, Texas, Washington, and Wyoming. Two others, New Hampshire and Tennessee, limit their state income tax to dividends and interest income only. State income tax rates vary but are lower than federal tax rates. Both federal and state income tax rates can change from year to year.

Some local governments (cities, counties, townships) have an income tax. Tax rates may vary depending on whether you are a resident or a nonresident. Nonresidents are people who earn income in the area but do not live there.

Social Security and Medicare

Social Security is a social insurance program with its beneficiaries being retired individuals, widows and survivors, and people with disabilities. Social Security benefits are paid when a person retires or becomes disabled. The program may also pay benefits to survivors and/or dependents of an insured person in the event of the person's death.

Medicare is a health insurance program for people age 65 or older. Certain people younger than age 65 can qualify for Medicare, such as those who have disabilities

and certain other medical conditions. The program helps with the cost of health care, but it does not cover all medical expenses or the cost of most long-term care (such as a nursing home).

Social Security's Old-Age, Survivors, and Disability Insurance and Medicare's Hospital Insurance are financed primarily by employment taxes. Tax rates for Social Security apply to earnings up to a maximum amount per year. In 2010 the maximum amount was $106,800. Medicare is also financed in part by monthly premiums deducted from Social Security checks. The 2010 Social Security tax rate is 6.2 percent for an individual employee. The 2010 Medicare tax rate is 1.45 percent for an individual employee.[2] Social Security taxes are sometimes called FICA taxes because they are collected under the authority of the Federal Insurance Contributions Act (FICA).

Other Payroll Deductions

Deductions may be made from your pay for items you have requested, such as the insurance plans or stock option plans discussed earlier. Another deduction that you might request is a payment to a health savings plan. These plans allow you to save money to pay for future medical

©ISTOCK

Dear Savvy Admin

Dear Savvy Admin:

When I'm out or away from my desk, my supervisor and a few of my coworkers sometimes need to check or "try out" data in the financial spreadsheets I keep (I use *Excel* 2007). More than once, they have inadvertently messed up formulas or changed data. I back up my files, but what else can I do to protect my formulas and data from being changed while allowing people to access my spreadsheets to get information they need?

Frustrated

Dear Frustrated:

Excel has a variety of protection features. It sounds as though the best option for you is to password-protect your files so that users can view them, change data, and even change formulas but are not able to save their changes, except under a different filename. This Password to Modify feature is available through the Save As dialog box.

Get your supervisor's approval first, and let everyone who accesses your files know what to expect.

Savvy Admin

2 U.S. Internal Revenue Service, "Publication 15 (2010), Circular E, Employer's Tax Guide," IRS. gov, http://www.irs.gov/publications/p15/ar02. html (accessed March 2, 2010).

expenses. The money you set aside in the plan is not subject to federal income taxes when you contribute it. When you withdraw the money, it is not taxed as long as it is used for medical expenses.

Some companies may encourage you to deduct money from your pay to be given to a nonprofit organization that you wish to support. For example, United Way is a nonprofit organization that supports education, health, and other community needs. Companies may encourage employees to support such organizations and offer payroll deduction for contributions. You might want to have money deducted from your pay and deposited in a savings account. Some companies perform this service for employees.

Financial Forms and Transactions

As an administrative assistant, you may be required to prepare or check financial forms such as petty cash records, payroll registers, purchasing records, and bank reconciliations. It is important that you understand the purpose of these forms in order to prepare or check them correctly.

Petty Cash

Petty cash is money kept on hand to pay small fees or charges incurred by the company or to reimburse employees for such charges. Using cash is sometimes more convenient than writing a check for small items such as a delivery fee. The amount of money in the petty cash fund varies by company; $200 is a typical amount. One or two people are in charge of the petty cash fund. When money is taken from the fund, a petty cash voucher is prepared showing the amount, the date, the reason for the payment, and the company or person to whom the payment is made. A cash register or sales receipt that shows this information may be used instead of the voucher. A running balance is also kept of the fund. When the fund reaches a certain low level, the fund is replenished from the cash account. A petty cash record is shown in Figure 14-6 below.

Payroll Register

A payroll register shows the earnings, deductions, and net pay for employees. **Net pay** is final earnings after taxes and other deductions are made. Each employee may receive a payment record that shows the same information as his or her entry on the payroll register. If employees are paid by check, the information is shown on the stub of the check. If employees are paid by automatic deposit, the payment information is provided separately. At the end of the year, the company gives each employee a Wage and Tax Statement (called a W-2 form) that shows payment information for the year. A portion of a payroll register is shown in Figure 14-7 on page 268.

Figure 14-6 Petty Cash Record

Petty Cash Record							
Date	Deposit	Payment	Balance	Receipt No.	Description	Received By	Approved By
2/1/20--	200.00		200.00		Deposit to petty cash		Maria Diaz
2/3/20--		18.53	181.47	1011	Pizza for overtime workers	Joe Brooks	Maria Diaz
2/7/20--		5.65	175.82	589	Delivery fee	Tim Hawks	Maria Diaz
2/10/20--		12.50	163.32	10056	Postage	Connie Wong	Maria Diaz

Figure 14-7 Payroll Register

Payroll Register									
January 31, 20--									
Employee No.	Employee Name	Regular	Overtime	Total	Income Tax	FICA	State Tax	Health Insurance	Net Pay
5782	Allenson, B.	2,150.00		2,150.00	236.50	164.48	64.50	123.00	1,561.52
5793	Bribes, W.	1,088.00		1,088.00	119.68	83.23	32.64	123.00	729.45
5714	Cantrell, T.	2,840.00		2,840.00	312.40	217.26	85.20	76.00	2,149.14
4598	Ellis, J.	2,010.00		2,010.00	221.10	153.77	60.30	123.00	1,451.83
5563	Perez, M.	1,600.00		1,600.00	176.00	122.40	48.00	76.00	1,177.60
5689	Wang, H.	3,445.00		3,445.00	378.95	263.54	103.35	123.00	2,576.16

Purchase Transactions

In many companies, employees in the purchasing and accounting departments order goods and process all payments. In a small company, the administrative assistant may order items and request payments. If it is your responsibility to order items and request payments, review all the related documents carefully.

- A purchase requisition is a document that shows items requested and an approval to make the purchase. The approval is typically given by a manager or other authorized person.

- A purchase order is a document sent to a vendor that details the items being purchased, the shipping and billing addresses, payment terms, and related information. If items are ordered online, an order summary or record may serve the same purpose as a purchase order.

- A receiving report or an initialed packing slip verifies that the items ordered have been received by the company.

- An invoice is a bill from a vendor requesting payment for the items.

- A voucher is a document that shows the vendor name, invoice date, terms, items purchased, and amount owed. An approved voucher authorizes payment of the invoice.

If you are responsible for ordering items, make sure the needed approval has been given for the purchase. This approval might be a signature on a purchase requisition or an e-mail from an authorized person.

A purchase requisition is shown in Figure 14-8 on page 269. You may be given the company from which to purchase items, or you may need to do research to find the best source for the items.

Communicating @Work

Administrative assistants often key or file documents that have sensitive information about employee salaries, performance evaluations, benefits, or health records. This information is considered confidential. Never discuss the information you may see or read with persons who are not authorized to know the information.

Take precautions to protect confidential information while it is in your care. For example, do not leave a file with confidential information displayed on your computer screen when you leave your desk. Close the file when someone comes into your office or cubicle. Place hard-copy documents in a folder or drawer where they will be out of sight. Check your work area every evening to make sure that all documents are put away. Discuss confidential topics by phone only in an area where you will not be overheard by others.

Figure 14-8 Purchase Requisition

Purchase Requisition

Requested by: Karen Roberts, Customer Service   **Date:** October 17, 20--

Vendor of Choice	Item	Quantity	Unit Price	Total
Office Supplies and Such 426 Monroe Street Somerset, KY 42502-0426	HP Printer Cartridge XL24 Black	3	$21.95	$65.85
			Total	$65.85

Account No: 73300   Purchase Approval   Date

Joe Park   10/17/20--

Your company may have one or more approved vendors from which you can order. For example, you might be authorized to order office supplies from only one or two companies. For other items, you may be free to select the company.

When the items arrive, check the packing slip to make sure that all items listed on the slip are in the package. Compare the packing slip and items received with the purchase order or order summary to verify that the items received are the items you ordered. When the invoice for the items arrives, check it against the purchase order and packing slip or record of items received to verify that the invoice covers only items you received and that the amounts are correct. If everything is in order, prepare a voucher to request payment of the invoice. A voucher is shown in Figure 14-9 on page 270.

If you order online, the items may be charged to a company credit card or the company's account with the vendor. In that case, forward the checked packing slip and order document to the accounting department personnel who will pay the credit card bill or company account with the vendor.

The terms shown on the voucher in Figure 14-9 on page 270 are 2/10, net 30. If the payment is made

within ten days of the invoice date, a 2 percent discount can be taken from the invoice amount. If the payment is made after the tenth day, the full amount is within 30 days. Many businesses pay their bills in time to take advantage of discounts.

Bank Reconciliation

A bank reconciliation is the process of comparing and checking company records against those shown on a bank statement. A bank reconciliation is typically done each month. In a large company, this task is usually handled by personnel in the accounting department. In a small company, an administrative assistant may do the bank reconciliation. By completing a bank reconciliation, you will:

- Confirm that deposits made during the month have been properly recorded by the bank.

- Verify that the checks processed during the month were written by the company (and that no unauthorized checks have been processed).

- Identify checks written by the company that have not yet been presented to the bank for payment.

- Note any service charges or other fees on the bank statement that need to be entered in the company records.

Figure 14-9 Voucher

Voucher

Voucher No.   4589   **Date:**   October 24, 20--

Pay To: Office Supplies and Such
                 426 Monroe Street
                 Somerset, KY 42502-0426

For the Following (Supporting documents are attached.)

Invoice Date	Terms	Invoice No.	Gross Amount	Discount	Net Payable
10/24/20--	2/10, net 30	3479	$65.85	$1.32	$64.53

Payment Approval   Date

Joe Park   10/24/20- -

■ Note any interest paid on the account that needs to be entered in the company records.

■ Determine the adjusted cash balance as of the reconciliation date.

Using a spreadsheet program is an efficient way to complete a bank reconciliation. You can create a standard form and simply update the information each month. Figure 14-10, on page 271, shows the information that should be included in the reconciliation.

1. The heading information (name of company, form name, and date) appears at the top of the worksheet.

2. The check register information appears on the left side of the worksheet. Enter the check register balance on the current date. Subtract bank fees and add interest earned to the check register amount to find the adjusted check register balance.

3. The bank statement information appears on the right side of the worksheet. Enter the bank statement balance. Outstanding deposits and checks are those that are not shown on the bank statement. Compare the company records to the bank

©ISTOCK

Writing @Work

As an administrative assistant, you may be asked to communicate information about benefits, salary, or health care claims to employees, department managers, or personnel in the human resources department. Communications that contain sensitive information should be sent in a hard-copy document placed in an envelope—not by e-mail.

Communications sent by e-mail are not secure or private. They may be accidentally sent to the wrong person or reviewed by personnel in the information technology department as part of routine checks.

Figure 14-10 Bank Reconciliation

W. C. Chang Company
Bank Reconciliation
August 31, 20--

Check register			Bank statement		
balance 8/31/--	$22,440.30		balance 8/20/--		$20,569.89
Deduct:			Add:		
Service charge	12.00		Deposit in transit		2,851.10
Add:			Deduct:		
Interest	336.60		Outstanding checks		
			No. 1188	198.70	
			No. 2000	110.10	
			No. 2003	347.29	
					656.09
Adjusted check register			Adjusted bank		
balance 8/31/--	$22,764.90		balance 8/31/--		$22,764.90

statement to identify outstanding deposits and checks. Add outstanding deposits and subtract outstanding checks to find the adjusted bank balance.

The adjusted check register balance and the adjusted bank balance should be the same amount. If the two numbers are not the same, recheck the numbers and formulas in the worksheet. Once the balance numbers are in agreement, record bank fees and interest in the company records or forward that information to the person who handles that task. File the bank statement for future reference.

Key Terms

401(k) account

403(b) account

assets

balance sheet

budget

cash flow statement

fiscal year

income statement

liabilities

loss

net pay

owner's equity

petty cash

profit

stock

Summary

◼ A goal of businesses is to make more money than is spent in operating the business.

◼ The amount of money made in a given time and the financial condition of a business are shown in financial statements such as income statements, cash flow statements, and balance sheets.

◼ A budget is a plan that includes projected income and expenses for a business for a given time period.

◼ In addition to salary or wages, many organizations offer benefits to employees. Typical benefits include paid time off (vacation, holidays, and sick days), group health insurance plans, retirement plans, and stock option plans.

◼ Health insurance costs for members of a group plan are usually lower than when individuals purchase health care insurance on their own, making this a valuable employee benefit.

◼ Tax-deferred retirement plans and defined benefit plans are two options offered by some employers.

◼ Employers may deduct money from your pay for items such as taxes, insurance, retirement plans, or stock purchase plans.

◼ As an administrative assistant, you may be required to prepare or check financial forms such as petty cash records, payroll registers, purchasing records, and bank reconciliations.

Bookmark It. *For convenient access to activities, links, and valuable career resources for administrative professionals, visit the companion website for this text:*

www.cengage.com/officetech/fultoncalkins

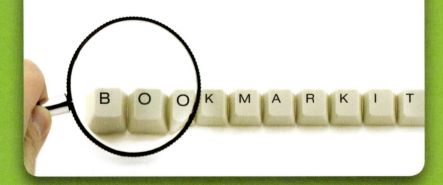

Discussion Questions

1. What information is shown on an income statement, a balance sheet, and a cash flow statement?
2. What is the purpose of a budget?
3. List and describe four types of employee benefits.
4. List and describe four types of payroll deductions employees might have.
5. What is the purpose of a petty cash fund?
6. Describe the following documents related to purchase transactions: purchase requisition, purchase order, receiving report, invoice, and voucher.

Critical Thinking

Petty cash fund You work as an administrative assistant for a small company and are in charge of the petty cash fund. Another administrative assistant, Gloria, asked to borrow $40 from the fund until payday, which is in two days. A personal loan is not stated as specifically against company policy, but it is also not listed as an approved use of petty cash. To keep Gloria's goodwill, you decide to make the loan and not record it in the petty cash records. Typically, no one else reviews the records, and you think only you and Gloria will know about the loan.

On the way home that day, you are in an accident and will not be able to report to work for two weeks. Your manager has asked you to send an e-mail with details about things your temporary replacement needs to handle. What will you say about the petty cash fund? Should you have made the loan to Gloria? Why or why not?

Build Workplace Skills

1. **Financial statements** Which financial documents (income statement, balance sheet, cash flow statement, budget) would typically show the following information:
   a. Profit or loss for a given period of time
   b. Assets and their value on a given date
   c. Expenses for a period of time
   d. Money paid out during a period of time
   e. Beginning and ending cash balance for a period of time
   f. Projected income for a period of time
   g. Income as a percentage of sales
   h. Owner's equity on a given date
   i. Liabilities on a given date
   (Learning Objective 1)

Planning Notes

Learning Objectives

1. Describe financial statements for organizations.
2. Describe common employee benefits.
3. Describe and calculate employee payroll deductions.
4. Describe and prepare financial forms.

Critical Thinking; Activities 2, 4, 5

Activities 1, 3, 8,9; Above & Beyond

Activities 6, 7

2. **Employee benefits**   Interview in person, by phone, or by e-mail a person who is currently working and receives employee benefits. Ask the person to describe the benefits received and to tell how important each benefit is (without revealing confidential details). Write a short report that includes the person's job title, place of employment, and job duties. Summarize the information about this person's employee benefits and their importance. (Learning Objective 2)

Communicate Clearly

3. **Payroll deductions**   Open the *Excel* file CH14 Payroll from the data files. All employee earnings are subject to FICA deductions totaling 7.65 percent. Edit the expense report to correct errors in spelling, capitalization, formulas, and numbers. (Learning Objective 3)

4. **Budget message**   Your supervisor asked you to send an e-mail to all department members reminding them that requests for budget items in the equipment category are due to her next Monday. Write the e-mail as requested, including the date. Remind the recipients that they should include complete information about the equipment requested including the costs and why the equipment is needed. Include any other details you think would be helpful. Send the e-mail to your instructor.

5. **Research for budget**   Your supervisor has requested that all budget requests for the equipment category be submitted by next Monday. You think the department could benefit from having a color printer. Research color printers and find one to recommend for purchase. Write an e-mail that gives the printer name/brand, model, description, cost, and reasons why you think the printer should be purchased. Send the e-mail to your instructor.

Develop Relationships

6. **Employee salaries**   You work as the only administrative assistant for a small company. The department manager and other department employees often invite you to join them for lunch. They like to have lunch at local restaurants, which can be expensive.

   You want to be friendly and enjoy the company of the other employees, but eating out so often is putting a strain on your budget. The other employees all make considerably more money than you do and don't seem to think twice about the cost of meals. What can you say or do to keep the goodwill of your fellow employees and stay within your lunch budget?

7. **Purchase request**   You are the administrative assistant in the information technology department of your small company. You are responsible for ordering supplies for all printers. You received an approved purchase requisition for three printer cartridges, all the same. As you were preparing to order the cartridges, you realized that the company does not have a printer that uses these cartridges.

   Thinking a simple mistake had been made, you sent an e-mail to Joe Teal, the person who submitted the request, asking him to verify which cartridges he needs. Joe answered your message saying, "The purchase request I submitted was approved and lists the correct cartridges. Please process the order immediately." What should you do? Why might Joe be defensive in this situation?

> ## Use Technology

8. **Bank reconciliation**   Use a spreadsheet program and the following information to complete a bank reconciliation:

   - On June 30 of the current year, the check register for Carson Consulting Company shows a balance of $35,184.64.

   - The bank statement dated June 25 shows a balance of $35,850.56.

   - You have identified one outstanding deposit of $450 made on June 26.

   - You have also identified two outstanding checks: No. 3478 for $150.98 and No. 3488 for $256.89.

   - The bank charged a service fee of $10.00.

   - The bank statement shows interest earned of $718.05.

   (Learning Objective 4)

9. **Social Security estimate**   Access the Social Security Online website. A link is provided on the website for this book. Go to the Benefit Calculators section. Follow the directions provided to enter information and get an estimate of your Social Security retirement benefits. Print the Your Retirement Benefit Estimate page. Since this page contains private information, you are not asked to submit it to your instructor.

> ## Above & Beyond

Investment research   To learn more about financial statements, read articles online such as "Beginners' Guide to Financial Statements" on the U.S. Securities and Exchange Commission website. A link is provided on the website for this book.

Select two Fortune 500 companies in which you would consider investing. A list of Fortune 500 companies can be found on the *Fortune* website. A link is provided on the website for this book.

Visit the website for each company and access the company's financial statements. After reviewing the statements, write a paragraph that tells which company you would choose for investment and why. Cite information from the financial statement to support your choice.

Planning Notes

Part V

Professional Profile

Michael Hertlein

Paralegal
Intellectual Property Issues
Dinsmore & Shohl Attorneys
Cincinnati, Ohio

Michael Hertlein is a paralegal working on intellectual property issues for Dinsmore & Shohl Attorneys, a large law firm in Cincinnati, Ohio.

Michael believes that confident people are more likely to succeed. "One should project an image of success at all times. Positive body language is crucial because it sends the correct message to those who may be evaluating your performance."

Asking appropriate questions can help you gain confidence and self-sufficiency in the early days of a new job. "I constantly asked questions," recalls Michael. "A keen eye for detail is a must in my field. I was fortunate to be surrounded by a team of wonderful secretaries, paralegals, and attorneys with years of experience whom I could rely on for advice."

Michael advises new employees to act as if they are always being evaluated. Workplaces are open spaces where "people are always watching and listening. Your actions are essentially public and can certainly serve to propel you forward toward new opportunities."

Michael encourages students to explore resources at school to prepare meticulously for the job application and interview process. "The interviewee has only a small window to give the interviewer a glimpse at his or her strengths. This is your brief chance to shine. Bedazzle interviewers by conducting practice interviews at your school's career planning center.

"One should project an image of success at all times. . . . Your actions are essentially public and can certainly serve to propel you forward toward new opportunities."

"Know that most jobs are highly competitive, but that you can separate yourself from the flock of applicants. This can be accomplished through achieving high grades, participating in relevant extracurricular activities, and interning for the organization you hope to work for." Above all, Michael says, "Know that if you work hard, more often than not, you will be rewarded for your dedication."

Career Success

Chapter **15** Seeking Employment

Chapter **16** Leading with Confidence

Ready, Set, Plan

©ANTHONY STRACK, GALLO IMAGES/GETTY IMAGES

Use this space to plan your work in this section. Record the due dates for reading assignments and other activities for each chapter. If you are working with a team or partner, record the schedule for team meetings. Do you need a list of phone numbers or e-mail addresses? Don't forget your other commitments: work, other classes, and family.

Do I qualify?

Administrative Assistant

Property management firm seeks responsible worker to interact with tenants and handle administrative duties such as:

- Document tenants' property concerns
- Send e-mail announcements
- Input data into *Excel*
- Answer a steady volume of incoming calls
- Create and publish memos and other communications
- Manage the schedule for conference rooms

An achievement-oriented demeanor, professional dress, and experience in property management are required.

©MARK WRAGG, ISTOCK

CHAPTER

15

Learning Objectives

1. Identify sources of job information.

2. Research organizations and prepare a letter of application and a resume.

3. Develop job interview skills.

4. Develop skills for job advancement and job changes.

Seeking Employment

Sources of Job Information

Throughout this course, you have improved your skills and have positioned yourself to become an administrative professional. Stop now and reflect for a few minutes on your skills. As you reflect on both your hard skills (computer competency, writing skills, presentation skills, and others) and your soft skills (interpersonal, teamwork, and verbal communication skills, for example), you need to think about a career path. What type of organization interests you? In the long term, where do you want your career path to go?

It is highly unlikely you will work for only one or two organizations during your career. You need to develop proficiency not only in looking for a job, but also in finding one that will make the most of your strengths and the directions you wish your career to go. Stop for a few moments to review your strengths and your weaknesses and consider where you want to be in your career in five or ten years.

Once you have seriously taken the reflective step of thinking about what your skills are and where you want to go, you are ready to begin thinking about the steps you must take to identify a job that fits your skills and what you want to achieve.

One of the first things to do as you look for a job is to get all the information you can about available job opportunities. Information is available through the sources listed here:

- Networking
- College placement offices
- Newspaper advertisements
- The Internet
- The United States federal government, United States Postal Service, and state governments
- Employment agencies
- Direct contact with companies and other organizations

Networking

Networking is making contacts with people who may help you in an activity, such as your job search or career growth. Most of us already have an extensive social network including our relatives, friends, and others. As you begin looking for a job, you will want to develop a job-related network. How do you do that? Here are some suggested steps:

- Let people know that you are searching for a job. Contact individuals you know who work for firms where you would like to work. Ask for leads and referrals.

- Contact professional organizations. For example, you may contact the local chapter of IAAP. Contact administrative professionals who are already employed. Contact managers you know; ask for referrals for any job openings that exist. Try to obtain at least three or four names from each person with whom you speak.

- Ask administrative professionals who are employed in the field how they obtained their positions and what they like or dislike about their jobs.

- Keep a record of every person with whom you talk—his or her e-mail or telephone number and any comments.

College Placement Offices

Many colleges and universities have placement offices. The counselors in these offices aid students in career planning. Job fairs are a relatively common type of service offered to students. Businesspeople invited to these fairs include representatives from major companies in the area who are seeking employees. Additional services offered by placement offices include:

- Materials on specific careers
- Writing assistance for application letters and resumes
- Interviewing assistance
- Testing

You will want to visit the placement office in your college (assuming one is available) for assistance that the personnel in this office can provide.

Newspaper Advertisements

Although job advertisements are carried in most newspapers all week, the Sunday newspaper is generally the paper that carries the most possibilities. Look in the Jobs section and under Administrative Professionals and/or Secretaries.

The Internet

Internet sites that provide job search information, often called **job boards**, allow you to browse job listings by company, industry, location (country, state, city), and pay. On some of these sites, you may post your resume, network, and get advice on successful job application techniques. A **resume** is a concise document that lists your background, education, skills, and experience related to work.

You can use the Internet to research the typical salaries for administrative professionals. For example, IAAP usually has information on its website for salaries of various job titles for administrative professionals. You can then compare salaries for specific jobs with typical salaries.

The Internet has a variety of resources for job seekers, including tips for resume and cover letter preparation and interviewing. Additionally, many organizations allow you to post your resume directly on their website. You will learn more about writing and posting resumes on the Internet later in this chapter. Several websites that provide job search information are listed on the website for this textbook.

Federal and State Government Jobs

Federal government jobs are available through the USAJOBS website. A link to this website is provided on the website for this book. This website allows you to choose the location you desire (U.S. government jobs throughout the world are listed), the job category, and the salary range or pay grade range you want. A sample search result for USAJOBS is shown in Figure 15-1. You may also want to review the positions available on the U.S. Postal Service website and state government positions available through individual state government websites.

Employment Agencies

Both private and state-operated employment agencies are available in most areas. Tax dollars support state-operated employment agencies. You can take advantage of the free services provided by these agencies. The website of the state-operated agency for California is shown in Figure 15-2 on page 281. The site allows employers to enter job listings, browse resumes, and find qualified workers. Job seekers can search online for jobs in California and enter a resume to match with job openings listed on the site.

Private employment agencies charge a fee for their services. For some jobs, the fee is paid by the employer. For other jobs, you may be responsible for paying the fee. When private employment agencies advertise jobs in newspapers, they may include the word *fee-paid*, meaning the employer pays the fee. When you go to a private employment agency, ask who is paying the fee and the amount. You may be required to sign a contract with a private agency. The contract should include the fee, if required. Read the contract carefully before signing it.

Figure 15-1 USAJOBS Website

Source: U.S. Office of Personnel Management, *USAJOBS*, http://www.usajobs.gov (accessed October 23, 2009).

Some agencies handle temporary work assignments. If you are uncertain about the type or size of organization where you want to work, you might want to work in several organizations as a temporary employee for a period of time. Without any long-term commitment, you can gain an understanding of various jobs and decide where you want to work as a full-time employee.

Direct Contacts

If you are interested in obtaining a position with a certain organization or in a particular type of business, contacting the organization or business may yield successful results. The contact may be made in person by visiting the organization or by sending a letter and resume. Individuals who are most successful using this approach are those who have a gift for selling themselves. Before you engage in this approach, find out as much as you can about the organization you plan to contact, as discussed in the next section of this chapter. Knowledge of the organization where you are applying is always helpful, no matter what job approach you select.

Do not restrict your job search to direct contacts only. Using this approach can be a time-consuming process, often with little success. If you do use direct contact as one of your approaches, be certain to dress professionally and take several copies of your resume when you visit a company to complete an employment application. Prepare to make a professional impression even on visits when you only plan to drop off an application.

Figure 15-2 State-Operated Employment Agency Website

Source: California Employment Development Department, *CalJOBS*, http://www.caljobs.ca.gov (accessed October 23, 2009).

Researching and Applying for Jobs

Once you have identified sources of information about jobs, you are ready to do research on the organizations and apply for jobs. Having information about an organization will help you create a letter of application and resume that will show your qualifications to your best advantage. As you conduct your research, select several organizations of interest to you. Do not place all of your hopes on one organization.

Research Organizations

Before applying for a job with an organization, spend time learning about the organization—its mission and vision, its financial history, its products or services, its reputation, the length of time it has been in business, and how it treats employees. How do you do this? There are several possibilities.

Since many organizations have websites, the best place to start is probably the company's website. Review everything on the site, paying particular attention to the organization's mission and vision statement and the products and services offered by the organization. Other suggestions for finding information about the organization include the following:

- Read periodicals or websites that profile organizations in the United States. For example, *Fortune* provides a list of the 100 best companies to work for in the United States. *Working Mother* lists the 100 best companies for working mothers. Similar lists are available for other groups from other organizations.

- Ask friends, relatives, and acquaintances what they know about the organization.

- Obtain an annual report of the company. Large companies often have the reports posted on their websites.

- Consult your local chamber of commerce.

- Ask your college placement office for information.

Prepare a Letter of Application

A **letter of application** is sent to a potential employer to state your interest in a job and to transmit your resume. This letter is generally the first contact you have with a potential employer and is key, along with your resume, to obtaining an interview.

The letter must sell your abilities to the employer. The person reading your letter gets a favorable or unfavorable impression of you from the content of your letter, your writing skills, and the format of the letter. This letter must be free of keying or spelling errors. If you make mistakes in the letter, you have little chance of getting an interview. Think of this letter as your chance to say to a prospective employer, "I am the person who can do the job; my work is always well written and free of errors." Conversely, a poorly written letter, with keying and other errors, suggests that you are disorganized, sloppy, unfocused, and ill suited for employment.

Technology @Work

USAJOBS and many other job boards allow users to create *search agents*, also called *job scouts or job agents*. Search agents are programs that automatically search job listings and retrieve jobs matching criteria you set. For example, you might request jobs in a certain geographic area. The results are sent to you by e-mail at an interval you select, such as daily or weekly. You can review the jobs listing and respond to jobs that interest you.

The basic goals of a letter of application are as follows:

- State your interest in the position.
- Provide general information about your skills (specific information appears in your resume) and sell your skills (let the reader know you have something to offer the organization).
- Transmit your resume.
- Request an interview, providing your contact information.

Use Proper Format   Block style is a commonly used style for a letter of application; however, modified block style is also appropriate. Both mixed punctuation, with a colon after the salutation and a comma after the complimentary close, and open punctuation are appropriate. If you need to review letter and punctuation styles, refer to the Reference Guide near the end of this textbook.

You may be posting your letter and resume online. This possibility will be discussed in a later section of this chapter.

Address the Letter Appropriately   Be certain that you address the letter appropriately. Reread the address several times and proof the address that you have keyed against the position advertisement. You do not want to key the wrong title, misspell the recipient's name, or even send the letter to the wrong person. Never use "To Whom It May Concern" as a salutation. If a name is not given in the job vacancy notice, use the organization name and address given, with "Ladies and Gentlemen" as a salutation.

Figure 15-3 on page 283 provides an example of a letter of application. Notice that the four basic goals of a letter of application are followed carefully in the three paragraphs of the letter. Notice that the top of the letter includes the sender's address, telephone number, and e-mail. A resume will also include this information; however, if the letter and resume get separated, this approach allows the organization to contact the sender.

Prepare a Resume

The resume, a concise statement of your background, education, skills, and experience, is an important part of your job application packet. Just as the letter of application is a sales document, so is the resume. It represents a very important product—you. A resume typically has these parts:

- Heading
- Career objective
- Education
- Relevant skills/professional skills
- Accomplishments
- Professional affiliations (if there are numerous affiliations that relate to the job) and military service

The resume parts may have different names. In preparing these headings, pay attention to the words that most clearly state your credentials and that relate to the job listing. Also, these headings may appear in a different order on the resume depending on whether the resume is in chronological or

workplace wisdom

When conducting a job search, you must learn to handle rejection without becoming discouraged. Do not take rejection personally. You may receive more "we have no openings" than "we are hiring for several positions." When the economy is growing and unemployment is low, you may be able to find a job within a few weeks. When the economy is slow and unemployment is high, finding a position can take several months.

Figure 15-3 Letter of Application

Elaina Diaz

2445 Edgecliff Road
Dallas, TX 75218-2445
E-mail: ediaz5@web.com
Phone: 214-555-0148

May 21, 20--

Ms. Jean LeJuan
Human Resources Department
Dallas Business Systems
1510 Eastern Drive
Dallas, TX 75202-1510

Dear Ms. LeJuan

Your job announcement for an administrative assistant came to my attention through your posting on the Employment Opportunities page of your website. Please consider me an applicant for this position.

After reading the qualifications you are seeking, I believe my skills and experience make me a strong candidate. My qualifications include the following:

- An associate's degree in administrative systems from Mountain Peak College
- Work experience as an administrative assistant
- Excellent human relations and communication skills
- Knowledge of computer software, including Microsoft Word, Excel, Access, and PowerPoint

You will find a resume enclosed, which gives further details about my experience and skills. May I have the opportunity to discuss my qualifications with you? Please call me at the number above to arrange a time when we can discuss the position and my qualifications.

Sincerely

Elaina Diaz

Elaina Diaz

Enclosure: Resume

Evaluating Possible Employers

When evaluating an organization as a possible employer, you will want to find answers to questions such as these:

↗ What are the organization's services or products?

↗ Is the organization multinational? Does the organization have branches in other states?

↗ What has been the profit picture of the organization for the last several years?

↗ Is the organization financially secure?

↗ Is the organization growing?

↗ What is the reputation of its chief executive officer?

© IMAGES COPYRIGHT YURI ARCURS 2009. USED UNDER LICENSE FROM SHUTTERSTOCK.COM

↗ Does the organization have a good reputation in the community?

↗ Is there a good relationship between the employer and the employees?

↗ Is the organization an equal opportunity employer?

↗ Are there opportunities for advancement?

---

functional order. Whichever order you use, follow these guidelines when preparing a resume:

■ Always be accurate and honest when listing information on your resume.

■ Keep the resume short—preferably one or two pages.

■ Target your resume to each job. Highlight those areas of your background or work experience that fit the position you want.

■ If you are a recent graduate and have held only part-time jobs, list them.

■ If you have not had any paid work experience, list volunteer jobs or leadership positions you have held.

■ Do not use personal pronouns (*I, me, you*). They are unnecessary and detract from the impact of the resume.

■ Describe your qualifications and skills in specific terms using action verbs; avoid vague language.

■ Check your spelling and grammar usage. Read and reread the resume several times, and ask someone else who is a good proofreader and grammarian to read it also.

■ Avoid using abbreviations, with the exception of your degree.

■ Take advantage of professional help in writing your resume. Check web sources, talk with your college placement representatives, and visit a bookstore or library for materials on resume preparation.

■ Print your resume on quality paper.

■ Use a professional, neutral e-mail address, such as rlsmith@yahoo.com. Never use an e-mail address such as fungirl@msn.com or partyhappy@msn.com or some equally unprofessional address.

Information on a resume may be presented in chronological order or functional order and in printed or electronic format. In determining the type of resume to prepare, you must consider your purpose and background and the requirements of the potential employer.

Chronological Resume   A **chronological resume** is a document that gives an applicant's work experience in order with the most recent experience listed first. This type of resume is the most common and most preferred format for a resume. It works well for showing progress and growth if the jobs listed reflect increasing responsibility. Figure 15-4 on page 286 illustrates the format of a typical printed resume in chronological order.

Writing @Work

Follow these tips for writing application letters:

- Personalize each letter by reading and writing to the job notice published by the organization. Do not assume one letter is appropriate for all organizations.

- Address the letter to a specific person. If you do not have a name, call the company or check with the placement office, agency, or person who told you about the job.

- Use three paragraphs—an opening paragraph in which you provide a brief statement of your interest, a middle paragraph in which you describe your abilities, and a closing paragraph in which you request an interview, providing your contact information. You should mention that your resume is enclosed in the second or third paragraph.

- Keep the letter short; put details in the resume.

- Use correct spelling, punctuation, capitalization, and grammar. Use the spell and grammar check on your computer.

- Key the letter in proper form using an acceptable letter style.

- Print your letter on high-quality bond paper. If you do not own a printer that produces quality work, have your cover letter and resume professionally printed.

- Send an original letter for each application. Do not send photocopies.

©ISTOCK

Functional Resume A **functional resume** is a document that gives the skills and qualifications of an applicant for a particular job rather than focusing on work experience. In this type of resume, the same information is included as in a chronological resume; however, the organization is different. Your education, experiences, and activities are clustered into categories that support your career goals.

The functional resume works well for individuals who have good educational backgrounds and skills but little or no work experience. It also works well if there are periods when an individual did not work; for example, if a woman took a break from her career to have a child. The functional resume de-emphasizes the gaps and emphasizes skill sets. Figure 15-5 on page 287 shows a printed functional resume.

Resume References A **resume reference** is a person who knows your academic ability and/or work skills and habits and is willing to recommend you to employers. A reference should be able to verify part of the information on your resume. Generally, you should not put your references on your resume. The resume is a place to highlight work experiences and skills. However, you should have a list of references prepared. The reference list should be taken with you to all job interviews; you may need to list references on an application, or the interviewer may ask you for them.

Get in touch with your references before a job search. Let them know you are looking for a job, and ask whether you can use them as a reference. Confirm the addresses and phone numbers of your references, as well as their current employment and job title/duties. A thoroughly completed reference section on an application can be a determining factor in the hiring of one applicant over another.

Electronic Resume An **electronic resume** is a document that gives qualifications and work history for an applicant in an electronic (rather than printed) format. An employer may request that you submit an electronic resume, or you may want to post an electronic resume on a job board. Although the information presented in an electronic resume should not differ significantly from that in a printed resume, the format of the information should be different. Electronic resumes are often scanned by a computer program for keywords that match words found in the related job listing. Because the resume

Figure 15-4 Chronological Resume

Elaina Diaz

2445 Edgecliff Road
Dallas, TX 75218-2445
E-mail: ediaz5@web.com
Phone: 214-555-0148

CAREER OBJECTIVE

A position as an administrative assistant with the opportunity to use technology and human relations skills

EDUCATION

Mountain Peak College, Dallas, Texas
Associate's Degree in Administrative Systems, May 20--
Courses studied: Business communications, organizational behavior, management, English, psychology, administrative procedures, and computer software

COMPUTER SKILLS

Keyboarding at 100 wpm; proficient in Word, Excel, Access, PowerPoint, Internet research, and web page design

EMPLOYMENT HISTORY

Intern, Admissions Department, Mountain Peak College, September 2005 to May 2010
- Prepared spreadsheets using Excel
- Keyed correspondence using Word
- Prepared first draft of admission letters for students
- Filed correspondence on hard drive and disks
- Handled student inquiries, answered the telephone, and assisted in designing class schedules

Records Management Assistant, LakeSide Manufacturing, Dallas, Texas, September 2001 to August 2005
- Maintained computer records for the entire company
- Assisted new clerical employees in setting up appropriate records storage methods

Receptionist, Martin Technology, Inc., Dallas, Texas, January 1998 to August 2001
- Greeted visitors and answered the telephone
- Keyed correspondence

ACTIVITIES/HONORS

Speech Club
Service Learning—tutored tenth-grade students
Delivered food for the Meals on Wheels program
Most Outstanding Student, Business Department

Figure 15-5 Functional Resume

Robert O'Malley

445 Maple Street
Dallas, TX 75218-9445
E-mail: romalley5@web.com
Phone: 214-555-0098

CAREER OBJECTIVE

A position as an administrative assistant with the opportunity to use my technology, communication, and human relations skills

PROFESSIONAL EXPERIENCE

While employed in the Business Division of Summerdale Community College, I performed the following duties:

- Communicated in writing and verbally with students, faculty, and the public
- Communicated by telephone with students, faculty, and the public
- Keyed syllabi, tests, and correspondence for faculty
- Employed human relations skills while working with 15 faculty members and 50 students
- Filed physical and electronic records
- Assisted students in solving problems with schedules
- Completed research on curriculums at other colleges
- Used Microsoft Office to prepare and search documents, spreadsheets, databases, and electronic presentations

EDUCATION

Summerdale Community College, Dallas, Texas
Associate's Degree in Administrative Systems, May 2009

EMPLOYMENT HISTORY

Intern, Business Division of Summerdale Community College, September 2008 to May 2009
Served in United States Army, June 2006 to July 2008
Clerk at Johnson's Hardware Store, Dallas, Texas, March 2005 to May 2006

ACTIVITIES/HONORS

Member of International Association of Administrative Professionals
Dean's list at Summerdale Community College

may be scanned, the format of the document should be simple, and it should contain keywords that relate to the job listing. Follow these guidelines when preparing an electronic resume:

- Use a single-column format that does not exceed 65 characters per line. Begin all lines at the left margin.

- Use a common font, such as Arial, Times New Roman, or Courier, and a font size of 11 or 12 points.

- Put your name, address, phone number, and e-mail address each on a separate line.

- Pay attention to the words in the job advertisement or job description and use these words in your resume. Also, use action words such as *wrote*, *organized*, *managed*, *collaborated*, and *researched*.

- Do not use italics, bold, underlines, lines, shadows, or other decorative formatting. Do not use graphics.

Figure 15-6 on page 289 shows a functional electronic resume. Notice that it does not contain bold, bullets, lines, or underlines and all text lines begin at the left margin.

Job Interview Skills

A **job interview** is a meeting between a job applicant and a potential employer to discuss a job and the applicant's qualifications. In the interview, the employer will judge your appearance, personality, human relations skills, self-confidence, and other traits. The interviewer will question you about your experience and abilities, as identified in your letter of application and resume. The interview is an opportunity for the prospective employer to get to know you and for you to get to know the interviewer and to learn more about the organization.

Employment Portfolio

You may wish to prepare an employment portfolio to take with you to interviews. A **portfolio** is a compilation of samples of your work and other career-related information. The information and work samples should be arranged attractively in a binder or should be in an electronic format, such as web pages. This format is sometimes called an e-portfolio. Some possible items to include are:

People @Work

RECRUITER

A recruiter works in the human resources department of a company. Recruiters search for job candidates to fill positions at the company. They may travel to college campuses and job fairs to talk with job seekers.

Recruiters may also screen, interview, and test applicants, deciding whether to recommend them for jobs. Recruiters must be knowledgeable about the company's personnel needs as well as company employment policies, wages, and benefits. They must also stay informed about laws and regulations related to hiring practices. If you apply for a job with a large organization, you may have contact with a recruiter.

- Your resume
- Awards or honors received
- Education, training, or certifications
- Letters you have written that demonstrate your writing style
- Research reports you have produced that demonstrate your ability to conduct research and present the research in an attractive format
- Spreadsheets, graphics, and electronic slides you have created to demonstrate your knowledge of software

Be certain that the work you choose is of the highest quality. Have someone who is knowledgeable in your field review your work carefully. Take seriously the individual's critique and make the necessary changes.

Pre-Interview Nervousness

Feeling nervous before an interview is natural. However, you want to control your nervousness. View each interview as a learning experience. After the interview, write down what went right and what went wrong. Concentrate on the positives; try not to make the same mistakes a second time. The more

Figure 15-6 Electronic Resume

ROBERT O'MALLEY

445 Maple Street
Dallas, TX 75218-9445
E-mail: romalley5@web.com
Phone: 214-555-0098

CAREER OBJECTIVE

A position as an administrative assistant with the opportunity to use my technology, communication, and human relations skills

PROFESSIONAL EXPERIENCE

2008 to present: Intern, Business Division of Summerdale Community College
Communicated in writing and verbally with students, faculty, and the public
Communicated by telephone with students, faculty, and the public
Keyed syllabi, tests, and correspondence for faculty
Employed human relations skills while working with 15 faculty members and 50 students
Filed physical and electronic records
Assisted students in solving problems with schedules
Completed research on curriculums at other colleges
Used Microsoft Office to prepare and search documents, spreadsheets, databases, and electronic presentations

June 2006 to July 2008: Served in United States Army

EDUCATION

Summerdale Community College, Dallas, Texas
Associate's Degree in Administrative Systems, May 2009

ACTIVITIES AND HONORS

Member of International Association of Administrative Professionals
Dean's list at Summerdale Community College

interview experiences you have, the more you will learn. Here are several suggestions that will help:

- Research the organization.

- Research national and local salaries for administrative professionals. Knowing about typical salaries will help you feel confident when responding to questions about salary.

- Practice interviewing by having a friend ask you questions.

- Use stress reduction techniques, such as exercising, getting the proper amount of sleep, and engaging in positive self-talk.

- Plan something to do the night before the interview so you do not spend your time worrying about the interview. Go to a movie or dinner with a friend.

- Be certain you know the exact time and location of the interview. When traveling to the interview location, allow time for unexpected delays.

Multiple and Team Interviews

You may have more than one interview for a particular position. For example, a human resources professional may interview you first. Next, you may interview with your prospective supervisor. Finally, you may have a group interview with your prospective team members.

A team interview may be with two or three or even five or six people. Although this type of interview sounds intimidating, it need not be.

Follow these tips for a successful team interview:

- When introductions are made, pay careful attention to the individuals' names.

- Focus on each individual as the person asks questions.

- Listen carefully to the questions asked and answer them succinctly.

- When you ask a question, ask it of the group. If one group member asks you a question you did not understand, address that person and ask for clarification of the question.

- Make eye contact with people when answering a question.

- If you find yourself getting nervous, glance occasionally at people who have given you positive feedback—ones who have a friendly face, open body language, and positive reactions to your responses. Say to yourself, This person likes me; I am doing well.

- Thank the group when the interview is completed. Use their names, if possible; it shows you were paying attention.

©ISTOCK

Dear Savvy Admin

Dear Savvy Admin:

I have my first job interview for an administrative assistant position next week. Do you have any advice for me?

Anxious Applicant

Dear Anxious Applicant:

My best advice is to spend a lot of time preparing what you're going to say and practicing how you'll say it. An HR executive remarked that the biggest problem among the many job applicants she interviews is lack of preparation. They don't know what they want to say to her about why they'd be a good candidate for the organization, or they haven't thought about how they're going to say it. They're also not ready to provide examples of what they've contributed to other organizations and of their leadership abilities.

Make a list of likely interview questions. Spend some time thinking about how to respond to each question in a way that shows strongly that you are a good match for the position. Use solid, specific examples of what you've contributed to past employers or what you've done in school or extracurricular activities. Then *practice*. Good luck!

Savvy Admin

Occasionally organizations will conduct an interview by telephone or via a videoconference. For example, assume you are applying for a job in Boston. Rather than go there, you are being interviewed in Columbus, Ohio, where you live. The organization arranges for you to interview by phone or perhaps go to a facility that has teleconferencing capabilities.

If you are going to take part in a virtual interview, you need to be well prepared. When a camera is involved, most people get nervous. However, your goal is to relax and treat the situation as if the person interviewing you were in the same room.

Helpful Interview Hints

Observe these suggestions to help you prepare for an interview and to make a good impression during the interview.

Before the Interview Get a good night's rest so that you will be alert during the interview. Determine what you should take with you. You should have several copies of your resume in a folder. Put a list of your references in the folder that shows the full name, address, e-mail address, and telephone number for each reference. Put your resume, references, wallet, cell phone, and so forth in your briefcase. Put a pad, pen, and pencil in your briefcase in case you need to take notes or fill out an application. Arrange your briefcase in an orderly manner so you will not have to shuffle papers during the interview.

© ISTOCKPHOTO/DEAN SANDERSON

A team interview may involve two or more interviewers and one job applicant.

Dress and Grooming

Dress conservatively, even if you are applying for a position in an organization that is in a creative line of work, such as art and design. For both men and women, a suit is appropriate; women may also wear a conservative dress. Wear a color that looks good on you. Keep your jewelry to a minimum. Do not wear dangling earrings or bracelets that jingle, excessive makeup, or cologne. Be sure to keep your cell phone turned off or left on mute.

Greetings

Greet the receptionist with a friendly smile, stating your name and the purpose of your visit. If you have to wait for the interviewer, do so patiently. Once you are in the interviewer's office, make appropriate eye contact with the interviewer. Shake his or her hand with a firm (but not tight) grip. Wait to sit down until invited to do so.

During the Interview

Show genuine interest in what the interviewer says; be alert to all questions. Try to understand your prospective employer's needs and describe how you can fill them. Follow these suggestions:

- Be prepared to tell the interviewer about yourself— a commonly asked question at the start of the interview. Keep the conversation on a professional level.

- Answer questions both thoroughly and concisely; do not talk too much.

- Be enthusiastic; demonstrate pride in your skills and abilities.

- Do not criticize former employers, instructors, schools, or colleagues.

- Do not tell jokes, argue with the interviewer, or brag about yourself.

At the Close of the Interview

Try to determine what the next step will be:

- Will there be another interview?

- When can you expect to hear the results of the interview?

Reiterate your interest in the job (that is, if you are still interested). Smile pleasantly and thank the interviewer. Smile and thank the receptionist as you leave.

Interview Follow-Up

After the interview, promptly write a follow-up letter. The letter should include the following: (1) a thank-you for the opportunity to interview, (2) a recap of your skills and abilities, (3) a statement of your continued interest in the job (if this is true), and (4) a reminder of the next steps you agreed on in the interview, such as when the decision is going to be made.

If no action is taken concerning your application within a reasonable time (one to two weeks), a second follow-up letter or a call may be advisable. The second letter should merely remind the employer of your continued interest in the job. Depending on the situation, you may want to make a third contact with the organization. Being persistent shows your interest in the job, and the organization views it as a plus. However, you do not want to annoy the employer. Use good judgment in determining how many follow-ups are appropriate in each job situation.

After the interview, you may decide you are not interested in the position. In that case, you should promptly send a courteous letter expressing your appreciation for the interview and explaining that you do not wish to remain a candidate for the position. Although you are not interested in the present position, you may be interested in a position with the company in the future.

Interview Evaluation

If you are interested in a job but do not get it, you may receive a generic reason from the organization. Most organizations do not give you exact reasons because of legal problems that may occur. You may also do very well in the interview and still not get the job. There simply may have been someone more qualified or with more experience than you have.

In any case, play back the experience in your mind. Note the questions you had trouble answering, the questionable reactions from the interviewer, and any errors that you believe you made. Think about how you can correct errors before the next interview. Review your thoughts with a trusted adviser. Ask the person how you might improve. A job rejection is no reason to become depressed. Do not lose confidence in your skills and abilities. Learn from each interview situation. Maintain a positive attitude.

Job Offer Evaluation   In addition to evaluating yourself in the interviewing process, you need to ask yourself if the organization lived up to your expectations. When evaluating whether you want to work for the organization, ask these questions:

- Do my skills and the position match?

- Is the work environment one in which I will be happy and will prosper?

- Will I have a chance to work with people I can respect and admire?

- Will the work be interesting?

- Will I be able to learn from the job duties and the people?

- Are the benefits and compensation packages acceptable?

Your goal is to find the right position for you. You will spend the major part of each week on a job, and you need to feel happy and productive in your job.

Job Advancement and Changes

Once you have successfully completed the interviewing process and have accepted a job offer, your task is to combine your skills and knowledge in performing the job well. Listen to what coworkers and supervisors tell you. Observe and learn what is expected and accepted in the workplace. Make certain you have a clear understanding of your job duties and how you will be evaluated. As you learned in Chapter 1, many companies provide job

Employment Applications

You may fill out an employment application form provided by the prospective organization before or after the interview. In some organizations, all applicants fill out the form. Other firms ask only those people who are seriously being considered for a position to fill out the application. Follow these suggestions when completing an employment application:

- Read the entire application before starting to complete it.

- Print unless your handwriting is extremely neat.

- Answer every question completely. If a question does not apply to you (such as military experience), put NA, meaning "not applicable." Leaving a space blank can give the impression that you overlooked the question.

- Check your spelling. Carry a pocket dictionary so you can look up words you do not know how to spell.

- Have all information with you that you need to fill out the form—dates you attended college, dates of employment, complete addresses of employers, and references. Carry your Social Security card with you.

- Be honest. State accurately the experience and skills you have. However, do try to state what may be negative information in a positive manner.

descriptions that detail the responsibilities of particular jobs. If you are not given one, ask for it. If a job description does not exist, ask your supervisor to go over your duties with you.

Perform Successfully

Listen to what your supervisor and coworkers tell you. Pay attention to what is happening in the

© ISTOCKPHOTO/IOFOTO

Thank the interviewer as you leave an interview.

organization and learn daily from the people with whom you work and your supervisors within the organization.

It is your responsibility to know what your job is and to do your job with commitment and professionalism. Recollect what you learned about professionalism in Chapter 2. A professional does not wait for her or his employer to describe every aspect of the job. As a professional, you are responsible for not just doing what is expected of you but exceeding expectations. Be certain that you consistently produce quality work in a timely manner. If you are not able to complete a task in the assigned timeframe, do not blame someone else. Accept the fact that you did not complete the task on time and look for ways that you can be more efficient. Ask yourself a series of questions:

- Did I understand the scope of the task?
- Did I seek information that I needed to complete the task?
- Did I work efficiently?
- Did I use my time wisely?
- If I encountered unexpected problems that I could not solve, did I ask for help?
- Did I let my employer know that I would not be able to complete the task on time?
- Did I volunteer to work after hours to get the job done?

Grow from the Performance Appraisal

How often performance appraisals are done varies from company to company and even from position to position. However, if you are a new employee, a performance appraisal is usually done at your six-month anniversary. Some organizations provide employees with evaluation procedures during a new employee orientation process. If you do not receive information concerning evaluation procedures, ask your supervisor. If a form is used, ask for a copy.

Communicating @Work

Read the evaluation tips below to help you understand how to conduct yourself during an evaluation and ways that you can grow and learn from the experience.

- ↗ Listen to what the evaluator is saying and maintain eye contact with the evaluator.
- ↗ Discuss the issues openly and honestly.
- ↗ Maintain a calm and professional demeanor.
- ↗ Provide the evaluator with important information relating to your performance—information the evaluator may not have.
- ↗ Accept negative comments as a criticism of your performance, not of you as an individual.
- ↗ Resolve to correct your mistakes. Tell the evaluator you will do so.
- ↗ Discuss with your evaluator how you can improve your performance.
- ↗ If the evaluator is not clear about the direction you should take in the future, ask for clarification. Writing objectives that fit the unit's strategic plan can help you know what you should accomplish.
- ↗ Accept praise with a smile and a thank-you.

A fairly common procedure during the performance evaluation is to ask you to evaluate yourself, paying attention to the job description that you were provided when you first took the job and any planning documents of the company that detail goals that need to be accomplished. For example, if your unit has a planning document, you and your supervisor may have used it as a basis to determine your job responsibilities and establish your goals. Then, during the evaluation period, use the planning document to determine if you have accomplished your goals.

Leaving a Job

You may decide to leave a job voluntarily, or you may be given no choice. Whatever your reasons for leaving (whether you are unhappy with a position and decide to leave on your own, you are looking for greater opportunities than you are being provided, or you are forced to leave), you must be professional in handling the exit.

The Exit Interview   Most companies conduct exit interviews with departing employees. An **exit interview** is a meeting between an employee who is leaving the company and a company representative. The purpose of the meeting is to learn the impressions the leaving employee has of the company and possibly the reason why the employee is leaving. An impartial party (such as a staff member in the human resources department) generally conducts the interview. The employee's immediate supervisor is not involved.

An exit interview is not a time to get even, to make derogatory remarks about a supervisor, or to unduly criticize the company. Keep in mind the old adage about not burning your bridges. If you are leaving on your own, you may wish to return some day. Regardless of your reason for leaving, you will probably need a reference from the company. Be honest and professional in the exit interview. For example, if you are leaving for a job that has greater opportunities for growth, say, "I've decided to accept a position with greater responsibilities." You do not need to give detailed reasons for your move.

A Layoff or Termination   In your career, you may have to face the situation of being laid off

Show a positive attitude in an exit interview.

or fired. Assume first you are being laid off. The situation may be a downsizing of the company where other jobs are being eliminated in addition to your own. Keep in mind that you did not cause the situation. Even though the situation is difficult, the skills, abilities, and experience you gained from your job will help you find another one. Remain positive and begin to think about what you want to do next.

What if you have been fired? Your feelings of fear, rejection, and insecurity are normal. However, it is not a time to blame yourself or feel sorry for yourself. It is a time to take a hard look at your skills. Listen to what your employer tells you about your performance. What can you learn for the future? What steps do you need to take to ensure that you do not find yourself in the same situation again? In what areas do you need to improve? Talk with family, friends, and your closest advisers. Realize that the job may not have been the best one for you. Commit to finding a job that will better match your skills and abilities.

Key Terms

chronological resume

electronic resume

exit interview

functional resume

job board

job interview

letter of application

networking

portfolio

resume

resume reference

Summary

- Information about job openings is available through networking, college placement offices, newspaper advertisements, the Internet, the United States federal government, the United States Postal Service, state governments, employment agencies, and direct contact with companies and other organizations.

- A resume is a concise document that lists your background, education, skills, and experience related to work. It may be arranged in chronological or functional order.

- Before applying for a job with an organization, you should spend time learning about the organization to help you create an effective letter of application and resume.

- A letter of application is sent to a potential employer to state your interest in a job and to transmit your resume. This letter is key, along with your resume, to obtaining an interview.

- A resume reference is a person who knows your academic ability and/or work skills and habits and is willing to recommend you to employers.

- A job interview is a meeting between a job applicant and a potential employer to discuss a job and the applicant's qualifications. A job applicant may have more than one interview for a position.

- A portfolio is a compilation of samples of your work and other career-related information. When the information is in an electronic format, such as web pages, it is sometimes called an e-portfolio.

- After an interview, the job applicant should promptly write a follow-up letter thanking the interviewer and restating interest in the job.

- To advance on the job, listen to supervisors and coworkers to help you perform successfully. Learn from performance appraisals and informal feedback on your work.

- Whatever your reasons for leaving a job, you should be professional in handling the exit.

Bookmark It. *For convenient access to activities, links, and valuable career resources for administrative professionals, visit the companion website for this text:*

www.cengage.com/officetech/fultoncalkins

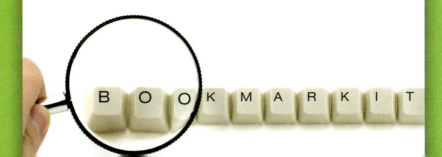

Planning Notes

Learning Objectives

1. Identify sources of job information.

2. Research organizations and prepare a letter of application and a resume.

3. Develop job interview skills.

4. Develop skills for job advancement and job changes.

 Critical Thinking Activity 4

 Activities 1, 2, 9, 10; Above & Beyond

 Activities 3, 5, 6, 7, 8

Discussion Questions

1. What are some common sources of information about job openings?

2. What is the purpose of a resume?

3. What is a job board?

4. What are some questions to which you should seek answers when researching an organization in preparation for applying for job?

5. What are four goals of a letter of application?

6. What is the difference between a chronological resume and a functional resume?

7. What is the purpose of an interview follow-up letter?

Critical Thinking

Interview skills   Robin McKnight graduated with a two-year degree a year ago. Robin was an A student; however, she was very shy and introverted. She was considered a loner by most of her classmates. She stayed away from all extracurricular activities. Because she was not certain where she wanted to work, she decided to try a number of different types of jobs through a temporary agency. During this past year, she worked for four companies. Her supervisors always praised her work; she was offered full-time employment at two of the organizations. Robin has gained confidence in her social skills. In fact, she was given a party by her colleagues and supervisor when she left three of the organizations. She has decided that she wants to work as an administrative assistant in a health-related facility—either a hospital or a research facility. She applied for two jobs recently, both in her preferred field; however, she was not offered either job. Robin had these experiences during the interviews:

- When asked about her present job, Robin stated that she did not work at the present time. She did not explain her work experiences during the past year.

- When asked about her college experiences, Robin said that she made good grades but did not do anything outside of her classes.

- When asked about her strengths, Robin said that she was a capable employee, but she had much to learn.

- When she was asked by the interviewers if she had any questions, she replied, "No."

- Robin was very nervous during each interview.

Robin knows she is capable; she has proven that in her performance at four different companies during the last year. However, she is still not very confident. What advice would you give Robin?

Build Workplace Skills

1. **Job information sources**   Use a local telephone directory and the Internet to search for sources of job information in your area. Prepare a list to include private and public employment agencies, school or college job placement offices, local or regional newspapers that contain job ads, job boards or other Internet sites with job listings, and persons with whom you can network regarding a job search. (Learning Objective 1)

2. **Research an organization** Identify a company or other organization for which you would like to work. Research the organization to find answers to questions such as those listed below. Write a summary of the information you find. (Learning Objective 2)

   - What are the organization's services or products?
   - Is the organization multinational? Does it have branches in other states?
   - What has been the profit picture of the organization for the last several years?
   - Is the organization financially secure?
   - Is the organization growing?
   - What is the reputation of its chief executive officer?
   - Does the organization have a good reputation in the community?
   - Is there a good relationship between the employer and the employees?
   - Is the organization an equal opportunity employer?
   - Are there opportunities for advancement?
   - To what name and address should a letter of application be sent?

3. **Letter of application** Assume the organization you researched earlier has an opening for an administrative assistant. Write a letter of application for the position, assuming the position was posted on the organization's website. Indicate your resume is enclosed. (Learning Objective 2)

Communicate Clearly

4. **Revise a letter** Open the *Word* file CH15 Letter from the data files. This document contains the body of a letter of application. Revise the text and add information as needed to make this an effective letter of application for an administrative assistant position posted on a company website (Learning Objective 2).

5. **Resume** Prepare a print resume to send with the letter of application for an administrative assistant position that you wrote earlier. Use the format (chronological or functional) that will best present your qualifications and experience. (Learning Objective 2)

6. **Interview questions** A list of typical job interview questions appears below. Write an answer to each question. Assume that you are interviewing for an administrative assistant position at the organization you researched earlier. (Learning Objective 3)

   - What do you know about our organization?
   - Why are you interested in our organization?
   - Why do you want this position?
   - What do you consider the ideal job for you?
   - Why did you choose your major area of study?
   - What was your academic average in school?
   - What honors did you earn?
   - In what extracurricular activities were you involved?
   - Which courses did you like best? Least? Why?
   - How have the classes you completed as part of your major helped you prepare for your career?
   - If you disagreed with something your supervisor asked you to do, what would you do?

Planning Notes

Planning Notes

- What type of work atmosphere do you prefer?
- Is a sense of humor important at work? Why or why not?
- Tell me about a conflict you have had with someone in the work environment. How did you handle the conflict?
- How do you handle pressure?
- How would your previous employers or teachers and coworkers describe you?
- Have you ever been fired or asked to resign from a position?
- Why did you leave your previous job?
- Have you had any problems with previous supervisors?
- What are your greatest strengths?
- What do you not do well?
- Why should I hire you?

Develop Relationships

7. **Exit interview**   Ramona is leaving her job as an administrative assistant for a higher-paying position at another company. In her exit interview she was asked, "What did you like least about working here?" Ramona said, "My supervisor often gave vague instructions about the tasks he assigned to me. When I would ask for more details, he would usually say, 'I don't know. You figure it out!'"

   Do you think it was wise for Ramona to make this statement? Why or why not? How could you respond honestly to such a question and keep the goodwill of the company? (Learning Objective 4)

8. **Overstating qualifications**   Cory recently interviewed for a position as an administrative assistant. The interviewer asked Cory if he was proficient in using *Microsoft Access*. Cory indicated that he was, although he had only had a brief training course in using *Access*. What might be the consequences of this statement if Cory gets the job? Is overstating your qualifications a good way to start a relationship with an employer? (Learning Objective 3)

Use Technology

9. **Search agent**   Visit the USAJOBS website. Read about ways to use a search agent. Set up a search agent to find job listings that interest you. Submit to your instructor a printout of one of the job listings the search agent gives you. (Learning Objective 1)

10. **Electronic resume**   Revise your resume that you created earlier for submitting in electronic format. (Learning Objective 2)

Above & Beyond

Electronic portfolio   Create an electronic career portfolio. Include samples of your work, your resume, any school/work awards or honors you have received, and any other career-related information that you think would be of interest to an employer. Save the files as web pages. Create a main web page that introduces you and has links to the other pages.

Medical Assistant Supervisor

Community health clinic seeks experienced medical assistant with strong administrative skills and a background in primary care. Duties include:

- Train and supervise medical assistants
- Perform patient intake procedures
- Assist in supervising clinic flow and activity
- Ensure supply stocks and equipment maintenance
- Represent clinic at local meetings as requested
- Promote opportunities for feedback from medical staff to improve service

Candidate must have discretion, good judgment, organizational or management ability, initiative, and excellent communication skills.

Do I qualify?

©MARK WRAGG, ISTOCK

CHAPTER **16**

Leading with Confidence

Leading and Managing

Leading with confidence is an important ability to develop as you grow in your career as an administrative professional. It will serve you well throughout life, regardless of what profession you choose. As you assume positions of greater responsibility in the workplace, you may have one or more people reporting to you. Even if you do not become a manager or supervisor, you may have the opportunity to assume other leadership roles, such as leading a team or part of a team. This chapter examines practical concepts of leadership and management.

Defining Leadership and Management

The verb *to lead* has been defined as "to guide on a way especially by going in advance"; "to direct on a course or in a direction"; or "to direct

Learning Objectives

1. Explain the difference between leadership and management.

2. Describe major leadership and management theories.

3. Describe common leadership styles.

4. Describe and begin developing qualities of effective leaders.

5. Describe and begin developing skills and strategies for successfully leading people.

the operations, activity, or performance of."[1] The capacity to lead well is more than filling a position or an office. It is a philosophy, an attitude, and a practice in the workplace. **Leadership** within an organization can be defined as the act of inspiring and motivating people to achieve organizational goals.

Management in a business setting is the act of organizing and directing people to accomplish organizational goals. Chapter 1 provided an overview of the responsibilities of management. You learned that management is considered a subset of leadership, and the responsibilities associated with these two roles overlap. Some key functions of management are planning, organizing, managing information, recruiting and hiring, and evaluating. If an organization is to be successful, management functions must be understood and carried out effectively.

Leadership and management are complementary but are different in concept, purpose, and process. A manager organizes and coordinates, while a leader motivates and inspires.[2] An effective leader stimulates employees to do more than they thought they could. A manager provides purpose as he or she directs employees to a goal. Leaders keep the long run in mind, while managers practically consider the short term. While this chapter focuses on leadership, remember that the most effective managers are also effective leaders, and conversely, effective leaders are also effective managers.

Leadership and Management Theories

To become an effective leader, you will find it useful to read the work of respected writers in the fields of leadership and management. Some key ideas of several writers on these topics are described below.

Robert Greenleaf on Leadership
Robert Greenleaf was a management consultant and director of management research for the American Telephone and Telegraph Company (AT&T). In a

1 "lead," Merriam-Webster Online, http://www.merriam-webster.com/dictionary/lead (accessed April 13, 2010).

2 Alan Murray, "What Is the Difference Between Management and Leadership?" *The Wall Street Journal*, http://guides.wsj.com/management (accessed April 22, 2010).

People @ Work

PROJECT SPECIALIST

A project specialist works for a project manager to assist with multiple projects. This person performs a variety of tasks depending on the organization's function and the projects that are currently in progress. Duties include managing financial accounts, supervising bookkeepers and temporary workers, organizing reports, overseeing the payment of contract work, knowing and understanding regulations associated with the industry (such as tariffs for transportation), writing and submitting reports to government agencies, creating budgets, and providing general assistance with project-related tasks.

If no proprietary software is available for management of project financial accounts, the project specialist uses spreadsheet and database software such as *Microsoft Excel* and *Microsoft Access* to track expenditures and send reports. He or she also trains bookkeepers and temporary workers in the use of the software. As an administrative professional, you may work with a project specialist to complete reports and do data entry related to ongoing projects.

©ISTOCKPHOTO.COM/ALi RAO

1970 essay, he introduced the concept of **servant leadership**, a topic on which he wrote and lectured for many years. According to Greenleaf, a servant-leader is a person who becomes a leader out of the desire to serve others. Businesses should devote themselves as much to the development of their employees as to providing products and services for their customers. Many companies have adapted the idea of servant leadership with the idea that helping employees to grow and succeed makes them better employees and improves their value to the company.[3]

Technology @Work

As a leader, you may need to gather and compute information for reports and meetings. Function formulas in *Excel* are an efficient way to do this.

Scenario 1: You have a financial account with multiple subcodes to track expenditures in different areas (such as travel, salaries, and equipment). You create a spreadsheet and use the IF function so that *Excel* tracks finances in each subcode.

Scenario 2: Your supervisor owns a small food distribution service that distributes food to multiple restaurants in the metro area. She wants you to tell her which type of food distributed brings in the most money. You have a spreadsheet that contains all the distributions. You use the SUMIF formula to have *Excel* consider all the food items distributed and sum the items that are coded "Southwest," "Asian," and "Italian." With three new numbers, your supervisor has information that may help her expand or change her business.

Peter Senge on Leadership   Peter Senge is a senior lecturer at the Massachusetts Institute of Technology and the founding chair of the Society for Organizational Learning. In his writing, he encourages leaders to build **learning organizations**—organizations in which a shared vision of the future allows the organization to move forward in the accomplishment of significant goals and objectives. Senge identifies three important roles for leaders:

- *Designer:* As designers, leaders create the guiding ideas for an organization, such as its purpose and mission, and they design the practical methods, such as policies and processes, for carrying them out.

- *Teacher:* As teachers, leaders are coaches and facilitators. They arrange means for people, including themselves, to learn from one another.

- *Steward:* A steward is a caretaker. As stewards, leaders care for the people they lead and the purpose or mission for which they're responsible.[4]

Peter Drucker on Management   Peter Drucker was a political economist, consultant, author, and teacher, considered by many to be the father of modern management. He developed the idea of decentralization in organizations, the delegation of authority and functions that many companies practice today. He also proposed the concept of **management by objectives**, in which managers and employees set goals together and make a plan for achieving them. Drucker believed that employees did not need to be managed too closely. Managers should tell them what they wanted done, how the results would be measured, and what the

3 Robert K. Greenleaf, *Servant Leadership: A Journey into the Nature and Legitimate Power of Greatness* (Mahway, N.J.: Paulist Press, 2002), 27, 154–155.

4 Peter Senge, *The Fifth Discipline: The Art & Practice of the Learning Organization* (New York: Doubleday, 2006), 321–338.

reward would be and then should step back and trust them to do the work.[5] He considered that employees were a company's most valuable assets.

Stephen Covey on Leadership Stephen Covey is the vice chairman of FranklinCovey, a company that provides consulting and training services in leadership and other subjects to businesses. His books include the bestselling *The 7 Habits of Highly Effective People*. Covey defines leadership as "communicating to people their worth and potential so clearly that they come to see it in themselves." He outlined the following four roles of leadership:

■ *Modeling*: An effective leader sets a good example. He or she inspires trust through character and competence.

■ *Pathfinding*: Involving others in setting goals helps to earn their commitment and to ensure that leaders and followers agree on what is important.

■ *Aligning*: An effective leader makes sure that an organization's structures, systems, and processes are consistent with its values and that they facilitate work rather than setting up roadblocks.

■ *Empowering*: Leaders empower employees by setting commonly understood goals and agreed-on guidelines and then letting employees decide how to accomplish the goals, while being available to provide support as needed.[6]

Jim Collins on Leadership Jim Collins is the founder of a management laboratory, a teacher of executives and CEOs, a university professor, an author, and a researcher on leadership. In his book *Good to Great*, he lists five levels of leaders and asserts that the great leader is the Level 5 leader. Figure 16-1 shows Collins's five levels of leadership.

5 Charles Handy, "The Handy Guide to the Gurus of Management," British Broadcasting Corporation, http://downloads.bbc.co.uk/worldservice/learningenglish/handy/drucker.pdf (accessed April 14, 2010).

6 Stephen Covey, *The Eighth Habit: From Effectiveness to Greatness* (New York: Simon & Schuster, 2004), 98, 114, 233–234, 256–257.

Figure 16-1 The Five Levels of Leadership

Level 5 Executive
Builds enduring greatness through a paradoxical blend of personal humility and professional will.

Level 4 Effective Leader
Catalyzes commitment to and vigorous pursuit of a clear and compelling vision, stimulating higher performance standards.

Level 3 Competent Manager
Organizes people and resources toward the effective and efficient pursuit of pre-determined objectives.

Level 2 Contributing Team Member
Contributes individual capabilities to the achievement of group objectives and works effectively with others in a group setting.

Level 1 Highly Capable Individual
Makes productive contributions through talent, knowledge, skills, and good work habits.

Source: Jim Collins, "Good to Great". Copyright © 2001 by Jim Collins. Reprinted with permission from Jim Collins.

Leadership Traits

You probably have encountered people whom you consider to be good leaders. What makes you put someone into that category? Is it a person's effectiveness at getting things done? Is it the respect he or she shows others, the ability to guide people, or the level of trust and rapport that person establishes with others? The following are several important traits of an effective leader.

Integrity

Integrity is the firm, consistent application of ethical standards at a personal level. It is considered the most important factor in leadership and is the cornerstone of good leadership. A cornerstone is the first stone laid in a foundation and is the reference point for all other measurements and dimensions used in the construction of a building. Leaders with integrity earn people's trust because they can always be relied on to "do the right thing." Leaders with integrity set the standards in their organizations.

General Ronald Fogleman, a former U.S. Air Force chief of staff and member of the Joint Chiefs of Staff, believes that leaders with integrity have four characteristics: they are sincere, they are consistent, they have substance, and they are good finishers.[7]

- *Sincerity:* Their actions match their words. People are loyal to leaders with sincerity.

- *Consistency:* Leaders with consistency always act with integrity. For example, they never discriminate based on friendship or positions. They always apply the rules fairly.

- *Substance:* Integrity is more than appearance. Leaders with integrity have the internal strength to persevere even through difficult times.

- *Good finishers:* Good leaders persevere until a task is completed, and they always perform at their maximum in accomplishing a task.

Leadership traits can be developed and improved with experience.

Emotional Maturity

Emotional maturity is an important part of leading others. Effective leaders are not driven by emotion. They understand the kinds of occurrences that tend to make them angry or irritated or that trigger other negative feelings. Good leaders have developed ways of managing their negative emotions so that they don't affect their work and don't show.

In his book *The 7 Habits of Highly Effective People*, Stephen Covey advises adopting a set of carefully selected principles and values and then working to subordinate your feelings to those values. Instead of simply reacting, you choose the way you are going to respond.

In one scenario, Covey asks readers to imagine arriving at work one day to find that nothing has been accomplished. Commitments have not been fulfilled, and no one has done his or her job. You are tired and "beat up." You could become angry. You could recall similar situations in the past and begin making judgments of people, which would probably make the situation worse. Instead, you choose to respond in a "mature, wise, self-controlled manner." You are cheerful and pleasant; you pitch in and start to help. Your reaction has the positive effect of stimulating the conscience of your employees.[8]

7 Ronald R. Fogleman, "The Leadership-Integrity Link," *Concepts for Air Force Leadership* (Maxwell AFB, Ala.: Air University Press, 1983), http://www.au.af.mil/au/awc/awcgate/au-24/fogleman.pdf (accessed April 13, 2010).

8 Stephen R. Covey, *Principle-Centered Leadership* (New York: Simon & Schuster, 1991), 43.

Commitment to Learning and Development

Effective leaders realize that there will never be a time when they "know it all." They are eager to learn, and they learn continually: from what they observe, from what they read, and from their subordinates, competitors, and peers. Former Kimberly-Clark CEO Darwin Smith, who took a wavering company and built it into a highly successful consumer paper-products business, said, "I never stopped trying to become qualified for the job."[9] Smith was committed to continual learning.

Besides continuing to learn, good leaders are also constantly engaged in **self-development**, which is the effort to improve yourself professionally. In his book *A Class with Drucker: The Lost Lessons of*

the *World's Greatest Management Teacher*, William Cohen writes that Peter Drucker had four vehicles for self-development:

- *Reading*: Drucker read constantly and regarded reading as the source of his wide-ranging knowledge.

- *Writing*: He wrote throughout his life, beginning early in his career.

- *Listening*: As a young adult, Drucker took part in intellectual conversations with visitors at his parents' home. He valued these conversations and later conversations he had with others.

- *Teaching*: Drucker said that "the best way to learn is to teach" and that "I teach to find out what I think." Teaching, Cohen points out, "requires extensive preparation and organization of ideas."[10]

9 Jim Collins, *Good to Great: Why Some Companies Make the Leap . . . and Others Don't* (New York: HarperCollins, 2001), 20.

10 William A. Cohen, *A Class with Drucker: The Lost Lessons of the World's Greatest Management Teacher* (New York: AMACOM, 2008), 237–238.

workplace wisdom

You may experience a variety of emotions at work. For example, you may sometimes be frustrated, angry, jealous, impatient, or disappointed. It is important to manage your emotions so that you remain positive and professional regardless of the situation. Here are a few tips for handling your emotions on the job:

Realize they are your emotions. You can't eliminate them, but you can work through them so that you establish and reinforce positive habits for the future.

Be curious about your motives and the thoughts surrounding them. Curiosity will help you to see situations more clearly and to control your responses to negative emotions.

Keep your perspective, and try to understand situations from all sides. Look actively for the positive.

Be grateful. Remind yourself of the good things in your life. Consider making a "thankfulness" list.

Make positive self-talk (see Chapter 2) a habit.

Rest, eat well, and take care of yourself physically and emotionally so that you are prepared for whatever comes your way.

Cohen identifies several principles for self-development that Drucker followed, principles Cohen believes that Drucker would recommend for managers:

- Be prepared.
- Be true to your commitments.
- When change occurs, take immediate action.
- Be flexible.
- Establish fixed goals, but vary strategy as necessary.
- Don't be afraid to take risks.[11]

On the job and especially in school, people are frequently told what they are supposed to learn and do. In contrast, continual learning and self-development are up to the individual. Good leaders know that they need to take the initiative to keep learning and developing themselves professionally.

Other Qualities

Effective leaders have several other important qualities. They include self-knowledge, confidence, vision, and the ability to make decisions.

Self-Knowledge   Good leaders know themselves. They capitalize on their strengths, concentrate on developing those strengths, and try to make their weaknesses immaterial.

Confidence   An effective leader sees herself or himself as competent and able to do the job. A good leader has had success, even small successes. Cohen, who has written more than fifty books and has held executive positions at several companies, wrote that "a little success counts just as much as a big success as far as building self-confidence and knowing that you will succeed in the future."[12]

Vision   Effective leaders have vision. **Vision** is a picture of an organization's future. Without vision, there is no forethought or foresight about what the focus of the organization should be.

Having vision does not necessarily mean the leader knows the exact path that the organization will need to take to fulfill the vision, but it does mean the leader knows where the organization is headed.

11 Cohen, *A Class with Drucker*, 239.

12 Cohen, *A Class with Drucker*, 37.

©ISTOCK

Writing @ Work

As you develop leadership skills, your vocabulary also will need to develop. This is part of growing professionally and of being perceived as a professional. Skills in expression are necessary for making your point and for people to see you as competent.

Develop a habit of being conscious of words. Are there words people use (in writing or conversation) that you have never heard or do not initially understand? Take the time to jot them down, discover the meaning, and then use them in your own writing so that you will remember them. Below are a few words to help get you started. Try using each word in a sentence.

adaptive (adj.)	having the capacity to adjust
attainable (adj.)	within one's capacity to achieve, gain, or obtain
contingent (adj.)	likely but not certain to happen; not logically necessary
inept (adj.)	lacking aptitude, fitness, sense, or reason; not suitable; generally incompetent
innovative (adj.)	new
static (adj.)	showing little change

Source: Definitions adapted from Merriam-Webster Online, http://www.merriam-webster.com (accessed April 18, 2010).

Visionary leaders must also have the courage to act on their vision. Darwin Smith, the CEO of Kimberly-Clark, made a monumental decision to sell the paper mills that had been the backbone of the company for years. He had a vision of what the company could become if it moved into different, more lucrative markets and then made the plucky move to sell the mills.

Decision Making   A good leader makes decisions and takes responsibility for those decisions. In making decisions, he or she follows a thoughtful decision-making process like the one described in Chapter 2.

Leadership Styles

Leaders have different **leadership styles**, or patterns of behavior. You are probably familiar with some of these styles from supervisors you have had at work, coaches on sports teams, and leaders you have had in other capacities in your life.

The leadership style affects the performance of the people who are being led or supervised. Some people work better or more comfortably with one leadership style than with another.

Though they often prefer a particular style, effective leaders use a variety of styles for different situations. For example, there are times when a leader must make a decision with little or no input from those on his or her team, and there are times when a leader can allow the team to make a decision. The changing of leadership styles for different situations is called **situational leadership**.

Many leadership styles have been identified. In a study of schoolchildren, psychologist Kurt Lewin and two associates identified three common leadership styles: the autocratic style, the democratic style, and the laissez-faire style, described on the next page. Figure 16-2 describes three additional leadership styles that are found in the workplace. These styles were identified by Daniel Goleman, a psychologist and writer.

Figure 16-2 Leadership Styles

Style	Description	Objective	Decision Making
affiliative	Emphasizes the importance of teamwork. Used to motivate employees in stressful times or to help reconcile team divisions. Praise used often, so leaders must guard against perception that mediocre performance is acceptable. Leaders are empathetic and good at building relationships and managing conflict.	Create harmony	Very collaborative and useful for team building
coaching	Used to help employees improve performance and hone skills for the future. Focuses on delegating and getting to know team members. Usually leads to loyalty but can be misconstrued as micromanaging. Leaders are empathetic and capable of building on employees' potential.	Build strengths for the future	Employees are very involved.
pacesetting	Leaders set exciting, challenging goals for employees and ferret out those working below expectations. Can contribute to a negative work climate. Best used with a highly motivated team. Often done poorly. Leaders are very driven and often very critical. Have high standards and much initiative.	Perform tasks to a high standard	Employees are expected to know what to do. Little guidance is given.

Source: Daniel Goleman, "Emotional Intelligence: Issues in Paradigm Building," in *The Emotionally Intelligent Workplace,* ed. Cary Cherniss and Daniel Goleman (San Francisco: Jossey-Bass, 2001), 42.

Autocratic Leadership

An autocrat is a person who has complete control over others. The **autocratic leadership style** is one of control. The leader directs and closely supervises the work that is done. He or she has complete authority; employees have no input into the decisions that are made. The autocratic style is appropriate for some situations when close control is very important. It used to be a common style in business, but for many years, it has been used less often. Organizations and leaders tend to favor other styles that do not involve such close control and give employees more latitude to make decisions.

Democratic Leadership

As the name implies, the **democratic leadership style** is one in which employees share in authority, decisions, and plans. It is a popular style in the workplace, one that both managers and employees often favor. In general, when the leadership style is more flexible, the morale of the organization is better and attitudes are more positive. Employees enjoy being able to work with less supervision, and having a voice in plans and decisions makes them feel more valued. This leadership style is commonly used in teams.

Laissez-Faire Leadership

Laissez-faire is French for "let people do as they choose."[13] When a leader uses the **laissez-faire leadership style**, employees generally lead themselves. The leader is not involved in directing or controlling tasks. He or she may only monitor employees' progress in completing them and respond to requests for assistance. This leadership style is appropriate when employees are skilled and responsible and the tasks they are to do are clearly defined.[14]

---

13 "laissez faire," Merriam-Webster Online, http://www.merriam-webster.com/dictionary/laissez faire (accessed April 13, 2010).

14 Marie Dalton, Dawn Hoyle, and Marie Watts, *Human Relations* (Cincinnati: Cengage, 2011), 243.

Leading Organizations

When you are new to leading an organization (or even a team), it is helpful to go back to fundamentals and ask these five essential questions posed by Peter Drucker:

1. "What is our mission?" What is it that we are trying to achieve?

2. "Who is our customer?" Whom are we serving?

3. "What does the customer value?" What is it that the customer wants?

4. "What are our results?" And how do we define those results? In other words, how do we measure achievement of our organizational mission?

5. "What is our plan?"

Leaders are often responsible for developing an organization's vision. The vision is similar to the **mission**, which is the organization's reason for being or its purpose. The mission is why your organization does what it does. It is the end product of what you want the organization to be remembered for. Without a strong focus on organizational goals, organizations can flounder in indecision and misdirection.

Organizations or teams need to have clearly defined goals and objectives. Drucker defines *goals* as "a set of three to five aims that set the organization's fundamental, long-range direction." *Objectives* are similar but set "specific and measurable levels of achievement."

Source: Peter Drucker, *The Five Most Important Questions You Will Ever Ask About Your Organization* (San Francisco: Jossey-Bass, 2008), 2, 100.

Leading People

Leadership has been discussed throughout this textbook. The responsibilities of team leaders described in Chapter 5, such as defining goals, setting objectives, establishing procedures, and performing administrative tasks, are often also the responsibilities of other types of leaders. Chapter 10 described the leader's role in planning, organizing, and conducting meetings; management responsibilities were outlined in Chapter 1.

Leading people is an acquired ability that you can develop by paying attention to leaders in both your professional and your personal life, as well as being intentional in your pursuit of good leadership qualities and skills. As you read about the skills and strategies below, think about their practical application for you in your current roles—student, employee, family member, etc.

Leading by Example

An effective leader is someone who sets an example. Do you want your employees to have a good work ethic, not complain, and work toward the common goal of the team? Do you have a good work ethic? Do you not complain? Do you work toward the common goal of the team? The power of modeling the conduct you expect from others is often underestimated. Effective leaders approach

Effective leaders invest in relationships with their employees.

IMAGE COPYRIGHT YURI ARCURS 2010. USED UNDER LICENSE FROM SHUTTERSTOCK.COM

the task of directing other people by holding themselves accountable and avoiding double standards.

Young adults in leadership positions sometimes experience challenges due to their age and lack of experience, particularly when the group they are leading includes people who are older than they are. If you find yourself in such a situation, leading by example can be especially helpful. For what you lack in age, make up for in character. Convey the qualities of patience, compassion, integrity, modesty, and confidence. Be honest, do not talk about others in a derogatory way, and do not use sarcasm. Be professional.

Investing in Relationships

Good leaders get to know the people with whom they work. They invest time in talking with their employees and are genuinely interested in them. Developing relationships with employees is a personal touch that isn't manipulative but rather is unselfish and based in an outgoing, friendly attitude.

Think about some of your favorite teachers in school. These teachers were most likely the ones who asked about your basketball game, wanted to know if you enjoyed the past weekend, asked how you were feeling after a bout with the flu, or just made sure you understood the class material and were comfortable asking questions. Their leadership showed genuine care and affected your attitude or performance. It made them approachable and made you more likely to participate.

Many leaders demonstrate their investment in people and relationships by involving employees in the decision-making process as much as possible. Leaders who ask for input or pose a problem and ask for solutions and options are showing that they value the opinions and abilities of their employees. When employees feel they are trusted and valued, they are empowered and are encouraged to do an excellent job. They are also more likely to step up in confidence and themselves be leaders in other situations.

It is easier for a leader to rely on an employee's abilities and skills if the leader knows the employee well and knows what that person is capable of doing. Understanding an employee's capabilities means more than knowing whether that person has the technical skills necessary to complete a task. It can include, for example, knowing the employee's capacity for finishing a job, admitting when she or he needs help, working well with customers, or remaining calm when problems occur. A leader who thoroughly understands what employees do well will be able to make good decisions when delegating key responsibilities. This makes the leader more efficient, effective, and trusted by higher-level management.

Motivating Others

People are motivated to do work, and to do it well, by many different things. Motivation may be *extrinsic* (from outside a person) or *intrinsic* (from within). For employees, an extrinsic motivation might be a salary increase or the opportunity for advancement. Examples of intrinsic motivators include the desire for personal recognition and the feeling of satisfaction from a job well done.

Good leaders find out what motivates each employee and use that knowledge, as far as possible, to encourage employees to have a positive attitude about their jobs and to do their best work. For example, if you know that an employee likes getting frequent feedback on his performance so that he can improve, you might give him feedback more often than you would another employee. If an employee is interested in finding ways to improve her skills and abilities, you might arrange for her to attend an occasional workshop or class.

Many studies about what motivates people have been done, and many theories have been developed. Figure 16-3 is a survey that has been given to hundreds of thousands of employees. It lists factors that employees have rated as important to them in their jobs, ranked from the most important to the least important.

One difficult but helpful strategy for motivating those around you is to get them to take leadership of a task, not just do the task. If they take responsibility for a task, they will have the desire to complete it, the task or goal will be valued more, and the resulting product will be of higher quality. To encourage responsibility and motivate people, include them in the process of planning, and consider and use their contributions if at all possible.

For an example of how this might be done, suppose that a proposal and presentation on a project are due at the end of the month. The project manager assigns an employee who is working on the project to prepare all the materials—the proposal and a *PowerPoint* presentation—and to give a portion of the presentation. The employee takes responsibility because he or she has been given a higher degree of trust and wants the presentation to go well. The leader provides help and encouragement and asks for status reports, but otherwise lets the employee

Figure 16-3 Factors That Motivate Employees

- Work with people who treat me with respect
- Interesting work
- Recognition for good work
- Chance to develop skills
- Working for people who listen if you have ideas about how to do things better
- A chance to think for myself, rather than just carry out instructions
- Seeing the end results of my work
- Working for efficient managers
- A job that is not too easy
- Feeling well informed about what is going on
- Job security
- High pay
- Good benefits

Source: Cohen, *A Class with Drucker*, 221–222.

work independently, while making it clear that she or he expects results.

On a broader note, Collins suggests that the problem of motivation disappears, for the most part, if you have the right people in the organization. Leaders should first be concerned with who is on their "bus." If they can get the right people on the bus and the wrong people off, then they can decide where to drive the bus (in what direction to take the organization to move it from "good" to "great"). The right people will provide their own motivation, in the form of an inner drive to do their best and to be part of building the organization.[15]

©ISTOCK

Being Responsible for Others

What is your responsibility to the people you lead? Effective leadership is, to some degree, servant leadership. Effective leaders make sure their team members have the skills, equipment, supplies, and training they need to do their work. Good leaders provide clear and precise directions so that employees know what is expected of them. They check in periodically to make sure work is going well, and they make themselves available for questions and support. Good leaders examine assignments and responsibilities to ensure that employees' skills are being used efficiently.

Effective leaders are concerned for their employees' welfare

15 Collins, *Good to Great*, 41–42.

Dear Savvy Admin

Dear Savvy Admin:

I have an administrative assistant who needs additional skills in web page design and *Microsoft Access*. I see her as a long-term employee and want her to move up with our growing company. I know she wants to develop professionally. Can you suggest sources for training?

Team Leader

Dear Team Leader:

I can suggest several sources. Professional organizations for administrative assistants offer webinars, courses, videos, and conferences. Local community colleges have classes in *Access* and web page design. Four-year colleges often have continuing education programs that address local business needs such as English as a second language, computer skills, motivating teams, and customer service.

I applaud your desire to keep good employees and invest in their training! A small investment now can pay you back in a loyal, skilled, and long-term employee!

Savvy Admin

and committed to their professional growth. Whenever possible, they work with employees to try to resolve problems. For example, suppose you supervise a new employee who is not completing assignments properly. You have to ask three or four times before he does a task, and sometimes it is only partly done. After investigating the problem, you conclude that he is not avoiding work, wasting time, or having personal problems. He is simply forgetting deadlines and some of the details of assignments.

You decide to sit down with him and outline some steps he can take to ensure he completes tasks. You provide him with tools, such as a new planner or a company-provided PDA. You follow up with accountability and let him know you are investing in his future: you want him to succeed and to be productive and efficient.

Good leaders are advocates for their employees with upper-level management. For example, they may request raises and bonuses when appropriate, and they share credit for the group's successes. Additionally, effective leaders look for opportunities within the organization that may benefit the employees they supervise, such as the chance to take a professional development class.

Resolving Conflict and Other Problems

Chapters 5 and 10 discussed the leader's role in resolving conflict and some other types of problems. Effective leaders not only act to solve problems that arise but also look for situations and events that might create problems and try

Communicating @Work

E-mail tips for leaders:

↗ Use the groups feature in your e-mail software to efficiently send e-mail to groups, teams, or departments. Double-check group lists to make sure no one is inadvertently omitted.

↗ Be careful that your texting language doesn't creep into your e-mail or other correspondence (KWIM?). Communicating effectively and professionally at work differs from communicating in your personal life.

↗ Use the spelling checking feature of your e-mail software to check your messages before sending them.

↗ Consider using salutations to personalize messages when appropriate.

↗ Use the *cc* (carbon copy) feature of your e-mail to keep everyone "in the loop." This option sends a copy of the message to someone in addition to the recipient in the *To* field.

to prevent them from occurring. In investigating problems, an effective leader "goes on a fact-finding tour." He or she observes activities and processes, listens to people's accounts, and asks questions, sometimes hard questions. Good leaders use a procedure for problem solving, like the procedure outlined in Chapter 2.

Communicating

When leading others, it is very important to clearly communicate your expectations to them. Writing down your goals will help you to make them concrete and precise. Arrange a meeting in which you explain your goals and determine deadlines. Communicating simple goals and deadlines is often overlooked, and employees are left trying to ascertain what a leader wants.

When you give directions or information verbally, remember that it is not enough simply to speak clearly. You need to take steps to ensure your listeners understand. Repeat what you have said in another way. Ask, "Does anyone have any questions?"

Don't underestimate the power of face-to-face communication. Looking an individual or group of people in the eye helps you gauge their understanding and any resistance. In the time that it would take to compose an e-mail with all the details, you could meet.

Good written communication skills are equally important. Failing to communicate goals, deadlines, directions, and information so that they are understood can have serious consequences. Follow the guidelines for written messages in Chapter 7. Keep in mind that effective written messages are courteous, correct, concise, clear, and complete. Whenever possible, set your messages aside, including e-mail messages, before you send them. Allowing as little as 20 minutes between preparing a message and sending it can help you identify unclear writing and missing information.

Leaders must follow up on both verbal and written communication. For verbal communication, provide a written summary of what was said. Send reminders of deadlines and assignments when appropriate. Arrange for periodic status reports on assignments. Note dates that assignments and status reports are due to you in your planner, as well as dates on which you should send reminders. Be proactive in giving the people you supervise information you think they might need.

Good leaders listen actively and use effective listening skills. Not listening effectively may mean not having all the information or having incorrect information, which impacts your ability to get tasks accomplished correctly and on time. Reflective listening will help you develop a rapport with employees. Truly listening means that you value what the other person says and that you are seeking to understand his or her point or perspective. Use the advice in Chapter 7 on listening, verbal, nonverbal, and written communication and in Chapter 10 on presentations to develop and improve your communication skills.

Delegating

Delegating is giving the responsibility for a task to another person. A leader who delegates is able to get more accomplished. Sandra Gurvis, the author of *Management Basics*, identifies three reasons why delegating effectively is important:

- ■ It enables the manager to spend time on more important tasks.

- ■ It is an excellent way of developing people who wish to advance in the organization.

- ■ It is highly motivational.[16]

A common problem in delegating is not providing all the information the person will need to complete the assignment, so that when it is done, it is not done correctly or completely. Before you delegate, think carefully about the task. Work out the details of what you want the person to do. Try to anticipate questions. Write down your directions so the person can refer to them later.

Give the assignment in person, if possible, so you can answer any questions that immediately arise.

The ability to delegate work successfully is an important leadership skill.

IMAGE COPYRIGHT HELDER ALMEIDA 2010. USED UNDER LICENSE FROM SHUTTERSTOCK.COM

Arrange for the employee to check in with you periodically, and make yourself available for these exchanges. Make sure the employee knows to come to you with questions, problems, or requests for additional support.

Delegating can be challenging because it requires you to relinquish control. You will need to trust team members to complete their assignments responsibly. You will also have to give them the authority they need. In addition, delegating requires you to allow employees to make mistakes.

Let your subordinates do all the planning and organizing for their assignments. They might not do it the same way that you would, but that does not matter as long as they do it well. They might do it in a better way, and everyone would learn something valuable in the process.

Evaluating

Effective leaders offer both informal and formal feedback on an employee's work. Frequent, constructive feedback shows employees how you expect work to be done and helps them to improve. Formal appraisals assess long-term performance, typically against a set of previously established goals, in order to improve performance that is inadequate and to reward performance that is exceptional.

16 Sandra Gurvis, *Management Basics: A Practical Guide for Managers,* 2nd ed. (Avon, Mass.: Adams Business, 2008), 117.

Informal Feedback Informal feedback can be invaluable to productivity, morale, and motivation. Take the time to tell employees what you think of a task or project they have recently finished, and do not hesitate to make a positive summary of past projects in meetings. An informal or formal meeting to ask, "So how do you think that went?" gives the team member ownership and value in the process and provides insights for you as the leader.

Keep negative observations to a minimum. Workers with a genuine willingness to learn and grow will carefully consider your comments, evaluate themselves, and strive to improve.

Performance Appraisals Different companies use different procedures for performance evaluations. The interval of time between appraisals, as you have learned, also varies. To prepare for and conduct a performance appraisal, you should generally plan to complete these tasks:

■ Take the time between appraisals to document instances of good performance and performance that could be improved.

■ If your organization requires the employee to do a self-evaluation, allow adequate time and provide the appropriate form(s).

■ In preparing your evaluation, review any goals that were established for the employee during the last appraisal and the documentation in your files. Be thoughtful, honest, and objective in your observations.

■ Begin the evaluation session by explaining the goals of the evaluation and how the session will proceed.

Informal feedback can be invaluable to productivity, morale, and motivation.

© 2010 STOCKBYTE/JUPITERIMAGES CORPORATION

■ Stay focused on the topics at hand. Praise the employee for work that was well done. If improvements are needed, give examples of what you expect. Be clear about your expectations.

■ Give the employee an opportunity to talk.

■ If improvement is needed, develop a plan with the employee, and put it in writing. Set interim dates, if necessary, to check that the needed improvements have been made.

■ Set goals together for the period until the next evaluation.

Key Terms

autocratic leadership style

delegating

democratic leadership style

integrity

laissez-faire leadership style

leadership

leadership styles

learning organization

management

management by objectives

mission

self-development

servant leadership

situational leadership

vision

Summary

- The ability to lead with confidence will serve you well throughout life, regardless of what profession you choose.

- The capacity to lead well is more than filling a job. It is an overall practical philosophy in the workplace in which an individual motivates and inspires others as the organization achieves its goals.

- Management in a business setting is the act of organizing and directing people to accomplish organizational goals. The responsibilities of leaders and managers overlap.

- Reading the work of respected writers in the fields of leadership and management will help you lead people more effectively.

- Traits that define an effective leader include integrity, emotional maturity, a commitment to learning and development, self-knowledge, confidence, vision, and the ability to make decisions.

- Leadership styles are patterns of behavior in leading others. Leadership styles affect performance in different ways.

- Leaders lead people as well as organizations. When leading organizations, leaders have to consider and at times develop the vision, mission, goals, and objectives of the organization.

- When leading people, effective leaders set an example, invest in relationships, motivate and take responsibility for others, problem-solve, communicate well, delegate, and perform informal and formal evaluations.

Bookmark It. *For convenient access to activities, links, and valuable career resources for administrative professionals, visit the companion website for this text:*

www.cengage.com/officetech/fultoncalkins

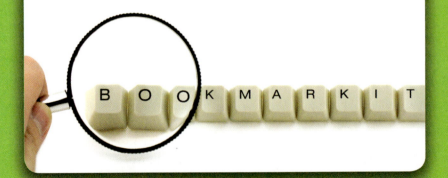

❯ *Discussion Questions*

1. If you had to write a summary of this chapter, what would be your topic sentence? Use your own words.

2. What is the difference between leadership and management?

3. Compare and contrast the ideas of two writers from the "Leadership and Management Theories" section of the chapter. Use only the information in the chapter, not outside sources.

4. Name three things you learned from the "Leadership Traits" section of the chapter.

5. Pick one leadership style and write a very short dialog (three or four verbal or e-mail exchanges) between an employee and his or her leader, who uses that style.

6. This chapter describes eight skills and strategies for leading people. For each one (e.g., leading by example), write a one-sentence summary.

7. What are some ways that leaders can demonstrate their investment in people?

8. Why are good written communication skills important for a leader? Are good listening skills more important or less important for a leader? Why?

9. What are some benefits and drawbacks of delegating?

❯ *Critical Thinking*

Flexible hours You work for Cabrera Manufacturing, which has 1,400 employees in three different locations. Several department heads have approached management about the possibility of offering flexible hours for employees (hours are currently 8 a.m. to 5 p.m. throughout the company). Management has formed a committee to gather information from all employees and particularly to consider what sort of flextime arrangement employees would like. You are the co-leader of this committee. How will you gather information from the employees and department managers? Are there questions you would ask each group? How do other companies use flexible schedules? Form a committee of 2–4 fellow students, do some research on flextime, and develop a plan for how your committee will do this assignment. If you will use a survey, write sample questions. Your plan will be reviewed by the senior vice president for employee affairs, so do a thorough job. (Learning Objective 5)

❯ *Build Workplace Skills*

1. **Leader interview** Interview in person, by phone, or by e-mail a person who holds a leadership position at a local business, such as a manager. Prepare a list of five or six questions. Ask what this person's view of leadership is, how he or she came to hold the current position, and what this person believes it takes to be an effective leader. Write a brief report of your findings. Include a comparison of what you learned from your interview with the information in this chapter. (Learning Objectives 4, 5)

Planning Notes

2. **Delegating**   Since the ability to delegate is often an important skill for leaders, develop a list of instances when delegating is appropriate (for example, when you are extremely busy and there is a task you know someone on your team can do well) and a list of times when delegating is probably not a good idea. You may use Internet resources to give you ideas. (Learning Objective 5)

3. **Leader from your past**   Think of a leader from your past experience whom you would consider to be a successful leader. This person might be a supervisor, teacher, youth group leader, or coach, for example. Compose a brief essay with the following parts: a general description of the person, two leadership traits that made him or her successful, how they were demonstrated by this leader, and what leadership style(s) you believe this person used most often and why. (Learning Objectives 3, 4)

> Communicate Clearly

4. **Leadership defined**   In your own words, define what successful leadership is and how leadership and management differ in an office setting. Consider what successful leadership "looks like" to you. Send this information in an e-mail to your instructor. (Learning Objective 1)

5. **Improve instructions**   Open the *Word* file CH16 Instructions E-mail from the data files. Revise the text and add information as needed to make these instructions from a supervisor to an employee complete and clear. Invent details as needed. (Learning Objective 5)

6. **Prepare and present**   With two or three classmates, develop a presentation using *PowerPoint* slides on integrity in leadership and how your personal integrity in areas such as downloading music, driving, taking tests, writing research papers, filling out a time sheet, and reporting sick leave relates to your ability to be a trustworthy leader. Deliver your presentation to your class or a group of classmates in person, or prepare a recorded version using screen capture software with audio. Your time limit is five minutes. (Learning Objective 4)

7. **Team member problem**   Locate the sound file CH16 Problem from the data files. Without pausing or stopping, play the file to hear Alberto telling his team leader, Ellen, about a problem. Play the file once more. What is the problem that Alberto is describing? If you were the team leader, what steps would you take to resolve it? (Learning Objective 5)

> Develop Relationships

8. **Team leader**   You have just been promoted to team leader at Combines Incorporated. You don't know any of the members of your four-person team, but you know that building relationships is important for effective leadership. Devise a one-page plan for developing relationships with individuals in your group. Consider how you will get to know your team members, establish a rapport, and develop trust. Also consider what leadership style you will use for most of your group interactions. (Learning Objective 5)

9. **Motivation** You have begun to work with your team from activity 8. You realize quickly that motivation could be an issue for one or two of your team members. What can you do to motivate them (and the others)? Prepare a *Word* document that will remind you to apply the strategies for motivating team members that you have chosen. Invent details about team members as needed. (Learning Objective 5)

> *Use Technology*

10. **Create a visual outline** Your supervisor will be giving a presentation on leadership to a local civic group. He has asked you to create a visual outline of topics related to leadership that he can use to stimulate ideas. Use the chapter and other sources for topics. Use the Shapes or SmartArt feature of *Word* or an online mapping tool to create your visual outline. Links to some of these tools are provided on the website for this text.

11. **Leader story** Imagine that you work for one of the following companies (or another company with the approval of your instructor): Procter & Gamble, General Motors, Apple, Google, Starbucks, Intel, Coca-Cola, BP, Cisco, Dell, or Target. You have been asked to create a profile of a leader in your company that will be presented at an annual company conference. Using *iMovie®*, *Windows Movie Maker*, or other video editing software, create a digital story of a successful leader from your company by describing this person's leadership qualities and skills and leadership style.

    Use pictures and copyright-free music from the Internet, if available. Add transitions, titles, and credits to provide a professional look to your movie whenever possible. (Learning Objectives 1, 3)

12. **Leadership theories** A vice president in your company is heading an effort to promote leadership in the organization. She has asked you to research the theories of two leading writers on leadership or management and to create a web page or set of web pages. This material will be posted on the company intranet for managers and other employees to review.

    Choose two of the leadership and management writers mentioned in this chapter, or choose other writers with the approval of your instructor. Research the leadership or management theories of these writers. Use *Word*, web design software, or a free website design site to make web pages or a website about their ideas. You should have at least two pages with images and summaries written in your own words. (Learning Objective 2)

> *Above & Beyond*

Overtime spreadsheet You work for Bradley and Cohen, a large air conditioner manufacturer and installation company. One of your many duties as office manager is to keep track of the office overtime schedule and budget. Today you will prepare a monthly summary and a chart.

Planning Notes

Planning Notes

a. Open the *Excel* file CH16 Overtime Hours from the data files.

b. Look at the formula for overtime pay for the first employee. The IF function is used to calculate the pay at 1 1/2 times the hourly rate if the overtime hours are 12 or fewer. If the overtime hours are more than 12, the formula calculates the pay at 2 times the hourly rate. Copy the overtime pay formula down to the next three rows to calculate pay for the other employees.

c. Enter a formula to calculate the total overtime pay for the week.

d. In cell E13, enter a formula that uses the IF function. If the total overtime pay for the week is less than or equal to the overtime budget, display "Yes" in the cell. If the overtime pay for the week is more than the overtime budget, display "No" in the cell. (Hint: Place quotes around "Yes" and "No" in the formula.)

e. Make copies of the worksheet to record the hours for the next three weeks. Change the dates at the top of the worksheets and on the worksheet tabs. Enter these hours for the employees:

	February 8–14	February 15–21	February 22–28
Emily Jones	4	4	5
Anita Morales	8	14	14
Hisao Nagano	4	3	2
Richard Wilson	12	5	3

f. Create another copy of the worksheet for monthly totals. Name the sheet February Totals and change the date at the top to February 1–28. The Overtime Hours column should show the employee's total overtime hours for the month. Change the overtime budget to reflect the total budget for the month.

g. Prepare a pie chart to show visually how overtime hours were distributed by employee in February. Name the chart FEBRUARY 20-- OVERTIME. Include a legend and use data labels to show percentages on each piece of the chart.

h. What conclusions can you draw from these data? Is there one employee who consistently works more overtime than others? If yes, why might that be the case? Is there one week of the month that has significantly more overtime than the others? Why might that be the case? (Learning Objective 5)

Reference Guide

Abbreviations

1. Use standard abbreviations for courtesy and personal titles, academic degrees, and professional designations.

Mr. Michael Khirallah	Dr. Cindy Bos
Ms. Shania Cole	Thomas Jones, Jr.
Mrs. Helene Chen	Nathan Portello, Ph.D.
Brian Edwards, CPA	

- Do not use a period after *Miss*. *Miss* is not an abbreviation.

- Use *Ms.* if you know a woman prefers that title or if you don't know her preference.

- Within the health care field, medical degrees are often written without periods.

- Professional designations such as CPA are written without periods when used alone but with periods when used with academic degrees.

- Do not use a courtesy title with an academic degree or with *Esq.* (*Esquire*).

Incorrect	Mr. Thomas McIntyre, M.B.A.
Correct	Thomas McIntyre, M.B.A.

- Do not "double" titles. A degree such as *M.D., J.D., Ph.D.,* or *D.D.S.* is a doctoral degree. Do not use *Dr.* and a doctoral degree together.

Incorrect	Dr. Elena Alonso, D.D.S.
Correct	Elena Alonso, D.D.S.

2. Most professional titles are spelled out. A professional title may be abbreviated if a person's full name is used.

   Professor Helen Vendler
   R. Adm. Grace Hopper

3. Use periods following initials and a space between first and middle initials.

   Dwight D. Eisenhower   T. S. Eliot

4. Familiar abbreviations for companies, professional organizations, and government agencies may be used in most professional writing.

   AIG   NYSE   IRS

   Abbreviations are sometimes part of a company's official name. Abbreviations that people have used for some companies' names have become official names.

   FAO Schwarz   AAA   FedEx

   Abbreviated names of companies and professional organizations are usually keyed in capital letters with no periods and no spaces between the letters. Always follow an organization's preference, however, in abbreviating names.

   AFL-CIO   P.F. Chang's

5. Use certain abbreviated expressions that are commonly employed in professional writing.

e.g.	*exempli gratia* (for example)
etc.	*et cetera* (and so forth)
i.e.	*id est* (that is)

   Other abbreviations, while not appropriate for business writing, may be used in forms, tables, and charts.

   acct.   dept.   pd.

6. Geographic names, such as the names of countries, should be abbreviated only in tables, business forms, and the like.

   United States is always spelled out as a noun and is usually abbreviated as an adjective.

   Dominic immigrated to the United States in 2009.
   In 2010, the U.S. population exceeded 309 million.

   Do not abbreviate compass directions when they are part of an address; use *North*, etc. After a street name, however, you may use *NW, NE, SE,* and *SW*.

7. When an abbreviation that ends with a period falls at the end of a sentence, use only one period. If the sentence ends with a question mark or an exclamation point, place the question mark or exclamation point directly after the period.

   The next speaker will be Hannah Tierney, R.N.
   Is that flight at 8:15 a.m. or 8:15 p.m.?

8. Use periods with *a.m.* and *p.m.* (in lowercase letters) to designate time.

   6:00 a.m.   4:30 p.m.

9. Use the United States Postal Service state abbreviations (two capital letters, no periods) in letter addresses.

   Dr. Alan Mossavi
   State College
   1800 College Street
   Somerset, KY 42501-1800

   Avenue, Boulevard, etc., are usually spelled out but should be abbreviated to avoid having a single long line in a letter address.

10. Do not abbreviate days of the week or months of the year.

- A company, an organization, or a profession will often use abbreviations that are commonly used within that group in internal correspondence.

- Do not use an abbreviation if you are not sure your reader will understand it.

- Sometimes introducing an abbreviation makes sense. If you are preparing a business report that refers repeatedly to the Agency for Healthcare Research and Quality, for example, using the agency's abbreviation, AHRG, will be easier for your reader. Spell out the term the first time you use it, with the abbreviation in parentheses. After that, use the abbreviation only.

> The Agency for Healthcare Research and Quality (AHRQ) has issued a report on patient safety.

Active and Passive Voice

Voice is the form of a verb indicating whether the subject is engaging in the action or receiving the action. A verb is in the *active voice* when the subject performs the action.

> Max *caught* the basketball.
> The voters *chose* the delegates.

A verb is in the *passive voice* when the subject receives the action.

> The basketball *was caught* by Max.
> The delegates *were chosen* by the voters.

The active voice is more direct and concise, so you should use it most of the time. The passive voice is appropriate for these uses:

- When you do not know, or when it does not matter, who or what performed the action.

  > The package was delivered this afternoon.

- When you want to emphasize the receiver of the action.

  > Gina was selected to represent the company.

- To avoid sounding as if you are assigning blame.

  > The payment was received after the due date.

Capitalization

1. Capitalize the first word of every sentence, including a quoted sentence.

   > He said, "Those prices are not a good indicator."

   Do not capitalize a quoted sentence preceded by *that* or woven into the sentence in another way.

   > Maya observed that "the board needs to refocus on retention."

2. Capitalize the days of the week, months of the year, and holidays.

   > Monday   May   Labor Day

3. Capitalize *proper nouns*—the names of specific people, places, and things.

   > John G. Hammitt   Beacon Street
   > Kazakhstan   the Boston Marathon

the East Building   Honda Civic
the Business Club   History 101
the Merrimack River   the Nikkei 225
the Renaissance   the Civil Rights Movement

Do not capitalize *common nouns*—names that do not refer to a particular person, place, or thing.

> supervisor   street
> country   race
> building   sedan
> club   history class

- *The* is not usually capitalized before a proper noun, but it is capitalized if the company or organization does it that way.

  > *The New York Times*
  > The Walt Disney Company

4. Capitalize proper adjectives.

   > Indian   Latino   Jewish

5. Capitalize courtesy titles and official titles that come before personal or proper names.

   > Ms. Giacomini
   > Deputy Chair Aidan Joffe
   > Professor Harry Sanders

   > **But** My psychology professor, Harry Sanders, has published a book on personality theory.

   Do not capitalize official titles that come after a name, except for titles of high-ranking national, state, and international officials. Those titles are also capitalized when they are used in place of a personal name.

   > Skylar Blum, vice president of sales
   > Sonia Sotomayor, Associate Justice
   > The President spoke about the economy.

   Do not capitalize titles used as a general term of classification or occupational titles.

   > A U.S. senator is elected to a six-year term.
   > Kelly is an administrative assistant.

6. Capitalize directional words like *north* when they are part of names for regions or localities but not when they simply show direction.

   > the Midwest   northeast of the city
   > the South   the southern United States
   > the West Coast   Go west for 15 miles.

7. In a letter, capitalize the salutation and the first word of the complimentary close.

   > Dear Ms. Riviera   Sincerely yours

8. Capitalize nouns used before numbers, except for such common words as *page*, *line*, and *sentence*.

> We are on Flight 1683.
> You will find the material on page 15.

9. Capitalize the first word, the last word, and all main words in headings and the titles of literary and artistic works. Do not capitalize articles (*a, an, the*), coordinating conjunctions (*and, but,* etc.), and prepositions of four or fewer letters unless they are the first or last word.

> Researching and Applying for Jobs
> *For Whom the Bell Tolls*
> *Saving Private Ryan*

10. The names of specific departments within the writer's company or organization are sometimes capitalized.

> our Customer Service Department

Collective Nouns

A *collective noun* is a word that is singular in form but represents a group of persons or things. For example, the following words are collective nouns: *committee, company, department, public, class,* and *board.* These rules determine the form of the verb to be used with a collective noun:

1. When the members of a group are thought of as one unit, the verb should be singular.

> The committee *has voted* unanimously to begin the study.

2. When the members of a group are thought of as separate individuals, the verb should be plural.

> The staff *are* not in agreement on the decision that should be made.

3. If the sentence seems unclear or awkward, you may address the problem by inserting the word *members* after the collective noun and using a plural verb.

> The staff *members are* not in agreement on the decision that should be made.

Misused Words and Phrases

A or *an* before *h*

The letter *h* can have a hard sound or can be silent. When using *a* or *an* before a word beginning with *h*, use *a* when the *h* has a hard sound and *an* when the *h* is silent.

Hard Sound	Silent
a house	an hour
a historical event	an honor

Accept, except, expect

- To *accept* an assignment is to agree to undertake it.
- *Except* is seldom used as a verb; it is usually a preposition.

> Everyone except Ralph attended the meeting.

> To *expect* someone is to believe that person will come.

Advice, advise

Advice is a noun meaning a recommendation; *advise* is a verb meaning to counsel.

> She did not follow my advice.
> Your attorney will advise you.

Affect, effect

The verb *affect* means to influence or to change. *Effect* is usually used as a noun and means a result.

> The new law will affect many corporations.
> What will be the effect on the economy?

All, all of

Use *all*; *of* is redundant. If a pronoun follows *all*, reword the sentence.

> Check all the items.
> **Instead of**   All of them are going.
> **Use**   They are all going.

All right, alright

All right is the only correct usage; *alright* is not appropriate for business usage.

Among, between

Among is used when referring to three or more persons or things; *between* is used when referring to two persons or things.

> The inheritance was divided among the four children.
> The choice is between you and me.

Appraise, apprise

Appraise means to set a value on; *apprise* means to inform.

> The house was appraised at $300,000.
> Pablo apprised me of the situation.

Bad, badly

Bad is an adjective; *badly* is an adverb.

> He feels bad about forgetting the meeting.
> The team played badly last night.

Can, may

> *Can* means to have the ability or power to do something; *may* means to have permission.

>> Elise can repair almost anything.
>> You may leave when you finish your work.

Capital, capitol

> *Capital* is used unless you are referring to a building that houses a government.

>> Austin is the capital of Texas.
>> We toured the U.S. Capitol in Washington.

Cite, sight, site

> *Cite* means to quote, *sight* means vision, and *site* means location.

>> She cited several authoritative references.
>> That is a pleasant sight.
>> The task force will recommend a site for the new building.

Complement, compliment

> *Complement* means to complete, fill, or make perfect; *compliment* means to praise.

>> His handouts complemented the presentation.
>> The manager complimented Apurva on his attention to detail.

Farther, further

> *Farther* refers to distance; *further* refers to a greater degree or extent.

>> The store is a mile farther down the road.
>> We will discuss the matter further on Friday.

Fewer, less

> Use *fewer* to refer to items that can be counted. Use *less* to refer to items that cannot be counted.

>> There were fewer speakers than last year.
>> Payroll takes less time with the new software.

Good, well

> *Good* is an adjective. *Well* is typically used as an adverb but may be used as an adjective when referring to the state of a person's health.

>> You did a good job on the project.
>> The team performed well in the playoffs.
>> I feel well.

In, into

> *In* means located inside an area or limits; *into* means in the direction of the interior or toward something.

>> Katie is sitting in the third row.
>> She went into the conference room.

Its, it's

> *Its* is the possessive form of *it; it's* is the contraction of *it is.*

>> The company posted its quarterly earnings.
>> It's probably going to rain.

Lead, led

> As a verb, *lead* means to be first or in charge, to take to, or to carry on. As a noun (and adjective), it means an element. *Led* is the past tense and past participle of *lead.*

>> Emma leads the committee now.
>> Tendo led it last year.
>> They tested the building for lead paint.

Like, as

> The conjunction *as* introduces a clause (a sentence part with a subject and a verb). In business writing, *like* is used only as a preposition.

>> Sales were up as we expected.
>> I want a car like Sam's.

Lose, loose

> *Lose* is a verb that means to misplace. *Loose* is most often an adjective. It means free or not restrained.

>> Did you lose your cell phone?
>> The dog ran loose in the yard.

Percent, per cent; percentage

> *Percent* is always spelled as one word; *per cent* is incorrect. *Percentage* is also one word and is the preferred word when a number is not used.

>> Caleb received 56 percent of the vote.
>> The percentage of votes she received is not known.

Principal, principle

> *Principal* as an adjective means *main;* as a noun, *principal* means the main person or a capital sum.

> *Principle* is a noun meaning a rule, guide, or truth; it never refers to a person directly.

>> The principal character in the play is John.
>> The principals in the case are present.
>> One of the company's principles is environmental responsibility.

Than, then

>Than* is a conjunction that compares two or more people or things.

>>Conor has more experience than Naima.

>*Then* is usually an adverb and means at that time. It answers the question *when* of the verb.

>>Then we will go to dinner.

That, which

>*That* and *which* are relative pronouns (pronouns that relate or refer to nouns or other pronouns in a sentence), and they introduce dependent clauses (clauses that have a subject and verb but cannot stand on their own).

>- *That* is used to refer to things or people. It introduces a clause that is essential to the meaning of the sentence.

>- *Which* is used to refer to things. It introduces a clause that contains nonessential information. A comma is used before *which* but not before *that*.

>>The seminar that was held last week focused on time management.

>>The first seminar, which was held last week, focused on time management.

There, their, they're

>*There* is almost always used as an adverb. *Their* is a possessive adjective. *They're* is the contraction for *they are*.

>>We went there after lunch.
>>Their flight was delayed two hours.
>>They're bringing the trustees to the meeting.

To, too, two

>*To* is most often a preposition, so it is followed by a noun or pronoun in the objective case.

>>Alaina is going to the conference.

>*Too* is an adverb. It means also, besides, very, or excessively.

>>That presentation was too long.

>*Two* is a number. It is usually an adjective that tells how many.

>>You have two assignments this morning.

Who, whom

>*Who* is used as the subject of a verb or as a predicate pronoun (a pronoun used to complete the meaning of the verb *be*, as in *Who is she?* *Whom* is used as an object of a verb or preposition.

>- Use this quick check for *who* or *whom*: If you can substitute *he or she*, *who* is correct. If you can substitute *him* or *her*, *whom* is correct. You may need to rearrange the sentence a little.

>>Who do you think will be hired?
>>(I think *he* will be hired.)

>>Whom should I cont.act for more information?
>>(You should contact *her*.)

>>Marita is a manager who gets things done.
>>(*She* gets things done.)

>>Kabuo is the candidate whom I prefer.
>>(I prefer *him*.)

Who's, whose

>*Who*'s is the contraction for *who is* or *who has*. *Whose* is an adjective that shows ownership or possession.

>>Leona, who's been taking accounting classes, got the position.

>>Whose cell phone is on the table?

Your, you're

>*Your* is a possessive adjective. *You're* is the contraction of *you are*.

>>Your supervisor called.
>>You're going to be late if you don't hurry.

Number Usage

1. Spell out numbers from one through ten; use figures for numbers above ten.

   >We ordered nine PDAs and four tablets.
   >Lakshmi prepared 60 letters.

2. If a sentence contains related numbers any of which is over ten, use figures for all the related numbers.

   >Please order 12 boxes of business cards, 2 reams of paper, and 11 boxes of envelopes.

   >(The numbers are related: they all refer to office supplies.)

   >**But** The company offers 15 different wellness seminars, each of which lasts two hours.

   >(The numbers are not related. *Fifteen* refers to seminars, and *two* refers to time.)

3. Numbers in the millions or above may be expressed with a figure and a word for easy comprehension.

> 3 billion (rather than 3,000,000,000)

4. Spell out numbers at the beginning of a sentence.

> Five hundred books were ordered.

For larger numbers, rearrange the wording of the sentence so the number is not the first word.

Instead of   Six thousand three hundred and seventy-two employees enrolled in the new plan.

Use   We enrolled 6,372 employees in the new plan.

5. Spell out indefinite numbers.

> A few hundred voters turned out for the local election.

6. Use figures to express dates written in normal month-day-year order. Do not use *st, th,* or *d* following the date.

> May 9, 20--
> **Not**   May 9th, 20--

If the date stands alone or comes before the month, use *st, th,* or *d* with the figure that represents the date.

> The meeting is on the 9th.

7. To express times of day, use figures with *a.m.* and *p.m.;* spell out numbers with the word *o'clock*. In formal usage (formal written invitations, for example), spell out all times.

> 9 a.m.   eight o'clock in the evening

Do not use zeros with on-the-hour times, except when used together with times that are not on the hour.

> Your flight to Detroit leaves at 11 a.m.

But   Your flight to Detroit leaves at 11:00 a.m., and your connecting flight to Boston leaves at 2:05 p.m.

Use the words *noon* and *midnight* alone, without the number *12*.

> noon   **Not**   12 noon

8. Amounts of money over a dollar are usually expressed in figures.

> $1,00-30 $3.27

Amounts of money under a dollar are expressed in figures with the word *cents*, except in statistical copy or when used together with amounts over a dollar.

> 79 cents
> **But**   I have petty cash receipts for $15.70, $8.09, and $.95.

9. Express percentages in figures. Spell out the word *percent*.

> 10 percent

10. Spell out isolated simple fractions in words. Write mixed fractions and decimals in figures.

> one-half cut   5 3/4 hours   0.125 inch

It is a good idea to add a zero before decimals that are less than one so that the decimal point is not overlooked.

11. Use words for street names from First through Tenth and figures or ordinals for street names above Tenth.

> Third Street   14th Street

Write house numbers in figures, except for the number *one*.

> One Main Place   13 Brook Avenue

When figures are used for both the house number and the street name, separate them with a dash.

> 122—33rd Street

12. Use figures for the larger of two adjacent numbers.

> We ordered three 8-gallon sharps containers.

Parallel Construction

Parts of a sentence that are parallel in meaning should be parallel in structure. Writers should balance a word with a word, a phrase with a phrase, a clause with a clause, and a sentence with a sentence. Parallel parts of a sentence should be grammatically the same.

> Your goals should be *clear, realistic,* and *they should be reachable*.
> (adjective, adjective, and clause—not parallel)

> Your goals should be *clear, realistic,* and *reachable*.
> (adjective, adjective, and adjective—parallel)

> *Tyne interviews the applicants,* and *they are tested by Oren*.
> (active voice and passive voice—not parallel)

> *Tyne interviews the applicants,* and *Oren tests them*.
> (active voice and active voice—parallel)

A common mistake in parallelism occurs with the use of *correlative conjunctions,* such as *both–and, either–or, neither–nor, not only–but also,* and *whether–or*. The text that follows the two conjunctions should be parallel in structure.

> Priya not only *handles administrative tasks* but also *some clinical duties*.
> (verb plus object and noun phrase—not parallel)

> Priya handles not only *administrative tasks* but also *some clinical duties*.
> (noun phrase and noun phrase—parallel)

Plurals

1. To form the plural of most nouns, add *s*.

2. For nouns ending in *s, x, z, sh,* or *ch,* add *es* to form the plural.

address	addresses
box	boxes
waltz	waltzes
bush	bushes
watch	watches

3. When a noun ends in *y* preceded by a vowel, form the plural by adding *s*.

attorney	attorneys

   When a noun ends in *y* preceded by a consonant, change the *y* to *i* and add *es* to form the plural.

company	companies

4. When a noun ends in *o* preceded by a vowel, form the plural by adding *s*.

video	videos

   For nouns ending in *o* preceded by a consonant, the plural is formed in different ways (*s* is added, *es* is added, or either is acceptable). Consult a dictionary if you are not sure of the correct plural form for a noun ending in *o* preceded by a consonant.

5. For compound nouns consisting of separate or hyphenated words that include a noun, make the main or base part plural.

cross-examination	cross-examinations
runner-up	runners-up

   If no part of a hyphenated compound noun is itself a noun, make the last element plural.

trade-in	trade-ins

6. Add *s* to make numbers expressed in figures plural.

1800s	1099s

Possessives

1. To form the possessive of most singular nouns, add an apostrophe plus *s* ('*s*).

   > My sister's name is Sheila.
   > Thomas's office is down the hall.

   If a singular noun ends in a silent *s*, or if adding an apostrophe plus *s* would make the word difficult to pronounce, add just an apostrophe.

   > What is the Peace Corps' mission?
   > What is Ms. Luebbers' address?

2. To form the possessive of a plural noun ending in *s*, add just an apostrophe (').

   > The managers' decision was unanimous.
   > The Garcias' house sold for $575,000.

3. To form the possessive of a plural noun not ending in *s*, add an apostrophe plus *s* ('*s*).

   > The children's play area is on the lower level.

4. Rules 1–3 apply to compound nouns as well.

   > The mayor-elect's plans are impressive.
   > The copy editors' hours have been cut.

5. To show joint possession, make the last element possessive.

   > Have you seen Megan and Jeffrey's apartment?

   To show individual possession, make each element possessive.

   > Mantero's and Ria's job descriptions overlap.

6. The possessive form of personal pronouns is written without an apostrophe.

   > This book is hers.
   > She will deliver yours tomorrow.

Pronouns

1. A pronoun agrees with its *antecedent* (the word or words to which the pronoun refers) in number (singular or plural), gender, and person (first, second, or third).

   > *Roger* wants to know if *his* new computer has been delivered.

   > *Marty and Tomie* are bringing *their* cameras.

   > *The company* issued *its* annual report. (not *their* annual report)

   See also Collective Nouns.

2. When a pronoun has an indefinite pronoun, such as *everybody,* as its antecedent, make sure the two pronouns agree in number.

   > *Everyone* should bring *his* or *her* company ID.
   > (not *their* company IDs)

   For lists of singular and plural indefinite pronouns, see the Subject-Verb Agreement section.

3. A singular pronoun is used when the antecedent consists of two singular nouns joined by *or* or *nor*. A plural pronoun is used when the antecedent consists of two plural nouns joined by *or* or *nor*.

   > Either *Elizabeth* or *Olivia* will need to bring *her* tablet.

   > Neither the *medical assistants* nor the *nurses* have received *their* benefits packet.

4. When the antecedent consists of a singular and a plural noun connected by *or* or *nor*, the pronoun agrees with the noun that is closer to it.

> When *Jamie* or *the managers* give *their* opinions, you should listen.

5. Use *who, whom,* and their compounds (such as *whoever*) when referring to persons. Use *that* when referring to people or things. *Who* refers to an individual person or group; *that* refers to a class or type.

> Shoko, *who* heads the recycling committee, will present the new program.
>
> He is the type of candidate *that* we like to employ.
>
> The building *that* I work in is LEED-certified.

Use *which* and *whichever* when referring to things.

> The reservation, *which* was made two weeks ago, was for a smoke-free room.

Use *which* to introduce a clause that is not essential to the meaning of the sentence. Use *that* to introduce a clause that is essential to the meaning of the sentence. A comma is used before *which* but not before *that*.

See also the *That, which* entry in the Misused Words and Phrases section.

6. Nominative case pronouns (*I, you, he, she, it, we, you, they, who,* and *whoever*) are used as subjects.

> *He* maintains the company's website.
> (subject of the sentence)
>
> Alexander, *who* lives in Salem, commutes to Boston by train.
> (subject of a dependent clause)

Use a nominative case pronoun after a *linking verb* (a form of the verb *be*).

> It was *she* who got the promotion. (**not** *It was her*)

7. Objective case pronouns function as direct objects, indirect objects, or objects of prepositions. These pronouns include *me, you, him, her, it, us, you, them, whom,* and *whomever*.

> Kyle asked *him* for a list of clients.
> (pronoun as direct object)
>
> Mr. Komnick gave Elizabeth and *me* a new assignment.
> (pronoun as indirect object)
>
> Look for *them* near the registration desk.
> (pronoun as the object of a preposition)

8. Possessive case pronouns show ownership. These pronouns include *my, mine, your, yours, his, her, hers, its, our, ours, your, yours, their, theirs,* and *whose*.

> *Whose* cell phone is this?

9. Two pronouns that are often confused are *who* and *whom*.

- *Who* is used as the subject of a verb or as a predicate pronoun (after the verb *be,* to complete its meaning).

> *Who* is making the arrangements for the conference?
> *Who* is the manager of that division?

- *Whom* is used as an object of a verb or preposition.

> To *whom* does Grant report?
> (object of the preposition *to*)
>
> *Whom* can we expect to give the welcoming address?
> (direct object of the verb *expect*)

For a quick check on using *who* or *whom,*, see the *Who, whom* entry in the Misused Words and Phrases section.

10. Reflexive pronouns serve to emphasize that the subject receives the action of the verb. Reflexive pronouns include *myself, herself, himself, themselves,* and other *-self* or *-selves* words.

> I intend to do the painting *myself*.

Be careful not to use a reflexive pronoun as a subject.

> **Incorrect** Roberto and *myself* will attend the webinar.
> **Correct** Roberto and *I* will attend the webinar.

Punctuation

Correct punctuation is based on accepted rules and principles. Punctuation is important if the reader is to correctly interpret the writer's thoughts.

Period

1. Use a period at the end of a declarative sentence or an imperative sentence.

> Jake works for the prosecutor's office.
> (declarative sentence)
>
> Please send me a copy of the report.
> (imperative sentence)

2. Use a period after an initial and after the courtesy titles *Mr., Mrs.,* and *Ms.*

> J. D. Salinger   Ms. Tabitha Todd

3. Use periods in academic degrees that follow a person's name.

> Yichen Tan, M.D., has joined the medical staff of Metropolitan Hospital.
>
> Within the health care field, medical degrees are often written without periods. Professional designations such as *CPA* (*certified public accountant*) are written without periods when used alone but with periods when used with academic degrees.
>
> Kirsten Brownstein, M.B.A., C.L.U., will speak on personal financial planning.

4. Use periods with *a.m.* and *p.m.* to designate time.

> 10 a.m.   4:30 p.m.

5. Use a period between dollars and cents. A period is not required when an amount in even dollars is expressed in figures.

> $42.65 $25

6. Use a period to indicate a decimal.

> 3.5 bushels   12.65 percent

See also Abbreviations.

Comma

1. Use a comma before a coordinating conjunction (such as *and, but, or, nor,* and *yet*) that links independent clauses. The comma may be omitted in a compound sentence if the clauses are short or closely connected in subject matter.

> Hakeem works from 9 to 5, but MacKenzie uses the flextime option.
>
> We sent a proposal and they accepted it.

2. Use a comma to separate an introductory word or phrase from the rest of the sentence.

> Unfortunately, Mr. Weinstein has another commitment that day.
> On their lunch hour, Jordan and Breana often go jogging.

The comma may be omitted after a short introductory element such as *then*.

3. Use a comma to set off a dependent clause that precedes a main clause.

> When the guests arrive, Adesina will welcome them.

4. Use a comma to set off *nonessential elements*—words, phrases, and clauses that could be left out of the sentence without affecting its structure (it would still be a sentence) or meaning. In speaking, you would pause before and after these words, phrases, and clauses.

> The survey showed, however, that our staff needs more training in call management skills.
>
> My supervisor, Ms. Snowe, has been with the company for 14 years.
>
> Our group, which had never lost a debate, won the grand prize.

5. Use commas to separate three or more items in a series.

> Companies look for employees with effective speaking, listening, writing, and presentation skills.

6. Use a comma to separate *coordinate adjectives* (adjectives that independently modify a noun).

> She had a large, receptive audience.

To determine whether adjectives are coordinate, try using *and* between them.

> *a large and receptive audience*

Compare the adjectives above to the adjectives in this sentence:

> The *old clock* tower is being repaired.

Could you say *old and clock tower? Old* and *clock* are not coordinate adjectives, and a comma should not be used.

7. Use commas to set off quotations from the rest of the sentence.

> Vincent said, "I suggest we try a face-to-face conference instead of an online meeting."
>
> "I think that's an excellent idea," Kristina responded.
>
> "Sirena," said Travis, "how could it be implemented in your area?"

8. Use a comma to set off the name of a city from the name of a state or country.

> Our southern branch is located in Atlanta, Georgia.

9. Use commas to set off the second and all following items in complete dates and in addresses.

> The anniversary party was planned for June 18, 20--, at the city park pavilion.
>
> Marguerite's new address is 10 State Street, Skagway, Alaska.

Do not use a comma when the date has only two parts or uses the word *of*.

> I earned my degree in June 20--.
> The wedding will take place on the ninth of April.

10. Use a comma after the complimentary close in a business letter when mixed punctuation is used.

> Sincerely yours,

11. Use a comma to separate personal and professional titles that follow names. The personal titles *Jr.* and *Sr.* may appear without the comma if that is the person's preference.

> William R. Warner, Jr.
> Ramona Sanchez, Ph.D.

12. For numbers greater than zero, use a comma to separate the digits into groups of three. Do not use a comma in parts of a number that are less than zero (decimals), street names and numbers, and years.

> 50,000 members $3,575,000
>
> **But,** 3.14159   1930 (year)

Comma Splices   A *comma splice* is a sentence that contains two or more independent clauses joined by a comma.

I walked home, then I had dinner.

Here are three ways to correct a comma splice:

- Make two sentences.
  I walked home. Then I had dinner.

- Add a coordinating conjunction.
  I walked home, and then I had dinner.

- Replace the comma with a semicolon.
  I walked home; then I had dinner.

Semicolon

1. Use a semicolon to separate independent clauses that are not joined by a coordinating conjunction (such as *and, but, or, nor,* or *yet*).

   > Moya handles accounts payable; Frank does payroll.

2. Use a semicolon between independent clauses that are joined by a conjunctive adverb, such as *besides, however, nevertheless, still, then,* or *therefore,* or by a phrase such as *as a result* or *for example.*

   > I purchased three instructional DVDs; however, only two of them are in stock.

   > Max is a considerate supervisor; for example, he ordered ergonomic chairs and keyboards for his staff.

3. Use semicolons to separate a series of items that contain commas.

   > This year's outstanding employees are Emaan Yazdan, Marketing; Henry Wright, Technical Support; and Anna Wang, Personnel.

Colon

The colon is most often used to direct the reader's attention to what comes after it, usually a list.

1. Use a colon following introductory expressions such as *the following, thus,* or *as follows.*

   > The following officers were selected: president, Helen Edwards; vice president, Torayye Ramey; treasurer, Ralph Moline.

   The colon must always be preceded by an independent clause, except when the listed items are on separate lines.

2. Use a colon after the salutation in a business letter when mixed punctuation is used.

   > Dear Ms. Carroll:

3. Use a colon to separate hours and minutes when indicating time.

   > 2:10 p.m.

Question Mark

Use a question mark after a direct question.

> When do you expect to arrive in Philadelphia?

An exception to this rule is a sentence phrased in the form of a question when it is actually a courteous request.

> Will you please bring me the files.

Exclamation Point

The exclamation point is used to express sudden or strong emotion and to give urgent warnings or commands. Use it rarely.

> Congratulations!
> I can't believe it!
> Watch out!

Dash

The dash is most often used in place of commas, parentheses, a colon, or a semicolon when special emphasis is desired.

> This is not a revision of an old book—it is a totally new book.

> These sales arguments—and every one of them is important—should result in getting the order.

A short dash, known as an en dash, is used to separate ranges of numbers.

> pages 32–35

Apostrophe

1. Use an apostrophe to show ownership or possession.

   > the assistant's PDA   the paralegals' request

   See the section on Possessives for additional examples.

2. Use an apostrophe to indicate the omission of a letter or letters in a contraction.

   > it's (it is)
   > couldn't (could not)

Quotation Marks

1. Use quotation marks to enclose a person's exact words (a direct quotation).

   > The author writes, "Too-frequent use of certain words weakens the appeal."

   > Jessup said that Ms. Carrero was "truly the best teacher that I have ever had."

   When you interrupt a quoted sentence to identify the speaker, end the first part of the sentence at a logical place, and start the second part with a lowercase letter.

   > "Do you think," said Lisa, "that it might be worth our time to take a second look at the figures?"

   When the break occurs between sentences, end the first part with a period. Begin the new quoted sentence with a quotation mark and a capital letter.

   > "Your idea definitely has possibilities," said Fabrizio. "Can you explain it more?"

2. Do not use quotation marks for an indirect quotation. The statement must be the exact words of a person for quotation marks to be used.

   > Jack said that he would have the report ready by 10:30.

3. Use quotation marks to set off titles of parts of works such as these:

   - Chapters of books

   - Newspaper or magazine articles

- Songs or television episodes
- Sections of websites

Use italics to set off titles of complete works such as these:

- Books
- Newspapers or magazines
- Albums or television series

Do not use italics, underlining, or quotation marks for website titles.

4. Follow these guidelines for punctuation with quotation marks:

- Place periods and commas inside quotation marks.

   "I took a class in medical law and ethics," she replied.

   Garrett said, "I completed an internship in the public defender's office."

- Place semicolons and colons outside quotation marks.

   I downloaded "Ashokan Farewell"; have you heard that song?

- Place question marks or exclamation points inside the quotation marks if they are part of the quoted matter and outside the quotation marks if they punctuate the entire sentence.

   Jaecar asked, "Are you coming with us to the seminar?"

   Did you read the part that said, "Listening is the communication skill that many people use the most"?

Parentheses

Parentheses are used to set off additions to a sentence that are not necessary to its meaning. Unlike the dash, parentheses tend to de-emphasize what they set off. Use parentheses to enclose explanations, references, directions, and numbers and letters of listed items.

Our personnel costs (including benefits) are much too high.

An additional 45 percent of our customers (Figure 1) would like a live chat feature.

To download the software, (1) go to the Downloads page of the company intranet, (2) click *Interoffice Scheduler*, (3) create a six-character password that includes letters and numbers, and (4) follow the instructions on the screen.

Hyphen

1. The hyphen is used in most compound adjectives that precede a noun and in some compound nouns and verbs.

   That was a *time-consuming* project.
   My *brother-in-law* works at the Pentagon.
   Try not to *second-guess* your decision.

2. The hyphen is also used in spelled-out compound numbers, phone numbers, nine-digit ZIP Codes, and simple fractions.

   Thirty-five employees attended the meeting.
   555-9120   45213-1419   two-thirds

3. The hyphen is used to divide words between one line of text and the next. Word processing software does end-of-line word division automatically. If an occasion occurs when you need to divide a word and you are not sure where to break it, or if you want to check whether a word break is correct, you can use the Word Division rules in this Reference Guide or consult a dictionary.

Spelling Rules

1. Use this guide to determine which comes first, *i* or *e*:

   Put *i* before *e* except after *c* or when sounded like *a* as in *neighbor* or *weigh*.

   review   receipt   freight

   This rule has numerous exceptions, such as *either, neither, conscience, foreign, leisure,* and *seize.*

2. When a word ends in a silent *e*, drop the *e* before a suffix that begins with a vowel.

advertise	advertising
guide	guidance

   There are exceptions to this rule, like these:

dye	dyeing (distinguished from *dying*)
notice	noticeable (keeps the *c* sound soft before *a* or *o*)

   Keep a final silent *e* before a suffix that begins with a consonant unless another vowel precedes the final *e*.

hate	hateful
true	truly

   As with most spelling rules, there are a few exceptions, such as this one:

nine	ninth

3. When a word ends in *y* preceded by a consonant, the *y* is usually changed to *i* before adding a suffix, except for suffixes beginning with *i*.

modify	modifier	modifying
lonely	lonelier	

   This rule also has a few exceptions, like this one:

memory	memorize

4. Double a final single consonant before adding a suffix that begins with a vowel when a single vowel precedes the consonant and (for words with more than one syllable) the consonant ends an accented syllable.

allot	allotted
bag	baggage
drop	dropped

remit	remitted
run	running

This rule has a number of exceptions, including words with the final consonant *w*, *x*, or *y*.

fix	fixed
tow	towed

When the accent shifts to the first syllable when a suffix beginning with a vowel is added, do not double the final consonant.

refer	referred	reference

5. When the final consonant in a one-syllable word is preceded by a single vowel, do not double the final consonant before a suffix beginning with a consonant.

ship	shipment
bad	badly

6. When a word ends in *ie*, drop the *e* and change the *i* to *y* before adding *ing*.

lie	lying
die	dying

Subject-Verb Agreement

1. Verbs must agree with their subjects in person and number. A singular subject takes a singular form of a verb. A plural subject takes a plural form of a verb.

> *Andrew works* in our New Orleans office.
> *Ishan and Kelsey work* in our San Diego office.

2. Disregard intervening words, phrases, and clauses when establishing agreement between subject and verb.

> *One* of the men *needs* additional training.
> The *request* for new computers *is* on Mr. Woo's desk.

3. The following pronouns are always singular and require a singular verb:

another	either	neither	other
anybody	everybody	no one	somebody
anyone	everyone	nobody	someone
anything	everything	nothing	something
each	much	one	

> *Everyone plans* to attend the meeting.
> *Neither is* an ideal solution.

4. *Both*, *few*, *many*, *others*, and *several* are always plural and require a plural verb.

> *Several were* asked to make presentations.

5. *All*, *none*, *any*, *some*, *more*, and *most* may be singular or plural, depending on the noun or pronoun to which they refer.

> *Some* of the supplies *have* arrived.
> *Most* of the paper *was* recycled.

6. When the subject consists of two nouns and/or pronouns connected by *or*, *either–or*, *neither–nor*, or *not only–but also*, a singular verb is required if the nouns and/or pronouns are singular, and a plural verb is required if they are plural.

> *Jane or Himanshu has* the letter.
>
> Neither the *managers* nor the *administrative assistants have* access to that information.

7. When the subject is made up of both singular and plural nouns and/or pronouns connected by *or*, *either–or*, *neither–nor*, or *not only–but also*, the verb agrees with the noun or pronoun that is closer to the verb.

> Either *Ms. Rogers* or the *assistants have* access to that information.
>
> Neither the *men* nor *Bonita is* working.

8. *There* and *here* are never the subjects of a sentence. When a sentence begins with one of these words, look elsewhere for the subject.

> There *are* the ticket and the itinerary.
> (*The ticket and the itinerary* is the subject.)

9. Use a singular verb with words or phrases that express periods of time, weights, measurements, and amounts of money.

> Three hours *is* a very long delay.
> Two hundred dollars *is* my limit.

10. *The number* has a singular meaning and requires a singular verb; *a number* has a plural meaning and requires a plural verb.

> *The number* of requests *is* surprising.
> *A number* of people *are* planning to attend.

11. Geographic locations are considered singular and used with a singular verb when referring to one location. When reference is made to separate states or islands, the plural form is used with a plural verb.

> The United Arab Emirates *is* made up of seven states.
> The Caribbean Islands *have* distinct cultures.

See also Collective Nouns

Tips for Writing and Editing

When addressing anyone, use terms that show respect. Remember that all assistants are not female and all executives are not male. If you answer the telephone and hear a woman's voice, do not assume she is an assistant and ask to speak to her supervisor. Do not refer to a woman as a girl or a young lady or use any other term that can sound gender-biased. Do not refer to a man as a boy or a guy.

Avoid statements such as *Each manager should submit his timesheet* by doing one of the following:

- ■ Use the plural of the noun and pronoun.
  All managers should submit *their* timesheets.

- Delete the pronoun or replace it with an article.
  Each manager should submit *a* timesheet.

- Use *he or she*
  Each manager should submit *his or her* timesheet.

Word Division

1. Divide words between syllables.

   moun-tain   base-ment

2. Avoid dividing words of five or fewer letters.

3. Do not divide one-syllable words.

   helped   eighth

4. If a single-letter syllable falls within a word, divide the word after the single-letter syllable.

   regu-late   sepa-rate

5. If two single-letter syllables occur together within a word, divide between the single-letter syllables.

   evalua-tion   radi-ator

6. Divide between double consonants except when the base word ends in a double consonant. In that case, divide between the base word and the suffix.

   neces-sary   commit-ted

   call-ing   careless-ness

7. Divide hyphenated compound words at existing hyphens only.

   two-thirds   self-control

8. Avoid dividing a date, a personal name, or an address. If it is absolutely necessary, maximize readability by doing the following:

   - Divide a date between the day and the year.
     (November 5, / 20--)

   - Divide a personal name between the first name and the surname. (Kazuo / Miyamoto)

   - Divide an address between the city and the state.
     (Lansing, / Michigan)

10. Avoid dividing figures presented as a unit.

    $20,000   36,108

11. Do not divide contractions.

    he'll   wouldn't

12. Avoid dividing words at the end of the first and last lines of a paragraph.

13. Do not divide the last word on a page.

14. Do not divide after a one-letter syllable at the beginning of a word or before a one- or two-letter syllable at the end of a word.

    around (not a-round)
    lately (not late-ly)

Document Formats

Letters

Business letters are typically formatted in block or modified block style. Open or mixed punctuation can be used with both letter styles. Figure 1 shows a block letter with open punctuation, and Figure 2 shows a modified block letter with mixed punctuation.

Figure 1 Block Letter with Open Punctuation

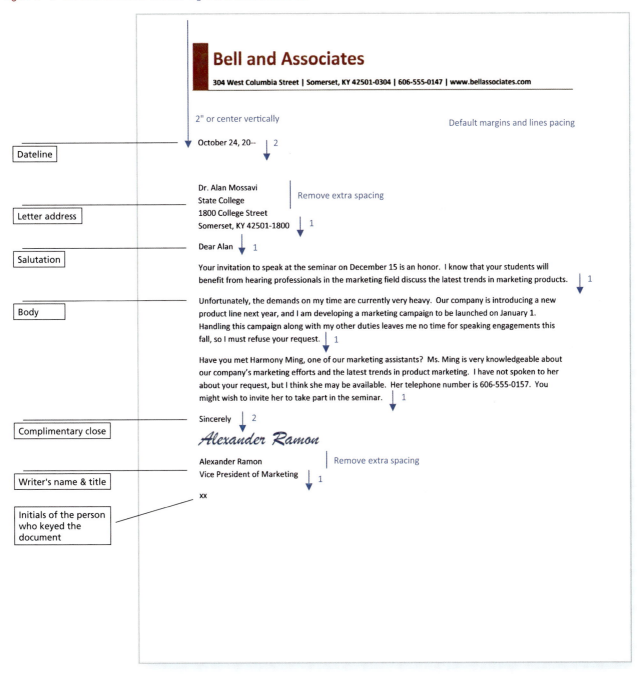

Figure 2 Modified Block Letter with Mixed Punctuation

Office Solutions

4540 Eastgate Boulevard, Cincinnati, OH 45245-4540   513-555-0125

May 12, 20--

Tab at about 3.25"

Ms. Janet Waldon
Johnson Company
3574 Kennedy Avenue
Cincinnati, OH 45213-3574

Dear Ms. Waldon:

Thank you for inviting me to make a presentation on document printers. We have several models of ink jet and laser printers for sale, and I will be happy to present information about them to your company. A brochure describing our most popular printer is enclosed.

Your suggested time for the presentation, 3 p.m. on May 20, is convenient for me. I will provide information on several printers. I will also bring three printers that I think would be good choices for your company based on the information you have given to me. You will be able to see these printers in action and judge the quality of the printouts. I will also provide the information on the cost of refill cartridges that you requested.

Please call me if your company has any special printing needs that we have not discussed so I can address those needs in my presentation. I will call you on May 19 to reconfirm our meeting at your company location.

Sincerely,

Anita Diaz

Anita Diaz
Sales Representative

tr

Enclosure

Enclosure

c   Scott Marlin, Account Manager
         Alicia Stokes, Buyer

Copy notation

Tab at 0.5"

Envelopes

You can use *Word's* Envelopes feature to create an envelope for a letter that is open in *Word*. The letter address will be inserted automatically in the Delivery address field. Key the return address in the Return address field. Choose to print the envelope or add it to the letter document for later printing.

The address on an envelope should be located in an area that can be read by the U.S. Postal Service's automated equipment, such as an optical character reader. Figure 3 shows the OCR area for a letter-sized envelope.[1] When you use word processing software to create an envelope automatically, the address will be placed properly. When you place a label on an envelope or create an envelope address manually, be sure the address is placed in the OCR read zone.

Figure 3 OCR Read Area for Letter Envelope

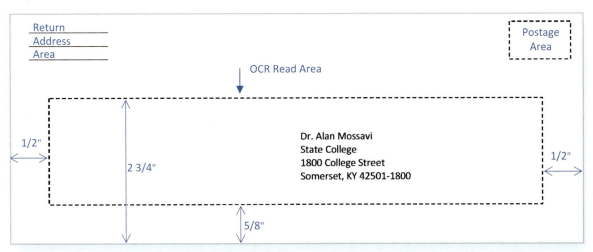

Place notations that affect postage (for example, REGISTERED and CERTIFIED) below the stamp position (line 8). Place other special notations (such as HOLD FOR ARRIVAL, CONFIDENTIAL, and PLEASE FORWARD) two lines below the return address.

Large Envelopes (No. 10, 9, 7 3/4)   Fold a letter for insertion in a large envelope in the following manner:

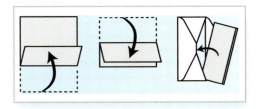

Small Envelopes (No. 6 3/4, 6 1/4)   Fold a letter for insertion in a small envelope in the following manner:

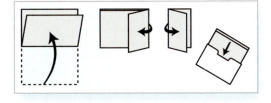

1 U.S. Postal Service, *Domestic Mail Manual*, "Address Placement," http://pe.usps.com/text/dmm300/202.htm#wp1047150 (accessed July 27, 2009).

Memorandums

Memorandums (memos) are short messages that may be printed with a letterhead, on plain paper, or with a company name at the top of the page. Memos that do not contain confidential or sensitive information may also be sent as e-mail attachments. Figure 4 shows a memorandum.

Figure 4 Memorandum

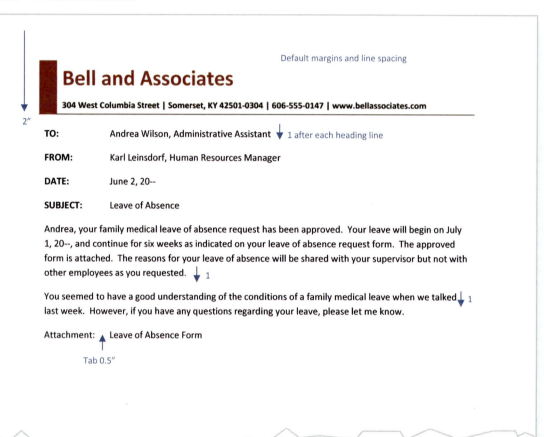

Second-Page Headings

If a memo or letter is more than one page long, a heading should be placed on the second and following pages. The heading should include the recipient's name, Page 2 (or the appropriate number), and the date. Figure 5 shows a sample second-page heading.

Distribution Lists

If you are addressing a memo to a large group of people (generally six or more), use a generic classification, such as Department Managers, in the To line. Include a distribution list at the end of the memo giving the names of the recipients. Figure 5 shows an example of a distribution list for a memo.

Figure 5 Second-Page Heading and Distribution List

Default margins and line spacing

Department Managers | Remove extra spacing
Page 2
May 18, 20--

You will have 30 minutes of free time following lunch. Please plan to make and return calls and answer messages during that time. During the retreat sessions, plan to devote your full attention to the team activities.

jm

Distribution List
    Alice Chang
    Roberta Garcia
    Howard Humble
    Dewayne Mannsfield
    Brenda Mason   Remove extra spacing
    Amy Pierson
    Gary Roberts
    Jerry Swartz
    Richard Watson
    Tom Wilson

Business Reports

Formal business reports usually contain several parts as listed below. Not all reports will contain all these parts.

- Executive summary
- Title page (Figure 6)
- Table of contents (Figure 7)
- Body (Figures 9-12)
- Bibliography or reference section (Figure 8)
- Appendix

Formal business reports are typically prepared in manuscript style. The body of the report includes a main title and side headings to identify parts of the report. Software features, such as the Title and Heading styles in *Word*, are typically used to format titles and headings. The report paragraphs are formatted using 1 or 1.15 line spacing with 10 or 12 points of blank space between paragraphs. The paragraphs are not indented. Tables, charts, or other visual aids may be included in the report body or an appendix. Footnotes or endnotes are used to cite sources of material used in the report. A bibliography or references page lists sources at the end of the report. An appendix may be used to provide additional details or related information mentioned in the report.

Figure 6 Report Title Page

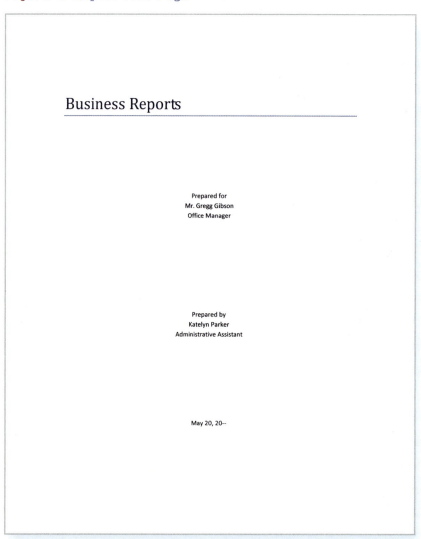

Figure 7 Report Table of Contents

Table of Contents

ii

Figure 8 Report Bibliography

5

Bibliography

Fulton-Calkins, Patsy and Stulz, Karin. *Procedures and Theory for Administrative Professionals* (Cincinnati: Cengage, South-Western, 2009) p. 166.

Stolley, Karl. "Avoiding Plagiarism." *The OWL at Purdue*. http://owl.english.purdue.edu/owl/resource/589/01/ (accessed April 27, 2009).

Figure 9 Report Body, Page 1

Business Reports

Introduction

Numerous reports are prepared in the workplace. These reports may be informal ones of two or three pages, or they may be formal reports containing the table of contents, body of the report (with footnotes or endnotes), bibliography, and appendices. Because reports are often presented orally, in addition to distribution of the written copy, *PowerPoint* slides can be an effective visual.

Planning and Organizing

Effective writing is based on determining the purpose or goal to be accomplished, analyzing the reader/audience, gathering the appropriate information, organizing the content, determining graphics, drafting the report, editing, proofreading, and preparing the final document.

Determine the Purpose or Goal

Business messages generally have one of three primary objectives: to inform the reader, to request action or information, and/or to persuade the reader to take action or accept an idea.[1] Some business messages have more than one objective. For example, the objectives may be to inform and persuade. To determine the goal of a report, ask these questions: Why am I writing this report? What is the objective? What do I hope to accomplish?

Analyze the Reader

If your employer is not clear with you concerning who is receiving the correspondence, do not be afraid to ask. It is important that you analyze the reader before you begin to write. Ask questions such as these about the reader(s):

- How much does the person receiving the document know about the subject?

- What is the educational level of the reader? Is the reader familiar with technical jargon that might be used?

---

[1] Patsy Fulton-Calkins and Karin Stulz, *Procedures and Theory for Administrative Professionals* (Cincinnati: Cengage, South-Western, 2009), p. 166.

Figure 10 Report Body, Page 2

2

- What effect will the message have on the reader? Will the reader react favorably or unfavorably to the message?

- Does the reader come from a different background? If so, what is that background? When the reader is from another country, you need to take additional steps to make certain that you are clear and not offending the reader in any way.

Gather the Appropriate Information

You may check the organization's files on the subject, talk with your employer concerning any background information, and/or research the topic. Most reports involve some type of research. The research may be primary research—the collecting of original data through surveys, observations, or experiments. The research also may be secondary research—data or material that other people have discovered and reported via the Internet, books, periodicals, and various other publications. Be sure to give credit to sources of the material used in the report. Purdue University's Online Writing Lab offers this advice:

> While some cultures may not insist so heavily on documenting sources of words, ideas, images, sounds, etc., American culture does. A charge of plagiarism can have severe consequences, including expulsion from a university or loss of a job, not to mention a writer's loss of credibility and professional standing.[2]

Organize the Content

Make an outline of the key points that should be covered; arrange your points logically. Brainstorm with others if the project is a collaborative one. Write down everything that comes to mind. Then group your ideas, getting all similar ideas together. Next, determine which idea logically goes first, which second, and so on. The basic organizational structure uses a three-pronged approach. The first part of the document conveys the purpose of the report. The second part supports, informs, and/or convinces the reader. The last part states the desired results, the action, or a summary of the findings.

Determine Graphic Needs

If the report requires tables or graphics, determine what the needs are and who is responsible for preparing the tables or graphics. You may be responsible if the graphics are minimal. With the graphic capabilities of computers, many graphics can be produced with relative ease. The graphic should contain enough information to be easily understood without having to read the text that precedes it. A sample pie chart that might be included in a report is shown on the following page.

---

[2] Karl Stolley, "Avoiding Plagiarism," *The OWL at Purdue,* http://owl.english.purdue.edu/owl/resource/589/01/ (accessed April 27, 2009).

Figure 11 Report Body, Page 3

3

Compose and Edit

Working from an outline of the topics to be included and keeping the reader in mind, write a first draft of the report. Review the first draft to see if the message achieves your objectives and how it could be improved. Consider questions such as the following when reviewing the first draft.

- Are the paragraphs effective?
- Is the sentence structure appropriate?
- Is the report written in active voice?
- Is the report written in a positive tone?
- Is the readability level appropriate?
- Is the message concise, clear, correct, courteous, and complete?

Parts of a Report

An informal report may have only one or two parts, with those parts being the body and an executive summary (a one- or two-page summary of the report). An informal report is written in conversational style. Personal pronouns such as *I*, *you*, *me*, *we*, and *us* may be used. Contractions are usually acceptable in an informal report. Before you begin writing a report, be certain that you determine whether the report is considered formal or informal.

Executive Summary

The executive summary is a one- or two-page summary of the document. It is written for the busy executive who wishes to preview the report but does not need a detailed understanding of all aspects of the report. The executive summary contains these parts: background, major findings, and recommendations.

Figure 12 Report Body, Page 4

4

Title Page
The title page contains information such as the title of the report; the writer's name, title, and department or division; and the date the report is being submitted.

Table of Contents
The table of contents lists each major section of the report and the page number of the first page of that section. Although a table of contents is not required in an informal report, it helps the reader find particular parts of the report. If numerous tables and illustrations are within the report, list the title of each one with the respective page number. This procedure helps the reader quickly locate and scan the data presented.

Body of the Report
The body is divided into sections using side headings. Use *Word's* Heading styles to format the side headings. The first section typically introduces the topic of the report and may give reasons for creating the report. Research methods used in gathering data for the report may be described. Research findings or a discussion of issues related to the report topic make up most of the body of the report. The body may end with a section that gives conclusions or recommendations.

References
All references used in a report should be included in a bibliography or reference section. Reference citations or footnotes are usually placed at the bottom of the page in the body. If endnotes are used, they are placed at the conclusion of the document. Internal citations appear within the context of the document.

Appendix
A formal report may contain an appendix that includes supporting information such as tables and statistics. Items in an appendix are listed as Appendix A, Appendix B, and so on. The appendix is the last part of the report.

Proofreaders' Marks

When proofreading printed documents, use proofreaders' marks to indicate changes or corrections. Commonly used proofreaders' marks are shown below.

Figure 13 Proofreaders' Marks

PROOFREADERS' MARKS

SYMBOL		MARKED COPY	CORRECTED COPY
‖	Align	$298,000 $117,000	$298,000 $117,000
～	Bold	The meaning is important.	The **meaning** is important.
≡	Capitalize	bobbie caine	Bobbie Caine
⌒	Close up space	Use con cise words.	Use concise words.
ℰ	Delete	They are happyy.	They are happy.
∧	Insert	Please make copy.	Please make a copy.
#	Space	Show alot of examples.	Show a lot of examples.
___	Italicize	The Sacramento Bee	The *Sacramento Bee*
stet	Ignore correction	He is an effective writer.	He is an effective writer.
/	Lowercase	Sincerely Yours	Sincerely yours
↶	Move as shown	I am only going tomorrow.	I am going only tomorrow.
⌐ ¬ ∏ ⊔	Move left, right, up, or down	Mr. Herschel King 742 Wabash Avenue Skokie, IL 60077	Mr. Herschel King 742 Wabash Avenue Skokie, IL 60077
¶	Paragraph	The file is attached.	The file is attached.
ⓢⓟ	Spell out	7209 E. Darrow Avenue	7209 East Darrow Avenue
∽	Transpose	The down up and motion	The down and up motion
⌐	Use initial cap only	FORMATTING A MEMO	Formatting a Memo

Glossary

401(k) account A tax-deferred retirement plan for employees of private companies and corporations (Chapter 14)

403(b) account A tax-deferred retirement plan for employees of nonprofit organizations or educational institutions (Chapter 14)

A

accession log A file containing a list of the numbers that have been used in a numeric filing system (Chapter 11)

accountability An obligation to answer to others regarding your behavior, the completion of a task or responsibility, or adherence to a standard (Chapter 3)

agenda A document that lists the topics to be discussed at a meeting (Chapter 10)

alphabetic storage method A filing system that uses the letters of the alphabet to determine the order in which a record is filed (Chapter 11)

assets Money and anything of material value owned by an organization (Chapter 14)

audio conference A meeting in which more than two people in at least two locations participate via telephone (Chapter 10)

autocratic leadership style A leadership style in which the leader closely controls subordinates and makes all decisions (Chapter 16)

B

balance sheet A financial document that shows the assets, liabilities, and owner's equity of an organization on a given date (Chapter 14)

blog A web-based journal, also called a weblog, in which participants express their opinions, thoughts, and feelings (Chapter 9)

boilerplate text Standard text used in documents (Chapter 12)

broadband A form of digital data transmission that uses a wide range of frequencies to achieve high-speed and high-capacity transmissions (Chapter 9)

budget A plan that includes projected income and expenses for a business for a given time period (Chapter 14)

business etiquette Accepted professional behavior in the workplace and at business functions (Chapter 2)

bylaws Written policies and procedures of an organization (Chapter 10)

C

cash flow statement A financial document that shows incoming and outgoing cash for a given period (Chapter 14)

character A combination of personal standards of behavior or traits, such as integrity and moral strength (Chapter 4)

chronological resume A document that gives an applicant's work experience in order with the most recent experience listed first (Chapter 15)

cliché A trite expression or phrase that has been overused and is not effective (Chapter 8)

code of ethics A written pledge to make responsible, moral decisions (Chapter 4)

coding Marking a record with the name, subject, location, or number that was determined in the indexing process (Chapter 11)

cohesion A quality of an effective team by which the team "sticks together" and operates as one (Chapter 5)

committee A work group generally established for an ongoing purpose (Chapter 10)

communication A process that occurs when a message is sent by one person and received and understood by another person or other people (Chapter 7)

communication barrier Anything that interferes with successful communication, such as noise, previous experiences, or biases (Chapter 7)

computer virus A program designed to infect, destroy, or interfere with computer operation (Chapter 9)

consulate An office of a government in a foreign city that acts to assist and protect citizens of the consul's country (Chapter 13)

core values Long-term attributes that don't change from day to day or situation to situation (Chapter 4)

corporation One of the three basic forms of a business, owned by stockholders who buy shares of stock in the business (Chapter 1)

credentials Evidence of someone's qualifications, competence, skills, or knowledge (Chapter 8)

credible Believable or trustworthy (Chapter 8)

critical thinking Breaking problems or questions down into small parts and examining them to find solutions or reach conclusions (Chapter 2)

cross-functional team A team composed of individuals from several different functional groups within an organization (such as the engineering, marketing, and quality control departments), usually brought together to solve a problem or work on a project that requires their expertise (Chapter 5)

cross-reference A note or document that shows an alternate name or subject by which a record might be requested and indicates the storage location of the original record (Chapter 11)

customer Someone who buys or uses the products or services of a company or organization (Chapter 6)

customer focus A commitment to providing high-quality customer service to all customers (Chapter 6)

customer service The ability of an organization to consistently give customers what they want and need (Chapter 6)

D

database A collection of records about one topic or related topics (Chapter 11)

delegating Giving the responsibility for a task to another person (Chapter 16)

democratic leadership style A leadership style in which the leader shares authority, decisions, and plans with subordinates (Chapter 16)

demographics Characteristics of a group of people such as age, gender, race, education, and income level (Chapter 8)

downtime Time when you are not accomplishing a specific task (Chapter 3)

duplexing Copying on both sides of a sheet of paper (Chapter 12)

E

editing Reviewing and revising a message to improve its form and content (Chapter 7)

electronic resume A document that gives qualifications and work history for an applicant in an electronic (rather than printed) format (Chapter 15)

electronic whiteboard A device that has the ability to electronically scan images drawn or written on it and transfer the data to a computer where it can be edited, printed, or e-mailed (Chapter 8)

empathy Understanding or concern for someone's feelings or position (Chapter 6)

emphatic listening Hearing and offering feedback that shows you have understood the message (Chapter 7)

ethics Guidelines or accepted beliefs about what is right or wrong, good or bad (Chapter 4)

e-ticket An electronic ticket that represents the purchase of a seat on a passenger airline, usually through a website or by telephone (Chapter 13)

evaluative listening Hearing and trying to understand and judge what is being said (Chapter 7)

exit interview A meeting between an employee who is leaving a company and a company representative (Chapter 15)

expense report A document that lists travel and other business expenses for an individual for a specified time period (Chapter 13)

external customers People or other organizations that buy or use the products and services provided by the organization (Chapter 6)

F

feedback Honest and constructive information from an employer about how well you are doing your job and how you might improve your performance (Chapter 2)

firewall A software program that monitors information as it enters and leaves a computer as a security measure (Chapter 9)

fiscal year A 12-month period used for accounting purposes (Chapter 14)

frequent flyer program An incentive program that provides a variety of awards after the accumulation of a certain number of mileage points (Chapter 13)

functional resume A document that gives the skills and qualifications of an applicant for a particular job rather than focusing on work experience (Chapter 15)

G

geographic storage method A filing system in which records are arranged by geographic location (Chapter 11)

government entity An office, department, or agency that carries out a function of state, local, or national government (Chapter 1)

groupthink A situation in which the members of a team tend to suppress divergent ideas and to make their opinions and decisions conform to those of the group (Chapter 5)

H

heterogeneous group A group of people with dissimilar backgrounds and experiences (Chapter 10)

homogeneous group A group of people with similar backgrounds and experiences (Chapter 10)

hotspot A public location that offers computer network access via a Wi-Fi connection (Chapter 9)

human relations skills Abilities that allow one to interact with others effectively (Chapter 6)

I

important records Records that are necessary to an orderly continuation of a business and are replaceable only at considerable cost of time and money (Chapter 12)

incentive A reward or encouragement (Chapter 3)

income statement A financial document that shows the income, expenses, and profit or loss of an organization for a given period of time (Chapter 14)

index A listing of the names or titles used in a filing system (Chapter 11)

indexing Determining the way a record is to be filed—the name, the subject, the number, or the geographic location—according to the procedures defined for the filing system (Chapter 11)

informal roles Roles on a team that are not articulated or assigned but that members recognize as needing to be filled and take on (Chapter 5)

informative listening Hearing and trying to understand and remember the information being presented (Chapter 7)

instant message An electronic message sent and received by two or more people who are connected to a network at the same time (Chapter 9)

integrity The firm, consistent application of ethical standards at a personal level (Chapter 16)

interactive whiteboard A large display board connected to a computer that is used to capture images and notes or access computer programs or the Internet (Chapter 8)

interference Anything that stands in the way of progress (Chapter 3)

internal customers Departments or employees within an organization who use the products or services provided by others within the organization (Chapter 6)

intranet A computer web that is for access and use by employees or members of an organization and is not generally open to the public (Chapter 8)

IP telephony The transmission of voice over a private IP network or a public IP network such as the Internet (Chapter 9)

itinerary A document that gives travel information such as flight numbers, arrival and departure times, hotel and car reservations, and appointments (Chapter 13)

J

jet lag The feeling of exhaustion following a flight through several time zones (Chapter 13)

job board A website that allows you to browse job listings and sometimes to post your resume (Chapter 15)

job interview A meeting between a job applicant and a potential employer to discuss a job and the applicant's qualifications (Chapter 15)

K

key operator A person who has been trained to operate and handle problems with equipment (Chapter 12)

L

laissez-faire leadership style A leadership style in which employees generally lead themselves (Chapter 16)

leadership The act of inspiring and motivating people to achieve organizational goals (Chapter 16)

leadership styles Patterns of behavior in leading others (Chapter 16)

learning organization An organization in which a shared vision of the future allows the organization to move forward in the accomplishment of significant goals and objectives (Chapter 16)

letter of application A letter sent to a prospective employer that states your interest in a job, provides general information about your skills, transmits your resume, and requests an interview (Chapter 15)

liabilities Debts of an organization that must be paid in the future (Chapter 14)

limited liability company A form of business that combines the tax advantages of a partnership with the limited liability of a corporation (Chapter 1)

listening Hearing and trying to understand a message using the sounds you hear (Chapter 7)

live chat Exchanging text messages in real time via a computer or other device such as a cell phone (Chapter 6)

local area network (LAN) A computer network that links computers and other devices over a small geographical area (Chapter 9)

long-range planning The process of defining an organization's long-term mission, assessing the current business environment, anticipating changes in the environment, and developing strategies for achieving the mission (Chapter 1)

loss In accounting terms, the amount by which expenses exceed income (Chapter 14)

M

mail merge A feature of word processing software that allows you to create personalized letters, labels, or envelopes for large mailings (Chapter 12)

management The act of organizing and directing people to achieve organizational goals (Chapter 16)

management by objectives An approach to management in which managers and employees set goals together and make a plan for achieving them (Chapter 16)

metadata Information about data, such as the author, structure, and subject of the data (Chapter 11)

metropolitan area network (MAN) A network that links computers and other devices across a city or region (Chapter 9)

microform Microimage media such as microfilm and microfiche (Chapter 11)

minutes A document that serves as a record of a meeting (Chapter 10)

mission An organization's reason for being or purpose (Chapter 16)

modem A device that converts the digital signal from a computer to an analog signal that can be transmitted through an ordinary phone line (Chapter 9)

morals Principles or rules for behaving in the right manner (Chapter 4)

N

net pay Final earnings after taxes and other deductions (Chapter 14)

networking Making contacts with people who may help you in an activity, such as your job search or career growth (Chapter 15)

nonessential records Documents that have no future value to the organization (Chapter 12)

nonprofit corporation A form of business that is similar to a for-profit corporation, but generally exempt from income taxes and qualifying as a charitable organization for donors (Chapter 1)

nonverbal communication Sending a message without spoken or written words (Chapter 7)

numeric storage method A filing system in which records are arranged in a numeric sequence (Chapter 11)

O

opportunity A good chance, prospect, or timing (Chapter 3)

owner's equity The financial claims to the assets of an organization by the owner or stockholders after all debts have been paid (Chapter 14)

P

partnership One of the three basic forms of a business, an association of two or more people as co-owners of a business (Chapter 1)

passport An official government document that certifies the identity and citizenship of an individual and grants the person permission to travel abroad (Chapter 13)

periodic transfer A system by which active records are transferred to inactive status at the end of a stated time (Chapter 12)

perpetual transfer A system by which records are continuously transferred from the active to the inactive files (Chapter 12)

petty cash Money kept on hand to pay small fees or charges incurred by a company or to reimburse employees for such charges (Chapter 14)

phishing Using an online message that seems to be from a legitimate source to gather personal information (Chapter 9)

pitch An attribute of sound that can be described as high or low, as in a low-pitched voice (Chapter 7)

portfolio A compilation of samples of your work and other career-related information (Chapter 15)

priority Something that merits your attention ahead of other tasks (Chapter 3)

procrastination The act of putting something off that you find difficult or boring (Chapter 3)

professional An employee who looks, speaks, writes, and behaves in a manner that reflects well on the employer and on the employee (Chapter 2)

profit In accounting terms, the amount by which income exceeds expenses (Chapter 14)

progress Forward movement toward a goal (Chapter 3)

project team A team developed for a clearly defined project with a beginning and an end (Chapter 5)

proofreading Reviewing and correcting the final draft of a message (Chapter 7)

publishing Sending a message to the receiver or making the message available to the receiver (Chapter 7)

R

record Information stored on any medium that is received or created by an organization and provides evidence of an event, activity, or business transaction (Chapter 11)

records management The systematic control of records from the creation or receipt of the record to its final disposition (Chapter 11)

records retention schedule A document that specifies how long various types of records should be kept (Chapter 12)

reflective listening Hearing and offering feedback that helps the speaker think about her or his feelings or objectives (Chapter 7)

resume A concise document that lists a person's background, education, skills, and experience related to work (Chapter 15)

resume reference A person who knows your academic ability and/or work skills and habits and is willing to recommend you to employers (Chapter 15)

S

S-corporation A type of corporation that has 75 or fewer stockholders (Chapter 1)

self-confidence Belief in yourself and your abilities (Chapter 2)

self-development The effort to improve yourself professionally (Chapter 16)

self-discipline Your own control over what you do, as well as how and when you do it (Chapter 3)

servant leadership A philosophy and style of leadership in which the leader serves the needs of followers (Chapter 16)

shareholder An investor who has purchased stock representing a portion or share of a business (a corporation); also known as a stockholder (Chapter 1)

situational leadership The changing of leadership styles for different situations (Chapter 16)

smartphone A full-featured mobile phone that includes many of the functions of a handheld computer (Chapter 9)

sole proprietorship One of the three basic forms of a business, owned and controlled by an individual (Chapter 1)

spam Unwanted and unsolicited electronic messages (Chapter 9)

spyware A program that runs on a computer without the permission of the user to gather personal information, often through an Internet connection (Chapter 9)

stakeholder A person or group that has a vested interest in a decision or action (Chapter 4)

status report A report to a supervisor on the progress of a team's activities (Chapter 5)

stock A share of ownership in a corporation (Chapter 14)

strategic planning The process of defining an organization's long-term mission, assessing the current business environment, anticipating changes in the environment, and developing strategies for achieving the mission (Chapter 1)

strategy A plan of action for achieving a goal (Chapter 6)

stress The worry and anxiety you feel when you react to pressure from others or yourself (Chapter 3)

subject storage method A filing system in which records are arranged by their subject (Chapter 11)

synergy The interaction of people or things that can accomplish more than the sum of the individual parts (Chapter 10)

system A group of independent but interrelated elements that make a unified whole, such as the departments or units in a business (Chapter 1)

T

task force A work group formed to deal with a specific issue or problem (Chapter 10)

team A group of people who work together towards a common goal (Chapter 5)

team norms Habits or unwritten rules of operation for a team (Chapter 5)

telecommunications The transmission of electronic information (text, data, voice, video, and images) from one location to another (Chapter 9)

template A model for creating similar items (Chapter 12)

tone An attribute of voice that conveys the attitude or emotional state of the speaker (Chapter 7)

travel agency A company that offers travel advice and makes travel arrangements for clients (Chapter 13)

U

useful records Records that are needed for the smooth, effective operation of an organization (Chapter 12)

V

values Personal beliefs about what is right and wrong (Chapter 4)

verbatim Word for word (Chapter 10)

video conference A meeting in which two or more people at different locations use equipment such as computers, video cameras, and microphones to see and hear each other (Chapter 10)

virtual assistant A self-employed administrative assistant who works from a virtual office to provide off-site administrative and/or personal assistance to clients (Chapter 1)

virtual team A team that primarily meets electronically (Chapter 5)

visa A document granted by a government that permits a traveler to enter and travel within that particular country (Chapter 13)

vision A picture of an organization's future (Chapter 16)

visual aid An object or image that listeners can see and that will help them understand a message (Chapter 8)

vital records Records that cannot be replaced and should never be destroyed (Chapter 12)

voice mail A system that plays a recorded announcement and records and stores telephone messages (Chapter 9)

W

web meeting A meeting in which two or more people at different locations communicate and share information via computers and a network connection, such as the Internet or a local area network (Chapter 10)

webcast A broadcast that is similar in nature to a television broadcast and takes place over the World Wide Web (Chapter 10)

webinar A seminar presented over the World Wide Web (Chapter 10)

wide area network (WAN) A network that connects computers and other devices over the largest geographical area—perhaps hundreds of thousands of miles (Chapter 9)

wiki A website or group of web pages on which anyone can add, edit, or delete content (Chapter 9)

work ethic An inner drive to work hard and well (Chapter 2)

Index